Geoff Tibballs is the author of the bestselling *Mammoth Book of Jokes* and *The Mammoth Book of Dirty Jokes* as well as many other books including *Business Blunders* and *Legal Blunders*. A former journalist and press officer, he is now a full-time writer who lists his hobbies as sport, eating, drinking and avoiding housework. He lives in Nottingham, England, with his wife and daughters.

THE MAMMOTH BOOK OF
WEIRD
BUT TRUE

EDITED BY
GEOFF TIBBALLS

RUNNING PRESS
PHILADELPHIA · LONDON

Constable & Robinson Ltd
3 The Lanchesters
162 Fulham Palace Road
London W6 9ER
www.constablerobinson.com

First published in the UK by Robinson,
an imprint of Constable & Robinson, 2011

A copy of the British Library Cataloguing in Publication
Data is available from the British Library

UK ISBN 978-1-84529-934-7

1 3 5 7 9 10 8 6 4 2

First published in the United States in 2011 by Running Press Book Publishers

9   8   7   6   5   4   3   2   1
Digit on the right indicates the number of this printing

US Library of Congress Control Number: 2010941554
US ISBN 978-0-76243-728-3

Running Press Book Publishers
2300 Chestnut Street
Philadelphia, PA 19103-4371

Visit us on the web!
www.runningpress.com

Printed and bound in the UK

CONTENTS

INTRODUCTION

WHEN WE WATCH the television news or read the daily papers, often it's not the major stories of the day that have the greatest impact. We all know the world is awash with corruption, war and economic strife and we don't necessarily want to be reminded about it 24/7, which is why media outlets, in an attempt to lighten the mood, scour the world in search of weird news stories. You know the sort of thing: Taiwanese Man Marries Barbie Doll, Woman Swallowed By Fridge, Moose Steals Bicycle or Driver Blames Crash On Pterodactyl. These quirky news items (a disproportionately high number of which, incidentally, seem to occur in Romania) are guaranteed to send us off to work or bed with a smile on our faces and the thought that maybe the world isn't such a terrible place after all. They restore our faith in the absurdity of the human race. How else can you explain why a drink-driving suspect would eat his own underwear to beat a breath test or why a 33-year-old woman would pose as her 15-year-old daughter to enrol at high school because she had always wanted to be a cheerleader? These are just two of the hundreds of true stories that I have unearthed from the four corners of the globe, covering topics such as crime, sex, health, animals, sport, relationships, travel, work and deaths. So if you have ever doubted the saying that truth is stranger than fiction, read on.

Geoff Tibballs

1

1

ANIMAL CRACKERS

MAN CAUGHT WITH PIGEONS DOWN PANTS

A 23-year-old Australian man stopped by customs officials at Melbourne airport in 2009 was found to have a live pigeon stuffed down each leg of his pants. The man was searched after disembarking from a ten-hour flight from Dubai. First, officials discovered two bird eggs hidden in a vitamin container before a further search revealed that the man was wearing tights under his pants – and inside each leg was a live pigeon wrapped in a padded envelope. An undeclared aubergine was also found in his luggage. A customs spokesman said: "We have no idea of his motives."

CAMEL HUMPS FIRE HYDRANT

A sex-starved male camel at a zoo in Wichita, Kansas, alarmed keepers by taking a fancy to a fire hydrant in his enclosure. When Tommy's mate died in 1993, he turned his affections to the hydrant, vigorously rubbing himself against it for hours on end until officials at Sedgwick County Zoo eventually decided to remove it. His embarrassed keeper, Julie Fritz, said of Tommy's misplaced passion: "If it's during public hours, I just go hide somewhere. What can I say? The camel doesn't have a life."

GIRAFFE MASTERMINDS CIRCUS BREAKOUT

A giraffe was the brains behind a mass escape of animals from a travelling Dutch circus in 2008. After the giraffe kicked a hole in their cage, 15 camels, two zebras and an unspecified number of llamas and potbellied pigs made a dramatic dawn break for freedom. They were later found wandering around an Amsterdam suburb before being rounded up by police and circus workers.

GOAT ACCUSED OF ARMED ROBBERY

Police in Nigeria arrested a goat on suspicion of armed robbery in 2009. Vigilantes seized the black and white goat, claiming that it was an armed robber who had used black magic to transform himself into an animal in order to escape after trying to steal a car. A spokesman for police in the eastern state of Kwara confirmed: "The goat is in our custody. Witnesses saw some hoodlums attempting to rob a car. One escaped while the other turned into a goat."

WOMAN CHASED HOME BY CRAZED SKUNK

A woman in Salem, Massachusetts, was chased for more than 15 minutes by a rabid skunk in 1997. Carmen LaBrecque, 51, encountered the skunk on her way home and it proceeded to harass her all the way back to her property, constantly snapping at her heels. Once there, she was unable to slow down sufficiently to open her front door and reach safety, so instead she had to run around her yard, making sure to stay at least a foot ahead of her demonic pursuer. On one lap, she was handed a cell phone by her elderly mother from inside the house and managed to call the police. Her trauma finally ended when, alerted by the police, an animal control officer arrived on the scene and shot the skunk.

STONED WALLABIES MAKE CROP CIRCLES

The mysterious appearance of a series of crop circles in Tasmanian poppy fields in 2009 was found to be caused by stoned wallabies which were eating the poppy heads and hopping around aimlessly. "We have a problem with wallabies entering poppy fields, getting as high as a kite and going around in circles," announced the state's top lawmaker Lara Giddings. Deer and sheep were also seen to "act weird" after eating poppies in Tasmania.

BEAR PASSES OUT AFTER BEER-DRINKING BINGE

A bear passed out on the lawn of a resort in Baker Lake, Washington State, in 2004 after drinking 36 cans of beer. The black bear had broken into campers' coolers and used his teeth and claws to puncture the cans, but after his marathon drinking session he decided to sleep it off. Wildlife agents noted that the bear only drank Rainier Beer and ignored all other brands.

MAN STALKED BY LOVELORN EMU

A **MAN FROM** Mobile, Alabama, had to fend off an amorous female emu with a boat paddle after the bird had fallen in love with him and stalked him for days. The six-foot-tall, 150-pound emu first showed up at the home of Ed and Ann Stuardi in 1998, drinking from a bird bath and eating berries in their yard. They responded by feeding it dog food but their affection for the feathered visitor began to wane when it started following Mr Stuardi around with an enthusiasm bordering on obsession. He tried to frighten off his suitor by firing a gun into the air but the emu simply stood there, looking at him forlornly. It then started making noises deep in its throat, which Mr Stuardi unfortunately failed to recognize as its mating call. The next thing he knew, he was being forced to keep it at bay with the paddle before fleeing to the safety of his home where he and his wife finally decided to call the police for help. Diane Roberts, director of the local Animal Rescue Foundation which captured the bird and took it away, said: "I've never seen an emu hold hostages but this was mating season and she took a fond liking to him. She was absolutely intent that this was her mate. Hopefully she will meet another emu and forget all about Mr Stuardi. After all, he is a married man." ●

"EXTINCT" BIRD SEEN ON WAY TO COOKING POT

A quail that was thought to have been extinct for decades was spotted alive in 2009 – on its way to a cooking pot. Worcester's buttonquail was previously known only through drawings based on dead museum specimens but when a live bird was captured by hunters in a Philippine mountain range, a film crew was on hand to take pictures. Michael Lu, president of the Wild Bird Club of the Philippines, was delighted by the find but admitted that it was unfortunate that the rare quail would probably end up medium rare.

RADIOACTIVE CAT MISTAKEN FOR BOMB

A driver in the US was stopped by police on suspicion of being a terrorist after his radioactive cat was mistaken for a bomb. The man was flagged down when his vehicle triggered an isotope signal on specialist radiation detectors that were being used by anti-terror agents to monitor passing highway traffic. However a search of the car revealed nothing more sinister than the owner's cat which had undergone radiotherapy for cancer three days earlier.

BULLS EXPLODE AFTER POWER LINES COLLAPSE

Seven bulls exploded and caught fire after overhead power lines fell on a dairy farm near Auckland, New Zealand, in 2009. Three of the animals were electrocuted after the lines collapsed and the other four were killed when they walked into the live area. Farmer Dave Taylor was alerted to the incident by a phone call from his father, who was driving on a nearby motorway, telling him his cows were exploding.

TORTOISE STARTS HOUSE FIRE

A couple from Bracknell, Berkshire, returned home in 2008 to discover that their house had been set on fire by their 70-year-old pet tortoise. Fred, a female tortoise, had been brought inside after coming out of hibernation early and was placed in a tank under a heat lamp in order to stay warm. But while Emma Fox and partner Paul Butler were out shopping, Fred piled dry straw under the lamp, causing it to catch fire and send flames spreading through the house. Although much of the couple's furniture was destroyed, Fred emerged unscathed.

CHIMP MAKES NUISANCE CALLS

A light-fingered chimpanzee bombarded staff at a Scottish safari park with nuisance calls in 2001 after stealing a cell phone from a keeper's pocket. For three days and nights workers at Blair Drummond Safari Park near Stirling were pestered with mysterious calls. They were on the verge of calling the police when keeper Gary Gilmour recognized the shriek of a chimp on the other end of the line. The culprit was 11-year-old Chippy who must have snatched the phone from Gilmour's jacket while the keeper was cleaning out the chimpanzee enclosure. The cheeky chimp then kept pressing various numbers stored in the phone's memory and hitting the redial button.

DOG SWALLOWS $750

When her dog swallowed $750 from a purse, Debbie Hulleman managed to recover most of the cash . . . by sifting through the animal's poop. Pepper, an eight-year-old labrador cross, snatched the notes from a purse belonging to a friend of Hulleman's mother in Oakdale, Minnesota. The dog quickly vomited up some of the cash and then Hulleman noticed a $50 bill hanging from a pile of dog faeces. After that it was simply a question of waiting for nature to take its course. She eventually managed to reclaim $647 but the rest was damaged beyond repair. The soiled money was then exchanged for fresh currency at a bank.

WOMAN CONFUSES GOLDFISH WITH PIRANHAS

A woman from Saransk, Russia, lost most of the flesh from two of her fingers when she attempted to clean her son's fish tank, unaware that it was full of piranhas. As she tried to catch the fish, they launched a frenzied attack on her hand, clamping their razor-like teeth onto her fingers. She finally managed to free herself from the hungry predators by banging them against the side of the tank. After undergoing extensive surgery, she told doctors that she was trying to do her son a favour and had thought the tank's occupants were just well-fed goldfish.

DRUNKEN MONKEYS RAID VILLAGE

A gang of drunken monkeys rampaged through an Indian village in 2005 after stealing a specially prepared alcoholic brew. The animals snatched the liquor – made from marijuana leaves in readiness for a religious festival – from pots stored outside the villagers' huts in Baralapokhari and proceeded to run amok. The residents hit back at the inebriated attackers with sticks and eventually drove them away, but not before several monkeys had passed out and three humans had been injured.

HORNY BULL LUSTS AFTER FARMER

A Polish farmer finished up in hospital in 2008 after a bull chased him around a field because it thought he was a cow. The amorous bull tore off 68-year-old Stan Markowski's clothes after catching the scent of cows on them at the dairy farm in Wies Dlugie. His daughter explained: "The bull smelt my dad who had just been with cows and thought he was a cow ready for mating. But when my dad pushed him off, the bull went mad and began to charge and toss him around the field, tearing his clothes and hurling him to the ground. He eventually managed to get away and ran home – terrified, bleeding and completely naked."

RECLINING CHAIR SWALLOWS TERRIER

Firefighters in Chicago were forced to saw a mechanical reclining chair in half in 2010 to rescue a small dog that had been swallowed by the contraption. Eighty-seven-year-old Ken Makris phoned the emergency services to report that his terrier, Ebonyser, had got trapped in the chair after its electrical controls stopped working. The crew of three managed to take the chair apart and free Ebonyser who suffered nerve damage in the ordeal but was said to be well enough to go for a walk the following day.

PARROT STEALS TOURIST'S PASSPORT

When a tour bus stopped on a highway on New Zealand's South Island in 2009, a wild kea parrot spotted a Scotsman's passport in a bag in the luggage compartment and flew off with it into dense bush. Police admitted that it was unlikely the passport would ever be recovered in the vast Fiordland rainforest. The unnamed passport holder lamented: "My passport is somewhere out there in Fiordland. The kea's probably using it for fraudulent claims or something."

MAN SWAPS WIFE FOR GOAT

A Bulgarian farmer swapped his wife for a goat – because she couldn't give him kids. Stoil Panayotov, 54, reportedly exchanged his third wife for Elena, an eight-year-old goat, at a livestock market in Plovdiv in 2008. He was quoted as saying: "The day before, a friend told me that he has had no luck with women and that he really liked my wife. The goat has given birth to three kids and my wife to none, so the deal was more profitable to the goat owner. I got a second-hand goat and he got a brand new wife."

LIVE ALLIGATOR FOUND IN CAR REAR WINDOW

Police officers on night patrol in Texas pulled over a motorist for erratic driving but when they shone their torches into the vehicle they found a six-foot-long alligator staring menacingly at them from the rear window. The alligator, which had been travelling in the back seat, had crawled up to the area behind the headrests to form a deterrent that was infinitely more effective than any car alarm. The driver said he had found the reptile by the side of the road near Houston. He was charged with illegal possession of an alligator.

MAN CAUGHT SHORT IN LION'S CAGE

When a 19-year-old Venezuelan needed to answer a call of nature, he had a closer encounter with nature than he would have liked. For he chose to go to the toilet in an animal enclosure at a zoo, unaware perhaps that the occupant was a lion. The man was squatting with his pants around his ankles when the lion, taking exception to his presence, pounced. Luckily a friend managed to deter the beast with a brick, and the pair scrambled to safety.

US MILITARY CALLS UP PARROT FOR DRAFT

When Sharon Garmize, of Wright Township, Pennsylvania, received a letter from the US Selective Service in 1998 ordering Sam Garmize to register for the military draft, it came as something of a surprise – not least because Sam is a parrot. Sharon shrugged off the order, saying: "They probably wouldn't want him because he has only four toes, green hair and no teeth." She suspected that a family friend may have listed Sam as a family member in a survey a few years earlier because since then a bank had offered Sam a credit card with a $2,000 limit, a tuxedo shop had offered him a nice deal just in time for the prom, and a student foreign exchange programme had asked him to study abroad.

RANDY RHINO TRIES TO MATE WITH CAR

A rampant rhinoceros tried to mate with a visitor's car at West Midlands Safari Park in 2004. Dave Alsop had stopped his vehicle in the grounds to take pictures of Sharka, a two-ton white rhino, mating with female Trixie, but the amorous male quickly turned his attentions to the Renault Laguna. He attempted to mount the car from the side, denting the doors and ripping off the wing mirrors before Alsop drove off with a puffing Sharka in hot pursuit. "He was a big boy and obviously aroused," said Alsop. "He sidled up against us and the next thing I know, he's banging away at the car and it's rocking like hell." A spokesman for the park confirmed that Sharka had something of a reputation as a ladies' man but admitted that "rhinos are not particularly intelligent animals".

DONKEY JAILED FOR ASSAULT

Blacky the donkey spent three days in jail in Chiapas, southern Mexico, in May 2008 for assault and battery. The animal was locked up along with drunks and other miscreants after it bit and kicked two men. It was finally released when its owner paid a fine of $36 plus the injured men's hospital fees. Two months earlier, Chiapas police had thrown a bull in the slammer after it devoured corn crops and destroyed two wooden vending stands.

COWS EAT AIRPLANE

While visiting friends in 2004, Tony Cooper and Lisa Kingscott landed their 58-year-old, four-seater Auster J1N light aircraft in an isolated field at Kentchurch, near Hereford. They thought it would be perfectly safe there, but had reckoned without a group of hungry heifers. For when the owners returned to the field ready to make their journey home to Wiltshire, they found that cows had munched their way through the aircraft's fuselage, leaving the plane grounded with $15,000 of damage. After being forced to dismantle the plane and take it home by road, Ms Kingscott mused: "The animals only ate the white bits – I don't know why."

SHARK ATTACKS BOY IN BEDROOM

A 14-year-old boy survived a horrific shark attack in his own bedroom. Sam Hawthorne, from Dudley, near Birmingham, was savaged when he sleepwalked into a long-dead souvenir shark that was hanging on the wall. He was left with the creature – a holiday gift – embedded in his cheek and blood pouring from the wound. His mother was alerted by his screams but it took 15 minutes to prise the shark from Sam's cheek, leaving him with a nasty scar.

DEAD SKUNK MAIL CLOSES POST OFFICE

A post office in Summerville, South Carolina, was evacuated for several hours by emergency services in 2009 after they received a call about a suspicious package that was emitting a "bomb-smelling odour". But when firefighters examined the box, instead of finding a bomb, they found a dead skunk. "There was a horrible stink," said one firefighter. "The whole package just stank. At first we didn't realize what it was until a guy said: 'I'm expecting a skunk.'" The dead skunk was being delivered to a taxidermist.

AMERICAN WOMAN IS OBSESSED WITH RABBITS

When police raided the Hillsboro, Oregon, home of 44-year-old Miriam Sakewitz in October 2006, they found over 150 rabbits roaming around plus 88 dead ones in the freezer. However three months later she was said to have broken into the facility where the survivors were being cared for and stolen most of them back. She was subsequently found in Chehalis, Washington, with eight live rabbits and two dead ones in her car. Another 130 rabbits were recovered at a nearby horse farm. Charged with animal neglect, she was sentenced to five years' probation and was banned from owning or controlling animals. She was ordered not to go within 100 yards of a rabbit.

In the summer of 2007, Sakewitz was sentenced to three days in jail for violating her probation by keeping a rabbit in her house. Probation officer Susan Ranger said Sakewitz had cancelled counselling sessions and refused to open the door for unannounced visits. On one occasion when she did manage to gain entry, Ranger said she found no rabbits but did notice a half-empty ten-pound bag of carrots.

Having apparently kept her nose clean for two years, Sakewitz was arrested again in June 2009 after a maintenance worker summoned to her Portland hotel room to fix a broken television set saw a number of rabbits hopping around. Animal control officers removed eight adult rabbits, five young and a dead one from the hotel room. The judge sentenced her to 90 days in jail. The "Bunny Lady" was back in the hutch.

TURKEYS FOUND STUFFED WITH COCAINE

Two turkeys were cut open by drug smugglers and stuffed with five kilos of cocaine. Acting on a tip-off, police in Peru stopped a bus outside the city of

Tarapoto and discovered two bloated turkeys in a crate. Lifting up the feathers in the chest area they noticed a handmade seam, and when a vet opened the stitching on the birds, he extracted a total of 28 plastic capsules containing cocaine. The turkeys were said to be recovering well from their ordeal.

TALKING PARROT ONLY SPEAKS POLISH

Hayley Wilson paid over $600 for a talking parrot in Crediton, Devon – and then discovered that because of its previous owner the bird could only speak Polish.

GUINEA PIG BREAKS OUT FOR NIGHT OF RAMPANT SEX

A male guinea pig called Sooty had a night to remember in 2000 after escaping from his pen and tunnelling into a cage of 24 females. Two months later, he was the proud father of 43 offspring. Carol Feehan, owner of Little Friend's Farm in Pontypridd, South Wales, said: "We knew that he had gone missing after wriggling through the bars of his cage. We looked for him everywhere but never thought of checking the pen where we keep 24 females. We did a head count and found 25 guinea pigs – Sooty was fast asleep in the corner. He was absolutely shattered and when we put him back in his cage, he slept for two days." She added: "I'm sure a lot of men will be looking at Sooty with envy."

MONKEY KILLS CRUEL OWNER WITH COCONUT

A monkey that had been forced to climb trees to pick coconuts finally exacted revenge on his tyrannical Thai owner by hurling a coconut from the top of a tree with such force that it killed the man. Leilit Janchoom had employed the monkey – named Brother Kwan –– to pick coconuts which he would then sell. However witnesses said he was a hard taskmaster and if the monkey refused to climb trees, Janchoom would hit him. According to reports, the monkey eventually decided enough was enough and planned his bloody retribution. The dead man's wife said the monkey had "seemed lovable" when they bought him.

SAY IT WITH SHEEP

Instead of flowers, a Brazilian teenager came up with a novel Valentine's Day gift for his girlfriend – a pregnant sheep. Frederico Skwara bought Juliana

Magalhaes the ewe – called Waffle – after first checking with the girl's mother that she was enthusiastic about welcoming a sheep into the family home.

POLICE FIND 300 DEAD CATS IN FREEZER

Police in Sacramento, California, discovered 300 dead cats crammed into three freezers at the home of a 47-year-old man. They also found 30 live cats and the man's 81-year-old mother living in the house.

PANDAS VIEW PORN

Chinese scientists claimed to have sparked a baby boom among giant pandas by showing them DVDs of other pandas mating. Pandas are notoriously poor breeders but the "panda porn" programme seemed to pay off with 31 cubs being born in captivity in China in the first ten months of 2006, compared to just 12 the previous year.

STREET SWEEPER SUCKS UP DOG

A truck sweeping the streets of New York City sucked a dog to its death in 2008. Robert Machin had just finished walking his two Boston terriers and was about to load them into his car when he turned around to see one of the dogs, Ginger, being swallowed by the sweeping machine's round bristles.

PROTECTIVE RABBIT SCARES AWAY OWNER'S BOYFRIENDS

A jealous pet rabbit did its utmost to ruin owner Ruth Galloway's love life. Normally calm and placid, Rocky reacted badly when any boy became affectionate with the 23-year-old graphic designer and saw off four would-be suitors in just six months. Ruth allowed Rocky to roam the house in Birmingham, England, when male friends came to visit but as soon they started getting amorous, he would bite, scratch and nip their ankles. One boyfriend picked up Rocky and had his finger bitten, and another beau was chewed as he tried to feed him carrots. Ruth said: "Rocky may look all cute and fluffy but under the cuddly exterior lies an absolute psycho. It's obviously some kind of a macho male rabbit thing where he can't stand men getting near me. I can't cage him now though – Rocky and I come as a couple. I think he'll know when I find the right guy." One of Ruth's former boyfriends, James Phillips, commented: "He's a savage. It was like having a rottweiller in the house. Ruth's a lovely girl but I stopped seeing her because of the thing. In the end it was me or Rocky – and I got out."

ELEPHANT ROBS MOTORISTS

In 2007 it was reported that an elephant in India was deliberately blocking the road and refusing to allow drivers to pass until they gave it food. Motorists in the state of Orissa were forced to stop by the elephant which then searched inside the vehicle with its trunk for any tasty snacks. One victim said: "If you are carrying vegetables and bananas inside your vehicle, then it will gulp them and allow you to go. But if you do not wind down your window or open the vehicle door, the elephant will stand in front of the car until you allow him to carry out his inspection."

MAN SURPRISED TO BE BITTEN AFTER PUTTING RATTLESNAKE HEAD IN MOUTH

Showing off to friends after a few drinks, Matt Wilkenson, from Portland, Oregon, decided to put the head of one of his pet rattlesnakes in his mouth. But he nearly died when the snake bit him, putting him in a coma for three days. "It's actually kind of my own stupid fault," he admitted later.

LAWYER CLAIMS CLIENT'S ROOSTER OWNED DRUGS AND GUN

A creative lawyer told a court in the Philippines that 67 kilos of cocaine and a gun found in a rooster's cage belonged to the bird and not his client. Attorney Manuel Urbina insisted: "The drugs were in the possession of a rooster and two hens, and the law is very clear that whoever is in possession of the drugs is the one who should be accused."

WOMAN ACCIDENTALLY POSTS CAT

Edith Schonberg, from Rosdorf, Germany, accidentally sent her cat Felix in the mail after the animal sneaked unnoticed into a parcel that she was sending to her nephew. Felix was eventually freed when a worker at the sorting office heard the parcel miaowing.

SUICIDAL SHEEP LANDS ON WOMAN'S HEAD

An Austrian woman was taken to hospital with severe bruising in 2001 after a sheep jumped 33 feet from a railway bridge in Braunau and landed on her head. The ram was one of a number of animals that had broken out of a field but while the rest of the sheep were rounded up by a combination of farmworkers and police officers, this one beast decided to risk all by plunging from the bridge. A local police inspector said: "It panicked and leaped off the edge of the bridge. It did not fall or anything, my men said it actually jumped off, ten metres or so to the ground. It was practically suicide." The unfortunate woman was walking her dog – appropriately a German Shepherd – on a path beneath the bridge. At the sight of the flying sheep, the dog ran off and hid under a bush.

HORSE TESTS POSITIVE FOR ALCOHOL

A HORSE IN Romania tested positive for alcohol in 2008 after the cart it was pulling hit an elderly man who was sitting on a bench. Witnesses said the horse "looked out of control" despite owner Ion Dragan's attempts to restrain it. Dragan had just bought the horse from a fair, leading police to suspect that the animal might have been given alcohol to make it look stronger and healthier before being sold. Ion Iliuta, head of the local veterinary authority, said he was amazed when police asked him to establish the alcohol concentration in the horse's blood. "We never had such a request before," he said. "Maybe to see what kind of blood it is yes, but to find out if the animal was drunk, never." ●

MAN SMUGGLES MONKEY UNDER HAT

A man flying from Lima, Peru, to New York in 2007 smuggled a monkey onto the plane by hiding it under his hat. His fellow passengers were alerted to the deception when the marmoset emerged from beneath the headgear and perched on the man's ponytail, prompting several to ask him whether he knew he had a monkey on him. Man and monkey were detained on arrival in New York.

WOMAN THREATENS TO SUE ALLIGATOR

In 1997, Kim Novacs of West Palm Beach, Florida, announced her intention to file a $1 million lawsuit against an alligator that her husband had killed the year before. The six-foot-long reptile had scared the couple's young daughter, prompting Keith Novacs to shoot it, for which he was convicted of poaching. Mrs Novacs cited a 1993 Florida court case in which an endangered species was the named plaintiff and she argued that if an animal can be a plaintiff, it can also be a defendant, with the state's Game and Fish Commission liable for any damages.

ZOO TIGER FLEES FROM ITS PREY

A Chinese zoo's plan to restore a tiger's natural instincts by putting a live bull in its cage backfired in 2010 when the prey turned hunter. Keepers at Yancheng Zoo put the one-year-old bull into the adult white tiger's enclosure expecting the big cat to kill and eat the bull, as it would do in the wild. However when the tiger attacked, the bull turned the tables and charged angrily, forcing the tiger to flee in terror, much to the amusement of visitors. A zoo spokesman admitted afterwards that a live bull might have been too much for the tiger, adding: "We will try live chickens next time and build up from there."

PIGEON TAKES DIP IN CHOCOLATE FOUNTAIN

Staff at an Edinburgh confectionery shop got themselves in a flap after a pigeon swooped through an open door and took a dip in their chocolate fountain. They managed to get the bird out of the chocolate and out of the shop but then had to call the Scottish Society for the Prevention of Cruelty to Animals because it was unable to fly. Fiona Thorburn took the call on her first day in the job. She said: "I got the call to say there was a chocolate-coated pigeon walking along Rose Street in Edinburgh, and I thought it was some of my colleagues playing a trick on me." Her fellow SSPCA officer Colin Liddle added: "The chocolate was coated on its wings and right down its back. Because it was in a fountain, the chocolate was softer but by the time it came to us, it had started to set. So we actually just washed it straight away. We've had diesel spills, we've had oil spills – but never before have we had a chocolate-coated pigeon."

DACHSHUND CHEWS OFF OWNER'S TOE

A 56-year-old Illinois woman woke from a short nap in 2008 to find that her pet dachshund had gnawed off her right big toe. The woman had no feeling in her toes because of nerve damage from diabetes. A veterinarian surmised that a bandage wrapped around the toe because of a healing hangnail might somehow have proved irresistible to little Roscoe.

LLAMA WANTS TO MATE OUTSIDE HIS SPECIES

Belgian zookeepers became frustrated with a llama which tried to mate with everything except his partner. Xenos the llama at Antwerp Zoo tried to mount ponies, donkeys and even, somewhat ambitiously, camels, but showed no interest whatsoever in the female llama provided for him. His keeper believed the problem stemmed from the fact that Xenos grew up surrounded by other breeds of animal and did not see his first llama until he was an adult.

AUSTRALIAN RESTAURANT BANS GAY DOG

An Australian restaurant was ordered to apologize and pay compensation after barring a blind man because a waiter thought his guide dog was gay. When Ian Jolly's partner, Chris Lawrence, asked if she could bring a guide dog into the restaurant, the waiter misheard and thought she was asking if gay dogs were allowed. The answer, apparently, was no, and Mr Jolly and his dog Nudge were refused entry to Adelaide's Thai Spice even though he showed staff a guide dog information card. The restaurant was eventually ordered by the Equal Opportunity Tribunal to pay Mr Jolly $1,800 in compensation. The restaurant owners said: "The staff genuinely believed that Nudge was an ordinary pet dog which had been de-sexed to become a gay dog."

CHINESE MAN IS SOLD A PUP

A Chinese man who was sold a white Pomeranian dog as a puppy was shocked to discover a year later that it was really an Arctic fox. Mr Zhang, of Tunkou, paid over $100 for the "puppy" but became puzzled when it kept biting him, could not bark properly and its tail kept growing longer and longer.

GOAT SMASHES DOOR AT CALIFORNIA STRIP CLUB

A goat was so keen to get into a California strip club in 2010 that it barged down the doors before the club had even opened for business. The 150-pound goat was caught on surveillance tape butting and eventually smashing two large glass doors at Lynx Gentlemen's Club in Coachella. The goat had visited the club the previous day but had been chased off by the owner. A local goat farmer explained that male goats have two things on their minds: eating and females.

WILD MONKEY GIVES POLICE THE SLIP

A wild monkey outwitted the entire Tokyo police force in the autumn of 2008. The monkey – a Japanese macaque – was spotted running through crowded train stations and even urinating in public, but always managed to escape before police could catch it. In one weekend alone, there were ten sightings of the animal, which is believed to have hitched a train ride from nearby mountains to the city. One officer summed up the frustration of the police. "This monkey is driving us crazy," he said. "It's so agile, and we only have nets."

GRIEVING FAMILY BURY WRONG CAT

After staging a special burial service for their dead cat, a Scottish family returned home to find it alive and well and waiting for its tea. The Wilkersons thought their beloved Mouse had been killed by a car after finding the body of an identical cat near their home in Invergordon. So they wrapped the body in a bag and buried it under a shrub in a friend's garden. Lou Wilkerson said: "We had a little service for the cat, then laid it to rest. But a few minutes later, Mouse turned up and we realized it wasn't our cat that we had buried. We have no idea who the dead cat belonged to."

DONKEY IS COURT WITNESS

When Dallas, Texas, oilman John Cantrell became involved in a dispute with his neighbour, attorney Gregory Shamoun, the first witness in their court case was Buddy the donkey. Cantrell claimed Shamoun put Buddy in his backyard to annoy him, but Shamoun maintained that Buddy was there to serve as a surrogate mother for a calf. In a bid to resolve the case and to prove that the law really is an ass, Buddy was led into the courtroom but refused to say a word. Instead he simply twitched his large ears and swatted flies with his tail. Eventually the two men settled their dispute out of court.

ORANGUTANS CAUSE A STINK BY EATING SPROUTS

Keepers at Dudley Zoo, near Birmingham, requested gas masks in 2003 after its orangutans developed a taste for Brussels sprouts. One keeper moaned: "Orangutans are windy animals anyway but because of all the sprouts they are eating, there is quite a pong around here at the moment. Whoever draws the short straw gets to muck them out."

MAN DISSECTS GUINEA PIG IN SEARCH FOR SPY CAMERA

Under the influence of the drug methamphetamine, Benny Zavala, of Oxnard, California, became convinced that US government agencies had planted a camera in the head of his daughter's pet guinea pig to spy on him. So after he had starved the rodent to death in 2001, he ripped open its head, also checking its teeth, which he thought were bar-coded. Relieved that his paranoia was unfounded, he phoned relatives to report: "The good news is guinea bleeds. The bad news is guinea's dead." Zavala was given three years' probation and ordered to seek psychiatric and drug counselling. Deputy District Attorney Tom Connors said: "It's not often you have someone this paranoid from using drugs that they think a guinea pig is spying on them for the government."

PEACOCK WOOS PETROL PUMP

For more than three years a lovesick peacock in Gloucestershire made a daily walk from his woodland home to a nearby gas station where he paraded his plumage to a row of diesel and unleaded pumps. Mr P. was so besotted by the pumps that he often spent 18 hours at a time with them in the hope of fuelling romance. His owner, Shirley Horsman, explained: "He gets very amorous and the clicking of the petrol pumps makes the same noise as a peahen crying 'Come on, I'm ready!' Every time he hears someone filling up he thinks he's on to a good thing. He goes all day, every day, in the breeding season. He just minds his own business and looks forlornly at the petrol pumps. It's quite sad really."

POLAR BEAR IS HEALTH FREAK

A polar bear that was apparently a real health freak stole toothpaste and vitamin pills after breaking into a tourist camp in the Norwegian Arctic in 2001. Tour operator Arne Kristoffersen said: "Maybe he felt he had bad breath after eating seal all summer."

DOG DEVOURS DENTURES

A Jack Russell terrier named Desmond was rushed to hospital in Tyneside in 2007 after swallowing his owner's false teeth. The dog ate 62-year-old Marjorie Johnson's dentures while she was in the toilet.

AUTHORITIES SWOOP TO CAPTURE ORNAMENTAL OWL

The Wisconsin Department of Natural Resources went to a family's home with a large net in 2003 to snare and capture what they thought was an injured owl. In fact the reason the bird had been motionless for so long was that it was a $15 garden ornament bought from Wal-Mart. Even then the owner had to yank it from the ground and show the agent its metal feet in order to convince him that the owl wasn't real.

GOAT WAVES GOODBYE TO TV STARDOM

Footage of a goat who waves back when visitors wave at him became a huge hit on YouTube where he was seen by tens of thousands of people. The clip of Darren, an eight-year-old Anglo-Nubian goat from White Post Farm, Nottinghamshire, was shown on American and Australian TV and soon came to the attention of the producers of *Britain's Got Talent* who wanted the waving goat to appear on TV in 2010 in front of judges Simon

Cowell, Amanda Holden and Piers Morgan. They thought Darren could be the next Susan Boyle. However the farm owners politely declined the offer, stating that it was a long way for a goat to travel for a five-minute trick and adding that, anyway, the show was not right for Darren.

SEX-CRAZED PARROT APPOINTED GOVERNMENT SPOKESBIRD

A rare flightless parrot, which became an international celebrity after attempting to mate with the head of a TV presenter, was named a conservation ambassador by the New Zealand government in 2010. The YouTube clip of Sirocco, the kakapo, trying to mate with zoologist Mark Carwadine's head on the BBC show *Last Chance To See* attracted over 1.6 million viewings and propelled the bird to overnight stardom. As one of just 124 kakapo still alive, Sirocco, who also has his own website and, naturally, a Twitter stream, was seen by New Zealand Prime Minister John Key as the ideal creature to promote the country's wildlife. Key said of Sirocco: "He's very media-savvy, he's got a worldwide fan base, and people hang on every squawk that comes out of his beak."

MOUSE GIFT IN CRACKER

New Zealand grandmother Betty Lawrence received an unwelcome surprise when she pulled a Christmas cracker and a rotting mouse popped out. She had just sat down to Christmas dinner with 20 relatives but said that the dead mouse "ruined my appetite for the rest of the day".

LION'S INGROWING TOENAIL KEEPS TOWN AWAKE

A lion with an ingrowing toenail kept residents of the Brazilian town of Industrial awake at night in 2004. Maruk was living in the town's zoo but he roared so loudly from the pain that local people thought he was right outside their homes. A police spokesman said: "We have received a lot of complaints, but what can we do? Arrest the lion?"

DECAPITATED RATTLESNAKE BITES MAN

A man in Prosser, Washington State, ended up spending two days in hospital in 2007 after being bitten by a beheaded rattlesnake. Danny Anderson had decapitated the snake with a shovel but when he reached down to pick up the severed head, it bit his finger. He took the head to hospital with him in his pickup truck.

WOMAN MURDERED BY MOOSE, NOT HUSBAND

A man arrested in Sweden on suspicion of murdering his wife was cleared after police decided she was probably killed by a moose instead. Ingemar Westlund found the body of his 63-year-old wife Agneta by a lake close to the village of Loftahammer in 2008. He was arrested and held in police custody for ten days but the case against him was dropped nine months later after forensic analysis revealed moose hair and saliva on his wife's clothes. Experts stated that the moose – or European elk – can become unusually aggressive after eating fermented apples in gardens.

DACHSHUND DEFIES ODDS TO MATE WITH ROTTWEILLER

Rusty, a tiny dachshund owned by Dale Adams of Peterborough, Cambridgeshire, proved that size isn't everything by fathering a puppy by a giant rottweiler bitch named Cassey. The odd couple produced Tinky, which Mr Adams described as looking like a miniature stretched version of her mother. "I have no idea how little Rusty managed to seduce Cassey," he added. "She's a big dog, so he either used my stepladder or he did it while she was asleep."

RAMPAGING GOAT PUTS THREE IN HOSPITAL

Three people were hospitalized after an angry goat invaded a Melbourne nursing home in 2010 and went on a rampage that ended only when it was caught by police. The billygoat wandered on to the grounds of the On Luck Chinese nursing home after escaping from a nearby enclosure. When a gardener at the home tried to shoo the animal away, it butted him and then attacked an elderly man who had to come to his aid. A woman who had witnessed the fracas injured her ankle as she ran for help.

CIRCUS CHIEF GOES ON THE RUN WITH ELEPHANT

A circus director went on the run with an elephant in 2003. The man and the female elephant named Kenia went missing in Dessau, Germany, shortly after another elephant he owned was put down. As German police launched a nationwide hunt for the pair, they insisted that finding an elephant was "not as simple as it sounds".

FAMILY SHOCKED AS GOLDFISH COMES DOWN CHIMNEY

A family sitting around the fireside at their home in Northampton, just before Christmas 1999, received an unexpected visitor down the chimney – a goldfish. The skydiving fish bounced off the hot coals, landed on the hearth and survived with nothing worse than a few damaged scales. It was thought to have fallen down the chimney after being dropped by a hungry heron that was perching on the roof.

DEER INVITED TO TAKE PART IN SALT TASTE TEST

Moose and reindeer at a Stockholm wildlife park were invited in 2007 to form a taste panel to help decide which type of salt should be used to de-ice Sweden's roads in winter. The National Road Administration planned to introduce a new, sweeter blend of road salt but did not want to attract wildlife to the highways. So they presented 14 hoofed panellists with different flavoured blocks of salt and opted for the one the animals liked the least.

POODLE SUES RESTAURANT

A Los Angeles lawyer instigated legal proceedings in 1996 on behalf of his co-plaintiff, his pet poodle, claiming that the dog's constitutional rights had been violated by a restaurant which had ordered it to leave. The claim was dismissed.

RARE GOAT ACCIDENTALLY HANGS ITSELF IN ZOO

An exotic goat at Canada's Calgary Zoo accidentally hanged itself in 2009 after it became entangled in a rope and then fell off a log. The zoo said that the Turkmenian markhor had been playing with a ball on the end of a rope – a toy designed to stimulate the animal.

NORWEGIAN ARMY BESTOWS KNIGHTHOOD ON PENGUIN

A penguin at Edinburgh Zoo has been knighted by the Norwegian Army. Nils Olav first become an honorary member of the army in the 1970s after a young lieutenant named Nils Egelien was so taken by the penguins at the zoo that he made one of them a lance corporal. Over the years, the king penguin was promoted through the ranks to colonel-in-chief in the Norwegian King's Guard, and then in 2008, with the permission of King Harald V, Nils Olav was granted a knighthood. The bird, who regularly inspects the troops, has also received medals for long service and had a four-foot bronze statue built in his honour. Officials pointed out, however, that the knighted penguin is not the original Nils Olav – he died in the 1980s.

HUMAN MOTHER RAISES LIZARD AS HER SON

A Thai woman was allowed to keep an endangered monitor lizard as a pet because she believed the reptile was possessed by the spirit of her dead son. Chamlong Taengniem, whose 13-year-old son Charoen died in a motorcycle crash, said that the lizard slept on her son's mattress and loved his favourite drinks – milk and yoghurt. Convinced by her story, crowds of people flocked to her house on the outskirts of Bangkok to shower the lizard with gifts and hunt for numbers for the state lottery on its skin.

BEAR STEALS HUBCAP FROM CAR – THEN GIVES IT BACK

A few weeks after having all four hubcaps stolen from her car, Azra Noonari was offered a new one – by a bear. Mrs Noonari, from Luton, Bedfordshire, was on a family outing to nearby Woburn Safari Park when the car in front stopped in the bear and wolf area. "There was a bear ahead of it," she said, "so I stopped too and started taking pictures. Then I saw it take a hubcap off the car in front and start walking towards us. It put the hubcap down and then banged on our window, as if it was trying to get my attention. It was almost like it wanted to give me the wheel cap – maybe it thought I needed it."

MAN TIES HIMSELF TO SHEEP AFTER BEING REFUSED ACCOMMODATION

After 20 landlords refused to let him share accommodation with his pet sheep, an Argentinian man registered his protest by tying himself to the ewe. "I don't see why I shouldn't be allowed to live with my sheep, as I have done for all my life,'" said the man who had recently moved to Buenos Aires from the country. "She's very tranquil, the ideal companion to share a flat." He confirmed that he would remain tethered to the sheep until they found somewhere to live together.

HUNGRY COWS LICK NEIGHBOUR'S HOUSE

Cows from an adjacent farm licked a house in Hawkins County, Tennessee, causing $100 of damage. The cows, which lived in a field next to the house, poked their heads through a fence, ripped off a screen window, cracking the glass in the process, and pulled down a gutter. Nobody connected with the case could explain what had suddenly made the house so tasty.

WOMAN FINDS BAT IN BRA

A Norwich hotel receptionist walked around for five hours unaware that a baby bat was hiding in her bra. Abbie Hawkins believed the creature hid itself in the padding of her bra while the garment was hanging on the washing line the previous day. "I didn't notice anything when I put my bra on," she said, "and although I felt a slight vibration when I was driving to work, I thought it was my phone."

GUN-TOTING PARROT FOILS BURGLARY ATTEMPT

A parrot owned by a retired police officer foiled a break-in after the owner left the bird alone in his Kiev, Ukraine, apartment for a few minutes. When the ex-cop returned, he found three men stretched out on the floor with their hands behind their heads. The would-be burglars admitted sheepishly that when they broke into the flat they heard a voice call out: "Stop! I'll shoot! On the ground!"

BULLDOG WRECKS MASERATI

TV presenter Johnny Vaughan's $90,000 Maserati sports car careered into a parked van in 2002 – thanks to his three-year-old bulldog Harvey. Vaughan was driving Harvey home from a trip to the veterinarian in southwest London. He said: "I stopped because Harvey, who was in the front and had a sore tummy, looked like he needed the toilet. I got out of the car and went over to the passenger side. But when Harvey saw me, he leapt over to the driver's seat, pushing the gearstick up to 'drive'. Then the little critter jumped into the footwell beneath the steering wheel and pressed the accelerator down. The car shot forward with me chasing behind – and went straight into the back of a van with a huge crunch. I couldn't believe my dog had crashed my car." The impact caused around $16,000 damage, which Vaughan had to pay for himself since the insurance company did not have Harvey listed as a driver.

LEOPARD BREAKS INTO HOUSE TO WATCH TV

When her four-year-old son came into the kitchen to tell her there was a "tiger" in his room, a woman from Chandigarh, India, thought he was referring to a wildlife documentary on TV. However her amusement turned to horror when she peeked into the bedroom and saw a real leopard sprawled out on the bed. After the animal had been tranquilized with a dart, a forest department official revealed: "From what we understand, the leopard sneaked into the house and watched TV for over an hour. Then it apparently got bored, so it rolled over and went to sleep on the bed."

ZOO CREATES ZEBRAS BY PAINTING STRIPES ON DONKEYS

Unable to afford the cost of importing real zebras, a zoo in Gaza solved the problem by painting stripes on donkeys. Mohammed Bargouthi, owner of the Marah Land Zoo, stuck strips of masking tape to the donkeys and then painted over them with black hair dye. He said: "The first time we used paint and it didn't look good, but the hair dye worked much better. The children don't know, so they call them zebras and they are happy to see something new."

POLICEMAN ACCIDENTALLY KILLS RESCUED CAT

After rescuing an injured cat in 1998, a Gloucestershire policeman then contrived to kill it. Phil Groom spotted the cat at the side of the road near Moreton-in-the-Marsh and put it in a box on top of his car. But he then forgot all about it and drove off with the box still on his car roof. After only a few yards, the box fell off and went under the wheels of a car following behind. The distraught officer admitted: "I must have had my mind on something else."

COW KILLS MAN FOR SEX

A Chinese farmer was trampled to death under the hoofs of his cow in 2007 as she rushed to mate with an ox from a neighbouring village. The cow, who was on heat, took one look at her bovine suitor and dashed towards him, in her haste knocking over and stamping on the hapless farmer who died on the spot with hoof prints on his body.

HEROIN-ADDICTED ELEPHANT IN REHAB

A **FOUR-YEAR-OLD** bull elephant spent three years in rehab after becoming addicted to heroin. The animal, called "Big Brother", had been captured by traders in China who used bananas spiked with heroin to control him. When police arrested the traders a few months later and freed Big Brother, the elephant was found to be suffering from withdrawal symptoms and was sent to an animal protection centre for rehab. There, as part of his treatment, he underwent a year of methadone injections at five times the human dosage to wean him off his addiction. ●

RUNAWAY BULL ENDS UP IN SWIMMING POOL

A family in St Andrews, Scotland, were looking forward to enjoying their newly built swimming pool in the summer of 2008 – only for a runaway bull to get there first. Having broken free from its farm paddock, the bull ran three miles before plunging into the private pool. The pool's owner said of the bull's unexpected entry: "It was an 8.5 out of 10 dive."

IRATE GORILLA HELPS CAPTURE FLEEING ROBBER

Pursued by Johannesburg police investigating a robbery in 1999, Isaac Mofokeng jumped over a wall – and landed in the gorilla enclosure at the city zoo. There, Max the gorilla demonstrated his anger towards the uninvited guest by ripping Mofokeng's jeans and biting him on the buttocks. A shaken Mofokeng reacted by shooting Max in the jaw and shoulder before being detained by police. Max recovered after surgery; Mofokeng was sentenced to 40 years in jail.

PIGEON ARRESTED FOR DRUG SMUGGLING

A pigeon was arrested in 2008 for smuggling drugs into a high security jail in Bosnia. Guards at Zenica prison became suspicious when they saw four prisoners "visibly intoxicated" shortly after the pigeon landed on one of the windows. The pigeon was a pet of one of the inmates, and when he and three other prisoners tested positive for heroin, the pigeon was taken into custody. Police believe the drugs were sent from the town of Tuzla – 40 miles away – by being stuffed into tiny bags and attached to the pigeon's legs.

PUGS MARRY IN MICHIGAN

When Bobby met Gracie it was love at first sight and everyone said it would end in marriage – despite the fact that both partners had four legs, a sunken black nose and a wrinkled face. Sure enough in 2005 Bobby, a two-year-old pug, married his puppy sweetheart Gracie, a three-year-old pug, at Clinton Township, Michigan. Bobby waddled down the aisle, tail wagging, in top hat, black tuxedo and red bow tie. As he took his place at the altar, his tongue flopped out. Gracie, her nails painted pink, wore a puffy white gown. The groomsmen and maids of honour were chihuahuas in a ceremony that cost respective owners Susan Laurer and Cyndi Parise $1,200. "We are gathered here today," announced Pastor Joseph DeRose, "to celebrate the joining of the paws of Bobby and Gracie." The happy couple were wed to the tune of "Who Let the Dogs Out" and at the ensuing reception they tucked into a two-tiered, bone-shaped cake with a pink heart in the middle.

CHIMP MAKES MONKEY OF ZOO BOSS

A zoo director who banned his keepers from feeding the animals by hand following a series of accidents had his finger bitten off by a chimpanzee in 2009. Bernhard Blaszkiewitz forgot his own rule while showing VIPs around Berlin Zoo and offered Pedro the chimp some fruit through the bars. The chimp responded by grabbing the zoo boss's hand and biting his index finger with such force that it was left hanging by just a flap of skin. The keepers at the zoo appeared less than sympathetic. One said: "He has only himself to blame. We're all banned from doing that sort of thing and that chimp is known to be very aggressive. He's lucky Pedro didn't eat his finger."

DESIGNER SNAKE IN COLOUR CLASH

A man handed in his pet python to the RSPCA in Godshill, Isle of Wight, in 2006 because it did not match the colour of his newly decorated home.

JOGGER HOSPITALIZED BY KANGAROO

An Australian jogger out running near Melbourne had to be taken to hospital after being attacked by a kangaroo. While on his daily run, the man apparently became trapped between a male and female kangaroo, as a result of which he suffered a gash on his head plus minor scratches to his body. A paramedic reported that following the attack, the victim's jog turned into a sprint as he fled to a nearby house.

BIRD'S CALLS FOOL POLICE

When neighbours heard a woman's voice repeatedly crying "Help me! Help me!" from a house in Trenton, New Jersey, they called the police. Officers arrived and when nobody answered the door, they kicked it in – but instead of a damsel in distress, they found a caged cockatoo with a remarkable ability to mimic humans. It wasn't the first time that ten-year-old Luna had brought the authorities to the home of owner Evelyn DeLeon. Back in 2001, the bird cried like a baby for hours, prompting a visit by concerned state child welfare workers.

CHINESE BURGLAR EATS PET TORTOISE

A hungry Chinese illegal immigrant was jailed for a year in 1999 for breaking into a Hong Kong house and eating an expensive pet tortoise. Having entered the house, Chau Chao-ping, 22, ignored valuable possessions but spotted three tortoises in a hut. Desperate for food, he slaughtered the biggest tortoise, boiled it and ate it before fleeing, leaving the shell in a wash basin.

MOOSE UPSET BY UNRESPONSIVE CAR

A Norwegian moose mistook a Ford Ka for a would-be partner in 2001. He licked and dribbled on the car but when his ardour was not reciprocated, he defecated on it.

SEAGULL TURNS SHOPLIFTER

A seagull turned shoplifter in 2007 by strolling into a shop in Aberdeen, Scotland, and helping itself to packets of potato crisps from the shelves. The bird, nicknamed Sam, always swooped for packets of cheese Doritos, which he then ripped open outside and shared with other seagulls. Shop assistant Sriaram Nagarajan said: "He's got it down to a fine art. He waits until there are no customers around and I'm standing behind the till, then he raids the place." Sam became such a celebrity that locals even started paying for his crisps.

ARMY DEMOTES GOAT FOR UNRULY BEHAVIOUR

A British army regiment's ceremonial pet goat was demoted in disgrace after it marched out of line and tried to headbutt musicians at a 2006 parade to mark Queen Elizabeth II's birthday. Billy, mascot of the 1st Battalion, the Royal Welsh, was downgraded from lance corporal to fusilier after army chiefs decided that his wayward behaviour had ruined the ceremony before visiting dignitaries at the base in Episkopi, Cyprus. In an official statement Captain Crispian Coates said: "The goat, which has been the regiment's mascot since 2001, was supposed to be leading the march, but would not stay in line. He was reported for insubordination and after consideration, the commanding officer decided he had no option but to demote Billy." Another soldier present at the parade recounted how the goat "was trying to headbutt the waist and nether regions of the drummers". Captain Coates added that as a result of his demotion, soldiers were no longer expected to salute Billy as a sign of respect.

GERMAN DOGS ATTACK PARKED CARS

In a well-planned dawn raid, a pack of large boxer-like dogs launched a frenzied attack on six cars parked in a suburb of Munich in 2003. Their orgy of savagery left a trail of damaged vehicles with ripped-off fenders, mud flaps and licence plates. Police found teeth marks on the hubcaps and bodywork, which were covered in blood and saliva from the dogs. Residents said they saw the animals biting and snapping at the cars around 4.30 a.m. One witness said: "It was incredible. One of them leaped again and again with unbelievable force into the side of a car and bit into it like a lunatic." Police could offer no explanation for the uncharacteristic behaviour but warned: "If we see any dogs sniffing around cars, we'll be sure to get them."

WOMAN MISTAKES PLASTIC BAG FOR WILD BEAST

A woman from England's West Country rang the Royal Society for the Prevention of Cruelty to Animals in 2002 to report that the infamous "Beast of Bodmin" – a black panther-like big cat said to roam the Cornish moor – was outside her door and laying siege to her house. The "Beast" turned out to be nothing more dangerous than her new telephone books, which had been delivered in a black plastic bag.

FISH SNATCHES CASH

A young girl standing on a riverbank in England's Lake District was robbed of a £5 ($10) note by a trout leaping from the water.

PET CAMEL TRIES TO MATE WITH OWNER

A woman in Australia was killed by her pet camel after the animal apparently tried to have sex with her. The ten-month-old male camel – a 60th birthday present for the woman – had already come close to suffocating the family's pet goat on several occasions before, one day in August 2007, he suddenly transferred his lust to his owner. He knocked her to the ground, lay on top of her and displayed what the police delicately described as possible mating behaviour.

LION RECEIVES WAKE-UP CALL

A man trying to retrieve a cell phone which had been dropped in a lion's cage in Mexico was badly mauled when the phone suddenly rang and woke up the lion. Guillermo Orozco entered the cage at a Pachuca amusement park in 2000 after making a wager with a friend that he could safely collect the phone.

SNAKE SWALLOWS ELECTRIC BLANKET

A pet Burmese python needed surgery in 2006 after swallowing an entire electric blanket, including the electrical cord and control box. Owner Karl Beznoska, of Ketchum, Idaho, believed the blanket, which was in the snake's cage for warmth, must have become tangled up in the reptile's rabbit dinner. Veterinary experts said it would have taken the python – named Houdini – six hours to swallow the blanket. "Somehow he was unable to unplug the electric cord," said Beznoska. "At least he wasn't hooked up to the power or it could have been pretty warm in his stomach."

NURSES TOLD TO WALK IN PAIRS TO AVOID SQUIRREL ATTACKS

Nurses in County Durham were told to walk in pairs or carry umbrellas to protect them from attacks by marauding gangs of squirrels. The warning came in 2009 after a district nurse was left shaken and with "reddening of the scalp" when one squirrel jumped on her and another landed on her head while she was walking up to a farm. On her health and safety report form, she rated the "severity of incident" as "insignificant to catastrophic".

BUSINESSMAN FINDS MISSING PHONE – INSIDE DOG'S STOMACH

When Kamal Shah's cell phone went missing from the bedside table of his home in Nairobi, the Kenyan businessman thought his young son had taken it. But when he called the number from his land line, he was amazed to hear it ringing inside the stomach of his German Shepherd dog. A bemused Mr Shah said: "When I dialled the number, just about the last place I expected to hear it ringing was inside my dog." The dog underwent surgery to have the phone removed.

WHEELS IMPROVE TORTOISE'S LOVE LIFE

Arava the tortoise found that a set of wheels did wonders for her love life. The ten-year-old spurred tortoise was fitted with a customized skateboard by staff at Jerusalem's Biblical Zoo after her rear legs ceased to function, and the improved mobility provided by the strap-on board quickly led to romance with an amorous male.

POLICE OFFICER HANDCUFFS AGGRESSIVE SHEEP

After an escaped ewe assaulted his colleague, a New Zealand police officer subdued the animal by handcuffing one of its front legs to a back leg . . . but then suffered the additional embarrassment of having to call for backup when he realized that the key to the handcuffs was missing. Summoned to deal with a loose sheep, one of the two police constables pursued it into a garage before emerging a minute or so later with his clothing torn. The ewe then ran straight towards the second officer who managed to wrestle it to the ground before handcuffing it. Describing the first assault, Sergeant Andrew Bardsley of Dunedin police said: "Our officer came out of the garage looking a little the worse for wear. He was limping, with ripped trousers. We're still not sure exactly what happened in there."

CUSTOMS OFFICERS FIND REPTILES INSIDE GNOMES

In 2007, customs officers in Sydney, Australia, found seven snakes and eight lizards stuffed inside hollowed-out garden gnomes and other ceramic figures in packages that had been sent from England. Due to quarantine regulations, all the reptiles were put down. The gnomes were released without charge.

DOG PERFORMS HEIMLICH MANOEUVRE

A golden labrador saved his owner's life by giving her the Heimlich manoeuvre when she was choking on a piece of apple. Debbie Parkhurst, from Cecil County, Maryland, was struggling for breath until two-year-old Toby pushed her to the ground by putting his front paws on her shoulders and then jumped up and down on her chest, eventually dislodging the apple from her windpipe. "As soon as I started breathing," she said, "he stopped and began licking my face, as if to keep me from passing out. He was amazing even though I now have pawprint-shaped bruises on my chest."

ELITE SWAT TEAM STALKS SOFT TOY

Called to deal with a report of a panther prowling in a back garden in Wielkopolska, a crack Polish police SWAT team spent nearly an hour watching and stalking the deadly beast – only to discover that it was a life-sized soft toy. When the armed officers arrived at the scene, they immediately identified the creature as a black panther and prepared a stakeout. It was only after more than 45 minutes of playing cat and mouse that they became suspicious when the panther didn't even twitch a whisker as they started to approach it. A police spokesman insisted afterwards: "From a distance it really looked like a live animal."

RARE ROBIN EATEN BY BIRDWATCHER'S CAT

A rare American robin – one of just eight seen in Britain over the previous five years – flew 400 miles from Norway to Manchester in 2004, only to perish when it was caught and eaten by a birdwatcher's cat.

HORSE FOUND ON TWELFTH FLOOR

Police who were called to investigate a strange smell in an apartment block in Prokuplje, Serbia, soon discovered the cause – a dead horse that had been jammed into a ventilation shaft 12 storeys up. The stench from the putrefying remains was so noxious that officers ordered the building to be evacuated in case the overpowering fumes proved lethal. The police admitted they were at a loss to explain how someone managed to get a horse's body 12 storeys up and why the animal was then dumped in the shaft.

"GHOST" TURNS OUT TO BE CAT UP CHIMNEY

After hearing a repeated moaning sound, John Bambrick, from Cradley Heath, West Midlands, called a priest to exorcise his house before moving his family out to a relative's home. Later it was discovered that their "moaning ghost" was nothing spookier than a cat stuck up their chimney.

CAT CHASES BEAR UP TREE

A black bear that strayed into a garden in West Milford, New Jersey, in 2006 was twice chased up a tree by the family cat. The petrified bear was able to make its escape only when the cat's owner, Donna Dickey, called the hissing feline into the house. She described the pet – a tabby named Jack – as "territorial".

PARROT SPREADS THE F-WORD

A foul-mouthed parrot, who once told a vicar to "fuck off", has been teaching other birds at a Warwickshire wildlife centre how to swear. Barney the macaw told the vicar, a mayoress and two police officers to "fuck off" and called them "wankers" when they visited the centre. Now he has been teaching two other parrots – Sam and Charlie – his full repertoire of abuse, which includes such terms as "tits" and "bollocks".

MATING GOATS UPSET TOWN

Convenience store manager Carol Mendenhall was charged with allowing her four goats to have sex in her front yard in public view – a contravention of a town law in Dibble, Oklahoma. While freely admitting that her billy goat, Adam, had been servicing three females who were on heat at the time, Mendenhall launched a vigorous campaign that led to her name being cleared and the law repealed.

MOOSE STEALS BICYCLE

A hungry moose stole a bicycle that a Swedish couple had placed in their garden to stop the animal eating their rose bushes. The moose, dubbed Droopy Ear, had frequently visited the Vuoggatjalme garden of Bjorn and Monica Helamb to munch their roses, so eventually they decided to put the bicycle in front of the flowers as a barrier. Instead of being deterred, the moose leaned through the bicycle frame to get at the flowers and then sauntered off, with the bike hanging around its neck. The couple found the bicycle 500 metres from their house, mangled beyond repair.

MAN RESCUED AFTER PELTING BEARS WITH SNOWBALLS

A 35-year-old man had to be rescued by firefighters in 1998 after climbing into the historic bear pit in Berne, Switzerland, and pelting two bears with snowballs. He was taken to hospital with "considerable flesh wounds" to his legs and shoulder, sustained when the female bear expressed displeasure at the intrusion.

SEAL BREAKS INTO TROUT HATCHERY

A clever seal somehow broke into a fish hatchery in Cape Cod, Massachusetts, in 2009 and turned the place into an all-you-can-eat buffet, devouring untold numbers of trout before being discovered. The three-foot-long seal, which was later released on a beach, was described as looking "pretty full".

PYTHON MISTAKES GOLF BALLS FOR EGGS

An X-ray of a python in Australia showed that it had swallowed four golf balls after mistaking them for eggs. A veterinary at a wildlife sanctuary on the Queensland–New South Wales border explained: "People in the area have been putting golf balls under their brooding hens, pretending that they are eggs, to make the chickens happy. We think that the snake slithered into the back yard, thought the golf balls were real eggs and tucked in."

ZOOKEEPERS SUSPENDED FOR EATING THEIR ANIMALS

Two keepers at a children's zoo at Recklinghausen, near Cologne, Germany, were suspended in 2002 on suspicion of having eaten some of the animals in their care. Police believed the pair had slaughtered and barbecued five Tibetan mountain chickens and two Cameroonian sheep.

SHEPHERD ALLOWED SHEEP TO INTIMIDATE NEIGHBOURS

A 58-year-old Gloucestershire shepherd was given an Anti-social Behaviour Order in 2008 following accusations from his neighbours that he couldn't control his sheep. For more than 500 years commoners born in the Forest of Dean have been able to let their livestock graze freely, but Jeremy Awdry was banned from taking his animals into the village of Bream after his 500-strong flock were found straying into gardens and damaging fences. His woolly bullies were described as part of the "intimidation of people living in the area."

WOMAN PUTS EARRINGS ON BABY DEER

Bettie Phillips, of Hiddenite, North Carolina, was ordered to pay $250 to a wildlife centre in 1997 after police officers found a two-month-old deer in the back of her car with zircon-studded earrings in its pierced ears. Phillips said she had rescued the fawn from a busy road and had pierced its ears by hand, pushing the posts of the two earrings through the flesh. "I thought it would be pretty," she told reporters. "You can get a little kid's ears pierced. What's the difference between a person's and a baby deer's?" Ned Gentz, chief veterinarian at the local wildlife centre to where the deer was taken to be treated for mildly infected ears, remarked: "We're pretty used to the concept of people who think fawns are cute and want to adopt them. However, earrings are a totally new one on us. Just when you think you've been dealing with the issues of human interaction with wildlife for long enough that you've seen it all, somebody surprises you."

POLICE DOG SACKED FOR BEING TOO FRIENDLY

Buster, a two-year-old German Shepherd, was sacked in 2005 after failing to make a single arrest in his six months with South Yorkshire Police. His problem was that he was simply too nice. He ignored fleeing villains, let drunken yobs stroke him, disappeared at crucial moments to cock his leg, and even lay down for a rest while supposedly in hot pursuit of a suspect. His former handler, David Stephenson, admitted: "He just showed no interest in doing the job. He had no fire in his belly. It's not his fault. He's just a dog who wants to be friendly with everyone." The final straw came when Buster twice failed to locate criminals hiding in gardens – even walking straight past one of them.

FIREMAN MISTAKES SNAKE FOR HOSE

UKRAINIAN FIREMEN fled a burning building in panic in 2005 after one of them grabbed a hosepipe that turned out to be a ten-foot python. The fire crew had arrived to tackle a blaze at a Donetsk health club but when one firefighter tripped over what he thought was a hosepipe and reached to pick it up, he found to his horror that it was a live snake. The men were eventually persuaded to re-enter the building after the owner convinced them that the snake was a harmless pet. ●

COW GETS HEAD TRAPPED IN WASHING MACHINE DRUM

An inquisitive young cow got its head stuck in a washing machine drum that had been illegally dumped in a field in Cornwall. Probably thinking there was food inside the drum, the animal put its head in and was then unable to shake off the metal container. An RSPCA officer rescued the hapless heifer and returned her to the rest of the herd without her cranial attachment.

POLICE SAY MAN BOUGHT DRUGS WITH DEAD PIG

A man was arrested on a street corner in Syracuse, New York State, in 2009 for allegedly offering a slaughtered pig as part payment for a bag of crack cocaine. The police claimed that Angelo Colon paid Omar Veliz half a pig and $10 for a $50 bag of cocaine. Veliz said the pig was intended to be the focal point of a celebration for a relative who was being released from jail. Unfortunately while the two men were being arrested, a third party stole the pig.

FOX SNATCHES WOMAN'S HANDBAG

Police in Switzerland were outfoxed by a four-legged handbag thief in 2008. A woman was working outside in Riehen when a fox suddenly ran off with her handbag – containing her wallet and house keys – in its mouth. A passer-by gave chase but the fox was too quick for him and made its escape. The women reported the daring theft to the police who found the unopened handbag under a nearby bush. They deduced that the fox had discarded the bag because it was too bulky to take into its lair.

BEAR CAUGHT EATING PORRIDGE

In a tale straight out of a fairy story, a woman from West Vancouver, Canada, arrived home in 2006 to find a young bear eating porridge in her kitchen. Despite the presence of three police officers, the hungry bear, which had obtained the oatmeal by breaking into a ceramic food container, refused to leave the house until it had finished eating.

FALLING COW WRECKS CAR

A couple were driving along a highway near Manson, Washington State, in 2007 when a 600-pound cow plunged 200 feet from the sky and landed on the hood of their minivan, causing major damage. The cow – named Michelle – had fallen off a cliff.

PATROLMAN USES DOG TO START CAR

Breakdown patrolman Kevin Gorman managed to get a car to start by using the vehicle owner's dog. Despite changing the battery in her electronic key fob, Juliette Piesley could not start her car, but when AA patrolman Gorman arrived at the scene in Addlestone, Surrey, he discovered that its immobilizer chip was missing. Ms Piesley then realized that her dog George had probably eaten the chip, so the resourceful AA man placed the dog in the driver's seat and started the car first time with the key. Afterwards Ms Piesley acknowledged that from then on she would have to take George with her in the car at all times until events took their natural course.

JET FIGHTERS CAUSE DEATH OF SANTA'S REINDEER

The Danish Air Force paid $5,000 in compensation in 2006 to a part-time Santa Claus whose reindeer died of heart failure when two fighter jets roared overhead. The animal – naturally named Rudolf – was grazing at Olavi Nikkanoff's farm when the noise of the low-flying jets caused it to collapse and die, leaving his owner with the prospect of having only one reindeer to pull his sleigh that Christmas. Capt. Morten Jensen of the Danish Air Force said: "We got a letter from Santa complaining about his reindeer's death and looked into it seriously."

COCKATOO MOTHERS CHOCOLATE EGGS

A confused cockatoo spent more than two weeks trying to hatch a bowl of chocolate creme eggs. Pippa started protecting the Easter eggs when she spotted them on a table at Nuneaton and Warwickshire Wildlife Sanctuary. Her owner, Geoff Grewcock, said: "She went straight over, climbed on the creme eggs and that was it. She was convinced they were her eggs and wouldn't let anyone near them." He added that Pippa had "always been a bit nuts".

THIEF DISGUISES STOLEN FARM ANIMALS IN CLOTHES

A thief from Port of Spain, Trinidad, stole some farm animals one night in 1999 and dressed them in clothes in the hope that people would think they were humans. The sheep wore a dress while the goats wore shirts, pants and hats. The culprit was ultimately arrested not because of the dubious disguises but because police officers became suspicious when they saw the truck driving along without headlights.

LIZARD SWALLOWS TOY LIZARD

When young Finley Collins from Jacksonville, Florida, saw legs, a body and a head emerging from near the tail of her pet lizard, she thought it was giving birth. But it turned out that it was merely excreting a rubber toy lizard that it had swallowed some time before.

BLIND MAN ACCUSED OF BITING GUIDE DOG

A blind man was arrested in Edinburgh, Scotland, in 2005 after witnesses said he sank his teeth into his guide dog's head and then kicked the labrador-retriever mix because it apparently refused to help him across a busy street.

CHICKEN FINED FOR CROSSING THE ROAD

A chicken was fined $60 for illegally crossing the road in California. Ophelia, a black Polish hen, strayed onto the street in the rural town of Johannesburg, in violation of state law which bans livestock from highways. However Ophelia's owners, Linc and Helena Moore, appealed against the fine, arguing that the chicken was domesticated and therefore could not be considered as livestock, and a sympathetic judge eventually dismissed the case.

CIGARETTE-LOVING DOG RUN OVER ON WAY TO TOBACCONIST'S

A dachshund that got through ten cigarettes a day ever since he was a puppy defied repeated health warnings to reach the ripe old age of 24, only to be run over and killed in 2008 on his way to his favourite tobacconist's shop. Wolfgang Trierler, from Graz, Austria, quickly spotted General Edi's strange tastes after the previous owner had abandoned the dog. "We noticed straight away that he was in the habit of eating cigarettes. He used to eat the tobacco and the paper, and then chewed a while on the filter before spitting it out. But all of his teeth were fine." However, having munched his way through half a packet of cigarettes a day for virtually his entire life

– 168 in human years – he finally perished in pursuit of his addiction. "Poor Edi dashed out in the road in excitement right in front of a car," said a neighbour. "There was nothing anyone could do. I suppose you could say that cigarettes did ultimately damage his health."

RAMPAGING BADGER PUTS FIVE IN HOSPITAL

Five people were put in hospital in 2003 and two police officers were sent running for cover after Boris the badger went on a 48-hour rampage through the normally tranquil Worcestershire town of Evesham. The male badger, two and a half feet long and weighing over 30 pounds, began his reign of terror by biting two teenagers before savaging a man and a woman who were walking their dogs. He then attacked a householder investigating noises coming from his garage, sinking his teeth into the man's arms and legs with a ferocity which left his victim needing skin grafts. Meanwhile two police officers, called by residents who thought a prowler was on the loose, were forced to jump onto the bonnet of their patrol car when the snarling animal charged straight at them. Boris, who had escaped from a local wildlife centre, was eventually captured by the chairman of the Worcestershire Badger Society.

BEAR WITH SWEET TOOTH STEALS CAR

Police in New Jersey suspected a black bear of stealing a people carrier and taking it for a spin. They found the passenger window broken, the door panels damaged and the interior of the vehicle covered in bear hair. They thought the bear – probably attracted by sweets left inside – had accidentally released the handbrake, thereby allowing the car to roll 50 feet down the hill from the owner's house.

HEAVY BREATHING CALLS WERE FROM DOG

A US police dispatcher was alarmed by three late-night 911 calls because "the only communication was someone breathing". The calls were traced and three squad cars raced to an address in Lake Parsipanny, New Jersey, where the occupant, Sylvia D'Antonio, maintained that they had been made by her German Shepherd, Slayer. Ms D'Antonio claimed she had been teaching the dog to dial 911 in an emergency. She said: "She knocks the phone off the hook and then she steps on it."

HORSE BITES OFF MAN'S TESTICLE

A man was rushed to hospital in Indonesia in 2009 after a horse bit off one of his testicles. The man was unloading sand from a horse-drawn cart at a construction site in Sulawesi when the horse – named Budi – suddenly lunged at him and sunk its teeth into him. As bystanders put the victim in a car to take him to hospital, one noticed a lump of flesh on the ground. A witness said: "Luckily the horse did not chew up or swallow the testicle, but spat it onto the pavement."

SWAN FALLS IN LOVE WITH PEDAL BOAT

In a tale to rival *Romeo and Juliet*, an Australian black swan on a lake in Germany fell in love with a plastic pedal boat in the shape of a white swan. Swans choose a partner for life but Petra's mistake was to fall for a four-seater pedal boat designed to look like a swan. Visitors to Aasee near Münster looked on in amazement as Petra repeatedly circled her plastic lover, staring longingly at it and making crooning sounds, all classic signs of a swan in love. And when the pedal boat swan refused to fly south for the winter, Petra stayed too, defying the cold weather. Fortunately the local zoo took pity and gave both Petra and her boat boyfriend a place to spend the winter. Over the next two years, Petra was encouraged to strike up a rapport with real swans but the relationships always fizzled out and she returned to her boat mate, swimming patiently alongside it, apparently undeterred by its lack of feathers or by the fact that it was 50 times bigger than her.

CASINO CHICKEN RULES THE ROOST

Ginger the chicken shattered the dreams of dozens of punters at a Las Vegas casino in 2002 by sending them home empty-handed in a big money game of tic-tac-toe (noughts and crosses). The casino was offering $10,000 in a Chicken Challenge to anyone who could beat Ginger. The bird was placed in a glass cubicle along with a computer screen showing a video of a tic-tac-toe board. Whenever Ginger pecked the screen, a nought appeared on the corresponding place on the game board. Many tried their luck but after either suffering the humiliation of being beaten by a chicken or at best achieving a draw, they left, grumbling about the fact that the chicken always went first.

OVERWEIGHT DOG IS VISIBLE FROM SPACE

A **FAMILY FROM** Bournemouth realized their bull mastiff might be overweight when they discovered that he was visible from space. Using the Google Earth website, Boris's owners spotted him sprawled out on the lawn of their hotel. Fran Milner said: "My brother-in-law was on the Internet and looked at a satellite picture of our place. He zoomed in a little way and noticed a big brown blob on the grass in front of the sundial. Then he realized it was Boris in his favourite place." An average bull mastiff weighs nine stone but Boris tips the scales at 14 stone, largely because he begs guests for the remains of their full English breakfasts. ●

WOMAN HIDES SNAKES IN BRA

A 42-year-old woman tried to smuggle 75 live snakes into Sweden by hiding them in her bra. Officers became suspicious when they noticed that she kept scratching her chest, and on further inspection of her heaving cleavage they found dozens of baby grass snakes writhing around in her bra and six lizards crawling about under her blouse. The woman said she was planning to start a reptile farm.

WOMAN MUGGED BY EAGLE

A 69-year-old Austrian woman received the shock of her life in 2009 when she was mugged in the street by an eagle. Klara Maier couldn't believe her eyes when the bald eagle, with its seven-foot wingspan, swooped down from the skies and snatched her handbag. The bird then proceeded to rip the handbag open and check its contents. Police in Kundl later found the thief hiding in a field. They then traced it back to its owner who revealed that the woman's handbag just happened to be the same colour and shape as the bag in which the eagle's food was kept.

CHICKEN SURVIVES TWO DAYS IN FREEZER

Feeling peckish, a Chinese man took a chicken out of the freezer, only to discover that it was still alive. Gan Shugen said the bird – a gift from a relative – was wrapped in a thick plastic bag and with its legs tied so, assuming that it was dead, he put it in the freezer. But when he opened the freezer two days later, he received something of a surprise. "I heard weak sounds," he said, "and when I opened the bag, a red head popped out. She was still warm, and when I removed the tape, she could stand." In the light of the chicken's near-death experience, Gan promised that he would not eat the bird, but would look after it instead.

GERMANS ROCKED BY EXPLODING TOADS

Visitors to parks in Hamburg, Germany, had a new menace to contend with in 2005 – exploding toads. The mystery disease caused thousands of toads to swell up to three and a half times their normal size before suddenly exploding, scattering their entrails over a large area.

PUPPY SWALLOWS 40 PAIRS OF UNDERPANTS

A springer spaniel puppy with a taste for underpants had to undergo surgery in 2007 after devouring his 40th pair. Usually whatever Taffy eats – and that has included 300 socks and a set of car keys – emerges naturally from the other end but this pair of underpants refused to shift, forcing his owner, Staffordshire vet Eubie Saayman, to operate. But once he had recovered, Taffy was quickly up to his old tricks again. "I guess this is just his vice," said Mrs Saayman, adding that Taffy had also destroyed 15 pairs of shoes.

2

SEX MATTERS

WOMAN'S SEX ROMP WITH DONALD DUCK IN SATELLITE DISH

An unmarried 32-year-old woman from Tulsa, Oklahoma, with a long history of paranoid schizophrenia, became convinced that she was being wooed by Donald Duck and that the satellite dish recently installed in her neighbour's yard had been put there to enable the cartoon duck to communicate his true love for her. She spent hours hovering around the satellite dish until, one day in 1992, she finally undressed and climbed into it. She was found sitting in the dish masturbating, happy in the belief that she was consummating her marriage to Mr Duck.

WIFE SAYS HUSBAND HAD SEX WITH FROZEN CHICKEN

A wife filed for divorce in 2002 after saying she caught her husband of six months having sex with a frozen chicken. Jean Curtis, from Glasgow, Scotland, claimed that husband Ian – a former military policeman – was dressed in a blouse and rubber stockings as he lay on the sofa with the bird of his fantasies. She told reporters: "My jaw just dropped. I said: 'You dirty bugger, that's my Sunday lunch.' He was calm as you like and said, 'It's all right, we can still eat it.' I kicked him out."

SEX-STARVED WOMAN BOMBARDS EMERGENCY SERVICES

A 42-year-old woman from Koszalin, Poland, made 700 calls to emergency services, the local army headquarters and the town council demanding a man for sex. Hanna Wozniak told telephone operators that she would gladly start a fire if it meant that a hunky fireman would come round afterwards for sex. After the calls were traced back to her home, she told the police: "I was desperate for sex. It's been so long since I had someone in my bed."

WOMAN BITES OFF LOVER'S PENIS IN CAR SMASH

A passionate encounter between a boss and his secretary ended in a painful manner in 2009 when the impact from a car crash caused her to bite his penis off. The 30-year-old woman was performing oral sex on her boss in a car in a Singapore park when the car was struck by a reversing van. Immediately after the collision, the woman was heard to scream loudly before emerging from the vehicle with her mouth covered in blood. To add to the couple's woes, the entire incident was witnessed by a private detective who had been hired by the woman's husband to catch them in the act. The detective helpfully called an ambulance to take the injured man to hospital. His lover followed him there, carrying part of his penis.

SEX LINE CALLER'S VOICE SOUNDED FAMILIAR

An Italian man called a telephone sex line expecting to have a steamy chat but instead found that the woman on the other end was his wife, whereupon a $3-a-minute shouting match ensued.

CUSTOMER SUES AFTER BEING BASHED BY EROTIC DANCER'S BREASTS

A visitor to a strip club unsuccessfully sued for $15,000 in 1998 after claiming he suffered from whiplash, "mental anguish and loss of life enjoyment" as a result of being slammed in the head by the 60-inch HHH bosom of an erotic dancer. Paul Shimkonis, 38, of Tampa, Florida, compared the impact from dancer Tawny Peaks' outsize breasts to being hit with cement blocks, adding: "I haven't been right since."

"DOGGING" TRIO ARE HIT BY LIGHTNING

In an act of divine retribution, three men who were spying on a pair of passionate lovers through a high-powered telescope suffered burns after being struck by lightning. The trio had gathered in a derelict hut on a hillside near Taipei, Taiwan, to observe the lovers having sex in a nearby car but became so engrossed with the action that they failed to spot the storm brewing. The bolt struck the hut with such force that the three were lucky to survive. A police officer said: "When we saw them, their hair was standing on end and their stares were fixed."

FOOT FETISHISTS SWINDLED VICTIMS OUT OF 4,000 PAIRS OF SOCKS

IN A BIZARRE SCAM, foot fetishists Steven Bain and Steven Gawthrop swindled thousands of people in Southport, Merseyside, out of their socks in the 1990s. The two men shared a strange fascination with feet and would approach tourists in the resort's bars and clubs, paying revellers up to $7.50 for their socks under the pretence of collecting them for charity. They made sure to take pictures of the victims with their socks and then meticulously tagged each pair with the donor's name before wrapping them in sandwich bags. But it turned out that they were hoarding the socks for their own sexual gratification. When one of the men's flats was raided, police officers found 4,000 pairs of socks in bin bags in a cupboard. One officer described having to wade through an 18-inch carpet of smelly socks. "They were everywhere and anywhere," he said. "They were all over the furniture, hanging from lampshades and even in the microwave, frying pan and cooker. It was like there had been an explosion in a sock factory."●

MAN CAUGHT HAVING SEX WITH VACUUM CLEANER

A Polish building contractor working at a London hospital was sacked in 2008 after being caught having sex with a canister vacuum cleaner bearing the design of a happy, smiling face. A security guard spotted the man in the staff canteen, naked and on his knees with Henry the Hoover. When challenged, the man claimed he was simply vacuuming his underpants, which he said was "common practice" in his native country.

PAIR BREAK INTO WOMEN'S PRISON FOR SEX

Two men broke into the all-women's Tarrengower Prison at Maldon, Victoria, Australia, in 2003 in the belief that the inmates would be desperate for sex. After the pair had been apprehended by guards, a prison spokesperson commented: "We have a hard enough time keeping inmates in, let alone having to worry about keeping people out."

MAN INSERTS PENCIL IN PENIS

A Serbian man's plan to "put lead in his pencil" backfired when he needed emergency surgery after sticking a pencil inside his penis to keep it stiff during sex. Zeljko Tupic had previously experienced problems getting an erection so, leaving nothing to chance before a hot date, he slotted a thin pencil into his manhood. But when the pencil moved and became lodged in his bladder, he was forced to end the sex session and call an ambulance. The doctor commented: "At first the patient did not tell us what really happened, but X-rays proved the truth. He said he had no idea there were things like Viagra available but agreed that in future he will take pills before he takes any more chances with pencils."

WOMAN SPOOKED BY MONKEY BUSINESS

In an apartment parking lot in Lakewood, Colorado, in 1992, a woman was accosted by a man who exposed himself to her while wearing a rubber gorilla mask, a long black wig and a gorilla suit.

MAN INVITES HORSE FOR ORAL SEX

A 41-year-old man was arrested in Tucson, Arizona, in 1994 after appearing to tempt horses from the University of Arizona Agricultural Center towards him with food. What aroused the officers' suspicions was the fact that he was holding the food near his exposed penis as if inviting the animals to perform oral sex.

"MAGISTRATE CAUGHT MASTURBATING IN COURT"

A French magistrate was locked up in 2003 pending investigation after a local newspaper reporter claimed to have spotted him masturbating during a court case. The Bordeaux newspaper said the magistrate discreetly lifted up his ceremonial robe while a lawyer was presenting final arguments, undid his pants and "engaged in gestures that left nothing to the imagination."

WOMAN SNAPPED BY FLASH PHOTOGRAPHER

A woman in Bloomington, Minnesota, told police officers that a driver had pulled up alongside her on the highway on a bitterly cold winter's morning and had then flashed her by pressing a naked photograph of himself against his car window.

ROMANIAN HOOKERS OFFER TO DO CLEANING TOO

Their trade hit by economic recession in 2000, Romanian prostitutes tried to boost business by offering to do household chores for clients after having sex. A "sexual agent" in Bucharest revealed that many women in the sex business had added cooking and house-cleaning to their repertoire. He added: "We had to invent something because people don't have money and clients are rare. Men are happy because many of them live alone and the girls help them get rid of the three things which torment their lives: sex, cleaning and cooking."

BUTT SNIFFER STRIKES IN DEVON SUPERMARKET

Police in Devon announced in 2009 that they were hunting a man who repeatedly knelt behind a supermarket shelf stacker in order to smell his bottom. The man was caught on CCTV creeping up on the unsuspecting employee at least 20 times while he stacked shelves at a Co-op store in Plymouth. The footage showed him pretending to choose items from the shelves before suddenly crouching down behind the worker. "I had no idea what was going on," said the victim of the phantom butt sniffer. "I thought it was a bit strange that he was in the aisle for that long." Plymouth police confirmed that they were treating the incident very seriously.

DISAPPOINTED TO FIND STUNNING MODEL WAS TEENAGE BOY

A German man who bid $2,000 to win a night of passion with an exotic model was distraught to find out that his "date" was a teenage boy running an online scam. The man said: "I saw the auction on the Internet and put in a bid straight away. I watched every day for a week to see if anyone would outbid me but no one did and when I realized I had won I started preparing for the big night. I admit I did find it a bit strange that I got no reply to my emails to the model but on the auction site there was an address and a date, so I thought she was just trying to set a mood of mystery for the night. I decided to turn up at the address but when I got there, instead of a beautiful model I found some spotty little kid with a laptop. That was when I realized I'd been ripped off."

MAN FOUND DEAD WITH CONDOM OVER HEAD

A naked man was found dead in his bed at Newhaven, East Sussex, in 2007 after pulling a condom filled with laughing gas (nitrous oxide) over his head for sexual gratification. He had been watching the Eurovision Song Contest the previous evening.

JUDGE PUTS BRAKES ON CAR LOVER

A 45-year-old man from Edmonton, Canada, was jailed for three months in 2007 for indecently assaulting cars. Sandy Wong pleaded guilty to three counts of climbing onto cars in public and masturbating on them. He was first caught pleasuring himself with his pants down on top of a BMW sedan at a local Home and Garden show. Two months later he was spotted mounting a green Mini Cooper that was parked outside a Pizza Hut and finally a witness called the police after watching him in ecstasy on a Buick Century. A psychiatrist explained that Wong is sexually attracted to the roofs of certain classic cars because they are "curved like a woman's body". He added that Wong is also aroused by motorcycles and women's feet.

SEX GAME BACKFIRES

As part of a bizarre sex game, a Green Bay, Wisconsin, man handed his wife a shotgun and told her to point it at his scrotum and shoot, which she did. His mistake was in thinking that the gun wasn't loaded.

CLOTHED MAN SPARKS RIOT AT NUDIST ORGY

A Brisbane man who refused to remove his clothes at a raunchy sex party was blamed for starting a fracas at an Australian nudist resort in 2009. Police were called to the White Cockatoo resort, near Port Douglas, Queensland, which was promoting a month of hedonism to boost sagging tourism figures. Resort owner Tony Fox said the "mini riot" broke out after four naked female guests protested when confronted by the fully clothed man. "They felt uncomfortable with him eyeing them up," said Fox, "and I asked him to show some respect and take his clothes off."

MAN LAYS TABLE

A 40-year-old man was arrested in the US in 2008 for allegedly having sex with a picnic table. A neighbour in Bellevue, Ohio, called the police when he saw the man turn over a round metal table in his garden and sexually assault it. The local police captain, who disclosed that the man had been seen with the table on four separate mornings, said: "He was completely nude. He would use the hole from the umbrella and have sex with the table." The officer added that the case was a first in his book. "Once you think you've seen it all, something else comes around."

IRANIAN SEX CHANGE MAN WANTS IT REVERSED

An Iranian man who underwent a sex change to become a woman decidedly shortly afterwards that she wanted to reverse the operation because she found life as a woman unbearable in Iran. Maryam, formerly Mehran, told reporters: "I thought I would get used to it, but life has become painful and intolerable. There are so many restrictions for women in Iran. So I want another sex change."

PROSTITUTE ARRESTED FOR SLASHING HER PRICES

A Turin prostitute was arrested by Italian police in 2002 because she charged clients too little and thereby contravened the country's laws of competition. She was charged with fraudulently lowering prices in a public trade market and unfair competition in what police described as a blatant attempt to force other prostitutes out of business.

MAN FALLS ASLEEP ON CHAT LINE

Romanian pensioner Constantin Luican found that calling a chat line can be an expensive business. Far from being aroused by sultry tones of the telephone temptress, Luican fell asleep during the call and ran up a bill of $1,400. He refused to pay the bill because he said the line was boring.

SEX IN THE SEA IS INTERRUPTED BY RESCUE HELICOPTER

Belgian authorities launched a major rescue operation in 2005 after a couple were seen "struggling" in the sea – only to find that they were actually making love. The alert was raised after a man spotted the couple with his binoculars and contacted the coastguard. A Sea King rescue helicopter, a lifeboat and police officers were drafted in to help but when the pair were eventually pulled from the sea, it transpired that they didn't need rescuing at all because the thrashing about in the water was merely an act of passion. The girl was found to be wearing only her partner's boxer shorts while the man was completely naked.

PHONE SEX OPERATOR SUES FOR INJURY SUSTAINED ON THE JOB

A Fort Lauderdale, Florida, phone sex operator won a "minimal" workers' compensation settlement after claiming she was injured while regularly "pleasuring herself" at work. Her lawyer said she developed carpal tunnel syndrome in both hands from masturbating up to seven times a day while speaking with callers. He added: "She was told to do whatever it takes to keep the person on the phone as long as possible."

HOT STUFF IN THE KITCHEN

While Romanian Virgil Cures was cooking dinner in his kitchen in 2000, his girlfriend was giving him oral sex. But then he accidentally spilled hot oil on her, the shock of which caused her to clamp down hard with her teeth onto his penis. Surgeons worked for four hours to repair the damage to his organ but feared that it would lose its sexual function.

GARDENER ORDERED TO COVER UP NAKED GNOMES

A grandmother from the West Midlands was ordered to put clothes on her garden gnomes in 2009 following complaints from a neighbour that the naked ornaments were upsetting local children. The gnomes – one male and two female – had stood in Sandra Smith's Hunnington front garden for around 15 years but when a neighbour objected to their presence, Bromsgrove District Council ordered a cover-up. So Mrs Smith covered the trio's modesty in miniature T-shirts. The offended neighbour called the gnomes "childish" and "pathetic".

TEEN FILMED HAVING SEX WITH HORSE

A teenager was arrested in 2007 after CCTV cameras caught him having sex with a horse in a barn in Corvallis, Oregon. The owners had installed the video surveillance camera after previous assaults on the mare.

MANURE FETISHIST IS CAUGHT PLEASURING HIMSELF IN MUCK SPREADER

A man who gets sexual thrills from manure was jailed for 16 weeks in 2009 after being caught performing sex acts on himself in a muck spreader on a Cornish farm. David Truscott, 40, had broken into the farm and covered himself in animal waste. He then climbed into the spreader vehicle, where he was discovered wearing rubber gloves and playing in the slurry for "sexual reasons". Truro Magistrates' Court heard that Truscott had been convicted of a previous offence at the same farm in 2004. On that occasion the farmer found a trough filled with dung and tissues scattered around. He then noticed two hand prints and a "bottom print" where manure had been. Police who searched Truscott's home in Camborne found 360 pairs of women's knickers and containers of liquid sludge. Officers related how Truscott would walk into the farm to roll in manure and pleasure himself before washing in a cattle trough. His lawyers described him as a "peculiar man with peculiar habits".

WOMAN FALLS FROM TREE AT HEIGHT OF PASSION

A couple were enjoying passionate sex in a tree at Windsor Great Park . . . until the woman lost her grip and fell naked to the ground, breaking her leg.

MAN KIDNAPS BLOW-UP DOLLS FOR SEX

A burglar broke into three adult shops in Cairns, Queensland, Australia, in 2009, stole blow-up dolls and then had sex with them before callously dumping them. He took the inflatable dolls – named "Jungle Jane" – out to the rear of the shops, blew them up and after having his way with them simply abandoned them in an alley. One of the shop owners admitted: "It's a real concern that someone like that is out on the street."

STORE OWNER STAGES FANTASY RAID

A businessman in Prince Albert, Canada, was sentenced to 12 months in jail in 2002 for staging a sexual fantasy in which he hired someone to rob his store and tie him up naked with an unsuspecting woman.

BOMB SQUAD DISARMS SEX TOY

When the janitor of an apartment block in Gothenburg, Sweden, spotted a package humming and vibrating in a garage, he immediately called out the bomb squad. The area was cordoned off but when the device was disabled following a delicate operation, officers found that the "ticking bomb" was nothing more deadly than a vibrating sex toy.

STUDENT IS OFFERED LIVE TIGER IN EXCHANGE FOR VIRGINITY

A student who auctioned her virginity to pay for a master's degree in Family and Marriage Therapy received a bid from a zookeeper who promised her a live tiger in exchange for a one-night stand. Natalie Dylan, from San Diego, California, also claimed that over 10,000 men had bid sums of up to $3.7 million to have sex with her, although she noted that the highest cash bid had come with the condition that the act be recorded on video. She said she started the auction in 2008 after her sister Avia had successfully raised money for her own degree by working as a prostitute for three weeks.

JUDGE SENTENCES TEENAGE THIEF TO 30 MONTHS' CELIBACY

After pleading guilty to stealing handguns, 17-year-old Brandon Stevens was sentenced by Henry County, Illinois, Judge Clarke Barnes to 30 months on probation, 180 days in jail and a $2,000 fine – but the judge said Stevens wouldn't have to serve the jail sentence if he remained celibate for the duration of the probation period. Although the defendant was not charged with any sexually related crimes, Judge Barnes said: "There are a lot of good, logical reasons why this young man shouldn't be having sex with anyone's daughter. He's got no job, no employment and no high school diploma. We don't need more kids fathered by people with this kind of background." State Attorney Ted Hamer admitted that the order would be difficult to enforce. "Nobody's going to be spying on him or looking in windows. I think the judge just hopes he'll abide by the order."

GRIEF-STRICKEN MAN DIGS UP DEAD FIANCÉE FOR SEX

A man told police officers in Sorocaba, Brazil, that he had been so overcome with grief following the death of his fiancée that, three months after her burial, he had dug up her body, which still had her wedding dress on, and had sex with it. "I was desperate and needed her," he confessed.

EEL INSERTION NEARLY COSTS MAN HIS LIFE

A Hong Kong man put a live eel up his butt in the belief that he would derive enormous sexual pleasure from its writhing. Instead it proceeded to gnaw a hole in his stomach, and surgeons only managed to save the man's life by removing the eel from his intestine.

MARRIED COUPLE MYSTIFIED BY SEX TALK

Having spent years hoping for children, a married couple from Germany finally decided to seek help from a fertility clinic in 2004. But when the clinic asked them how often they had sex, they looked blank and said: "What do you mean?" A clinic spokesman told reporters: "We are not talking retarded people here, but a couple who were brought up in a religious environment and who were simply unaware, after eight years of marriage, of the physical requirements necessary to procreate."

LOVER LEAVES THE METER RUNNING

A cold-hearted Swedish taxi driver left the meter running while he had sex with a woman customer. He eventually sent her an invoice for $11,000, the bill including 25 instances of "sexual coitus", mileage, hotel and telephone costs, plus 25 per cent sales tax. However the court took a dim view of his actions, sentencing him to three years in prison and ordering him to reimburse the woman in full.

MINISTER ARRESTED OVER INDECENT SLIDE SHOW

A Texas minister was arrested in 2002 when, in the middle of his PowerPoint presentation on servitude, the wrong slides popped up on screen, showing his collection of pictures of naked young boys.

SEX SEEKER KEEPS CALLING POLICE DEPARTMENT

A 22-year-old New Yorker got his wires badly crossed when he tried to phone for a hooker in 2001. Although he had taken the number from a newspaper advertisement, he kept ringing the Colonie Police Department by mistake. Five times the police operator informed him that he had got the wrong number, but the caller just wouldn't take no for an answer. So when he phoned for a sixth time, the annoyed operator suggested meeting him at a local hotel for sex. When he showed up, her colleagues were waiting to arrest him.

EX-MALE BIKER WINS "MUM OF THE YEAR"

Karen Buckley, mother of three teenage children, was chosen as "Mum of the Year" by a Rochdale newspaper in 2003 having been nominated by her partner. After receiving her prize, it was revealed that she had previously been a biker named Tommy Buckley before undergoing a sex-change operation in 2000, and that she was in fact the father of the children.

COUPLE FINED FOR SEX IN CHURCH

A Nigerian couple were fined for having sex on the altar of their local church. Tolu Akintepe and his wife Bunmi told a judge they had been trying to spice up their love life when they were caught in the act by the pastor. Mr Akintepe said: "I thought it would be thrilling if we did it in the church, having the big guy upstairs watching us. I thought it was a little adventurous. My wife loved the idea." The pastor was less impressed and demanded they pay $150 damages for desecration. He also wanted them to clean the altar.

FREE STRIP SHOW PROVES COSTLY

Dozens of Russian motorists who abandoned their luxury cars to watch three women frolic naked on the banks of a Moscow river in 2006 paid a heavy price when thieves made off with the vehicles. Once the fleet of BMWs and Mercedes had been stolen, the women hastily grabbed their clothes and escaped in a waiting van.

INTRUDER COATS WOMAN IN CHOCOLATE

An intruder entered a woman's apartment in Virginia Beach, Virginia, in 1981 while she was asleep. He then forcibly covered her face and body with chocolate and vanilla cake frosting. He reportedly told his victim that she should have known this would happen if she left her door unlocked.

WOMAN SWALLOWS LOVER'S FALSE TEETH

A 38-year-old woman from Galati, Romania, spent two days in hospital in 2007 after accidentally swallowing her lover's dentures during a moment of passion. She told doctors she had been experimenting a "special type of passionate kiss" with her boyfriend.

BREAST IMPLANTS SAVE WOMAN IN CAR SMASH

A woman survived a serious car crash in Bulgaria in 2006 thanks to her silicone breasts which acted as airbags. Consequently the accident produced only two serious casualties – the breast implants themselves, which burst with the force of the impact leaving the woman deflated but relieved to be alive.

MAN CAUGHT IN COMPROMISING POSITION WITH CHICKENS

Patrolling San Francisco's Aquatic Park in 2003, police officers knocked on a car window. Inside they found a man with two chickens – one on his lap, the other in the passenger seat. "What's with the chickens?" asked one of the officers. "I'm going to take them home and eat them," came the reply. Then the officer ordered the man to "lift up the chicken." When the man did so, he was immediately taken into custody and the hens were examined for signs of sexual interference. Among the items of evidence was a 15-ounce jar of Vaseline with three feathers in it.

PASSIONATE LOVERS BOUNCE CAR OVER CLIFF EDGE

Two young lovers got so carried away while having sex in their car on a hill near Sarajevo in 2007 that the vehicle bounced over the edge of the cliff and plunged 30 feet into the Miljacka River below. Risto Bocic and Sonja Pasic, both 22, were pulled naked from the crumpled heap by passers-by who saw the accident. This latest incident at the popular courting spot prompted police to set up a permanent patrol on the hill.

BOGUS COP DEMANDS FREE SEX FROM BOGUS HOOKER

In an unlucky twist of fate, a Canadian man pretending to be a police officer demanded free sex from an undercover police officer pretending to be a prostitute. Flashing police ID, Trevor Blair Roszell approached the woman in Edmonton, Alberta, in 2001 and asked her for free sex – or at the very least a reduced rate. When she revealed her true identity, he rather went off the idea and ended up more than $500 out of pocket, courtesy of a fine for impersonating a police officer.

CANNIBAL FULFILS FANTASY OF EATING A FRIEND

A German computer technician confessed to killing and eating a man who apparently volunteered for his fate by replying to an Internet advert. A court heard in 2003 how horror films had fuelled Armin Meiwes' childhood fantasies of eating school friends. He began his plan in adulthood by advertising on the Internet for a well-built male who was prepared to be slaughtered and then eaten. After the victim, 43-year-old Bernd Jurgen Brandes, answered the advert in 2001, Meiwes took him back to his home in Rotenburg, where Brandes agreed to have his penis cut off. Meiwes then flambéed the member, but finding it lacking in flavour, decided to fry it instead. After both men had tasted it, Meiwes stabbed his victim repeatedly in the neck and dissected the corpse, capturing the moment on a camcorder. When police later searched his house, they found remnants of Brandes in a freezer. "I had the fantasy," said Meiwes, "and in the end I fulfilled it."

MAN FEELS A PRICK AFTER SEX WITH HEDGEHOG

Serbian Zoran Nikolovic was rushed to hospital in 2006 with severe lacerations to his penis after trying to have sex with a hedgehog. He had gone to a witchdoctor seeking a cure for premature ejaculation and the witchdoctor had apparently recommended having sex with a hedgehog. Happily the hedgehog was none the worse for its ordeal.

COUPLE ROBBED WHILE HAVING SEX IN BIN

A couple's romantic plan to have sex inside a large garbage bin was spoiled somewhat when they where robbed at knifepoint. The couple from Wichita, Kansas, had crawled inside the dumpster to have what police described as an "intimate moment" when they were rudely interrupted by two men, one armed with a pocket knife. The robbers made off with jewellery, the man's wallet and the couple's shoes.

LOVER'S HEART PIERCED IN SEX GAME

A 24-year-old Canadian man who asked his lover to carve a heart-shaped symbol on his chest during a rough sex game in 2007 nearly died when she accidentally pressed too hard and punctured his heart. Both had been drinking heavily before the sex session.

HYPNOTIST FINED FOR KISSING WOMAN "IN TRANCE"

A South Korean hypnotist was fined over $2,000 for stealing a kiss on a blind date with a woman he thought he had put in a trance. The 32-year-old man persuaded his 27-year-old date to let him hypnotize her during their first meeting arranged by a matchmaking agency. He told her: "You will plunge deep into a trance. You will feel thrilled all over your body, and if my hand touches your body, you will feel intense pleasure." Convinced that he had put her in a trance, he then went to kiss her, but the woman turned out to be very much alert and pushed him away. She did not feel intense pleasure, more a sensation of sexual harassment.

SEX BY THE METER PROVES COSTLY

A drunken Australian footballer was fined $150 in 2009 after loudly simulating sex with a parking meter. Police had been called to a disturbance on a street corner in Cairns, Queensland, where they found Adam Kelly dry-humping a parking meter and shouting out: "Yeah, baby, you know you want it." Prosecutor Michelle Long said Kelly was making expansive pelvic thrust actions at the meter to the disgust of passers-by. Kelly's lawyer said his client had been drinking with teammates to celebrate the end of the football season and that he did not remember much of the incident.

WOMAN BOOBS BY FLASHING BREASTS

As her husband dropped her off for work, a woman from Maine gave him a kiss followed by a quick flash of her breasts. Unfortunately she was seen by a passing cab driver who was so mesmerized that he drove into a nearby building, sending a lump of masonry crashing down onto the woman. "I'm not sure why I did it," said the woman when she had recovered from the ordeal. "I was really close to the car, so I didn't think anyone would see it."

TOURISTS CONTINUE ORGY IN BACK OF POLICE VAN

Five tourists who were arrested for filming their orgy on a Spanish beach continued their romp in the back of a police van. The quintet – a British couple, a Frenchman and two Swiss, all aged between 22 and 40 – were arrested for exhibitionism and transported in a van to the local police station in Benidorm. On arrival, officers opened the doors to discover one of the Swiss men having sex in the van with the British woman. After being told in no uncertain terms that carnal relations were strictly forbidden in the back of a police custody vehicle, the five were released.

ARSONIST BECOMES AROUSED BY SIREN

Arrested in 2002 for setting fire to cars, a Thai man claimed he did it because the sound of fire truck sirens gave him an orgasm. He admitted the truth only because nobody believed his first story – that he started the fires to relieve stress and get rid of a headache.

MAN RIDES LOCAL BIKE

A man in Ayr, Scotland, was found guilty of a sexual breach of the peace in 2007 after two cleaners at the hostel where he was staying caught him trying to have sex with a bicycle in his room. After receiving no reply when they knocked on 51-year-old Robert Stewart's door, they used a master key to unlock it and discovered him naked from the waist down holding the bike and moving his hips back and forth as if to simulate sex. Sheriff Colin

Miller told Stewart: "In almost four decades in the law I thought I had come across every perversion known to mankind, but this is a new one on me. I have never heard of a cycle-sexualist." Stewart had claimed the incident was a misunderstanding after he had drunk too much.

SEX HAS ITS OWN REWARD

Police officers in Juneau, Alaska, raided the hotel room of an Oregon man in 1995 and discovered cocaine plus $10,000 in cash. When questioned about the money, the man claimed that it had been given to him by a woman – whose name escaped him – as a reward for outstanding sex.

PENSIONERS HAPPY TO BE RIPPED OFF BY STRIPPERS

TWO **NORWEGIAN** pensioners who were robbed by strippers said they didn't really mind because it was the most fun they'd had for years. Arne and Oystein Tokvam, aged 73 and 80 respectively, invited the women to their home in 2001 after meeting them in a shop. The women then performed a striptease before saying they needed the toilet. When they failed to reappear, the brothers realized they had been robbed of nearly $7,000 in cash. "It's too bad about the money," said Arne philosophically, "but we have to take it with good humour. We're looking at it as entertainment. Very expensive, but absolutely entertaining." ●

MAN SELLS GIRLFRIEND'S FAVOURS TO PAY FOR LIVER TRANSPLANT

German singer Christian Anders announced in 2001 that he was allowing 20-year-old girlfriend Jenna Kartes to sleep with another man for a year – to raise money for a liver transplant. Anders agreed the deal, which carried an option for a 12-month extension, with millionaire Michael Leicher in return for the sum of 500,000 marks ($231,000). Anders explained: "I thought this 'indecent proposal' was a joke when we first spoke about it. But now Michael has produced a cheque and a contract. And to be honest I could use the money." Kartes said: "I will sleep with Michael because I love Christian. Perhaps he can then afford a new liver. Why should I feel like a prostitute about it?"

COUPLE CAUGHT HAVING SEX IN THE BRITISH LIBRARY

A passionate couple were thrown out of the British Library in 2001 after being caught having sex. Suspicions were aroused when an attractive young woman was seen heading into the gents' toilet near the rare books section. Library users then raised the alarm after the couple's loud moaning began to disturb their reading. A library spokesman said: "A couple were caught in what could be described as a high state of excitation. By the time staff were scrambled, they were already in the throes of an exchange about philosophy, judging by their cries. There is a lot of sex in the British Library – but usually just in the books."

FATHER TRIED TO KILL SON OVER SEX WITH FAMILY DOG

A 71-year-old man pleaded guilty to trying to kill his son after finding that he had been having sex with the family dog. Frank Buble, from Parkman, Maine, struck his 44-year-old son Philip several times with a crowbar before turning himself in to police. At his father's 2001 trial, Philip asked the judge if he could have his "significant other" – his dog Lady – with him in court while his father was being sentenced. Despite the begging letter, which carried Philip's signature and a hand-drawn paw print, the judge declined. Confirming that he preferred sex with animals to humans, Philip said that although he didn't want him to go to jail, he did feel his father "needs serious therapy".

BROTHEL CLOSES AFTER SAILORS EXHAUST HOOKERS

A brothel in Perth, Australia, was forced to shut its doors temporarily in 2002 because the arrival of the American fleet had left the hookers exhausted. The brothel owner said her establishment had taken 580 bookings in the three days since three US warships docked in the port and the sailors had tired out her girls so much that she decided to close rather than risk the brothel's reputation. "I have always offered a quality service," she stated. "I would not sell a man a hamburger if I thought my buns were stale."

MAN SUES OVER TEN-YEAR ERECTION

A former Rhode Island handyman was awarded more than $400,000 in a lawsuit over a penile implant that gave him a ten-year erection. Charles Lennon received the steel–plastic implant in 1996, some two years before Viagra became readily available. The implant was designed to allow impotent men to position the penis upward for sex and then lower it. However Lennon was unable to move his organ to the down position – and because of the resultant discomfort and embarrassment he could no longer hug people, swim, wear bathing trunks or ride a bike.

COUPLE HAD SEX ON POLICE CAR

A couple in Groningen, the Netherlands, were arrested in 2005 for having sex on the hood of a police patrol car. The pair were in such a state of arousal that they failed to notice that two officers were sitting in the car at the time.

MAN JAILED OVER SMELLY FOOT FETISH

David Donathon, of Medina, Ohio, was sentenced to one year in prison on telephone harassment charges – more specifically calling people and asking them whether their feet stank. Donathon's fetish for posing bizarre questions about foot odour led Judge Judith Cross to recommend that he be placed in a facility that deals with sex offenders. His lawyer said: "He realizes what he does is wrong, but he is unable to stop himself."

FLASHER IN A GAS MASK

A man exposed himself to women horse riders near Middlesbrough in 1986 while wearing a full-length wet suit, a gas mask and with two hot-water bottles hanging on a piece of string around his neck. The man, thought to have a rubber fetish, was fined for indecency and had his gas mask confiscated.

COUPLE DIED AFTER SEX IN HEARSE

A young Mexican couple were found dead in the back of a hearse in 1999. Jose Agustin Noh worked for a funeral home in Campeche and decided to have sex with his girlfriend, Ana Maria Camara Suarez, in his hearse, meanwhile leaving the engine running to provide air conditioning. But they died from carbon monoxide poisoning while sleeping off their tryst.

GUNMAN SNATCHES INFLATABLE DOLL

A 19-year-old man armed with an air pistol made off with an inflatable doll from a sex shop in Katowice, Poland, in 1998 after threatening to kill the saleswoman if she tried to stop him. At first the customer asked the shopkeeper to wrap up the brown-haired doll, which, equipped with a built-in vibrator, was priced at $80, but instead of paying he suddenly produced a gun. The culprit, who had visited the shop several times over the previous few days, was quickly arrested. Police said they were keeping the doll as evidence.

TEEN CAUGHT IN FLAGRANTE WITH MANNEQUIN

A teenager was caught in a compromising position with a female mannequin on display at an arts centre in Sioux Falls, South Dakota. Security guards found Michael Plentyhorse sprawled with the naked dummy on the floor with his pants and underpants down. The police said: "There was inappropriate activity between him and the mannequin." Guards patrolling the centre said they had noticed several times before that the dummy's clothes had been removed. However, Plentyhorse was found not guilty of indecent exposure as nobody else had been around when he snuggled up to the mannequin.

WOMAN'S DOG SINKS TEETH INTO FLASHER

Jacqui Jones was walking her German Shepherd cross Tara through a park in St Albans, Hertfordshire, in 2002 when a man suddenly appeared from behind a tree and exposed himself to her. But the flasher merely succeeded in arousing the dog, which leaped forward and bit him hard on the genitals.

She said: "I could see the man was in a state of excitement but Tara wiped the smile off his face. He hobbled away doubled up in agony."

DIVORCE THREAT AFTER PENIS EXTENSION SNAPS DURING SEX

Grigory Toporov, of Voronezh, Russia, has been threatened with divorce by his wife after his penis extension broke off during sex. He had the special prosthetic fitted because he did not measure up to his wife's expectations in the bedroom but she was horrified when the extension snapped off during a sex romp. A glum Mr Toporov said: "I told her I would get a new one but she wasn't having any of it. She said she was fed up with my failures in bed and wants a divorce."

MAN IN STICKY SITUATION WITH PADLOCK

A man in his fifties turned up at a fire station in Margate, Kent, with his penis stuck in a padlock. The keyhole had been superglued, forcing firemen to use hydraulic cutters to free him in a delicate two-and-a-half-hour operation. Apparently the man's unfortunate predicament was the result of a sex game that had gone wrong.

CRUSH FETISHIST DIES PLAYING FAVOURITE GAME

Bryan Loudermilk, of Okeechobee, Florida, used to become sexually aroused by allowing the family's SUV to roll over a board on his stomach as he lay in a shallow pit underneath – that is, until the game went wrong in 1999 and he died after being pinned beneath the vehicle's left rear wheel.

TRANSSEXUAL TOPLESS FIRE-BREATHER CAUSES CITY BLACKOUT

A woman who spat fire and danced topless on a high-voltage electrical tower caused chaos in parts of Seattle, blacking out homes and creating gridlock on surrounding roads. Ara Tripp, 38, from Olympia, climbed the 180-foot tower beside a freeway bridge one morning in 1999, took off her shirt and began dancing, occasionally taking swigs from a vodka bottle, spitting out the liquor and setting it on fire. Traffic on the bridge slowed to a standstill during the hour that Tripp remained up the tower and electricity was cut to 5,000 homes to prevent her being zapped by the 120,000 volts of juice flowing through power lines. She later revealed that she had planned the stunt for weeks to protest against discriminatory laws that allow men to take their shirts off in public but not women. Tripp was a man before undergoing a sex-change operation.

DOCTOR DISCOVERS WHY COUNTRY COUPLE COULDN'T CONCEIVE

A Romanian country couple went to see a gynaecologist in Zalau in 2001 to discover why, despite having regular sex, the woman had yet to become pregnant. When they began to explain how they were having sex, the gynaecologist immediately realized the problem: they were having anal sex. He sent them away with a pile of sex education leaflets.

MAN TELLS COURT OF SPECIAL LOVE FOR COW

Appearing in court on a charge of having sex with a cow, a man in Zimbabwe explained that because he was afraid of contracting AIDS from a human partner, he had developed a special, monogamous relationship with the animal. He went on to express his genuine love and affection for the cow, recited marriage vows and promised to remain faithful to her while serving his nine-month jail sentence.

LOVERS RUN OVER BY TRACTOR WHILE HAVING SEX IN FIELD

The earth moved for a Czech couple making love in a field in 2000 – when a farmer ran them over in his tractor. The pair had chosen what they thought was the perfect spot – a secluded meadow near the village of Brnicko – but were so gripped in the throes of passion that they were oblivious to the approaching farmer who was taking a shortcut across the meadow. His tractor drove over the woman's chest and the man's buttocks, injuring them both.

MAN STARTS FIRE TO AVOID HAVING SEX WITH WIFE

Too tired for sex with his wife, Svetin Gulisija, 26, from Seget, Croatia, hit upon the idea of distracting her by starting a fire in woods behind their house. However the fire spread rapidly causing over $20,000 damage and forcing the couple to be evacuated from their home. The good news for Mr Gulisija was that he didn't need to worry about having sex with his wife for another two years – the length of his jail sentence for arson.

MAN SUES OVER INFLATABLE DOLL

A Romanian man sued a sex shop on the grounds that his inflatable doll had lost her moan. He also complained that she went down too quickly. The shop in Brasov was fined $1,200 and ordered to provide the man with a new doll. The head of the local Consumer Protection Office confirmed: "The doll was losing air very quickly and due to a faulty electrical circuit it didn't make the expected specific sounds."

MAN CUT FREE AFTER SEX WITH PARK BENCH

POLICE AND paramedics were called to a Hong Kong park in 2008 after a man inserted his penis into a hole in a park bench and got stuck when he became aroused. After trying unsuccessfully to ease the pressure by removing some of his blood, they were forced to cut the bench from the ground and take it, with the man still attached, to a city hospital. There, doctors took four hours to cut him free. They said later that if he had been stuck for another hour, they would probably have had to amputate his penis. The man, who told police he thought it would be fun to have sex with a park bench, was described in reports as "lonely and disturbed". ●

ROBBERS' ESCAPE DELAYED WHILE ACCOMPLICES HAD SEX IN GETAWAY CAR

Four teenagers – three boys and a girl – were cruising around Raleigh, North Carolina, in 1997 looking for a place to rob before eventually setting their sights on a store. While two of the males then went into the store to carry out the robbery, the girl and the other boy hid the car in a dark spot, out of the view of prying eyes. However when the two robbers ran back to the getaway car after the raid, they found the doors locked, the windows steamed up and their two accomplices "in the act". Told to wait until the lovers had finished, the pair on the outside created such a commotion that witnesses were able to give police a good description of the car, leading to the eventual arrest of all four.

LAWYER SPANKED CLIENT TO PREPARE HER FOR COURT

A lawyer removed a 22-year-old client's panties and stockings, put her across his knee and repeatedly slapped her buttocks – actions which, he claimed, were designed to help prepare her to testify in court. Milo J. Altschuler, from Ansonia, Connecticut, told the woman that he needed to spank her to stop her fidgeting in the witness box so the judge wouldn't think she was lying. In his defence, Altschuler said he often threatened to spank clients if they gave wrong answers to his questions, but when another female client also complained about his tactics, he held his hands up and pleaded no contest to two counts of fourth-degree sexual assault.

WOMEN CLAIM TO HAVE BEEN RAPED BY GHOST

Two women went into a police station in Federal Way, Washington State, in 2008 to report that a ghost had been having sex with them against their will for the past two years.

DIAL M FOR MOTHER

A frantic mother called the police after mistaking the sound of passionate lovemaking as a cry for help from her daughter. The woman, from Devizes, Wiltshire, was woken by two phone calls in the early hours of the morning. Hearing moaning, groaning and shouting, she dismissed the first as an obscene call, but in the second she recognized her daughter crying "Oh my

God" and also heard a man's voice. Convinced that her daughter was being attacked in her bedroom 100 miles away, the mother dialled the emergency services and a police car sped to the house to investigate. There, the embarrassed daughter explained that at the height of passion either she or her partner had accidentally pushed an auto-dial button on their phone with a toe. Unfortunately on both occasions it was her mother's phone number.

COUPLE HAVE SEX IN CHURCH CONFESSIONAL BOX

An Italian couple in their early thirties were caught having sex in a church confessional box in Cesena, Italy, in 2008 while morning Mass was being said. The couple's lawyer said they had been drinking all night and realized they had gone too far.

HITCHHIKER BARES ALL TO GET LIFT

Struggling to get a lift in North Carolina while hitchhiking from Georgia to Virginia in 2000, a 43-year-old German woman decided that the best way to catch motorists' attention was to strip naked. Sadly for her the only driver who stopped was a police officer who immediately gave her a lift to the nearest sheriff's office on a charge of indecent exposure.

PRIVATE HAS PROBLEMS WITH HIS PRIVATES

A Romanian soldier collapsed and began convulsing uncontrollably at a barracks in Valcea in 2003 – because he was missing his girlfriend. After carrying out exhaustive tests on 21-year-old Adrian Busureanu, doctors at a military hospital diagnosed that he was suffering from "an acute case of sexual frustration". An army spokesman said: "He became feverish, delusional and finally hysterical after being apart from his girlfriend for two months." Busureanu admitted that life without her for so long had been "impossible".

DRIVER PLEASURES HIMSELF WITH PASTA JAR

A 46-year-old man was fined $500 after police caught him in his car with his penis in a pasta jar – near a location in Queensland, Australia, known as Nobby's Beach. Spotting him acting suspiciously, officers approached him but he drove off and led them on a low-speed car chase. When he finally stopped the vehicle, they discovered he had a 750-millilitre pasta jar around his manhood, and as they tried to restrain him, he continued to "pleasure himself in between bouts of wrestling." Police found a number of items in the car, including pornography, a homemade sex aid, women's stockings and a Jack Russell terrier.

WIFE PANICS AFTER HUSBAND TAKES VIAGRA

An 82-year-old Italian man became so excited after taking a Viagra pill that his wife called the police, fearing that he might have a heart attack. Carla di Stefano, from Palermo, said that although the police didn't actually do anything, their mere presence quickly cooled husband Giovanni's ardour.

SNEEZING FETISHIST ARRESTED FOR PEPPER ATTACK

An elderly man was arrested in Commerce, Texas, for blowing pepper into a female store clerk's face – because he apparently has a fetish for women sneezing. Police officers said the man twice blew the powdery substance into the face of the clerk at a hardware store checkout. After apprehending a suspect, Police Chief Kerry Crews revealed: "We found out he's got a problem. He becomes aroused by females sneezing. For me, this is a first."

ERECTION SAVES BURGLAR FROM JAIL

A German burglar escaped a prison sentence in 2006 because he was suffering from a permanent erection. Hardened criminal Maurice Baumann was sentenced to a year in prison for burgling homes in the town of Bielefeld but instead he entered hospital to undergo treatment for the unrelenting priapism from which he had suffered for several months. After a week's intensive course of injections and medication, doctors admitted they had only managed to get his manhood down to "half-mast".

CHAT LINE WORKER ATTACKED BY DISILLUSIONED CLIENT

A telephone sex line worker in Romania was attacked by one of her regular callers after he discovered what she really looked like. The woman from Ploiesti was recognized by her voice while buying parsley at the local market. She told police: "He said he was shocked and felt betrayed because he imagined I was a unique woman with ideal measurements." The woman, who used the work name Ella, described herself as "not looking so nice and one of my legs is a lot shorter than the other."

COUPLE CAUGHT HAVING SEX ON SUPERMARKET DAIRY DISPLAY

A London couple were caught enjoying sex in an all-night supermarket in 1999 "on a bed of margarine tubs, yoghurt, clotted cream and trifles". Michael Pallant and Danielle Minns were already giggling when they entered the Kensington branch of Sainsbury's at 3 a.m. He then put her in a shopping cart and pushed her down the aisle towards the dairy produce. Shortly afterwards, customers and staff heard muffled screams and a security guard was sent to investigate. Finding Pallant lying on Minns on the refrigerator, he asked them what they were doing, to which Pallant replied: "Chilling out." The lovers were fined $400. They told the court they had been very drunk.

ELECTRICIAN HAD SEX WITH PAVEMENTS

After being spotted on several occasions lying face down on paving stones in Redditch with his underpants around his ankles, electrician Karl Watkins appeared at Hereford Crown Court in 1993 charged with having sex with pavements. He was also alleged to have attempted to mount an underpass. He was jailed for 18 months but was back in court two years later on charges of simulating sex with black plastic bin bags. Watkins admitted that he had a fetish for "the feel and touch of the bin liners" and the court heard how he went out at night to lie in piles of garbage and had been found in wheelie bins and in the backs of garbage trucks. Apparently his ultimate sexual fantasy was to be in a garbage truck when the bin bags were crushed. He was put on three years' probation and ordered to seek psychiatric help.

ONE-NIGHT STAND ENDS IN EMBARRASSMENT

After meeting a stranger in a nightclub, a Berkshire woman enjoyed a night of wild passion at his luxurious home on a new development. But when she woke in the king-size bed the following morning, she found her lover gone and three people staring at her. They were the estate agent and two prospective buyers for the show house.

ARMPIT SNIFFER SENT TO JAIL

A Singaporean man with an armpit-sniffing fetish was sentenced to 14 years in jail and 18 strokes of the cane in 2008. Mohammed Ismail Ariffin, 36, was convicted of sniffing the armpits of 23 females, ranging in age from a nine-year-old girl to a 53-year-old cleaner. The court heard that he stalked his victims, following them into lifts, staircase landings or their homes. Following a report from a housewife that a man had smelled her armpit, police took a semen swab at the scene, which led them to Ismail.

MYSTERY ATTACKER MUTILATES BARBIE DOLLS

Over a six-month period between 1992 and 1993, 25 Barbie dolls in three department stores in Sandusky, Ohio, were sexually assaulted. The dolls were slashed in their private parts, leaving their breasts cut and their crotches mutilated. Police confirmed that Ken was not a suspect because he didn't have the balls.

IMPOTENT TURK SOUGHT PENIS TRANSPLANT FROM DONKEY

An impotent Turkish man tried to find a remedy for his problem by securing a penis implant from a donkey – but his desperate quest angered his family so much that one of his sons eventually shot him. According to newspaper reports, Mehmet Esirgen had twice bought donkeys, amputated their sexual organs and attempted unsuccessfully to persuade doctors to carry out a transplant. His family bitterly opposed the idea, so when the 52-year-old returned home from a trip to Ankara in 1997 with a third donkey, his son vented his frustration by shooting him in the leg. Esirgen remained unrepentant, vowing to acquire a fourth donkey as soon as he recovered from the bullet wound. "For a long time now," he was quoted as saying, "I have had sexual problems and I have spent all my pension funds to overcome them."

3
ARTISTIC PURSUITS

ACTORS FALL IN LOVE WHILE PLAYING PANTOMIME COW

A couple fell in love while playing a pantomime cow in a Lincolnshire drama group production of *Babes in the Wood*. Kevin Blackburn met Sharon Colley when they played the front and rear ends respectively of Daisy the cow for the North Hykeham Dramatic Society's 2002 show. Announcing their plans to marry, Mr Blackburn said: "It was love at first sight. It doesn't matter that I met Sharon when she was the rear end of a cow. You really need to get on together in those roles. I hope she'll always be my other half."

PERFORMING DWARF GETS PENIS STUCK TO VACUUM CLEANER

A dwarf performer at the 2007 Edinburgh Fringe Festival was rushed to hospital after his penis got stuck to a vacuum cleaner during an act that went hideously wrong. Daniel Blackner, or "Captain Dan the Demon Dwarf", was due to perform at the oddball Circus of Horrors with a vacuum cleaner attached to his penis by means of a special apparatus. However the attachment broke shortly before the performance and although Blackner managed to fix it using extra strong glue, he only allowed the glue to dry for 20 seconds instead of the recommended 20 minutes. So when he joined it directly to his organ, it formed a solid attachment. The audience thought it was hilarious – even when Blackner was taken to hospital. He admitted afterwards: "It was the most embarrassing moment of my life when I got wheeled into a packed Accident & Emergency with a vacuum attached to me."

WRONG PLASTER LANDS ARTIST'S MODEL IN HOSPITAL

When art student Kate Freeland asked budding actor Paul Fifield to model for him in 1995, he jumped at the chance. She explained that she was going to cover his body in plaster to create a lifelike male nude. So wearing only Y-fronts and a pair of socks, Fifield, from Girton, Cambridgeshire, struck a pose, but unfortunately Freeland made the mistake of using wall plaster instead of plaster of Paris for the full-body mould, leaving him in agony when she tried to break the solid cast. Firemen had to take him to hospital, where he was given an anaesthetic while the plaster was hammered off. "Kate had a book on how to do it," he said ruefully, "but I don't think she got further than the preface."

POP STAR ROBBED WHILE DRESSED AS PINEAPPLE

Japanese pop star Hideki Kaji was robbed of camera equipment worth over $3,000 in 2009 after three young men beat him up while he was dressed as a pineapple. Kaji was wearing the tropical fruit costume for a music video in Malmo, Sweden, but, having been left alone with the equipment while the camera crew went for a break, he was viciously attacked, sustaining a cut lip and a broken tooth. A police spokesman speculated that the pineapple outfit might have hindered Kaji's attempts at resistance.

FIRE EATER SEES PARTNER'S BREASTS GO UP IN FLAMES

An erotic dancer who was tied to a pole wearing just her g-string was rushed to hospital in 2005 after her fire-eating partner set her naked boobs alight. Maria Leeb and flamethrower Marc Miszler were performing at a lap-dancing club in Augsburg, Germany, but their hot routine came to a painful end when Leeb suffered burns across her chest. "I shouted at him that he was getting too close but he didn't stop," she said. "The oil and glitter that I rubbed on my body must have caught on fire." Miszler was given a ten-month suspended jail sentence for causing grievous bodily harm. Meanwhile Ms Leeb was planning to look for a new partner.

DRUNK DRIVER SUSPECT NAMES AND BLAMES SHANIA TWAIN

A suspected Canadian drunk driver escaped conviction in 2006 because he believed singer Shania Twain was helping him to drive. Matt Brownlee had been arrested for speeding along a street in Ottawa but the judge ruled that Brownlee was not criminally responsible because he suffers from delusions that female celebrities communicate with him telepathically.

CLEANER BINS ART EXHIBIT

A bag of garbage that was part of a Tate Britain work of art was accidentally thrown away by a cleaner in 2004. The bag, stuffed with old paper and cardboard, was a key ingredient in an exhibit by German artist Gustav Metzger that was said to demonstrate the "finite existence" of art. The message was clearly lost on the cleaner who binned it as rubbish, forcing Metzger to replace it with a new bag of garbage that enjoyed round-the-clock protection.

FIRE TURNED OUT TO BE TV IMAGE

Firefighters in Zurich, Switzerland, responding to an elderly woman's call to say her TV was burning, discovered it was tuned to a German channel that broadcasts the constant image of a fireplace in the early hours of the morning. A fire service spokesman said: "The fire was extinguished with the press of a button."

NUNS ACCUSED OF PORNOGRAPHIC EXHIBITION

An order of Catholic nuns was forced to close an art exhibition in 1994 after the sculptures and paintings on display were labelled "pornographic". The Sisters of Charity of the Incarnate Word had staged "Spiritual, Sensual, Sexual", by Houston artist Donell Hill, at their own gallery in San Antonio, Texas, but a deluge of complaints led to it being shut down after just one day. Callers to the church principally objected to the graphic pictures of genitalia in a religious setting, including one painting of an angel having sex on an altar. Even the archbishop declared himself "highly offended". Sister Alice Holden, the gallery director, said she had prayed before putting on the event but had decided to proceed because "sexuality is a tremendous gift from God".

POLICE SEIZE MUSICAL PROPS

The Stromness Drama Club in Orkney had to perform *The Sound of Music* without props in 2001 after their dummy guns and Nazi uniforms were handed over to the police by suspicious bosses at a Royal Mail sorting office.

TROUBLE IN THE WIND SECTION

Ken Lawrence, an oboist with the Kansas City Symphony Orchestra, was suspended in 1994 after one of the horn players complained that he had farted loudly during a rehearsal for *The Nutcracker*, "creating an overpowering smell".

AUDIENCE MEMBER INJURED BY FLYING SHEEP'S HEAD

A concert-goer in Oslo, Norway, was rushed to hospital after his skull was fractured by a flying sheep's head. The band Mayhem was carving up a dead sheep on stage when the animal's head flew into the audience.

ACADEMY CHOOSES BASE OVER SCULPTURE

When English sculptor David Hensel submitted a laughing head on a wooden plinth for exhibition at London's Royal Academy in 2006, he was surprised to see that only the plinth was put on show. It transpired that the Academy had thought they were two separate works and much preferred the simple support to the elaborately sculpted head.

LIBRARIANS NEED GRIEF COUNSELLING OVER DAMAGED BOOKS

After flooding from a burst water main damaged thousands of precious books in 1998, Boston, Massachusetts, Public Library staff were so overcome with grief that many had to undergo counselling. Some reported waking up in a panic while others complained of stomach upsets, headaches and uncontrollable weeping. A few were even so upset that they could not bear going into work to face the sight of muddy, damaged books. So the library arranged for anxious staff to attend a programme of grief counselling and encouraged them to express their emotions in departmental meetings. "It's a process just like when someone dies," explained the library's human resources director. "It's not just a job to any one of us."

RADIO STATION CHALLENGE PUTS FOUR IN HOSPITAL

When Birmingham-based radio station BRMB challenged contestants to sit on blocks of dry ice to win tickets and back-stage passes for a music festival, four of them had to be treated in hospital for severe frostbite. Three spent ten weeks in hospital recovering from extensive skin grafts following the Coolest Seats in Town event outside the station's headquarters in 2001.

PERFORMANCE ARTIST IS BITTEN BY DOG

For a 1999 display, San Francisco performance artist Zhang Huan took off all his clothes, lay on the floor, had an assistant smear his body with puréed hot dogs, and then invited eight dogs to lick him. However he got more than he bargained for when one dog – an Akita – sank its teeth into Zhang's bare butt, drawing blood. Afterwards the artist put a brave face on it, insisting: "If he hadn't bitten me, I would have been disappointed."

FOUR TOPS TRIBUTE BAND FAILED TO BE THERE

A Four Tops tribute band missed a sell-out gig in 2006 because their satellite navigation system had been set for Chelmsford instead of Cheltenham. As a result Viscount Oliver's Legendary Four Tops – based on the Motown band whose biggest hit was "I'll Be There" – ended up 140 miles from the venue. Their tour manager said: "Whoever tapped the place into the GPS got it wrong. Because they're American they don't know British geography very well."

NOVELIST MISTAKEN FOR VANDAL

When American horror author Stephen King walked unannounced into a bookshop in Alice Springs, Australia, for an impromptu book-signing session in 2007, customers in the store thought he was a vandal who was defacing the books and reported him to staff.

INSULTING ARTWORK SPARKS DIPLOMATIC ROW

To mark their 2009 presidency of the European Union, the Czech government spent $700,000 commissioning a sculpture that was supposed to celebrate European diversity. Instead artist David Cerny created an installation that insulted virtually every nation in the EU. His map of Europe depicted Sweden as an Ikea flat pack, Slovakia as a wrapped-up corpse, and Lithuania urinating on Russia, while France was represented simply by a banner that read: "Strike!" Bulgaria was particularly offended, having been portrayed as a Turkish toilet. Demanding that the sculpture be taken down, a leading Bulgarian politician protested: "I cannot accept to see a toilet on the map of my country. This is not the face of Bulgaria."

THIEVES STEAL HITLER FROM CANADIAN MUSEUM

Thieves stole a life-sized wax figure of Adolf Hitler – in full Nazi uniform – from the Criminals Hall of Fame Museum at Niagara Falls. The Führer, who was housed in a display case between Oklahoma City bomber Timothy McVeigh and 1930s US gangster Benjamin "Bugsy" Siegel, was noticed to have gone AWOL when the cashier walked through the museum at closing time one evening in 1999. She suspected the culprits simply walked out with the figure. "Hitler is a small man," she said, "so they wouldn't have much problem getting him out."

ISRAELIS LEFT SCRATCHING THEIR HEADS OVER LICE ART

When seven young artists from Berlin tried to turn head lice into a work of art in 2008, visitors to an Israeli museum were left scratching their heads. The Bat Yam Museum near Tel Aviv allowed the septet to live there for three weeks with lice in their hair in a bid to stretch the boundaries of art. They wore shower caps to prevent the lice from spreading but although acknowledging that it was an uncomfortable experience, they insisted that it was not a gimmick. "We are serious," said one. "The lice are part of the art."

LISTENER COLLECTS GRASSHOPPERS TO SEE ELTON JOHN

Canadian Brandy Elliott won two tickets to see Elton John's 2002 concert in Regina, Saskatchewan, by collecting 38,000 grasshoppers. Local radio station Z99 had offered the tickets to the sold-out concert to the listener who could collect the most grasshoppers over a two-day period. Ms Elliott was among 100 listeners to rise to the challenge and she beat her nearest rival by 6,000 grasshoppers after driving a truck rigged with five-foot-high netting through the pests' favourite haunts. Making her victory speech she revealed: "Every night when I went to bed, all I could dream about was grasshoppers – just bags and bags of grasshoppers. All I kept thinking was, 'Is this enough?'"

CYCLE RACK WAS PRICELESS RELIC

A statue that had been kept in the basement of a Southampton museum was eventually identified as being a valuable Egyptian piece dating back 2,700 years. Staff had been using it as a cycle rack.

TEXT BOOK ERROR DRIVES AUTHOR TO KILL WIFE

In 1996, New Jersey police charged 67-year-old Ukrainian–American mathematics professor Walter Petryshyn with clubbing his wife to death with a claw hammer. A friend said that Petryshyn had descended into paranoia and depression because he was afraid that he would become a laughing stock in the mathematical community as a result of a small error in his latest textbook, *Generalized Topological Degree and Semilinear Equations*. He was found not guilty of murder on the grounds of insanity.

ARTIST GROWS THIRD EAR

AN AUSTRALIAN performer had a third ear grafted onto his forearm – all in the name of art. Cyprus-born Stelios Arcadiou, known as Stelarc, revealed in 2007 that it had taken him years to find a surgeon willing to carry out the operation. The extra left ear, made of human cartilage, does not function but Stelarc said he hoped to have a miniature microphone implanted so that other people could listen to sounds that the ear picks up. "The microphone will enable a wireless connection to the Internet," he enthused, "making the ear a remote listening device for people in other places. For example, someone in Venice could listen to what my ear is hearing in Melbourne." ●

STALKER'S CLAIM WAS ONLY MAKE BELIEVE

In 1993 a court ordered Thomas Fry of Jensen Beach, Florida, to stop harassing singer Conway Twitty. Apparently 24-year-old Fry was convinced that Twitty, 58, was his son.

ARTIST POSES 1,250 NAZI GARDEN GNOMES

A German artist posed 1,250 black plastic garden gnomes in a town square in 2009 with their arms outstretched in the stiff-armed Hitler salute. Ottmar Hoerl created the exhibit in Straubing as a satirical protest at lingering fascist tendencies in German society.

DOG SACKED FOR STEALING THE SHOW

A canine actor was sacked from an Essex stage production of *Oliver* because he kept distracting the cast and audience. Bull terrier Bronx had been playing Bill Sikes's dog in the Southend Operatic and Dramatic Society's production until being ruthlessly relieved of his duties. His owner Edward James attributed Bronx's dismissal to his habit of flapping his leg and stamping. He explained: "Bronx got on stage when Bill was having a romantic moment with Nancy and did his dance, with his leg going up and down. Everyone started laughing."

ARTIST PRICES BANANA AT $15,000

Artist Michael Fernandes wanted to price his latest artwork at $15,000, even though it was merely a banana on the gallery's window sill. He did, however, change the banana on a daily basis, eating the old ones and putting progressively greener ones on display to illustrate the banana's transitory nature. Fernandes eventually lowered his price to $2,500, which was enough to attract interest from at least two collectors. Nevertheless Victoria Page, co-owner of the Halifax, Nova Scotia, gallery, thought it best to seek assurances from the prospective buyers. "It's a banana; you understand it's a banana?"

WOMAN CHARGED WITH KISSING PAINTING

A woman appeared in a French court in 2007 on charges of kissing a painting worth over $2 million. The art-lover was apparently so overcome with passion in front of the Cy Twombly work in Avignon that she felt she had to kiss it, leaving a red lipstick stain on the canvas.

MISTAKE HONOURS KING'S MURDERER

A typographical error led to a notorious murderer being honoured on a plaque instead of a distinguished actor. The plaque was meant to honour black actor James Earl Jones at a Florida event marking Martin Luther King Day in 2002 but instead it paid tribute to James Earl Ray – the man who killed the civil rights leader. The erroneous plaque read: "Thank you James Earl Ray for keeping the dream alive."

EXPLODING POTATO HALTS BALLET

Some 2,000 ballet fans had to be evacuated from London's Royal Opera House in 2001 after a baked potato exploded in a backstage microwave oven and triggered the fire alarm.

THE BEAVER MAGAZINE RENAMED TO END PORN MIX-UP

Canada's second oldest magazine, *The Beaver*, changed its name in 2010 because the title was frequently censored by Internet porn filters, thus preventing it from reaching new online readers. The Winnipeg-based magazine was launched in 1920 to celebrate the history of the fur trade but its publisher, Deborah Morrison, said the title had become something of an impediment online. Announcing a change to *Canada's History*, she said: "Several readers asked us to change the title because their spam filters were blocking it. Ninety years ago, it probably seemed the perfect name for a magazine about the fur trade. There was only one interpretation for the word then, but you're likely to find a lot of strange sites now if you search for the title of our magazine online."

MADONNA LOOKALIKE IS A MAN

Chile's most successful Madonna impersonator was revealed to be a man. Elias Figueroa has been obsessed with the singer since he was a schoolboy and now earns $12,000 a year – three times the national salary – as a Madonna lookalike. He says modestly: "I'm so good at playing Madonna, some people can't tell the difference between me and the real thing. They don't even realize I'm a man." Unsurprisingly he had yet to be granted a meeting with the real Madonna.

DUCK MORE EXPENSIVE TO HIRE THAN ACTOR

A London theatre dropped plans to hire a duck for a production because it cost four times more than an actor. English comedian Arthur Smith had wanted to hire the duck for a waddle-on part in his 2000 show *Arthur Smith Sings Leonard Cohen* but was quoted $375 to hire a Muscovy duck for a day – just $60 less than the union minimum wage for a West End human actor for a whole week. Smith said: "It is ridiculous to pay a duck so much. So we have decided to hire an unemployed actor, dress him in a duck suit and give him a bigger part."

TV PRESENTER THROWS TANTRUM OVER LACK OF CALLS

A Romanian TV presenter on a live phone-in quiz show threw a tantrum when no viewers called in. Adela Lupse started screaming at the camera, smashed the phone on the ground and then jumped up and down on it, yelling repeatedly: "I want the phone to ring now. Now! Call me now!" After the National TV station was fined $2,000 in 2009 for "unjustified violence", Lupse, who had been presenting the show for three years, admitted: "Maybe I was a bit over the top but I wanted to get people to call. There is a lot of pressure to get people to call in with the correct answer. It was a bad day."

MUSEUM DISCOVERS EARHART'S HAIR IS PIECE OF THREAD

An Ohio museum discovered in 2009 that an exhibit believed to be a lock of Amelia Earhart's hair was actually nothing more than a piece of thread. The Cleveland International Women's Air and Space Museum acquired the "lock" in 1986. It was said to have been recovered by a maid at the White House after pioneering aviator Earhart stayed there prior to her final flight in 1937. Eager to shed more light on the mystery of Earhart's disappearance over the Pacific, the museum lent a small sample of the artefact to a historian's organization seeking to match her DNA to other items found on the central Pacific island of Nikumororo. However the DNA analysis revealed the supposed cherished hair to be simple thread of no historical significance whatsoever. The museum described it as "a disappointing turn of events".

ARTIST CREATES BUSH PORTRAIT FROM PORN

British artist Jonathan Yeo has created portraits of George W. Bush and Paris Hilton in the form of collages using pieces of pornographic magazines. Yeo apparently came up with the idea after the White House cancelled his commission to paint Bush in 2004.

RECIPE TYPO CALLS FOR "FRESHLY GROUND BLACK PEOPLE"

An Australian publisher was forced to reprint 7,000 cookery books in 2010 after a typographical error in a pasta recipe called for "salt and freshly ground black people" instead of "salt and freshly ground black pepper". The mistake in the *Pasta Bible* recipe for tagliatelle with sardines and prosciutto had apparently prompted a number of complaints from readers. Penguin Group Australia's head of publishing said: "It was just a silly mistake. We're mortified that this has become an issue of any kind and why anyone would be offended, we don't know."

WOMAN WINS DAMAGES OVER HYPNOTIC TRANCE

In 1994, Ann Hazard, a 25-year-old woman from Edinburgh, Scotland, won a $32,500 settlement from a theatre that had employed a hypnotist in a stage show. The performer had brought Hazard on stage, hypnotized her and told her to leave "by the quickest exit", at which she stepped off the stage, tumbled four feet and broke her leg.

ACTOR INJURED DURING SUICIDE SCENE

A German actor's suicide scene during a stage play in Vienna in 2008 was a little more realistic than he had intended when he accidentally stabbed himself in the neck. Daniel Hoevels was meant to be using a prop knife that had been deliberately blunted for use onstage, but unbeknown to him the knife had been switched with a sharp one for the Saturday night performance of Friedrich Schiller's *Mary Stuart*. While Hoevels received stitches for his injury at a city hospital, Vienna police were investigating "bodily injury caused by negligence".

OVER-ENTHUSIASTIC CONDUCTOR RAMS BATON THROUGH HAND

While conducting the first act of the opera *Il Pirata* in Stockholm, Sweden, in 2001, 70-year-old Giovanni Impellizzeri became so animated that he inadvertently rammed his baton straight through his left hand. "I did not feel a thing," he said afterwards. "I just saw the baton sticking out of the hand and thought it looked funny. There was almost no blood at all. I quickly pulled it out, licked the wound, and the orchestra did not notice a thing."

GALLERY VISITORS FALL INTO EXHIBIT

In October 2007, three visitors to London's Tate Modern Gallery accidentally fell into a 167-metre-long crack in the entrance hall floor that formed an exhibit by Colombian artist Doris Salcedo. The fissure, which was a metre down at its deepest point, was designed to symbolize racial and social division in the world.

INFLATABLE DOG POOP LANDS ON CHILDREN'S HOME

A giant inflatable dog poop – an artwork by American Paul McCarthy – broke free from its moorings outside a museum in Berne, Switzerland, and left a trail of destruction in its wake. The installation, entitled "Complex Sh*t", came loose in strong winds and as it floated away it brought down a powerline before eventually landing on a nearby children's home, where it smashed a window.

PRIZE REVEALS WORLD'S WEIRDEST BOOK TITLES

Since 1978, Britain's *Bookseller* magazine has run an annual contest to find the strangest book title of the previous 12 months. Winners of the coveted Diagram Prize have included *How To Shit in the Woods: An Environmentally Sound Approach to a Lost Art* (1989), *How To Avoid Huge Ships* (1992), *Highlights in the History of Concrete* (1994), *Reusing Old Graves: A Report on Popular British Attitudes* (1995), *Greek Rural Postmen And Their Cancellation Numbers* (1996), *Bombproof Your Horse* (2004), *People Who Don't Know They're Dead: How They Attach Themselves To Unsuspecting Bystanders And What To Do About It* (2005), *If You Want Closure In Your Relationship, Start With Your Legs* (2007), and *The 2009–2014 World Outlook for 60-Milligram Containers of Fromage Frais* (2008).

THIEVES STEAL STATUE'S PENIS

Security cameras at a public library in Whangarei, New Zealand, captured a nighttime raid in which three masked men used a chisel to remove the penis of a wooden Maori figurine. Police said they were at a loss to explain the theft, particularly as a nearby statue of Tangaroa, the Maori god of the sea, was better endowed.

KIDNAPPERS SNATCH ARTIST TO PAINT PORTRAIT

Artist Niceforo Urbieta understandably feared the worst when he was seized at gunpoint in the street at Oaxaca, Mexico, in 1997, a cloth was thrown over him and he was driven to a mystery location. Imprisoned in the 1970s for his links to militant leftist groups, he thought this might be a political act, but instead his kidnappers told him: "There is a very rich lady who likes your painting a lot. She wants you to paint her." Provided with brushes by the kidnappers, Urbieta was held captive for the next four days while he painted a nude portrait of the young woman, who never spoke but, according to the artist, had long black hair and "a very well-formed body". She would pose for an hour at a time, Urbieta viewing her through a hole in the wall of an adjoining room. He was eventually released when the painting was finished. "It was totally absurd," he complained afterwards. "Looking at her through that hole, I felt like a voyeur."

$100,000 CHINESE VASE MADE INTO LAMP

A rare Chinese vase worth $100,000 in mint condition was listed in a 2008 sale for just $12,000 after a hole had been drilled in its base so that it could be used as a table lamp. The Dorset auctioneer said of the eighteenth-century Qing Dynasty porcelain vase: "I don't think the owners knew how much it was worth before they drilled the hole."

SLEEP DISORDER SPOKESMAN OVERSLEEPS, MISSES TV SPOT

Actor Tony Randall, who had been appointed spokesperson for US National Sleep Disorder Month, overslept on 9 May 1995 and missed a guest spot on the TV show *Wake Up America*.

EXHIBITION OF STOLEN ITEMS IS ROBBED

Organizers of a 2010 exhibition displaying stolen artefacts from history should not have been totally surprised when it was robbed. Burglars broke into the Jerusalem museum where the exhibition "Antiquities Theft in Israel" was showing hundreds of items that had been recovered from thieves, and made off with several valuable pieces, including a silver ring belonging to Alexander the Great.

NEWS CHANNEL INTERVIEWS WRONG MAN

In a classic case of mistaken identity, a man who had arrived at the BBC for a job interview ended up being interviewed as an IT expert on its News 24 channel. The mix-up occurred in 2006 when a producer went to collect the expert, Guy Kewney, from the wrong reception at BBC Television Centre in West London. There, a receptionist pointed the producer in the direction of Guy Goma, an economics and business studies graduate from the Congo, who was waiting for a job interview. The next thing Mr Goma knew, he was being whisked into a studio to answer questions live on air about the Apple court case. The interviewer, Karen Bowerman, noted that the guest seemed "very breathless and nervous", while for his part Mr Goma assumed it was all part of the job selection process. However he did wonder why the questions were not related to the data support cleanser job he had applied for. It was only after Guy Goma's short, vague TV interview that producers realized that Guy Kewney was still waiting in reception. Although Mr Goma described his unexpected screen appearance as "stressful", he generously said that he would be happy to go on air again in the future, if asked, "to speak about any situation".

ARTIST PLANS TO TURN MURDERER INTO FISH FOOD

Gene Hathorn, a convicted killer on death row in Texas, has given permission for Chilean-born artist Marco Evaristti to use his remains as fish food should his final appeal against the death sentence fail. Evaristti would deep-freeze the body of Hathorn, who was found guilty of killing his father, stepmother and stepbrother in 1985, and then turn it into fish food which visitors to an exhibition could then feed to goldfish. In 2000, Evaristti had a museum display in which he placed goldfish in electric blenders filled with water and invited visitors to turn them on.

ART STUDENT'S INVITATION SPARKS TERRORIST ALERT

In a bid to encourage Norwegian dignitaries and celebrities to attend his 2000 exhibition, a 29-year-old art student mailed out bottles of homemade beer to the great and good of Oslo. Alas the beer sent to Norway's parliament had not stopped fermenting, as a result of which the bottle exploded violently, showering the walls of the building's mail room with foul-smelling liquid just hours before a visit from the South Korean President Kim Dae-jung to collect the Nobel Peace Prize. Police immediately feared the parcel contained a chemical bomb, and reports began to come in of similar packages being received by other people in the city, including leading newspaper editors. As panic spread, the red-faced student called police to confess.

KNIT YOUR OWN HITLER

A London designer has produced a set of knitting patterns for making woolly models of the most evil dictators in history. Rachael Matthews's pattern book includes designs for Adolf Hitler, Saddam Hussein, Idi Amin, Pol Pot and a hand grenade. She calls the Hitler doll "Knitler".

FEMALE ARTIST STARTS AT THE BOTTOM

A Welsh artist was awarded a $30,000 National Lottery grant in 2009 – to study female bottoms. Sue Williams, 53, of Swansea, created plaster-cast moulds of women's butts in a bid to explore their place in contemporary culture. She also examined racial attitudes towards buttocks in Europe and Africa. The Arts Council of Wales, which awarded the grant, insisted: "There is a serious point to this research."

BLIND MAN OBJECTS TO "OBSCENE" PAINTING

In 2001, Fred Tarrant, a city councillor in Naples, Florida, demanded that a local art centre remove a controversial painting, which he described as disgusting and salacious, even though he himself was blind. The painting, by local artist Ted Lay, showed the Mona Lisa, Albert Einstein and Monica Lewinsky all sticking their tongues out, but Tarrant claimed that Lewinsky's tongue looked like a penis. He said various advisors had told him so.

VIEWER SUES TV WEATHERMAN OVER WRONG FORECAST

In 1996, an Israeli woman sued Danny Rup, the country's leading TV weather presenter, because of an inaccurate weather forecast which, she claimed, led her to catch flu by not wearing warm clothing.

MUSEUM SEEKS COMPUTER HACKER

The Ivar Aasen Museum in Norway was forced to advertise for a computer hacker after it inherited a vast collection of books and periodicals. The librarian cataloguing the bequest had entered 11,000 items into a database when he died suddenly – and nobody else knew the password.

RUSSIAN TV LAUNCHES CUT-PRICE VERSION OF *WHO WANTS TO BE A MILLIONAIRE?*

A Russian television station launched the country's first version of the big money game show *Who Wants To Be A Millionaire?* in 2001 with a top prize of barely $50. The hard-up station said it couldn't afford to pay more prize money but in acknowledgement of the fact that its jackpot was just 1,300 roubles as opposed to the UK version's equivalent of 41 million roubles, it moderated the show's title to *Who Wants To Be Fabulously Wealthy?*

FIRE-EATING SINGER SETS HOTEL ABLAZE

Steve McLennan, singer with avant-garde Australian rock band Freak Shop, breathed fire as part of his act. But while performing at the Star Hotel in Newcastle, New South Wales, on Christmas Eve, 1994, his crowd-pleasing antics backfired when the flames reached the ceiling and set the hotel ablaze. The fire put 11 audience members in hospital and left another four needing treatment for smoke inhalation. Some years later, McLennan reflected: "I'd been lighting fires since I set the front fence alight as a five-year-old. This was just an unfortunate moment. I guess I just got careless. I thought it was going to be the event that catapulted us into the next level. We all know what chickens did for Alice Cooper, and what bats did for Ozzy Osbourne. A little controversy never hurt anyone. But after that, wherever we were booked, venues copped grief from the licensing police, and it all turned very negative. The band self imploded a few months later when I set fire to the Cardiff Workers' Club."

WOMAN PUNISHES ENEMIES WITH MAGAZINE SUBSCRIPTIONS

An Ohio woman came up with an unusual way of getting even with people who had crossed her – she would sign their names to unwanted magazine subscriptions. In 1999, she was jailed for two months for forgery after being convicted of taking revenge on her enemies – including a job counsellor, a landlord and a neighbour – by signing them up to around 350 magazines.

SHAKESPEARE'S PLAYS STAGED IN CONVERTED TOILET

A BRITISH THEATRE company announced in 1999 that it was putting on a run of Shakespeare's plays in an old Victorian toilet. The Bog Standard Theatre Company spent three years and $6,475 converting the toilet in Malvern, Worcestershire, into a 12-seater venue with a tiny stage. "Shakespeare said all the world's a stage so I guess that includes toilets," reasoned the troupe's Dennis Neale. "Ironically we don't have room for a toilet of our own – the audience have to run across the road to public ones." ●

ARTIST CREATES PANIC WITH NAKED MANNEQUINS

Artist Liu Jin caused havoc in Shanghai in 2008 by hanging four naked mannequins from the outside of skyscrapers. Mistaking the dummies for potential jumpers, several worried residents phoned the emergency services while the shock caused one grandmother to be rushed to hospital after suffering a heart attack.

RAP FAN SENTENCED TO LISTEN TO BEETHOVEN

Convicted of playing rap music too loudly on his car stereo, Andrew Vactor, of Urbana, Ohio, faced a $150 fine. But the judge offered to reduce the fine to $35 if Vactor spent 20 hours listening to classical music by the likes of Beethoven and Bach. Champaign County Municipal Court Judge Susan Fornof-Lippencott said she wanted to force Vactor to listen to something he didn't necessarily like, just as other people had no choice but to listen to his loud rap music. Vactor accepted the classical alternative but only lasted 15 minutes and so had to pay the full fine.

ROTTING FISH CAUSES STINK AT EXHIBITION

"Majestic Splendour", a 1997 exhibition by South Korean artist Lee Bul at New York's Museum of Modern Art, consisted solely of rotting fish in sealed bags and glass cabinets. But after only a few hours on display, it was pulled by museum staff when the ventilation equipment failed and the stench became unbearable.

ARTIST UPSET BY SPELLING ERRORS

An educational mural created for Livermore Public Library in 2004 contained 11 spelling mistakes, including the names of such famous figures as Shakespeare ("Shakespere"), Einstein ("Eistein"), Michelangelo ("Michaelangelo"), Van Gogh ("Van Gough") and Gauguin ("Gaugan"). Miami artist Maria Alquilar was paid $40,000 by the California city to create the 16-foot circular mosaic made up of 175 historical names and cultural words – and when the storm erupted over her poor spelling she was paid another $6,000 plus travel expenses to make the corrections. Alquilar couldn't understand what all the fuss was about. She dismissed the errors as "unimportant", adding that people often spell her name incorrectly. "Anyway," she said, "none of us are particularly good spellers anymore because of computers". City officials confirmed that they were spell-checking Alquilar's replacement tiles.

POSTMAN MISTAKES ACTORS FOR MUGGERS

When he saw two men apparently mugging a woman while on his round in Bristol in 2007, postman Neil Filer sprang into action. He whacked one of the attackers on the back of the head with his heavy mailbag and battled to free the victim. It was only when he called for help that he was informed the two men and the woman were actors and that he had interrupted filming for a scene in the BBC hospital drama series *Casualty*.

ARTIST PROJECTS PENIS ON BUILDINGS

Spanish artist Jaime del Val has used cutting edge technology to project enlarged images of his penis onto public buildings in Madrid, including Almudena Cathedral and the Royal Palace. He apparently wanders the streets of the Spanish capital naked except for camera equipment attached to his genitals.

PRESENTER'S TOILET-TALK DROWNS OUT BUSH SPEECH

Instead of hearing a speech by President George W. Bush in 2006, CNN viewers were able to listen to a news presenter's conversation in the toilet. With her microphone not switched off as she took a toilet break, Kyra Phillips's private chat, in which she described her husband as "passionate" and her sister-in-law as "a control freak", was broadcast live over the President's speech. CNN duly apologized for "audio difficulties".

DEAD POET PURSUED BY TV LICENCE AGENCY

A German poet who had been dead for over 200 years was sent two letters by a TV licence-collecting agency threatening to instigate legal proceedings against him unless he quickly settled his monthly $25 bill. Friedrich Schiller had died in 1805 – long before the invention of either television or radio – but that did not prevent agency GEZ sending him two letters in 2008 demanding immediate payment. The letters were sent to a primary school bearing Schiller's name in the Saxony town of Weigsdorf-Köblitz.

Headteacher Michael Binder informed the agency that "the addressee is no longer in a position to listen to the radio or watch television" and attached Schiller's CV to his reply. GEZ responded by insisting that Schiller would only be exempt if he could prove that he did not own television or radio sets. After the confusion was finally cleared up, GEZ promised to alter Schiller's status in its computer system.

ANCIENT CARVINGS WERE FAMILY JOKE

Visiting the British Museum in 1994, 79-year-old Ted Ridings was strangely drawn to two stone faces that were on display. They were described as 2,000-year-old Celtic carvings but Ted recognized them as the work of his brother Leslie, who had created them in 1939 to resemble Hitler and Mussolini. Embarrassed museum officials quickly withdrew the exhibits.

SQUIRREL BLACKS OUT OLYMPIC FINALE

A squirrel hunting nuts in an electricity station caused an 80-minute blackout that shut down Switzerland's main TV station – just as the closing ceremony of the 2008 Beijing Olympics was about to begin. The blackout also hit coverage of motor racing's European Grand Prix in Valencia, silenced two Swiss radio stations and cut power to 6,000 homes in Zurich. The squirrel died in the incident after giving itself an 11,000-volt shock.

COMEDIAN INTERRUPTED BY ROBBERY CONFESSION

Rickey Smiley's stand-up routine at the Comedy Café in Macon, Georgia, in 2001 was interrupted by a heckler with a difference. Glenn Matthews jumped up on stage, grabbed the microphone and proceeded to confess to the bemused audience that he had robbed several banks. While the audience laughed, club officials called the police. Matthews was subsequently convicted of three counts of armed robbery.

DANE TURNS VOMITING INTO AN ART FORM

As part of her final year exams in 2002, Birgit Hansen, a Danish design and fine art student at the University of Ulster in Belfast, performed a piece called "Mother Land Father Tongue" which involved her reading aloud the text of a French philosopher while intermittently vomiting into a bucket.

"I was using the body in a way that I have never done before," she explained, "and I have generally received a positive response about it." Asked how she was able to vomit on demand, she replied: "It happened more easily than I expected. People thought it was amazing."

DONKEY RIDER BANNED FROM DRIVE-IN CINEMA

A New Zealand farmer was banned from a drive-in cinema near Wellington for watching movies on the back of a donkey. Theatre bosses said Geoff Roder blocked the view for others while sitting on the animal. The 35-year-old bachelor protested that he couldn't go to the movies without his donkey because he couldn't drive and, anyway, he added, the donkey was his only companion in life.

FAN WOOS SINGER WITH RUSTY WRENCH

A crazed male fan stalked American country music singer Barbara Mandrell over a 15-year period. Among the tokens of affection that he sent to her Nashville, Tennessee, home were a case of corn flakes, dirty clothes, four bicycles and a rusty wrench.

CHEF PREPARES TESTICLE COOKBOOK

Serbian chef Ljubomir Erovic has compiled what he claims is the first cookery book devoted solely to dishes made from animal testicles. His recipes, which include testicle pizza, battered testicles and barbecued testicles with giblets, require thorough preparatory washing and a very sharp knife. Erovic says: "The tastiest testicles in my opinion probably come from bulls, stallions or ostriches, although all testicles can be eaten – except human, of course."

100 THINGS TO DO BEFORE YOU DIE AUTHOR DIES

The man who co-wrote the best-selling adventure travel guide *100 Things To Do Before You Die* perished in 2008 after only doing half of them. Dave Freeman had already visited around 50 per cent of the places mentioned in his book, whose recommendations included a voodoo pilgrimage to Haiti, running with bulls in Pamplona, Spain, and nude night surfing in Australia. He died at the age of 47 in ironically dull circumstances after hitting his head in a fall at his home in Venice, California.

COMPOSER CREATES CHAMBER MUSIC

Norwegian composer Arne Nordheim made music using noises recorded at an Oslo sewage treatment plant. Whenever any of the city's 280,000 residents take a shower, brush their teeth or flush a toilet, it generates a noise in the plant; by attaching leads to a computer Nordheim was able to air the recorded sounds from 32 strategically placed speakers below ground. To the intense disappointment of music lovers everywhere, he said he was not planning to release a CD of his work.

ACTOR GETS DRUNK WHILE PLAYING A DRUNK

To add realism to his portrayal of a drunk in a 2010 performance of *Moscow – Petushki* by Russian satirist Venedict Yerofeyev, Austrian actor Marc Schulze drunk several shots of real vodka during the course of the show. At first the method acting went down well with the audience in Frankfurt, Germany, but gradually the alcohol took its toll and Schulze ended up getting so drunk that he collapsed on stage. One theatre-goer commented: "He was turning in a very realistic performance and it looked really impressive. I was amazed at how good his drunken staggering was and how he was slurring his words. But then he started missing lines, staring blankly at the other actors and generally looking confused. That was when the audience could tell there was something wrong and realized that he may not actually be acting. Finally he just collapsed." Theatre bosses ordered Schulze to stick to water in future.

LEG BREAST IMPLANTS EXPLODE

After having a drawing of a woman tattooed on his leg, Lane Jensen, from Edmonton, Canada, decided to make it more anatomically accurate by getting breast implants put in the leg. However within a few weeks the breasts had burst. Describing how fluid had started oozing out of the leg, Jensen said: "There was nothing wrong with the implantation procedure. My body just rejected it. I guess my girl wasn't meant to have 3D breasts."

SEAGULLS SWOOP ON PERFORMANCE ARTIST

British performance artist Mark McGowan has pushed himself to the limit in the name of art, rolling a monkey nut for seven miles along the streets of London with his nose, eating a corgi, and walking backwards for 11 miles with a 27-pound turkey on his head. But in 2008 his stunt to encourage Britons to holiday at home instead of travelling abroad, by burying himself up to his neck for 48 hours on Margate beach, had to be scrapped after aggressive seagulls began dive-bombing him. Fearing that the birds might peck out his eyes, he abandoned the challenge after only 30 hours. "I just lost it," he lamented. "Physically and mentally."

BBC ANNOUNCES NUCLEAR TESTS IN NORTH YORKSHIRE

A newsreader on BBC Radio Five Live mistakenly announced in May 2009 that North Yorkshire – instead of North Korea – had launched a programme of illegal underground nuclear tests. The newsreader declared: "There has been widespread condemnation of North Yorkshire's decision to carry out an underground nuclear test. The UN secretary general, Ban Ki-Moon, says he is deeply worried." A spokesman for Five Live said: "We are aware of the occasional tensions between North and South Yorkshire, but clearly this was a slip of the tongue."

SWEARING PARROT FIRED FROM FAMILY PANTO

Percy the Amazonian Green parrot was sacked from a production of the pantomime *Pirates on Treasure Island* in 1999 after saying "piss off mate" instead of "pieces of eight". Percy had been word perfect during earlier rehearsals of the production in Blandford Forum, Dorset, but suddenly unleashed a stream of profanities. Actor Mark Hyde, who played Long John Silver, on whose shoulder Percy sat, could not believe his ears. The rest of the cast stood shell-shocked, particularly when Percy then added: "Bugger off!" A spokesman for the theatre company said: "We could not risk him in a family production."

RINGO STARR LOSES HEAD IN TOPIARY ATTACK

One of the life-sized topiary figures of the Beatles at Liverpool South Parkway station was vandalized in 2008 – just a few weeks after they were unveiled. While the rest of the Fab Four remained untouched, drummer Ringo Starr's head was chopped off by an unknown assailant. The unscheduled hedge trimming was thought to be an act of revenge after Ringo had outraged some Liverpudlians by stating that there was nothing he missed about the city.

PREGNANT ACTRESS SUES OVER NOT BEING CAST AS VIRGIN

A British actress sued an opera company in 2001 after it rejected her for the part of a virgin on the grounds that she would have been heavily pregnant by the end of the show's run. Bethany Halliday, 27, took exception to the decision by the D'Oyly Carte company not to cast her as a blushing teenage daughter in a production of Gilbert and Sullivan's *The Pirates of Penzance* at London's Savoy Theatre. The company's general manager, Ian Martin, said the idea of a pregnant woman playing the role was absurd. "We were casting for the ladies' chorus, who all play the teenage virginal daughters of Major General Stanley and scream every time they see a man. It would not make sense to have a pregnant virginal daughter, and the heavily-corseted Victorian costumes would make it very difficult to disguise her pregnancy. What next? The Royal Shakespeare Company being forced to have a pregnant actress playing the female lead in *Romeo and Juliet*?" Ms Halliday lost her case.

ELDERLY WOMAN STARTLED BY NUNS

Some of the most frightening scenes in cinema history were caused by an elderly woman who fell asleep while watching *The Sound of Music* at a Birmingham picture palace in 1992. Waking with a start during the nuns' chorus, she created chaos and confusion because she thought she had died and was being welcomed to heaven. "It took several minutes to convince her that she wasn't dead," sighed the harassed manager, before adding: "We don't get many out-of-body experiences in Smethwick."

CALLER COMPLAINS ABOUT TIMING OF ECLIPSE

A woman phoned a radio station in South Australia during the December 2002 solar eclipse to express her unhappiness with tourism authorities for organizing a solar eclipse on a weekday when most people were at work. She suggested that next time the eclipse should be held at a weekend.

FOR BETTER
OR FOR WORSE

WOMAN IS MARRIED TO BERLIN WALL

A woman with a fetish for inanimate objects says she has been married to the Berlin Wall since 1979. Eija-Riitta Berliner-Mauer, whose surname means Berlin Wall in German, claims she fell in love with the concrete structure when she first saw it on television at the age of seven. She then began collecting pictures of "him" and saving up for visits, on the sixth of which they tied the knot before a handful of guests. While she remains a virgin with humans, she insists that she has a full, loving relationship with the wall. "I find long, slim things with horizontal lines very sexy," she says. "The Great Wall of China's attractive, but he's too thick – my husband is sexier." Thus she was mortified when most of the Berlin Wall was torn down in 1989. "What they did was awful," she complains. "They mutilated my husband." With her husband in pieces, she was so distressed that she has been unable to return to Berlin from her home in Liden, northern Sweden, and instead is said to have shifted her affections to a nearby garden fence.

WEDDING GUEST ARRIVES A YEAR EARLY

In 2007, Dave Barclay flew 4,000 miles from Canada to attend his friend's wedding in Wales, only to discover that he was a year early. Barclay, who was working as a teacher in Toronto, paid $1,000 for his air ticket and had his suit cleaned specially for the occasion after his pal Dave Best had informed him by email earlier in the year that he was getting married on July 6. However when Barclay arrived in Cardiff and asked for directions to the venue, he was told that the wedding date was actually July 6, 2008. "My mates are loving it, aren't they?" he sighed ruefully, before spotting a silver lining to the cloud. "At least it's assured me of a mention in the speech next year."

BEST MAN WEARS BRIDE'S DRESS

When Romanian bride Manuela Voicu went into labour at her 2002 wedding, the best man, Ion Vidican, put on her dress and stood in for her.

CAKE TRADITION ENDS IN BRAWL

Tracy and John O'Donnell of Westport, Connecticut, brawled on their wedding day in 1994 following a row over the traditional insertion of a piece of wedding cake into the bride's mouth. Tracy saw red because she thought her new husband was pushing the cake into her mouth too forcefully.

WEDDING PARTY CANCELLED OVER BRIDE'S BEARD

An Arab ambassador called off his imminent wedding celebrations and had his marriage contract annulled after he discovered that beneath her veil, his fiancée was cross-eyed and had a beard. The ambassador had only met his future bride a few times before the marriage was due to take place – and she had been wearing the niqab at all times. It was only after the marriage contract had been signed and shortly before the wedding party that he tried to kiss her and saw the optical impediment and facial hair. He immediately called off the celebration and filed for divorce claiming that he had been deceived by his mother-in-law who, he said, had shown his mother pictures of the bride's sister instead of the bride.

POLICE STOP BRIDE'S LIMO ON WAY TO CHURCH – TO GET NUMBER OF HIRE FIRM

Already running late for her wedding ceremony at Haydon Bridge, Northumberland, in 2001, bride Cheryl Ann Brown was horrified when a police car ordered the 46-foot-long stretch limo that was taking her to the church to pull over to the side of the road. The 21-year-old said: "The policeman had his clipboard in his hand and the limo driver had to get out and then come back. I assumed he was getting his driving licence but it turned out the police just wanted the phone number of the car hire firm for a force function! I couldn't believe it."

PUPPY LOVE: GHANAIAN WOMAN MARRIES DOG

Emily Mabou, of Aburi, Ghana, married her dog because she believed it possessed qualities she had seen only in her late father. She said the dog was kind, faithful and treated her with respect, just like her father but unlike any of her previous boyfriends. However her family boycotted the ceremony, which was presided over by a traditional priest, because they felt the wedding was "a stupid step to combat her loneliness".

BRIDE CATCHES GROOM WITH BEST MAN

A bride-to-be on the Greek island of Crete suffered a nervous breakdown on the night before her 2001 nuptials when she discovered the groom, wearing her wedding dress, in the arms of his best man. The ceremony was cancelled.

BEST MAN WAS CARDBOARD CUT-OUT

When racing car driver Andy Priaulx discovered that a hastily arranged event in Brazil clashed with his duties as best man at a wedding in Guernsey in 2007, he sent a life-sized cardboard cut-out of himself to the ceremony along with a pre-recorded speech. The six-foot-tall cut-out – created by a local sign-maker – stood next to the altar as Andy Richmond and Carlee Yates tied the knot. Carlee even danced with the cut-out at the reception.

BRIDE WEDS DRUNKEN GROOM'S BROTHER INSTEAD

A groom was so drunk when he turned up for his wedding at a village in India in 2007 that the teenage bride married his brother instead. After the groom "misbehaved with guests", the bride's family chased him away and promptly invited his sober brother to take his place.

COUPLE MARRY IN PUBLIC TOILET

When Jennifer Cannon and Doy Nichols of Lexington, Kentucky, decided to get married in New York they chose an unusual venue – a public toilet in Times Square. In keeping with the lavatory theme, the bride wore a dress made from glue, tape and toilet paper, the creation of Hanah Kim, winner of the coveted 2007 Toilet Paper Wedding Dress Contest.

BRIDE SPOTS IMPOSTOR BY HIS LACK OF DROOL

A wedding ceremony in Uganda was cancelled in 2002 when the bride suddenly realized that the man standing next to her was not the one she had agreed to marry. She spotted the difference because her original suitor drooled continually at the mouth. Apparently the bride's parents had subsequently conspired to have her married off to his older brother instead.

TAIWANESE MAN MARRIES BARBIE DOLL

A Taiwanese man tried to appease the restless spirit of his dead wife by marrying a Barbie doll. Chang Hsi-hsum, 46, married the 11-inch plastic doll during an elaborate ceremony at his local Buddhist temple in 1999. He believed the doll housed the spirit of his wife Tsai who had killed herself 20 years earlier because his family opposed their marriage.

DOCTORS REMOVE GRAIN OF RICE FROM BRIDE'S EAR

A bride who was showered with rice on the steps of a church after her wedding had to go to hospital to have one grain extracted from her ear. The reception at Lecco, Italy, was delayed for an hour until she returned from hospital.

POLICE HALT CEREMONY TO QUIZ COUPLE

A wedding service in Glauchau, Germany, was interrupted when police officers insisted on quizzing the happy couple about items that had been stolen from them the night before. Constanze and Rocco Zahn had reported the theft of a laptop and wedding presents from the groom's stag party but none of the guests had expected two over-zealous officers to take statements from the victims during their actual wedding ceremony. "Everyone thought Rocco was in trouble with the police when the officers waltzed into the ceremony and led him away," said one of the guests. "After all, the stag party was quite a wild one. But when we found out they were just taking statements, all the guests started booing and the officers left pretty quickly. There's a time and a place for these things."

"GROOM RUNS OVER BRIDE ON HONEYMOON"

A groom was accused by police of deliberately driving his car at his bride – while they were still on honeymoon. After a quickie wedding in Las Vegas in 2007, the newlyweds were driving near Salt Lake City, Utah, when they apparently started fighting in the car. Police said the bride got out of the car and started to walk away, whereupon the groom allegedly drove off the road and rammed her with the car, pushing her into a snow bank. A police source said the couple were "well known to the sheriff's office".

WOMAN MARRIES DOLPHIN

In a modest ceremony at Dolphin Reef in the Israeli port of Eilat, 41-year-old Briton Sharon Tendler married Cindy, a 35-year-old male bottlenosed dolphin, in 2006. Finally taking the plunge after 15 years of courtship, Tendler, who wore a white dress, a veil and had pink flowers in her hair, got down on one knee and gave Cindy a kiss – and a piece of herring. Although acknowledging that the wedding had no legal status, she said the ceremony reflected her true feelings for the animal. "It's not a perverted thing," she insisted. "I do love this dolphin. He's the love of my life."

GROOM WAS ALSO FATHER OF THE BRIDE

When a Los Angeles businessman learned that his fiancée had been conceived via artificial insemination, he was alarmed to discover that the sperm bank was the same one to which he had donated in his student days. So he obtained a court injunction to inspect the bank's records and found that he was, in fact, the father of his bride-to-be and 806 other children. The wedding was called off.

WEDDING GUESTS SHOOT DOWN AIRPLANE

Guests celebrating a wedding in a Serbian village in 2004 fired guns in the air in accordance with national custom and accidentally shot down a light airplane.

EXPOSED BRIDE CAUSES PRIEST TO HALT WEDDING

A priest in Turin, Italy, called a halt to a wedding in 2001 because the bride was showing too much cleavage. He refused to allow her into the church and asked the wedding party to disperse quietly. While the bride's mother saw no problem with the dress, the local church authority supported the priest's stance and emphasized the need for appropriate attire at religious ceremonies. Rather than risk incurring the wrath of another priest, the couple later decided to get married in a civil ceremony instead.

MAN ANNOUNCES INTENTION TO MARRY PILLOW

A Nigerian man who said he couldn't get a girlfriend because of his bad stutter, announced plans to marry his pillow. Twenty-six-year-old Lagos labourer Okeke Ikechukwu lamented: "Since I am a stutterer, ladies have always laughed at me whenever I try to talk to them. I have needs, and so I have taken to sleeping with my pillow in my arms ever since I was 16. I have grown to fall in love with it, and I intend to spend the rest of my life with it. Unlike a woman, it will cost me little or nothing to maintain. I think it will make the ideal mate for me."

GROOM SHOOTS BRIDE DEAD BY MISTAKE

Mistaking his fiancée for an intruder, a 62-year-old Florida man shot her dead on the eve of their wedding. He grabbed his gun and fired at a figure in the dark hallway of his home, thinking his live-in partner was still in bed. A relative said: "They loved each other. It was quite apparent."

BRIDE'S BOUQUET BRINGS BAD LUCK

The traditional throwing of a bride's bouquet for luck nearly ended in tragedy at a 2009 Italian wedding when the flowers caused a plane to crash. Following the ceremony near Plombino, Tuscany, the bride and groom had arranged for a small plane to fly overhead and for a passenger to throw the bouquet to a line of female guests. However the flowers became caught in the aircraft's rear rotor, causing the plane to catch fire, explode and crash to the ground. The passenger who threw the bouquet suffered two broken legs.

MAN FORGOT HE WAS MARRIED

An Australian man learned in 2008 that his marriage was invalid because he had forgotten that he had married someone else in a drunken haze 30 years earlier. The 67-year-old vaguely remembered meeting a "nice" blonde woman in Arizona in 1978 during shore leave from his job as a cook on an oil rig but had no idea that they had married. It was only when he was shown his signature on the Arizona marriage licence that the truth hit him. The news was broken to him by US immigration authorities when he applied to live in Hawaii with the person he thought was his wife. He said that she was very understanding about being temporarily relegated to girlfriend status.

SISTER-IN-LAW DOUSES BRIDE WITH BLACK PAINT

On her way to church in 2008, bride Nancy Rose stopped off to use the washroom at a coffee shop in Halifax, Nova Scotia. But as she returned to the car park she saw her sister-in-law, Michelle King, screaming and running towards her limousine with a can of black spray paint. King, who was married to Rose's brother, proceeded to douse the bride's gown and veil in sooty black paint before wrestling with the limo driver while the rest of the wedding party looked on in disbelief. As the driver tried to restrain her, King's tube top fell down, exposing her breasts but giving her a chance to flee. The animosity between the two women is said to have stemmed from a dispute at King's wedding the previous year over a bridesmaid's dress to be worn by Rose's young daughter.

GUESTS SMASH PRICELESS TEA SET IN TOAST ERROR

Like all proud fathers, Grigory Romanov, mayor of Leningrad, wanted only the very best for his daughter's 1980 wedding. To this end he persuaded the director of the city's Hermitage Museum to lend him Catherine the Great's irreplaceable, 200-year-old china tea set especially for the occasion. All went well until late in the proceedings one guest rose to his feet and accidentally dropped a cup. Thinking that this was a toast, the other guests interpreted it as a traditional gesture of good luck, whereupon they all stood up and hurled the entire service into the fireplace.

STAND-IN BRIDE IS SHORT CHANGED

When a 22-year-old Romanian man was jilted days before his wedding in 1998, his parents, anxious to spare their son's embarrassment and not wanting to see the money they had spent on the nuptials go to waste, decided to rent a bride for the day. So an old childhood friend named Mariana stepped in, dutifully rehearsing her lines and practising the ceremony with the groom whose family promised that in return for her trouble she would receive $100. Under Romanian tradition wedding guests donate money to help pay for the cost of the event but only two-thirds of the invited guests turned up on this occasion and some, surprised by the replacement bride, did not give generously. As a result, Mariana received just $3 – $97 short of the sum she was promised. To add to her woes, the groom took a shine to her and declared that he wanted the marriage to last.

BRIDE FINALLY SAYS "YES" AFTER 8,500 PROPOSALS

Following 8,500 proposals and 24 years of candlelit meals, Britain's Beverley Redman finally agreed to marry her partner Keith in 2000. Keith had tried to persuade her with romantic notes, dinners and trips to Ibiza but she had repeatedly turned him down. "I was frightened of committing myself," she said.

GROOM GETS COLD FEET, SETS WEDDING HOTEL ON FIRE

Unable to decide whether to stay with his wife or marry his girlfriend, a Japanese man tried to buy himself some time by setting fire to the hotel where the wedding was to take place. Tatsuhiko Kawata had been married to his wife since 1994 but had also been seeing another woman for three years and had promised to marry her in October 2008 at a hotel in the mountain resort of Hokuto. However on the eve of the ceremony, the still-married Kawata sought to delay events by spilling seven litres of petrol in the hotel and setting it on fire, causing minor damage and forcing several guests to evacuate the premises. Sentencing him to five years in jail, the judge described Kawata as "egoistic and short-sighted."

BRIDE IN RECEPTION FIGHT WITH BAND

A bride was arrested at her wedding reception in Port Chester, New York State, in 2008 after becoming involved in an argument with the band. She was accused of trashing a set of conga drums and breaking a speaker, causing $1,500 damage.

MAN WITH TAIL STRUGGLES TO FIND WIFE

An Indian man with a 13-inch tail announced in 2006 that although he had become an object of worship he was struggling to find a wife. Chandre Oram from West Bengal is regarded by locals as an incarnation of Hindu monkey god Hanuman but the tail, which he refused to have surgically removed, proved a turn-off for the ladies. He lamented: "Almost 20 women have turned down marriage proposals. They see me and agree but as soon as I turn around, they see my tail and leave."

"HERE COMES THE BRIDE" IS PLAYED ON CELL PHONE

When the organist failed to get to the church on time, bride Tracey Muxworthy walked down the aisle to the tinny strains of "Here Comes the Bride" played on a cell phone. The 2002 ceremony, at Aberdare, Wales, had been put back a few minutes in the hope that the organist would appear but when he still failed to show, Darren Medd, a friend of the groom, realized that he had the tune on his phone as a ringtone. So the phone was held next to a microphone as the bride made her way down the aisle. Mr Medd said afterwards: "It was probably the fastest wedding march you'll ever hear."

JAPANESE MAN MARRIES COMPUTER GAME CHARACTER

A Japanese man who became infatuated with a character in a computer game married the object of his desires in a solemn ceremony in Tokyo. The groom, who calls himself SAL9000, fell in love with Nene Anegasaki from the Nintendo DS game 'Love Plus' after a string of failed romances with girlfriends from other animated games. The wedding took place at the Tokyo Institute of Technology and was presided over by a priest. The groom, dressed in a white suit and tie, read his vows before Ms Anegasaki flashed hers up on the touch screen of his Nintendo. The ceremony was broadcast live on the Internet, with the groom's best man giving a speech and Ms Anegasaki's imaginary maid of honour posting an on-screen message declaring her joy at the union. Before jetting off with his new bride on honeymoon to Guam, the groom said: "I feel as if I have been able to achieve a major milestone in my life. Some people have expressed doubts about my actions, but this is really just about us as husband and wife. As long as the two of us can go on to create a happy household, I'm sure any misgivings about us will be resolved." However the groom then admitted that he had yet to inform his parents that he had even got married, let alone to a computer character.

BRIDE ATTACKS GROOM WITH WEDDING CAKE

The wedding of Brett Patrick to his wife Kathryn in Florida in 2001 ended acrimoniously when a late-night disagreement over wedding gifts erupted into violence. Police said the bride, who was ten-weeks pregnant at the time, threw wedding cake at her husband, punched him in the face, then kicked and beat him while he was on the ground. Officers arrived to find him covered in bruises, scratches and icing.

COUPLE MISCALCULATE THEIR ANNIVERSARY

Barry and Carol Watson of Cliftonville, Kent, booked a round-the-world trip to celebrate their silver wedding anniversary, only to discover that they were a year too early. Having spent two years planning the trip, they decided to go ahead with it anyway and were showered with gifts wherever they travelled but were too embarrassed to admit they had really only been married for 24 years.

IDENTICAL TWINS CHOOSE BRIDES BY DRAWING LOTS

A pair of identical Ethiopian twin brothers drew lots to decide who would wed whom after their parents arranged their marriage to a pair of identical twin sisters. Isamel and Ali Mohammed, both 27, had insisted their parents should look for twin sisters if they wanted them to get married and settle down. When suitable sisters were found, it proved impossible to distinguish them apart, so the brothers picked their respective brides by drawing lots.

"MAN TRADES DAUGHTER FOR BEER, MEAT AND MONEY"

A man was arrested in Greenfield, California, in 2009 after allegedly arranging for his 14-year-old daughter to marry a neighbour in exchange for $16,000, one hundred cases of beer and several cases of meat. Police said they learned of the deal after the man asked them for help in getting his daughter back after he failed to receive the promised money.

WEDDING ELEPHANT DESTROYS 20 LIMOS IN LOVE RAMPAGE

An elephant hired for a 2010 Hindu wedding in India caused over $400,000 damage in his desperate attempt to reach an in-heat female. The amorous elephant trampled 20 limos to try to reach the object of his desires in a nearby sugarcane field. When that failed, he smashed through a shopping mall before mounting and attempting to mate with a truck.

CHINESE MAN MARRIES HIMSELF

A Chinese man married himself in 2007 to make a statement about his dissatisfaction with reality. Liu Ye, who married a life-sized foam cut-out of himself wearing a bridal dress, said the ceremony made him feel "whole again" but admitted he was "maybe a bit narcissistic".

WEDDING PROPOSAL GOES UP IN FLAMES

Adam Sutton planned to make his proposal to high-school sweetheart Erika Brussee an occasion she would never forget – and he was right because it ended in the young couple being lucky to escape with their lives. His idea was to hire a pilot to take them up in a Cessna 172 airplane circling low over Rome, Georgia, in the summer of 2006 and to have family members on the ground holding up a tarpaulin saying "Erika, Will You Marry Me?" Everything went smoothly until the plane stalled at low speed, crashed into the airport runway and the nose burst into flames – just as Sutton was about to slip the ring onto her finger. The couple scrambled out with cuts and bruises, and as Brussee was loaded into an ambulance, she called out to Sutton's cousin: "Tell Adam I said yes."

SUICIDE BIDS PERSUADE PARENTS TO THINK AGAIN

When the parents of Huang Pin-jen and Chang Shu-mei refused to bless their 1996 Taiwanese wedding, the distraught couple decided to commit suicide. First, they drove a car off a cliff – but survived; next they tried to hang themselves – but survived; and then they jumped from the top of a 12-storey building – but survived. After that, the parents agreed to reconsider.

WOMAN MARRIES HOURS AFTER SHOOTING ATTACKER

As wedding days go, few were more eventful than the occasion in 2002 when former school principal Charlotte Ann Neely-White married Russell Roark in Pierce City, Missouri. The bride-to-be was making last minute preparations on the morning of the ceremony when a total stranger raced up in a car and threatened to detonate a bomb unless Neely-White gave him her pickup truck. But, wedding or no wedding, she was not about to hand over her beloved truck and told him: "No, sir, you go ahead and set the bomb off. My house needs work anyway." The stranger then tried to choke her with a riding whip, whereupon she shot him in the chest with a gun she had been handed and beat him around the head with a shovel. And she still got married three hours later. Asked why she had taken such a risk on that of all days, the 55-year-old replied: "Have you ever had anything you really love? Well, I love that truck." A police officer who attended the incident was full of praise. "This lady was calm as a cucumber," he said. "She can withstand anything. I admire her guts. He came right at her – he was wired. She didn't back down, and she knew she had to protect what was hers, and she did. I don't think I'd want to make her upset."

BRIDE SUES AFTER BUM WEDDING

An Italian bride sued a dress designer in 2006 after the stitching on her $4,000 bridal gown came apart at the altar and slid down, revealing her bottom to the entire congregation. Her lawyer said: "The priest concluded the ceremony and the couple were married but she was not able to have any proper photographs because she was semi-naked. The priest did not know where to look."

LIGHTNING STRIKES TWICE FOR UNLUCKY GROOM

When his second bride-to-be fell in love with the wedding invitation maker and promptly cancelled their forthcoming nuptials in 2001, it brought back painful memories for Romanian Sorin Archiudean. His first wife had run off with their wedding-day chauffeur just two weeks into their marriage.

POLICE RAID BRINGS COUPLE TOGETHER

A Kent couple got married in 1994 after being introduced by police officers conducting a drugs raid. At the same bar in Herne Bay, Cathy Snelson was waiting to meet a blind date while Dominic McDonnell was playing pool, but when police raided the establishment, the strangers were made to spend two hours sitting on the floor with their hands tied behind their backs before eventually being released. The enforced confinement led to true love, culminating in the pair being married – even though the police weren't invited to the wedding. "But I suppose we should have done," said Ms Snelson, "as they brought us together."

GROOM UPDATES FACEBOOK STATUS AT ALTAR

A GROOM interrupted his own wedding to get his cell phone out at the altar and update his relationship status on Facebook and Twitter. Immediately after the minister pronounced them man and wife, Dana Hanna, of Abingdon Maryland, whipped out his phone and changed his Facebook status from "in a relationship" to "married". He also Tweeted: "Standing at the altar with Tracy Page where just a second ago, she became my wife! Gotta go, time to kiss my bride." ●

MAN CUTS OFF PENIS OVER MARRIAGE DISAPPOINTMENT

Refused permission to marry a girl from a lower-class family, a 25-year-old Egyptian cut off his own penis to spite his family. After unsuccessfully petitioning his father for two years to marry the girl, the man reached the end of his tether in 2009 and heated up a knife and sliced off his reproductive organ. He was rushed to hospital but doctors were unable to reattach the severed penis.

BRIDE REJECTS GROOM OVER LOUSY MATHS

A bride in India dumped her husband-to-be in 2008 because he could not perform a simple mathematical sum. Sarita Kumari was all set to marry a man named Tinku but when the gathering reached the bride's house in Gopalganj district, some of the women present asked the groom to give the answer to the sum of three plus four. Poor Tinku didn't know the answer, whereupon the bride refused to marry him. After hasty consultation between the two families, she agreed to marry his younger brother, Pintu, instead.

WOMAN RUGBY-TACKLES FIANCÉ AT PRENUP PARTY

A woman from Poulsbo, Washington State, was thrown in jail after being accused of beating up her fiancé at their prenuptial party. The argument broke out after the woman's 12-year-old son told her he saw her fiancé kissing one of her women friends. Deputies said the bride-to-be ordered him to leave the house and then started hitting him in the face. When he did leave, she reportedly tackled him rugby-style, punched him again, threw his watch into the bushes and broke his glasses. The woman was arrested on suspicion of assault. It is not known whether the marriage took place.

PET DOG IS CHIEF BRIDESMAID

When Sonia Wilde married Steve Begley at Stockport, Cheshire, in 2005, she chose a very special chief bridesmaid – her dog Lucy Brown. The three-year-old collie cross even wore a pink frilly dress and bonnet for the service. Afterwards Sonia said: "Lucy Brown absolutely loved her dress. Whenever I got it out to try it on her, she would put her front paws up like she couldn't wait to get it on. She was really well behaved throughout the service. She got a little excited at the reception but we could tell she was happy."

BRIDE DELAYS WEDDING OVER FEAR OF VOMITING

A London bride postponed her 2008 wedding because she was afraid of vomiting. Emma Pelling said she had been unable to go through with her wedding to Gareth Heal because she suffers from emetophobia, an intense fear of vomiting. She added: "I have this recurring nightmare of being ill as a bride, running out of the church and abandoning my husband at the altar."

MARRIAGE PROPOSAL DRIFTS AWAY

Lefkos Hajji came up with a novel idea for proposing to his girlfriend Leanne: he hid a $12,000 engagement ring inside a helium balloon and gave her a pin so that she could pop the balloon as he popped the question. But as he left the shop, a sudden gust of wind wrenched the balloon from his grasp, leaving him to watch helplessly as the ring floated away over London. "I couldn't believe it," he said afterwards. "I just watched as it went further and further into the air. I felt like such a plonker. It cost a fortune, and when I told my girlfriend the story she went absolutely mad. Now she is refusing to speak to me."

BRIDE MARRIES WRONG MAN

An Indian woman married the wrong man in 2005 after the priest confused the groom with his brother. During the exchange of vows at the Muslim wedding in Uttar Pradesh, the priest said Mehraj instead of Siraj and the bride failed to spot the mistake. The blunder came to light the following morning when the groom's family saw the marriage document.

GERIATRIC NEWLYWEDS GIVEN BOOK ON PARENTING

When 90-year-old Max Gordon and his bride-to-be, 82-year-old Mollie Levy, requested a marriage licence in 1999, the clerk handed them a book – on parenting. Despite the fact that between them the couple had six children, 14 grandchildren and 17 great-grandchildren, under Florida law their union still needed safeguarding by the Marriage Preparation and Preservation Act of 1998, a statute designed to protect children from the fallout of failed marriages. So the elderly couple sat down together and dutifully read the book's advice about parenting – although Mollie had to read to Max because of his cataracts.

WEDDING DAY WAS ONE TO REMEMBER

Bebe Emerman intended to marry Steve Wolfe in a spectacular outdoor ceremony at California's Yosemite National Park in 1995, but a huge rainstorm literally blew their plans away. Then a flooded road forced guests to drive an extra 140 miles to the new indoor location. A wild squirrel nearly destroyed the cake and the wedding photographer was rushed to hospital with a kidney stone. "Everything that possibly could go wrong went wrong," recalled the bride. "I even dumped the back of my dress into the toilet."

GROOM WEARS DRESS TO RECEPTION

A factory worker from Barnsley stunned relatives by turning up to his 2008 wedding reception wearing a fitted bridal gown. Transvestite Dean Dudley

– also known as Deanne – has been wearing women's clothes since the age of six but his mother knew nothing about it – until the reception. However, his bride Robyn, who fell for him five years earlier when, as Deanne, he lent her a hairbrush in a ladies' toilet, remained unfazed, admitting: "He's a better looking woman than me."

WOMAN CANCELS WEDDING OVER FIANCÉ'S PORN CAREER

A woman cancelled her church wedding and country house reception in 2009 after discovering that her fiancé was a secret porn star. Haylie Hocking, from Bristol, only found out shortly before the big day that fitness fanatic Jason Brake made adult movies. A friend organizing her hen night had been searching online for a male stripper when she stumbled across a movie clip in which the male star looked like Jason. On checking the website, she realized it was Jason. "I don't know if I'll ever be able to trust a man again," sobbed Haylie.

FATHER SUES OVER UGLY BRIDE

A man from Belchertown, Massachusetts, announced in 2006 that he was suing friends who had arranged a marriage for his son, claiming that the bride was too ugly, had bad teeth, a poor complexion, and couldn't hold a conversation. Dr Vijay Pandey sought $200,000 in damages from a Maryland couple whose niece was the proposed bride. Pandey said that when he travelled to New Delhi to meet the woman he was "extremely shocked" by her appearance. In his lawsuit he alleged fraud, conspiracy and violation of civil rights resulting in emotional distress, and sought costs for travel and long-distance telephone calls.

WILDLIFE COUPLE ENJOY GIBBON-STYLE WEDDING

Two animal conservationists who met while working with gibbons tied the knot in a gibbon-style wedding ceremony at a Thailand wildlife sanctuary in 2004. Accompanied by a drum band, groom Sam Lake summoned his mate by imitating the call of a male gibbon, whereupon his bride, Norka Russin, responded with happy monkey calls while swinging down from a treetop into his arms. Afterwards the groom vowed: "Once the gibbon has chosen a mate it will not philander."

BRIDE ATTACKS GROOM WITH SHOE

While the reception was in full swing downstairs, the bride was attacking the groom with a shoe in their Scottish hotel room. Teresa Brown was still wearing her wedding dress when she assaulted groom Mark Allerton with the heel of her stiletto and ended up spending the rest of the weekend in a police cell. Brown was subsequently fined at Aberdeen Sheriff's Court for assault and vandalism. Her lawyer said: "She and her husband are still together although this incident has not helped."

RUST REMOVER SPOILS WEDDING BANQUET

Around 170 guests at a wedding banquet in northern China were rushed to hospital in 2008 when someone accidentally added powdered rust remover instead of salt. All the food was stewed in a big pot but the guests decided it tasted too bland, so one of them added what he or she thought was salt – several times over. Within an hour, the local hospital was packed with guests suffering from stomach pains, vomiting and diarrhoea.

KEEN HUNTERS GET MARRIED IN TREE

As fanatical deer hunters, David Cunningham and Mary Boyer decided that their 1999 wedding should reflect their favourite pastime. They took their vows high in a tree at a Reinholds, Pennsylvania, gun club with the bride wearing a full-length camouflage dress, complete with a veil made of a deer-hunting face mask. The path to the altar was lined with deer antlers and the groom was chased along it by a group of hunting companions. Among the 300 guests, many of whom also wore camouflage, were several life-sized rubber deer. A friend of the couple described it as "a unique occasion".

BRIDE'S JOKE FALLS FLAT

A bride who jokingly replied "I don't" during her wedding lived to regret it as the registrar promptly refused to go ahead with the ceremony. Tina Albrecht, 27, was to marry fiancé Dietmar Koch at a castle in Steyr, Austria, in 2007, but the wedding was called off after she tried to inject a little humour into proceedings by saying "I don't" before immediately correcting herself. Under an Austrian law designed to prevent forced marriages, if either party replies to the key question in the negative the wedding must be cancelled and cannot be rescheduled for a further ten weeks. Ms Albrecht said: "We had to send all our guests home. In retrospect my remark was probably not so funny."

LONELY MAN MARRIES GOAT

A Sudanese man was ordered to take a goat as his wife after he was caught having sex with the animal. Roused by a noise one night in 2006, the owner, Mr Alifi, rushed outside and found Charles Tombe with the goat named Rose. Mr Alifi said: "When I asked him, 'What are you doing here?', he fell off the back of the goat, so I captured him and tied him up." Mr Alifi then took him to a council of elders who ordered Tombe to pay him a $50 dowry for the animal because he had used it as his wife. An official explained: "In South Sudan if a man is caught sleeping with a girl, he is ordered to marry her immediately in order to save her honour and that of her family. That was why Tombe had to marry the goat." Tombe said he was drunk at the time.

GROOM CRASHES $400,000 CAR ON WAY TO CHURCH

A bridegroom crashed a $400,000 Lamborghini that his bride had hired as a treat for him to drive to the church. Abi Pattison-Hart paid $12,000 to hire David Gallucci a yellow Lamborghini Murciélago LP640 for their big day but he lost control of the 220 miles per hour supercar on his way to the ceremony near Bradford, West Yorkshire, ending up in a ditch and causing $250,000 of damage to the bodywork, suspension and wheels. He wisely waited until after the wedding before breaking the news to his bride.

MAN MARRIES WRONG TWIN

A Romanian dentist inadvertently married the twin sister of the woman he had fallen in love with. Vladut met Elena, whom he called the "love of his life", during a trip to France and they agreed to meet up again back in Romania. However Elena suffered an accident and decided not to stay in touch. Meanwhile Vladut bumped into her twin sister, Monica, at the seaside and thought it was Elena. She did not correct him and the pair married in 2001, remaining together for three years before Vladut realized he was living with the wrong twin.

WEDDING TOAST – FORTY TIMES OVER

When Paul and Lynne Davies of Stoke-on-Trent got married in 2008, they told friends and relatives that they didn't want any presents. So their 40 guests decided to play a prank on the couple – and each bought them a toaster.

BRIDE CAUGHT IN THE ACT WITH BEST MAN

Doctors had to separate a bride and best man after they were caught having sex in the toilets during a wedding reception in Varazdin, Croatia, in 2005. When a friend of the groom walked in on them unexpectedly, the shock caused a muscle spasm that meant they were unable to be pulled apart. A procession of wedding guests came to gawp at the hapless pair before doctors arrived with the intention of separating them. Unable to do so, they had to take the pair on a stretcher to hospital, where the bride was given an injection to relax her muscles, thereby enabling the best man to break free. Meanwhile the party continued after the groom announced that the celebrations were now to mark his divorce rather than his wedding.

TREES GET MARRIED IN INDIA

Two trees that had grown around each other were married by Indian villagers in 2006. It was hoped that the ceremony, conducted before 250 guests, would keep evil spirits at bay.

BRIDE GETS STUCK IN CHURCH DOOR

When 16-year-old Carly O'Brien from Gloucester, England, said she wanted a big wedding, she found a dress to match. Unfortunately the eight-foot-wide dress, which weighed 25 stone and had a 60-foot-long train, was so big that she became wedged in the church door for an hour and a half. It eventually required the combined efforts of 20 people to push her through the door and up the aisle and another 14 plus the groom to carry her out again at the end of the ceremony.

GROOM CHOKES TO DEATH ON BRIDE'S FALSE FINGERNAIL

A bridegroom died during his wedding ceremony in 2001 while licking honey from his bride's finger, an Iranian custom designed to guarantee that newlyweds' life together starts sweetly. Instead there were only tears as the hapless groom fatally choked on his beloved's false fingernail.

DEAD GRANDFATHER ATTENDS WEDDING

Upset that her grandfather would miss her 2003 wedding, having died two days earlier, a New Zealand bride and her family decided that he should be present anyway. So they took his corpse along to the wedding, leaving it in an open coffin inside the church during the ceremony.

GRIEVING BRIDE MARRIES CORPSE

After her lover drowned in a well, an Indian woman married his corpse. Members of the bride's family dressed the deceased like a groom and conducted the marriage ceremony on a decorated stage. Tulsi Devipujak, 20, had been prevented from marrying 25-year-old Sanjay Dantania while he was alive because they belonged to different castes.

WEDDING VIDEO MARRED BY BESTIALITY SCENES

Guests at a wedding in East Sussex in 1994 received an unwelcome surprise when they sat down to watch the video of the ceremony. The man filming the wedding had borrowed the camera from 59-year-old Derek Jeffrey, who had forgotten to erase the previous footage on the tape. Consequently the final shots of the smiling bride and groom joyfully embarking on their new life together were followed by a ten-minute movie of Jeffrey lying on a bed, wearing only his socks, and performing indecent acts with a neighbour's Staffordshire bull terrier called Ronnie. In court, Jeffrey admitted to having been drunk at the time but claimed that he had only been simulating sex with the dog. He was given a six-month suspended sentence.

MAN DROPS ENGAGEMENT RING FROM HOT AIR BALLOON

A vicar's romantic proposal to his girlfriend in a hot air balloon fell flat when he dropped the engagement ring and saw it fall 500 feet into woodland below. James Ng had hidden the ring in his camera case but as he and Sonya Bostic took to the skies above Ohio in 2009, the case slipped from his hand. The resourceful Mr Ng went through with the proposal, using a plastic tie twist in place of the ring, and after a week of scouring the three-square-mile area of woods he finally located the camera bag with the ring still inside.

BRIDE RUNS OFF WITH WEDDING PRESENTS

While the groom waited patiently at the altar, a bride in Portugal did a vanishing act. She was later spotted in Lisbon – and charged with the theft of almost $200,000 worth of wedding presents.

POP STAR MARRIES PINEAPPLE

IN 1970, German pop star Ramma Damma – aka Ulli Hopper – decided to get married to a pineapple. Having chosen his bride, whom he affectionately named Tippi, from a supermarket he drove her across the Scottish border to Gretna Green in a Jaguar car covered in green Astroturf. There, he and his pineapple were wed before returning together to his home in Munich. Now a champion of plant rights, he recalls: "I loved her. I wanted to marry her. We stayed in Gretna Green Hall Hotel and were married by a craftsman wearing a kilt. We enjoyed meals out and Tippi loved to go to the movies – especially ones about earthquakes – where she would sit on my lap when she got scared." ●

GROOM DIVORCES BRIDE OVER COLOUR OF MOTORBIKE

For a bride in Jharkhand, India, it was a tale of two marriages and a divorce in one night – all over the colour of a motorbike. Directly after his marriage to Farhana in 2007, Riyaz Ansari asked to see the motorbike that was gifted to him as a dowry but became so angry on discovering that it was black instead of red that, in spite of the bride's family's attempts to pacify him, he promptly divorced her. While the groom and his father were being beaten up by disappointed villagers, Yasin Ansari, a member of the groom's party, offered to marry Farhana, a gesture which the girl's family readily accepted.

INFLATABLE DOLL STANDS IN FOR HUSBAND

With Sheila Smith's husband Bob away on business and therefore unable to attend the couple's recommitment service in Ohio, friends brought along a life-size inflatable doll as a stand-in. They dressed the blow-up Bob in shirt, tie and trousers and taped on a head-shot photo of the real Bob.

JILTED BRIDE DRESSES DOG AS GROOM

Despite being cruelly dumped by Paul Fox two weeks before their wedding day, Emma Knight of Portland, Dorset, was determined that the reception should go ahead as planned. So she dressed her dog Dennis up as the groom, wore the $3,000 wedding dress and partied with her 100 guests. She had sold her house to pay for the wedding.

WOMAN WEDS EIFFEL TOWER

In a touching ceremony before a few invited friends in Paris, an ex-US Army soldier from San Francisco married the Eiffel Tower in 2007. Erika La Tour Eiffel (she legally changed her surname to reflect her union with the 1,000-foot iron monument) promised eternal love even though she also claims to be romantically attached to the Golden Gate Bridge. "I am a woman and this is a bridge, and despite our vast differences we are very much in love," she declared. A former archery champion with a passion for inanimate objects rather than people, Erika's first beau was her bow, Lance.

5

IN SICKNESS AND IN HEALTH

WOMAN SAT ON TOILET FOR A MONTH

A woman spent at least a month sitting on her boyfriend's toilet – so that by the time he finally contacted police she was stuck to the seat. Although Kory McFarren told investigators that he regularly took her food and water and had begged her every day to come out of the bathroom, 35-year-old Pam Babcock from Ness County, Kansas, apparently refused to move. Sheriff Bryan Whipple said it appeared that the woman's skin had grown around the seat. "We prised the toilet seat off with a bar and the seat went with her to hospital. The hospital removed it. She was not glued. She was not tied. She was just physically stuck by her body. It is hard to imagine."

PENSIONER BANNED FOR FARTING

In 2007, a social club in Devon banned a 77-year-old man from breaking wind while indoors. Retired bus driver Maurice Fox received a letter from Kirkham Street Sports and Social Club in Paignton which said: "After several complaints regarding your continual breaking of wind while in the club, would you please consider that your actions are considered disgusting to fellow members and visitors. You sit close to the front door, so would you please go outside when required." A club regular for 20 years, Fox said that the letter was a surprise because he had not been given a formal warning. "I think someone has complained about the noise," he said. "I am a loud farter, but there is no smell."

AROUSED FARMER FRACTURES HIS PENIS

A newly married Romanian farmer fractured his penis in 2005 after ogling his young wife while carrying a heavy sack of grain. Gheorghe Popa, 52, stopped work to watch his 25-year-old bride Loredana hang up some washing but he became over-excited and dropped the sack on his erect organ, snapping vital tendons and ligaments.

ANGRY HEART SCARE PATIENT CHASES PARAMEDICS

Experiencing chest pains which she feared could be the first symptoms of a heart attack, a Florida woman called the emergency services but asked that the ambulance refrain from using sirens or flashing lights. The message was obviously not relayed and when the paramedics arrived with their lights on and sirens wailing, she was apparently so angry that she jumped to her feet and chased them down the street, brandishing a rolling pin.

NIGERIAN WOMAN SAYS SHE HAS GIVEN BIRTH TO TORTOISE

A 30-year-old Nigerian woman, Tawa Ahmed, told worshippers at her church in 2000 that she had been pregnant for five years before giving birth to a one-kilogram tortoise. With the reptile sitting next to her, Ahmed told the crowd she became pregnant in Lagos but returned to her parents' home in Ondo after failing to give birth. The pastor of the Rock of Ages Gospel Church said he had organized a 14-day religious event to ease Ahmed's labour pains. He admitted to being "surprised" when she eventually gave birth to the tortoise.

MAN DRIVES CAR THROUGH DOOR TO SEE PSYCHIATRIST

Refused an appointment with a psychiatrist at a hospital in Izola, Slovenia, in 2002, 48-year-old Aleksandar Oven ran from the building and returned minutes later in his car, which he drove through a set of glass doors and down a 100-ft-long corridor to reception where he demanded to see a psychiatrist. Asked why he had done it, he replied: "I don't know – that's why I came here."

PATIENT HYPNOTIZES HIMSELF BEFORE OPERATION

A man from West Sussex hypnotized himself so that he could undergo extensive surgery on his right hand without an anaesthetic. Alex Lenkei, a registered hypnotist, put himself in a trance and said that he felt no pain during the 83-minute operation, even when a hammer, chisel and circular saw were used.

FLYING ELVIS SUFFERS BROKEN PELVIS

Paul Moran, a member of the Flying Elvi, a team of skydiving Elvis impersonators, broke his pelvis while jumping at the grand opening of the Glacier Parks Casino in Browning, Montana, in 2006. Other members of the troupe said the Las Vegas man appeared to misjudge the landing and hit the ground at 50 miles per hour.

THIEVES CUT OFF MAN'S "HOLY LEG"

Police in southern India were hunting for two men in 2007 who attacked a Hindu holy man, sliced off his right leg and then fled with it. The pair had gone to the village near Tirupati to seek the advice of 80-year-old Yanadi Kondaiah over a medical problem but after getting him drunk they used a sharp hunting knife to cut off his leg from the knee. While the victim remained mystified by the motive, police said he had told a number of local people about the supposed magical powers of his right leg. "This," said an officer, "might have motivated some people to take away his leg, hoping to benefit from it."

SURGEON CARVES INITIALS ON WOMAN'S ABDOMEN

A Manhattan obstetrician carved his initials on a female patient's abdomen after performing a Caesarean section because he felt he had done "a beautiful job." Dr Allan Zarkin was dubbed "Dr Zorro" by hospital staff after he had used a scalpel to etch "AZ" in three-inch letters into the skin of new mother Liana Gedz as she lay sedated in 1999. As well as surrendering his medical licence, Zarkin had to pay $1.75 million to Ms Gedz who said the incident left her feeling "like a branded animal". Zarkin's lawyer revealed that his client suffered from a brain disorder which sometimes impaired his judgement.

PARTY BET ENDS IN PENIS PAIN

At a party to celebrate the birth of his first child in 2001, Ioan Soaita of Sibiu, Romania, slid a wheel bearing over his penis for a bet. But when it came to removing the bearing, it wouldn't budge, so he resorted to using a circular saw. However the saw slipped, leaving him half the man he used to be. Surgeons managed to reattach the missing penis portion in a five-hour operation.

LEG THAT WAS TOO LONG IS NOW TOO SHORT

A Swedish police officer with one leg longer than the other was left with a new problem after a bungled operation took too much off the leg, leaving it several centimetres *shorter* than the other. The officer had approached a private clinic in Gothenburg to remove two and a half centimetres from his longer leg, but after four operations he was left with a leg that is now five and a half centimetres shorter and with the imbalance firmly on the other foot. To add insult to injury, the officer also suffered from back and knee pain following the surgery. The clinic conceded that the operation had not been an unqualified success.

PARAMEDIC IS CALLED TO HIS OWN EMERGENCY

A paramedic received an emergency message on his pager – to attend to his own suspected heart attack. Complaining of severe chest pains, Roger Flux took to his bed in Ashurst, Hampshire, while his wife called an ambulance, but moments later his pager went off, summoning him to his own address. After being released from hospital, he said: "The message was telling me to attend to a man with chest pains. Then I looked at the address and saw it was mine! At least it shows the system works. The whole idea is to get the nearest responder available to attend to an emergency – and I was certainly the nearest."

WOMAN HAS SURGERY TO LOOK LIKE HUSBAND'S EX-WIFE

A man in China persuaded his new wife to undergo plastic surgery so that she could resemble his first wife, who had been killed in a car accident three years earlier. Zhao Gang admitted: "I got married only because she looks a bit like my ex-wife and I want to have a chance to make up for my mistakes."

MAN GIVES BIRTH TO BABY GIRL

Thomas Beatie, a transsexual man, left hospital in Bend, Oregon, in 2008 after giving birth to a baby girl. Thomas, who was previously known as

Tracey, had his breasts surgically removed ten years earlier and started taking male hormones. He legally changed his gender, grew a wispy beard and married a woman but retained his reproductive organs so that he could one day get pregnant. Greeting the arrival of his baby, the proud father claimed: "The only thing different about me is that I can't breastfeed."

PARENTS DON'T HAVE A BEAN, BUT DAUGHTER DOES

After removing a troublesome bean from a young girl's ear, a Nairobi physician jammed it back in when her parents were unable to pay for the $6 operation.

"BOGUS DENTIST USED HOME IMPROVEMENT TOOLS"

Police said Alvaro Perez from Ecuador posed as a dentist for many years and had hundreds of clients on his books despite having no qualifications and using such basic implements to extract teeth as a power drill, household pliers and screwdriver. He was charged with deception in 2008 after one of his patients in Sampierdarena, Italy, complained about the excruciating pain he had suffered while undergoing surgery at the hands of Perez.

MAN CONDUCTS CASTRATIONS AT HOME

Having placed an advert for his services in specialist magazines, Edward L. Bodkin, from Huntington, Indiana, performed consensual castrations on at least five men using a variety of equipment ranging from cattle-farm implements to manicure scissors. He obtained permission from them to videotape the operations and to keep the severed testicles. After Bodkin was turned in by his roommate, police found nine jars in his apartment, each containing a testicle labelled either "L" for "left" or "R" for "right". The reason for the odd number was that excessive bleeding had apparently forced him to abort one castration. In 1999, 56-year-old Bodkin pleaded guilty to practising medicine without a licence. As for the patients' motives, prosecutor John Branham said: "I can't sit here as a reasonable human being and give you an intelligent answer to that."

FAKE BUS STOP KEEPS ALZHEIMER'S PATIENTS IN CHECK

Bogus bus stops have been erected outside German nursing homes to prevent Alzheimer's patients wandering off. "Our members are 84 years old on average," explained one clinic director. "Their short-term memory hardly works, but the long-term memory is still active. They know the green and yellow bus sign and remember that waiting there means they will go home. We will approach them and say that the bus is coming later and invite them back in for a coffee. Five minutes later they have completely forgotten they wanted to leave."

COSMETIC SURGERY ADDICT INJECTS COOKING OIL INTO FACE

A Korean woman addicted to plastic surgery ended up with a disfigured, bloated face after injecting cooking oil into it. Over a period of 20 years, Hang Mioku underwent so many plastic surgery procedures that her own parents didn't recognize her. To fuel her obsession, a doctor supplied her with a syringe and silicone so that she could self-inject, and when her supply of silicone ran out, she resorted to cooking oil.

SURGEON ACCIDENTALLY SEVERS PATIENT'S PENIS

A Romanian surgeon accidentally sliced off a patient's penis during an operation in 2004. Professor of anatomy Naum Ciomu was carrying out an operation for a testicular malformation at a Bucharest hospital when he cut off the man's penis with a scalpel in front of amazed nursing staff, then chopped it into three pieces before storming out of the operating theatre. He was ordered to pay the unfortunate patient, 36-year-old builder Nelu Radonescu, $795,000 compensation. Dr Ciomu claimed he lost his temper after accidentally cutting the patient's urinary channel. He said it was a loss of judgement due to personal problems.

HOMEMADE REMEDY TURNS PATIENT BLUE

When Paul Karason of Madera, California, suffered from stress-related dermatitis following the death of his father in 1994, he decided to treat it himself with homemade colloidal silver, an old medicine widely used before the discovery of penicillin. But the silver caused argyria, a condition that turned his skin permanently blue. As a result Karason has had to endure constant taunts of "Papa Smurf" for the past 15 years. What's more, the homemade medicine didn't even cure his dermatitis.

OHIO MAN DRILLS HOLE IN SKULL TO SEARCH FOR BRAIN

A MAN CREATED a stir in Ohio by walking into a police station with a nine-inch wire protruding from his head. He asked officers to help him locate his brain, explaining that he had drilled a hole into his skull but had failed to find anything by prodding. ●

BUMBLEBEE HAS SURPRISE BIRTH ON HEN NIGHT

A 30-year-old woman who didn't even know she was pregnant went into labour on a friend's hen night in 2008 while dressed in a bumblebee costume. Ally Ashwell was in Blackpool, Lancashire, to celebrate her friend's forthcoming wedding when she began to feel unwell. She returned to her hotel room, where, within minutes, she started to give birth.

IMPATIENT PATIENT LEAVES FINGER AT HOSPITAL

Fed up with waiting for more than an hour to be treated at a hospital in Lecco, Italy, a 47-year-old man left his detached finger with staff and shouted: "Take care of the finger when you have some time. I'm going home." The man had lost the finger in an accident at work and had carried it to the hospital in the hope that it could be reattached.

WOMAN PUZZLED BY NOISY BREASTS

After noticing for some time that her breasts made strange noises whenever she was in an airplane, a woman finally decided to seek medical answers. An X-ray at a clinic in Frisco, Colorado, revealed that her saline breast implants contained air bubbles and this caused her breasts to make a "swishing sound" when they were at high altitudes, where the outside air pressure was lower.

MAN WORE HEARING AID IN WRONG EAR FOR 20 YEARS

An elderly Leeds man was mystified why even a hearing aid failed to improve his hearing – until he discovered that for the past 20 years he had been wearing the appliance in the wrong ear.

PATIENT LEAVES HOSPITAL WITH HEART MONITOR

A 68-year-old patient hooked up to a heart monitor got up and walked out of a Los Angeles hospital in 1999 – with the six-foot-high machine in tow. "He didn't want to stay any longer," explained a hospital spokesperson.

WOMAN EXTRACTS 18 OF HER OWN TEETH WHILE HIGH ON DRUG

A 25-year-old woman pulled out 18 of her own teeth to stop a "luminous green and pink fly" choking her while she and her boyfriend were both high on the hallucinatory drug GHB. Samantha Court was found at her home in Horwich, Greater Manchester, in 2002 with her body covered in blood and 18 of her teeth either in a bowl or on the bed. She and Jason Morris had both consumed enormous amounts of the liquid drug, as a result of which they started seeing witches, clowns and floating furniture. Court said: "I turned to face my bedroom wall and a luminous green and pink fly flew out and down my throat. That's when it started choking me." She added that, after struggling to pull out the first tooth, "the rest seemed to just fall out" and she had felt no pain. The couple announced afterwards that they had decided to stop taking GHB.

CANADIAN MAN WINS $100,000 BET BY WEARING BREAST IMPLANTS

Professional gambler Brian Zembic won a $100,000 bet by getting breast implants and keeping them for a year. Under the terms of the 1996 wager, made with a backgammon friend, the Canadian agreed to wear breasts that were at least 38C in size and to pay for the surgery himself. Sixteen months later – even though he had long since won the bet – he was still wearing them, claiming that they really turned on women he met. One woman who was none too happy, however, was his wife. She only found out about his implants shortly before the wedding. Zembic said: "She broke down and started crying, 'They're bigger than mine!'"

EYEBALL DELIVERED BY MISTAKE

A guest at a hotel in Hobart, Tasmania, was startled to receive a foam box containing a single human eyeball. The box marked "Live human organs for transplant" was wrongly delivered to the hotel in 2008 by a taxi driver. An employee at the hotel said: "The guest brought the box with the eyeball to reception. I thought 'this is just too weird'. I went and put it in the fridge because I didn't know what else to do with it. It was more than a little disconcerting." An Australian Air Express spokeswoman blamed the error on "failure in an internal handover process".

DENTIST SUED OVER FAKE TUSKS

A Washington State dentist was sued by his assistant after temporarily implanting fake boar tusks in her mouth as a joke. Dr Robert Woo of Auburn put the tusks in while pig-lover Tina Alberts was under anaesthetic. He removed them before she woke up but first took photos of her which eventually circulated around the office. She felt so humiliated when she saw the pictures that she quit her job and took legal action. Dr Woo agreed to pay her $250,000 in an out-of-court settlement but he in turn successfully sued his insurers for $1,000,000.

RUSSIAN BURGLAR LOSES TESTICLE

A Russian burglar thinking a handicapped man's home would be an easy target received a nasty surprise when the homeowner whacked him between the legs with his crutch, forcing the intruder to leap out of the window – minus one of his testicles. The homeowner said: "I didn't understand at first what had fallen out of his pants. When I looked closer, I realized it was a testicle and put it in cold water." The burglar was later found unconscious and taken to hospital, where doctors had to amputate his entire scrotum to prevent gangrene.

DEPRESSED BANKER DROVE DOCTORS NUTS

An Australian banker had his testicles examined more than 300 times – mostly by female doctors – to help him deal with severe depression brought on by restructuring in the banking industry. Craig Bell invented stories about being hit in the groin with a bat or a ball in order to get himself examined at clinics in the Brisbane area.

SHEPHERD HAS HOLE DRILLED IN NEW TEETH SO HE CAN WHISTLE TO DOGS

Fitted with a new set of false teeth, shepherd Ronnie Collins was dismayed to find that he could no longer whistle commands to his dogs. Despite using his fingers and even taking his teeth out, he was unable to make a sound that was recognizable to his border collies. So the retired milkman from Bingley, Yorkshire, asked his dentist to drill a small hole through the two front teeth, which he could then whistle through. The unusual request paid off when Ronnie and his dog Bob won the International Sheepdog Society Supreme Championship in 2000. "I've always whistled through my teeth," he said, "but I found it impossible when I got the false ones. The dentist burst out laughing when I told him what I wanted him to do, but it's been a great success."

WOMAN NAMED WINK CHARGED WITH GLASS EYE THEFT

A woman with the surname Wink was charged with stealing 50 glass eyes from a hospital in Owensboro, Kentucky. CCTV footage allegedly showed Melissa Jane Wink leaving the hospital with the eyes, which were valued at between $20 and $50 each. They were later recovered from a house at which she was staying. Police were baffled as to the motive since apparently there isn't a great demand for glass eyes on the black market.

BOGUS FEMALE DOCTOR PERSUADES WOMEN TO STRIP

A woman posing as a doctor phoned a number of women in Portugal in 2002, informing them how they could have a mammogram by satellite.

She told the women – aged between 19 and 45 – that the service was free provided they followed the instructions, which were to strip to the waist and stand either at their window or on their balcony facing in the direction of a supposed satellite. They all fell for the hoax, including one woman who bared her entire body. Later the women were phoned with their "results", which merely provided the bogus lady doctor with the chance to describe graphically her own desires.

GIRL LOSES MEMORY AFTER BEING HIT ON HEAD BY FALLING TORTOISE

A 12-year-old girl was taken to hospital in Chongqing, China, after a three-pound pregnant tortoise plummeted from the sky and landed on her head. She suffered concussion and was unable to remember anything about the incident. The tortoise died from its injuries.

BEAUTY QUEEN DIES IN QUEST FOR FIRMER BOTTOM

Former Miss Argentina Solange Magnano, 38, died in 2009 after undergoing cosmetic surgery to sculpt her bottom. She underwent a gluteoplasty – a procedure which involves placing implants in the buttocks to improve their outline – but was rushed to hospital the next day suffering from a pulmonary embolism, apparently caused by complications arising from the surgery. A friend mourned: "A woman who had everything lost her life to have a slightly firmer behind."

SPIDERS MAKE THEIR HOME IN BOY'S EAR

After a nine-year-old boy complained about a popping sensation in his left ear in 2007, doctors in Albany, Oregon, found the culprits – a pair of nesting spiders. The spiders were removed from Jesse Courtney's ear by irrigation. One came out dead but the second was still alive.

MAN FEARS HE IS TURNING INTO A WOMAN

A father-of-five from Birmingham, England, has revealed his fears that he is slowly turning into a woman. Terry Wright, 60, started losing his hair and beard over ten years ago, and has since developed smooth skin, hot flushes and breasts. Blood tests have shown that he has abnormally high levels of the female hormone oestrogen. Terry, whose diminutive stature and slim build add to his femininity, moaned: "I get mocked by kids where I live who call me She-Man and other names. Once a child bumped into me and its mother said, 'Say sorry to the lady.' Doctors call me an 'interesting case' and 'unique' but I just want to go back to being a proper man."

MAN SLICES OFF PENIS IN PIZZA RESTAURANT

A 35-year-old Polish man burst into a London restaurant in 2007, jumped on a table, dropped his trousers and hacked off his penis with a knife in front of horrified diners. The man was subdued with CS gas before being rushed to hospital. It was thought he had a history of mental illness.

DEPRESSED WOMAN BRIDLES OVER "PSYCHO" LABEL

A woman from Palm Beach, Florida, who was battling depression, sued pharmacy chain Walgreens in 2005 after reading a printout attached to her prescription for a sleep aid. Typed in a space reserved for patient information was "Crazy!" In another field, it read: "She's really a psycho!"

PATIENT TOLD TO WALK OFF PAIN AFTER SHOOTING

After a Johannesburg security guard was shot in the side during a burglary in 2007, he went to hospital to have the bullet removed. One hospital turned him away because he couldn't afford the bills, another examined him briefly before telling him to "walk the pain off", and a third told him they couldn't do anything because he had started treatment elsewhere.

RELATIVE DISLODGES TRAPPED FOOD WITH VACUUM CLEANER

An 80-year-old Japanese man who was choking on a tasty paste called "devil's tongue" was saved by an emergency medical worker and a relative who managed to dislodge the stuck food with a vacuum cleaner. The pensioner from Osaka was eating sukiyaki when the chewy food became lodged in his throat. As he lost consciousness, the family called the emergency services who suggested a number of measures, all of which failed. As a last resort, the dispatcher told the 25-year-old granddaughter to insert the tube of a vacuum cleaner into the choking man's mouth. She switched it on, and out came the obstruction. Despite the success of the manoeuvre, Japanese medical services stressed that a vacuum cleaner should only be used in extreme circumstances and was no substitute for forceps where delicate removals were concerned.

MAN WORE NECK BRACE FOR 14 YEARS TOO LONG

After falling from a truck while at work in 1986, driver Herbert Scott was taken to Burnley General Hospital, where doctors suspected a broken neck and gave him a neck brace to wear. Due to a misunderstanding, he kept it on for the next 14 years, instead of the four weeks that the doctors had advised.

DOCTORS FIND CRACK IN MAN'S BUTT

When a 41-year-old man from Val des Monts, Quebec, suffered a seizure following a crack cocaine overdose in 2007, it disturbed his dog, a pit bull terrier, which promptly bit him in the neck just below the ear. Seeing this, the man's housemates, who police said were also under the influence of drugs, tried to rescue their friend from the dog by swinging at it with a baseball bat, but in their befuddled state they missed and instead hit the man in the face. He was then taken to hospital, where a plastic bag containing ten grams of crack cocaine was found in his rectum.

ONE FOOT IN THE GRAVE: MAN ARRANGES FUNERAL SERVICE FOR AMPUTATED LIMB

A Sicilian man who had his left foot amputated in 2002 gave it a full funeral service before burying it in a coffin. Having persuaded the surgeon to give him his foot back after the operation, Antonio Magistro, 56, asked for the limb to be buried in his future grave at the cemetery in Giojosa Marea. He said he hoped to join the foot in the grave "as late as I possibly can".

AMBULANCE DRIVER RUNS OVER PATIENT AND DEFIBRILLATOR

After a heart attack victim was resuscitated by another ambulance crew with the use of a defibrillator, a Montgomery County, Pennsylvania, paramedic arrived on the scene and tried to get his vehicle as close to the patient as possible. In doing so, he succeeded in running over not only the victim's ankle but also the defibrillator. Happily, the patient survived the double shock.

DRUNK UNAWARE OF KNIFE IN BACK

A Russian electrician who spent the night with a ten-inch knife embedded four inches deep in his back only found out when he got home and his wife saw it. Yuri Laylin, 53, received the wound from a blindfolded friend while playing a variation on Russian roulette during a vodka-fuelled night out in Vologda. Laylin said he felt no pain and had no idea what had happened until his wife saw him on the bed with the knife in his back. He said: "We had a few vodkas and I remember playing some silly games and someone had a large knife. I came home, went to sleep as usual and woke up when my wife started screaming." Doctors suggested that the amount of alcohol he had consumed had acted as an anaesthetic, numbing the pain.

MAN CHASED UP TREE BY INVISIBLE COPS

A 30-year-old man rang the St Cloud, Minnesota, police force in 2007 to complain after imaginary drug squad officers had chased him up a tree. When the real police arrived on the scene, they found him up the tree, still fearfully clutching his cell phone. They quickly realized that he was hallucinating under the influence of drugs. It took them some time to convince him that it was safe to come down.

PLASTIC SURGEON ALLOWS WAITER FRIEND TO HELP OUT

Dr Joseph Graves, a San Diego plastic surgeon, was convicted of negligence and had his medical licence suspended in 1997 after allowing a waiter friend to assist him in carrying out surgeries. The court heard that the waiter helped during liposuctions and the insertion of breast implants.

X-RAYS REVEAL JEWEL THIEF'S LOOT

A burglar who swallowed thousands of pounds worth of jewellery after being disturbed while robbing a first-floor apartment in Perth, Scotland, was caught when doctors X-raying him for a broken hip discovered the loot in his stomach. The suspect had tried to escape from the apartment by jumping from an icy window-ledge but he landed awkwardly in the street below and broke his hip. "He really could have done without that trip to hospital," said a police spokesman.

MOTHER SAYS SON WAS CIRCUMCISED BY GENIE

An Indonesian woman claimed in 2003 that a genie had circumcised her ten-month-old son while she was cooking breakfast. "When I heard Riyan crying," she told reporters, "I went straight to his bedroom and couldn't believe what my eyes saw. He had been circumcised." She said a local paranormal confirmed that it was the work of a genie.

THREE PAIRS OF PANTS STOP STRAY BULLET

A 53-YEAR-OLD bystander at a Philadelphia shooting escaped serious injury in 2000 when a stray bullet was stopped by the three pairs of pants he was wearing. Willie Marbury was waiting nearby for a bus but luckily the wayward bullet failed to penetrate all three pairs of pants, instead lodging in one of his many pockets. Police said they had no idea why Marbury happened to be wearing three pairs of pants. "We don't ask those types of questions," said an officer on the case. "Sometimes the answers frighten us." ●

TOOTHBRUSH SURGICALLY REMOVED FROM MAN'S RECTUM

In 2001, the British Dental Association reported that a 69-year-old man had to have a toothbrush surgically removed after using it to relieve the painful itch of haemorrhoids but then losing it in his rectum.

SUPERSTITIOUS TAIWANESE MAN WANTS PIG-LIKE SNOUT

A Taiwanese man asked a cosmetic surgeon to perform an operation to change his nose to the shape of a pig's snout so that it would bring him luck in 2001. According to traditional Chinese beliefs, the shape of a person's face determines their fortune, and in Chinese society pigs are regarded as a symbol of wealth. However the man's luck was out on this occasion as the surgeon flatly refused to carry out the bizarre alteration.

MAN SUPERGLUES CONDOM TO PENIS

A father-of-five required medical assistance in 2004 after supergluing a condom to his penis in an attempt to achieve a more effective form of contraception. When 43-year-old Romanian Nicolae Popovici donned the condom he decided it was too big, so for a tighter fit he stuck it on with glue, but was unable to get it off afterwards. A nurse who treated him commented disbelievingly: "He even said he thought the condom could be used several times and that he wanted it stuck on his penis so he could use it again later. We really struggled to remove it."

PARKING STRESS LEADS TO CANCELLED OPERATION

A surgeon cancelled a heart operation at Cardiff's University Hospital of Wales after taking an hour to find a parking space. He said he was so stressed by the experience that he was in no fit state to operate.

DENTIST EASED PAIN BY MASSAGING PATIENTS' BREASTS

California dentist Mark Anderson was accused in 2007 of inappropriately massaging the chests of 27 female patients. After allegedly fondling one woman, he asked whether she had undergone breast augmentation. When she replied in the affirmative, he is said to have remarked: "They did a good job." In his defence he claimed that the procedure was an accepted method of dealing with jaw pain.

MAN WORE THREE PAIRS OF CONTACT LENSES

A Chinese man had to have his contact lenses surgically removed after he didn't take them out for a whole year. Mr Liu had never taken the lenses out because he found it too difficult. After nearly 12 months of wear he began to feel his eyesight deteriorating, so he bought another pair of lenses and wore them on top of the old ones. When that failed to help, he put a pair of used contact lenses over the other two pairs, so that he was now wearing three pairs of lenses. The following day, his eyes reacted so badly to his makeshift optical treatment that he finally sought medical help, and a doctor found that the first lenses had actually grown into his eyes.

DOCTORS REMOVE PATIENT'S PENIS "JUST TO BE SAFE"

When 67-year-old mechanic Hershell Ralls went into hospital in Wichita Falls, Texas, in 1999 to have a cancerous bladder removed, he did not expect to wake up and find his penis missing too. Surgeons said they lopped off his penis because they thought the cancer had spread there – but it hadn't. Ralls, who said that doctors never warned him or his wife that amputation of the penis might be part of the surgery, recalled: "My wife had to hold my hand in the bed there. And she said, 'Honey, it's over. They got all the cancer.' And she waited a few minutes and then said: 'But they had to remove your penis.'"

BABY SURVIVES FALL THROUGH EXPRESS TRAIN TOILET

A newborn Chinese baby boy endured a traumatic introduction to the world in 1999 when he fell through the toilet of an express train, landed on the tracks and was nearly crushed to death by a passing train. The boy's mother, Yang Zhu, was nine months' pregnant and returning home by train near the city of Guangzhou when she started to suffer stomach pains. Her husband took her to the washroom where, to her great surprise, she gave birth into the toilet as soon as she squatted down. In a panic, she then ripped off the umbilical cord, as a result of which the baby promptly disappeared down the toilet. Three security guards spotted the baby lying in the middle of the tracks but before they could reach him, another train sped by, passing right over him. Amazingly he escaped with slight bruising and a small cut to the head.

MAN DEHYDRATED DESPITE TWO DAYS IN LAKE

After the water scooter he was riding broke down, Ricardo Enamorado was rescued from Lake Michigan in 1997, suffering from dehydration. Paramedics were baffled as to why he had spent two days on the water without drinking any, as Lake Michigan is a freshwater lake.

BOYFRIEND FORCED TO HAVE BREAST REDUCTION

A Chinese woman forced her boyfriend to have breast-reduction surgery because his man boobs made her look flat-chested. Doctors in Chongqing sucked out more than 200 millilitres of fat and tissue from the breasts of Zhang Jianguo to prevent his girlfriend, Xiao Feng, dumping him. Zhang, who is 5 feet 7 inches tall and weighs 15 stone, explained: "She said that whenever we went out, she felt embarrassed because my breasts were eye-catching compared to hers."

FORTY-SIX TEASPOONS REMOVED FROM MAN'S STOMACH

Surgeons in Taormina, Sicily, removed five and a half pounds of "inedible matter" from a man's stomach – including 46 teaspoons, two cigarette lighters and a pair of tongs. The man was described as "psychologically disturbed".

MOTHER RUNS OVER SON IN HOSPITAL PICK-UP

A man on his way out of hospital ended up back inside after his elderly mother ran him over when she came to collect him in her car. Ron Carter, 49, had just been discharged from Elliot Hospital, New Hampshire, and was walking to meet his mother Lillian, 84, when she accidentally hit him.

FATHER TRIES TO SWAP DAUGHTER FOR BOY

A Romanian soccer fan whose wife had given birth to a daughter in 2002 tried to bribe maternity nurses to swap the little girl for a boy. He claimed that he had always wanted a boy and that girls were more expensive. Upset because nurses would not comply with his request, he then refused to take his wife and daughter home.

SURGEON AMPUTATES WRONG FOOT

Shortly before an operation to have his gangrenous right foot amputated in 1995, William King, a 51-year-old diabetic, joked with staff at the University Community Hospital in Tampa, Florida: "Make sure you don't take the wrong one." When he awoke, King discovered to his horror that the surgeon had indeed removed the wrong foot, amputating the healthy left limb while leaving the gangrenous right one intact. After the unfortunate patient had been awarded $900,000 compensation, the hospital announced that it was introducing a foolproof new system to prevent any reoccurrence: in future the word "no" would be written in large letters in marker pen on all limbs that were not to be amputated.

CIGARETTES CAN DAMAGE YOUR HEALTH

Feeling powerful cravings for a cigarette, a patient at a hospital in Llanelli, South Wales, decided to light up secretly under the bedclothes while the nurses' backs were turned. Unfortunately he did so right next to his oxygen mask with the result that as soon as he flicked his lighter he blew himself up.

DOCTORS HAVE TO SEPARATE ENTANGLED LOVERS

Two Malaysian lovers who were having an affair got stuck together during sex and had to be rushed naked to hospital by ambulance. After the 50-year-old woman had taken a sexual stimulant, she became so excited that her 60-year-old lover was unable to disengage. In a panic, they called neighbours who in turn summoned the emergency services. Still joined together at their private parts and watched by intrigued villagers, the naked couple were carried gingerly to the ambulance and taken to hospital, where they were finally separated after being given an injection.

TIME-TRAVELLING DOCTOR SURRENDERS LICENCE

A chiropractor who claimed to be able to treat patients using time travel relinquished his licence to practise in 2006 after the Ohio State Chiropractic

Board ruled that he was suffering from a serious delusional disorder. State regulators had been investigating Dr James Burda, of Athens, who said he could treat ailments by travelling back in time to when the injury occurred. He called the skill bahlaqeem; medical officials called it malpractice. When asked initially about the case, a state spokesman replied: "Doctor who?"

GOOD SAMARITAN MUST PAY STRANGER'S HOSPITAL BILL

A Good Samaritan drove a sick woman to hospital in Germany – only to be landed with a $9,000 bill for her treatment. Resul Mor was driving home from work in Hamburg when he was flagged down by a man who asked him to take his desperately ill wife to the hospital's emergency room. On arrival Herr Mor was asked to sign a patient registration form, unaware that it committed him to settling any fees she couldn't pay. Two weeks later, the hospital sent him the bill, and judges subsequently ruled that he was legally liable and must pay up.

DOUBLE AMPUTEE IS GIVEN TWO RIGHT LEGS

A Dutchman who lost both legs in separate accidents complained that the health service had given him two false right legs. Jelle Wagt, from Assen, lost his right leg after falling into the hold of a ship in 1998 and lost his left leg in another accident three years later. He said the Dutch health service originally gave him a prosthetic right leg which was too long for him. They corrected that mistake but after his left leg was amputated, they sent him home with another right leg. "I didn't want to undress to try on the new prosthetic leg," he explained, "so I opened the bag when I got home. I was stunned to find a right foot on my left leg. I'd love to try to walk again but with two right feet it just doesn't feel comfortable."

RELIGIOUS ZEALOT SAWS OFF HIS OWN HAND

As a deeply religious individual, Norfolk, Virginia construction worker Thomas Passmore was alarmed to see a mark on his hand in 1994 that looked ominously like the demonic sign "666". Remembering the Biblical passage "If thy right hand offend thee, cut it off", he proceeded to do just that with a circular saw. When doctors tried to save the limb, he refused to agree to the operation, saying that he would go to hell if the hand were reattached. He then tried unsuccessfully to sue the hospital for $3 million on the grounds that they should not have paid any attention to what he said.

WOMAN INCUBATES BIRD'S EGG IN CLEAVAGE

A Norwegian woman spent several weeks using the warmth of her cleavage to incubate a bird's egg. After a local farmer found the abandoned curlew egg, Anne-Mette Smette, a 58-year-old former hospital midwife, initially tried to persuade a hen to incubate it but when the bird refused, she decided to tuck it down her cleavage instead. She even slept at night with the egg in place. Meanwhile her husband Knut was under strict instructions not to touch her breasts for fear of cracking the precious egg. "It's look but don't touch," he told a local newspaper wearily.

WOMAN IS ACCIDENTALLY GIVEN NEW ANUS

A German pensioner sued a hospital in 2008 after she checked in for an operation on her leg – and woke up to find she had been given a new anus instead. The clinic in Hochfranken suspended the surgical team concerned after they apparently mixed up the notes for two patients.

MAN KEEPS SEVERED LEG FOR 20 YEARS

A Chinese man has preserved his severed leg in formaldehyde for more than 20 years to warn people against the dangers of drink driving. Song Weiguo, who lost his left leg when his motorbike crashed into a tractor after he had been drinking in 1989, puts the amputated limb on display every year on the anniversary of the accident. He takes it out of its sealed tank and invites friends and people he suspects of drink driving to come and view it. "It scares the hell out of people," he says. "None of them ever drives after drinking again." His wife said his husband is obsessed with his severed leg and often talks about it in his sleep.

"DOCTOR" FOUND WITH DEAD DEER IN STOLEN AMBULANCE

A 37-year-old man reported missing from a Florida hospital in 2005 was found a month later in North Carolina dressed like a doctor and driving a stolen ambulance with a dead deer in the back. He was admitted to a North Carolina hospital for psychiatric evaluation.

WOMAN ADMITTED TO HOSPITAL WITH CAN OF HAIRSPRAY UP HER BUTT

A 37-year-old woman was admitted to hospital in Arad, Romania, in 2009 with a large can of hairspray stuck up her backside. She arrived at the clinic in extreme agony but refused to say how the aerosol came to be there, even after a successful operation dislodged the canister. The doctor in charge of the operation said: "She was very embarrassed. She was clearly in a lot of pain, however it got there."

DENTIST EXTRACTS PAYMENT FROM PATIENT

When a female patient's insurance company refused to pay the cost of her $600 dental work, her dentist allegedly took drastic measures to get his money back. She said that he turned up unannounced at her home in Germany with his medical instruments and, after tying her hands, forced her to open her mouth and removed the expensive bridgework. According to the victim, he never said a word throughout the procedure. The dentist faced charges of assault and theft.

SERIAL BELCHER IS BANNED FROM MARINE WORLD

Fourteen-year-old Joey Ramirez was banned from Six Flags Marine World in Vallejo, California, in 1999 for persistent belching. Officials claimed he belched loudly and deliberately in visitors' faces. His mother said: "He has a lot of indigestion."

DEER URINE PRANK FELLS STUDENTS

A dozen students at a school in Church Hill, Tennessee, had to be treated by paramedics for headaches and nausea in 2008 after someone poured deer urine into an air conditioning unit as a joke.

SURGEON SNAPS TATTOOED PRIVATES

A surgeon in Phoenix, Arizona, faced a disciplinary hearing for taking a photo of a patient's tattooed genitals during an operation and showing it to other doctors. The medic is said to have taken the photo with his cell phone while inserting a catheter into the penis of a strip club owner. The tattoo on the patient's penis read "Hot Rod".

LUMBERJACK ADDICTED TO KNITTING AFTER TRANSPLANT

A BURLY CROATIAN lumberjack planned to sue his local health authority after a kidney transplant left him addicted to housework and knitting. Stjepan Lizacic said he had not been warned about the possible side effects of being given the kidney of a 50-year-old woman. He complained: "I used to enjoy heavy drinking sessions with my pals, but now I have developed a strange passion for female jobs like ironing, sewing, washing dishes, sorting clothes in wardrobes and even knitting." ●

MAN ROBS BANK TO GIVE TRANSVESTITE LOVER NEW BREASTS

Austrian car mechanic Robert Steinwirt, 29, was jailed for six years in 2007 for robbing a bank in Grinzens to pay for his transvestite lover's breast operation. He stole $14,000 in the raid and went straight to a plastic surgeon who, suspicious that someone would pay up front for an operation with a large sum of cash, promptly alerted the police.

MAN WAKES TO FIND BARNACLE ON PENIS

To stay cool while sleeping naked on the beach, a man from Bor, Serbia, decided to rest his body in shallow water. But when he woke up, he found to his horror that he had a barnacle stuck to his penis. A female nurse at the local hospital tried unsuccessfully to remove it with tweezers until the man suddenly got an "unplanned erection" and she was finally able to prise away the barnacle.

WOMAN WITH "MULTIPLE PERSONALITIES" SUES SHRINK OVER GROUP THERAPY CHARGE

In 1997, Nadean Cool, of Appleton, Wisconsin, sued her psychiatrist, Dr Kenneth Olson, for convincing her that she had 120 separate personalities – including those of a duck and the devil – and then charging her insurance company $300,000 for group therapy. She won a settlement of $2.4 million.

CAT RUNS OFF WITH SEVERED TOE

A cat ran off with its owner's toe after he chopped it off in a freak accident and left it on the floor while he called an ambulance. Udo Ried, 41, was slicing bread in his kitchen in Lubeck, Germany, in 2005 when he dropped a large kitchen knife onto his bare foot, slicing off his second toe. He hopped to the bathroom to fetch a bandage but while he was on his cell phone calling the emergency services, his cat Fritz pounced on the bloody toe and ran off with it into the garden. Herr Ried tried to retrieve it but was in such pain that he was soon forced to give up the pursuit and wait for medical help. Lubeck Hospital said they would have been able to reattach the toe if the cat had not stolen it.

MAN GOES TO COURT TO GET HIS LEG BACK

As if he hadn't suffered enough by being shot five times, a Nebraska man then had to go to court to get his prosthetic leg back from prosecutors. Val McCabe's false left leg had been held since the shooting because the Box Butte County Attorney's office wanted to run tests on both the leg and a bullet lodged inside it. But a judge ordered them to return the limb to the victim because it was impractical for him to replace the $28,000 prosthesis. Police did, however, remove the bullet before handing back the leg.

6

TILL DEATH US DO PART

THANKFUL WORSHIPPER CRUSHED BY CHURCH ALTAR

A devout Catholic who believed his prayers were answered when he was rescued from an elevator was killed when he went to church to give thanks and the stone altar fell on him. Forty-five-year-old Gunther Link was so relieved to have been freed from the elevator that he rushed straight to the Weinhaus Church in Vienna, Austria, to thank God. There, he warmly embraced a stone pillar but his action caused the 860-pound altar to collapse and it landed on him, killing him instantly. He was found the next day by parishioners attending Mass.

MAN DIES TRYING TO RETRIEVE TOY FROM LION ENCLOSURE

When his child accidentally dropped a toy into the lion enclosure at Moscow Zoo in 2001, Anton Briesov sprang into action. Fetching a ladder, he boldly climbed down into the enclosure, hoping that the lions wouldn't notice. Alas his escape route was cut off when the ladder toppled over. Briesov managed to outrun the lions and climb to safety, only to drown in the moat surrounding the enclosure.

FLORIDA MAN PERISHES IN CAT FLAP

A 32-year-old man was found dead in St Augustine, Florida, in 2007 – wedged fast in the cat flap of his girlfriend's house. It appeared that he had been trying to get back into the house after she had kicked him out. A witness said: "His head was caught, like he was trying to reach up and unlock the door."

"PEEPING TOM" WARDER CRASHES THROUGH SKYLIGHT

A Mexican prison warder who apparently enjoyed watching inmates having sex with their wives during conjugal visits paid a high price for his fantasy in 1999. Raul Zarate Diaz was supervising his prisoners from the roof of the jail in Tapachula, a task which seemingly required him to carry a pair of binoculars and a pornographic magazine. However he tripped over an air vent, crashed through the skylight and plunged 23 feet to the ground, landing next to the bed where a prisoner and his wife were indulging in passionate lovemaking.

CORPSE WAS STILL PART OF THE FAMILY

A 77-year-old woman was treated by her son as an active part of the family even though she had been dead for four months. When police officers found her in 1997 – propped up on the sofa at her home in Bakersfield, California – the son told them he thought she was "demonically depressed" and would wake up any minute.

GERMAN TOURIST MISTAKEN FOR BABOON

A German holidaymaker out birdwatching at a hunting lodge in Namibia was shot dead by a guide who mistook him for a baboon. As soon as he realized his mistake, the guide put his gun to his head and killed himself.

EX-DEATH ROW PRISONER DIES REPAIRING TV

After years awaiting the electric chair in South Carolina, convicted murderer Michael Anderson Godwin finally had his sentence commuted to life imprisonment. Then in 1989, while sitting on the metal toilet in his cell, he tried to fix his portable TV set by biting into a wire and was electrocuted.

MAN WEARING CONDOM IS KILLED BY SNAKE BITE

A 40-year-old man was found dead next to a roadside in Thailand in 2008 with a cobra carcass in his hands and a condom on his penis. Wiroj Banlen had several snake bites to his body and the cobra had also been bitten several times, fragments of the reptile's skin being found in the dead man's teeth. The condom contained no semen, leading baffled police to speculate that Banlen was removing his trousers when the snake struck.

ROBBER DIES STARING DOWN THE BARREL

Would-be robber James Elliott from Long Beach, California, was mystified when his .38 calibre revolver failed to fire. So he peered down the barrel and pulled the trigger again. This time it worked . . . fatally.

MAN WEARING FISH SUIT FOUND DEAD NEAR RESERVOIR

The badly decomposed remains of Neil Wilson, from Melbourne, Australia, were discovered in a paddock near the Toolondo Reservoir in 1995 in what newspaper reports of the day described as a death "shrouded in mystery, tragedy, and a fish suit". Law enforcement officials said 49-year-old Wilson was wearing a heavy green plastic bodysuit, which he had apparently constructed from old waterbed material. The suit was designed with an external full-length zipper in the back along the spine, constricting his legs into a mermaid-like tail. Apart from the zipper, the only openings in the suit were two holes for the eyes. The suit enclosed his entire body like a maritime mummy costume, thus restricting movement and breathing. A second, yellow suit was found in his garage. Investigators learned that the deceased was taking medication at the time for epilepsy and diabetes and suggested that his unusual behaviour may have had a chemical basis, but locals had their own theories about the aquatic adventure. "He wanted to be a fish," said one, recalling incidents where Wilson would swing from a rope while wearing the suit at the lake.

ZAMBIAN MAN IN CLOTHES-LINE TRAGEDY

A man in Kitwe, Zambia, was electrocuted in 2000 when, having run out of space on his clothes line, he unwisely decided to hang the remainder of his wet washing on a live power line which passed his house.

STUDENT KILLED BY EXPLODING CHEWING GUM

A 25-year-old Ukrainian chemistry student was killed by what is believed to be exploding chewing gum. The student from Kiev Polytechnic Institute was found dead with his jaw blown off after working on a computer at his parents' house. He was known for his habit of dipping chewing gum in citric acid, but police found packets of both citric acid and an explosive material on a table in his parents' room, leading them to conclude that he may have confused the two packets.

END OF THE LINE FOR AVID FISHERMAN

Fishing in a 14-foot boat on Fox Lake, Illinois, in 1998, Daniel Wyman and an unnamed friend decided that they would have more success if they used an M250 firecracker to blast the fish out of the water. After lighting the powerful explosive, they threw it into the lake but seconds later a sudden gust of wind blew their lightweight boat over the firecracker. The resulting explosion sank the boat and caused Wyman to drown.

YOUNG LOVERS PLUNGE FROM ROOF DURING SEX

Brent Tyler and Chelsea Tumbleston, both 21, were killed in 2007 after they fell 50 feet from the sloping roof of an office in Columbia, South Carolina, while having sex. The naked bodies of the pair, who had recently graduated from South Carolina University, were found in the street by a stunned taxi driver. He duly informed the police who were mystified as to what had happened until they found the couple's clothes in a pile on the roof.

COUPLE ATTEND WRONG FUNERAL

Believing they had just sat through the cremation of their friend Roy Spencer, pensioners Maurice and Shirley Dodwell were understandably surprised when they arrived for his wake and he answered the door. It turned out that they had been to the funeral of another Roy Spencer in Cheltenham, Gloucestershire. Maurice said: "It was a terrible fright. I thought I'd seen a ghost. I had to go and sit in the car for a while because I was so shocked."

THIEF CRUSHED TO DEATH BY SAFE

A thief was crushed to death at an office in Huntington, New York, in 1996 while in the act of stealing a 600-pound safe. He apparently violated the cardinal rule of hauling a safe downstairs by standing on a lower step than the one that the safe was on. His efforts were destined to end in disappointment anyway as the safe was empty.

TRIO PLAY FOOTSIE WITH UNEXPLODED MINE

Three customers at a restaurant in Phnom Penh, Cambodia, thought it would be fun to play footsie with an unexploded antitank mine in 1999.

One of the three – a soldier – put the mine under the table, and then he and his friends began playing with it, stepping on it and tapping it with their feet. Other diners quickly fled the scene but the trio carried on the daring game for another three minutes – until the mine exploded, blowing them up.

MAN TAKES FATHER'S CORPSE FOR BIKE RIDE

After his 86-year-old father died, Flemming Pedersen asked staff at the Copenhagen hospital if he could spend some time alone with the body. He then dressed the rigid corpse in leather gear, boots, a crash helmet and dark sunglasses and walked it out of the hospital. Outside he strapped the body to the pillion seat of his Harley Davidson and for the next two hours drove around the city, visiting his father's favourite haunts. At one point he stopped at a bar, where he bought two bottles of beer and stuck a lit cigar between his dead father's lips. Pedersen junior explained that he had taken his father for one last ride so that he could have a chat with him. Despite receiving a $300 fine for improper treatment of a corpse, he added: "I wanted him to leave life this way. I'm sure he was happy to have been in the places he liked so much. Everybody should do what I did."

TALL MAN'S LEGS CUT OFF TO FIT IN COFFIN

Faced with the problem of how to fit a 6-foot 7-inch corpse into a standard-sized coffin, a South Carolina funeral parlour came up with a simple solution – an electric saw was used to hack off the lower parts of the dead man's legs. Allendale undertaker Michael Cave was stripped of his licence following complaints from the family of James Hines who had died in 2004. According to his widow, the deceased's legs were cut off between the ankle and calf and then placed alongside him in the casket. Mr Hines's body was only visible from the chest up at the funeral, during which several people had remarked that the casket looked too small.

BALLOONING PRIEST FLOATS TO HIS DEATH

A Brazilian priest who took to the skies strapped to 1,000 helium balloons in the hope of breaking a 19-hour flight endurance record perished when he crashed into the sea shortly after takeoff. Father Adelir Antonio di Carli took off from the port of Paranagua in April 2008 but soon called friends to say that he was crashing into the sea. The following day a cluster of colourful balloons was found in the shark-infested waters and his body was discovered three months later.

MAN INJURED BY BUS IS KILLED BY SECOND BUS

A New Delhi labourer survived being hit by a bus, only to be run over fatally by a second bus 20 minutes later. Raj Kumar was on his way to work when a bus hit him from behind. He was taken to hospital by taxi but on the way he said he felt fine and jumped out of the cab. As he crossed the road, another bus hit him, killing him instantly.

SUICIDE PLAN NEEDED MORE THOUGHT

A 16-year-old student and a 20-year-old former student of a high school in Buckingham, Pennsylvania, decided to kill themselves in 1999 by crashing a borrowed car into the walls of the school's gymnasium at 80 miles per hour. Although the impact caused $70,000 of damage, the kamikaze kids escaped unhurt because both were wearing seatbelts!

EXCESSIVE NOSE PICKING PROVES FATAL

A man from Manchester picked his nose so much that he bled to death. Ian Bothwell, 63, who suffered from dementia brought on by alcoholism, died from a terrible nosebleed brought on by constant picking.

MAN SHOOTS HIMSELF WHILE TEACHING GUN SAFETY

James Looney, 40, of Imperial, Missouri, was killed after accidentally shooting himself in the head while teaching firearms safety to his girlfriend. Witnesses said he was demonstrating how to use the safety mechanisms on several guns. He would put the guns to his head, ask his girlfriend if she thought the gun would go off, and then pull the trigger. The safety mechanism worked on the first two guns but was less successful on the third.

FRIENDS PUSH CORPSE THROUGH CITY STREETS

Two men who were found pushing their dead friend through the streets of New York in an office chair thought he was merely incapacitated. Virgilio

Cintron, 66, who had died from natural causes, was seen flopping from side to side in the chair while his two friends propped him up.

GRIEVING WIDOWER DIGS UP WIFE'S CORPSE TO HUG HER

A Vietnamese man dug up his wife's corpse and slept beside it for five years so that he could continue to hug her in bed. After his wife died in 2003, Le Van initially slept on top of her grave but 20 months later, fed up with the rain, wind and cold, he decided to dig a tunnel down into the grave in order to sleep with her. When his children found out about the unusual arrangement and prevented him from visiting the grave, Le then dug up his wife's remains and took them home. "I'm a person that does things differently," he admitted.

MAN TRIES TO SHOOT HIMSELF IN COFFIN

In a bizarre suicide attempt, a man from Podgorica, Montenegro, bought a coffin from a funeral director, climbed in and shot himself in the head. Milo Bogisic, 52, paid cash for the coffin and asked puzzled staff to wait while he wrote out his own obituary. Then he jumped into the casket, put a gun to his head and pulled the trigger before the shocked undertakers could stop him. However he survived because the bullet passed straight through his chin and nose, missing his brain. To rub salt into his wounds, the funeral company refused to give him a refund on the coffin.

SHEEP SHOOTS SHEPHERD

When a young Egyptian shepherd was found shot dead in the middle of the desert in 2001, the police were baffled by the absence of footprints in the vicinity. Then examination of his rifle revealed that he had forgotten to put the safety catch on before falling asleep next to his sheep. One of his flock had accidentally trodden on the trigger and shot him.

CACTUS TAKES REVENGE ON GUNMAN

One day in 1982, roommates David Grundman and James Joseph Suchochi decided to take pot-shots at cacti in the Arizona desert. After felling a small cactus by shooting it repeatedly in the trunk, Grundman became more ambitious and turned his gun on a 26-foot-high specimen, estimated to have been 100 years old. No sooner had he started shooting than a four-foot-long spiky arm of the cactus, severed by the blast, fell on Grundman, crushing him to death.

DEPRESSED MAN ON THE WRONG TRACK

A suicidal man decided to end it all by allowing himself to be run over by a train . . . only to lay down on the wrong set of tracks. Martin Rapos placed himself on the rails at Deiva Marina, Italy, in 2008 and waited for the express train from Genoa to hit him at 100 miles per hour. Instead he watched dejectedly as the train roared past him on an adjacent set of tracks.

WIFE WANTED TO PICKLE LATE HUSBAND'S PENIS

A German woman was reported to have hacked off her dead husband's penis in 2006 with the intention of pickling it as a happy souvenir of their marriage. Uta Schneider, 65, was said to have used a butcher's knife to chop off husband Heinrich's manhood in a Stuttgart hospital before wrapping it in foil and packing it into a lunchbox ready to take home. However she was spotted by a nurse and accused of mutilation. Uta told police: "It was his best asset and gave me so much pleasure. I wanted to pickle it for eternity. We called it his joystick."

WOMAN PLUNGES TO DEATH IN TITANIC TRIBUTE

A 31-year-old woman from Plymouth, Devon, who had been drinking for several hours on a ferry from Spain to England, plunged to her death in 2003 after apparently striking the famous outstretched arms pose of actress Kate Winslet in the movie *Titanic*. Emma Blackwell lost her balance, fell from the ninth deck and drowned. Her body was washed up on the French coast eight months later.

HUMAN HEAD DISCOVERY IS CASE OF MISTAKEN IDENTITY

Investigating an abandoned mining shed near Detroit, Oregon, in 2002, a hunter thought he had found a severed human head and immediately called the police. However Deputy Larry Taylor deduced it was the just the head of a mannequin when he noticed a price sticker on the forehead.

MAN WITH SHORT FUSE KILLED IN PIPE BOMB STUNT

A man who was fascinated with explosives blew himself up in 2002 after putting a homemade pipe bomb in his mouth and lighting the fuse. Kevin Barnes, 20, from Daventry, Northamptonshire, performed the stunt while his terrified flatmates and girlfriend looked on. The inquest heard he was a risk-taker with a quick temper.

MINISTER SHOT DURING FUNERAL TRIBUTE

Presiding at the funeral of a Korean War veteran in Champion, Ohio, in 1994, Rev. Thomas Gillum was accidentally shot in the face when the local guard of honour fired a four-gun salute.

BEDROOM GUITARIST BOUNCES OUT OF OPEN WINDOW

A 16-year-old business student from China plunged to his death in 2005 while imitating a rock star on the bed of his Singapore hostel room. Li Xiao Meng was playing the guitar and bouncing up and down feverishly on the bed but got so carried away that he bounced straight out of the open window, falling three floors to his death.

WOMAN CALLS 911 TWICE AFTER FAILED SUICIDE

A woman who deliberately shot herself in the head survived the suicide attempt and called 911 for help before passing out. But when firefighters, who were trained as emergency medical technicians, arrived at the woman's home in Soldier Township, Kansas, they thought she was dead. An ambulance was cancelled, and the firefighters and deputies waited outside the house to protect it as a crime scene. Meanwhile the woman regained consciousness and called 911 again, prompting the firefighters to rush back in and give medical assistance. The Shawnee County Sheriff admitted: "It was a mistake."

CYCLIST KILLED WHILE CROSSING AIRPORT RUNWAY

A cyclist crossing an airport runway in Sao Paulo, Brazil, was killed in 1997 when he was hit by a plane that was coming in to land. Marcelo Dias dos Santos couldn't hear the approaching plane because he was listening to his Walkman on headphones.

BODY IS MISTAKEN FOR HALLOWEEN DECORATION

The body of a woman seen hanging from a tree near Frederica, Delaware, in October 2005 went unreported for hours because passers-by thought it was a Halloween decoration.

MORGUE ATTENDANT DROPS DEAD AFTER DECEASED REVIVES

Morgue attendants at a hospital in Menoufia, Egypt, were naturally alarmed when Abdel-Sattar Abdel-Salem Badavi pushed open the lid of his coffin and shouted that far from being dead, he was still very much alive. In fact, one of the attendants was so shocked that he dropped dead on the spot.

GRANDMOTHER'S BRAIN SENT IN A BAG TO FAMILY

A New Mexico family were left grieving after the brain of their recently deceased grandmother was sent to them in a bag of personal belongings. The discovery was made after they detected a "foul odour" coming from the bag, which had been forwarded to them by a funeral home. The bag had been left inside a relative's truck overnight, and when family members opened it the next day, they found personal effects and a small bag labelled with their grandmother's name and the word "brain".

MAN SUFFERS HEART ATTACK JUST BEFORE CHEAP SEX

An 80-year-old grandfather from Split, Croatia, suffered a fatal heart attack in 2009 moments after negotiating a fee of $6 for oral sex with a local prostitute. The pair went to an abandoned house – their usual rendezvous – but as he dropped his pants, the excitement proved too much for him and he collapsed. A friend described the deceased as a man who was "looking for sex until his last breath".

FISHERMAN PAYS HEAVY PRICE FOR LOSING COUNT

Fishing with two friends in 2002, a Denton, Texas, man suddenly decided it would be a fun idea to discharge his gun into the lake. Then, for a laugh, he pointed the gun at his nose and pulled the trigger, confident that there were no bullets left in the barrel. He was wrong. Afterwards, one of the friends said the dead man simply "lost count of the rounds when he was firing the gun".

FRIEND IS LEFT SAUSAGES IN WILL

Every week for five years, Pat Vaughan treated work colleague Peter Fountain to a sausage sandwich as they met in the same café in Odiham, Hampshire, to discuss council business. When Mr Vaughan died of cancer at the age of 57, he left his friend $1,500 and a note: "Buy your own bloody sausage sandwiches!"

FARTING CLOWN BRINGS LAUGHTER TO DUTCH FUNERALS

A DUTCH CLOWN who specializes in farting has been hired to ease the tension at funerals. Clown Roelof van Wijngaarden believes one of the best tactics for making people laugh at funerals is to break wind loudly. He says: "Imagine adults following the coffin to the burial place. People are using their handkerchiefs, no one dares to speak a word. It's all very solemn. Imagine then this clown whispering to the children and at the same time letting out a fart. The children start to giggle and their parents get a smile on their faces. That's what we do, take the tension away." He adds on his website: "I only come when I have been invited by the deceased or by the family. We clearly discuss beforehand why someone wishes to have a clown at their funeral." •

MAN DISMANTLES GRENADE AND HIMSELF

In an attempt to dismantle a rocket-propelled grenade, a Brazilian man drove over it back and forth with his car. When the weapon still failed to break up, he attacked it with a sledgehammer. The resulting explosion killed him as well as destroying six cars and his workplace.

WILDERNESS EXPLORER FORGETS TO ARRANGE COLLECTION

Enthusiastic American amateur photographer Carl McCunn paid a bush pilot to drop him at a remote lake near Alaska's Coleen River in March 1981 so that he could study wildlife . . . but failed to make arrangements for the pilot to pick him up again the following August. A plane did circle overhead at one point but the hapless McCunn used the wrong emergency hand signals and thus merely succeeded in waving the plane away. When it became clear that nobody was coming to collect him, rather than starve in the wilderness, McCunn shot himself in the head. Shortly before blowing his brains out, he had written in his diary: "I think I should have used more foresight about arranging my departure."

SON PUTS FATHER'S ASHES UP FOR SALE ON EBAY

In revenge for being abandoned as a child, a Warwickshire man auctioned his father's ashes on eBay. The ad placed by William Ireland, of Atherstone, read: "Here are the ashes of my father, Kenneth Ireland, an adulterer who left a wife, two children and just £17 ($25) in her pocket. He never paid a penny towards his kids' upbringing."

MARRIED COUPLE DIE OF EXCITEMENT

Shy Japanese couple Sachi and Tomio Hidaka, both 34, waited 14 years before making love for the first time in 1992. Alas, the excitement proved too much for them and both died of heart attacks.

BUDDHIST MONK RUN OVER BY LAWNMOWER

A Buddhist monk was killed instantly in 2007 when he was run over by his own sit-on lawnmower as he cut the grass at his temple in Milton Keynes, Buckinghamshire. Rev. Sanji Handa was seen chasing the out-of-control machine and fell beneath it as he tried to climb back onto it. His dismembered body was found on a grassy slope at the ten-acre peace centre. It was reported that Rev. Handa had lost three fingers in a previous incident with a lawnmower.

BUNGLING BURGLAR STUCK IN CHIMNEY FOR 16 YEARS

The fully-clothed skeletal remains of a bungling burglar were found in a chimney in Natchez, Mississippi, in 2001. Calvin Wilson had last been seen alive in 1985. It is thought he had tried to burgle the premises but had got stuck in the chimney and died.

WIDOW HAS HUSBAND'S ASHES PUT IN EGG-TIMER

When Londoner Malcolm Eccles died of bowel cancer, his ashes were put in an egg-timer so that he could be with his widow in the kitchen while she cooked. Brenda Eccles said: "I can't boil an egg to save my life. He knew that and said I should turn some of his ashes into an egg-timer. Then he could help me and it would be a nice way of remembering him."

DRIVER BLINDED BY BUBBLE GUM

Abner Kriller of Albany, Australia, was blowing bubble gum while driving when it burst and stuck to his glasses. Temporarily blinded, he drove off the road and plunged down a hill to his death.

SKYDIVING PHOTOGRAPHER FORGETS TO PUT ON PARACHUTE

An experienced skydiver with over 800 jumps to his name made a fundamental – and fatal – error in 1988 when he forgot to strap on his parachute before jumping from a plane 10,000 feet above North Carolina. Ivan McGuire was filming a private lesson given by an instructor for a trainee. He had attached a video camera to his helmet and wore the power supply and recorder in a rucksack on his back. Jumping from the rear of the plane, he carefully captured the moment as student and instructor jumped from the front and pulled their ripcords. It was then, as McGuire reached for his own ripcord, that he realized to his horror that while remembering all his camera equipment, he had forgotten to strap on his parachute.

THE UNLUCKY FOUR-LEAFED CLOVER

Salvatore Chirilino was walking with his wife along the cliff top at Vibo Marina, Italy, when he spotted a four-leafed clover and picked it. Just as he was congratulating himself on his good fortune, his foot slipped on the wet grass and he toppled over the cliff edge, plunging 150 feet to his death.

TIN THIEVES POISON THEMSELVES

A dozen thieves stole a sizeable quantity of tin from a company in Gejun, China – unaware that the metal had been treated with arsenic and would therefore create a poisonous gas when exposed to water. It was raining at the time of the theft, and within 8 days eight of the gang were dead and another two were critically ill.

"ROTTING CORPSE" TURNS OUT TO BE MAN WITH SMELLY FEET

Police broke into an apartment in Kaiserslautern, Germany, after neighbours complained about a foul stench seeping on to the stairway. The windows and curtains of the apartment had been closed for a week, and the postbox was full of uncollected mail, leading to fears that there was a rotting corpse inside. On entering the apartment, however, officers found a man with pungent feet asleep in bed next to a pile of dirty laundry.

COVER BLOWN IN INSURANCE FRAUD

Sacramento, California, funeral director Melvin Lincoln was convicted of defrauding an insurance company in 1991 by trying to fake his own death and that of his wife. The deception was uncovered when the supposedly deceased Mr Lincoln tried to renew his driving licence.

THAI SISTERS ARE A PAIR OF REAL "LIVE WIRES"

A 57-year-old Thai woman, Yooket Paen, was walking on her farm in 1991 when she accidentally slipped on a cow pat, grabbed a naked live wire to steady herself and was electrocuted. Shortly after her funeral, her 52-year-old sister, Yooket Pan, was showing neighbours how the accident happened when she, too, slipped, grabbed the same live wire and was killed.

"CORPSE" LASHES OUT AT POLICE OFFICERS

Two off-duty policemen leapt into action when they found a corpse at an English country hotel, only to get the shock of their lives when he jumped to his feet and asked them angrily what they thought they were doing. Police Constables Mick Cotterill and Grant Darbey, who were guests at a party at the Botleigh Grange Hotel near Southampton in 1998, had tried to revive the man by checking his airways and loosening his clothing, unaware that he was an actor taking part in a murder mystery weekend. A Hampshire police spokesman said: "It was a bit of a surprise when the dead man made a full recovery in front of them."

FACTORY WORKER KILLED BY ROBOT

While working at a Kawasaki factory in Japan in 1981, 37-year-old Kenji Urada climbed over a safety fence to carry out maintenance work on a robot. In his haste, he failed to switch off the robot properly. Unable to sense his presence, the robot's powerful hydraulic arm kept on working and pushed him into a grinding machine with fatal consequences.

MAN DIES FOR THE LOVE OF HIS CAR

When 68-year-old Ivece Plattner found himself trapped in his car on an Italian level crossing with a train fast approaching, his first thought was to save his beloved Porsche. So instead of scrambling to safety, he ran along the track toward the oncoming train, waving his arms frantically in a bid to spare his car. The attempt was successful insomuch as the car received considerably less damage than its owner who was hit with such force by the train that he landed 100 feet away and could not be revived.

FINED FOR CELEBRATING NEIGHBOUR'S DEATH

A 63-year-old man from Ulrichtstein, Germany, was fined $5,000 in 2003 for celebrating his neighbour's death by loudly singing "It's a Wonderful Day".

SUICIDE BID SUCCEEDS – EVENTUALLY

Sevan Kevorkian, 36, from San Diego, California, tried to hang himself in 2008 but his bid was foiled when his girlfriend found him just in time and pulled him down. He reacted angrily to her intervention and the pair argued violently, attracting the attention of a passer-by who, in restraining Kevorkian, applied a wrestling hold to his carotid artery and accidentally killed him.

MAN DROWNS WHILE FLEEING FROM FIRE

Ioannis Philippou, 50, accidentally set himself on fire while huddled over a heater in his house in Kato Deftera, Cyprus, in 1990. To douse the flames, he ran out of the house and jumped into a nearby reservoir, where he drowned.

DEAD MAN IS GIVEN PARKING TICKETS

Police in New York City repeatedly ticketed an illegally parked Chevrolet Ventura for a month in 2009 without noticing that its occupant was dead. The body of the 59-year-old man was finally discovered after a marshal attempted to tow the vehicle, which had a number of summonses on the windshield, away from underneath a flyover in the city's Queens district. The deceased's daughter said: "The window was cracked open. I don't understand how no one noticed him. They just gave him tickets."

GIRLS KILLED AFTER LIGHTNING STRIKES THEIR BRAS

Two young visitors from Thailand were killed in 1999 after lightning struck their bras while they were sheltering under a tree in London's Hyde Park. The underwiring in their bras conducted the electrical charges straight to their hearts, killing them instantly.

BOTTOMS UP! HUSBAND HAD ADDICTION TO ALCOHOLIC ENEMAS

A man with an alcohol problem who was addicted to enemas died after receiving one based on sherry. Michael Warner, of Lake Jackson, Texas, died of alcohol poisoning in 2004 with a level almost six times the state's legal limit. Tammy Jean Warner said her husband had been addicted to enemas since he was a child. Unable to swallow liquor because he suffered from ulcers and heartburn, he often gave himself wine or sherry enemas as his body would absorb the spirits more quickly that way. Mrs Warner told reporters: "He did coffee enemas, he did soap, he had enema recipes. That's the way he went out and I'm sure that's the way he wanted to go out because he loved his enemas."

SUICIDE BID DUMPS ITALIAN IN SEWERS

In despair after separating from his wife, a 35-year-old bank clerk tried to drown himself in a river on the outskirts of Milan. But he hadn't realized that after a few hundred yards the river flowed underground to join the city's sewer system, and within moments of jumping in he was swept along on a tide of filth. The "indescribable" smell quickly made him change his mind about committing suicide. "I just wanted to get out of there," he said afterwards. "I wanted to live." He was eventually rescued from a manhole after a six-hour ordeal and a seven-and-a-half-mile journey through the stinking sewers of Milan.

WOMAN DIES AFTER HOLDING HER WEE FOR A WII

A Californian woman died in 2007 after trying to win a "Hold Your Wee for a Wii" contest run by a radio station in Sacramento. KDND 107.9 radio promised a Nintendo Wii to the person who drank the most water without going to the toilet. Twenty-eight-year-old mother-of-three Jennifer Strange was one of the participants but she complained of a severe headache hours after the contest and died later that day from water intoxication.

CORPSE WAS LIFE AND SOUL OF THE PARTY

When 35-year-old Ian Clifton passed out at a party in a Sheffield pub, his friends shaved one side of his head and took pictures of him with a blow-up doll. It was not until an hour later that one of the other partygoers decided to check for a pulse and found that there was none. Ruling that Clifton had died from accidental alcohol poisoning, the coroner remarked: "It is quite disturbing to think people were celebrating a birthday party in the presence of a corpse."

COMEDIAN CHOKES TO DEATH ON CUSTARD PIE

French comedian Yves Aboucher, 45, choked to death on a custard pie that was thrown in his face. He breathed in just as the pie landed and was suffocated by the foam.

NEW ZEALANDER DROWNS IN CAT BOWL

A New Zealand man died in 2001 after slipping on ice and drowning in his cat's water bowl. Peter Robinson, 28, hit his head in the fall at his home in Reefton and landed face down in the dish, where the one and a half inches of water was enough to cover his mouth.

HUSBAND SHOOTS WIFE WHILE INSTALLING SATELLITE TV

A man accidentally killed his wife in 2008 while trying to install satellite television in the bedroom of their Deepwater, Missouri, home. Unable to punch a cable through an exterior wall, Ronald Long decided to use his .22 calibre handgun to blast a hole. He fired two shots, the second of which hit his wife Patsy who was standing outside, wounding her fatally. Long told police he thought his wife and their two children were all inside the house when he opened fire. He added that he didn't own an electric drill and hadn't wanted to hire or buy one for such a small job.

MAN DIES AFTER RETIREMENT PARTY FUN

A 60-year-old transport company worker who was thrown into the air in celebration at his retirement party in Ritto, Japan, in 2007, died after his colleagues failed to catch him and he crashed to the floor.

SUICIDE JUMPER REFUSES TO PAY FOR DAMAGED CAR

A suicidal jumper who landed on top of a car in a Hong Kong street refused to pay for the damage she caused because she claimed the vehicle was illegally parked. Chung Kai-chiu's car was totally destroyed in the death bid but Lee Chen-fan protested that it should not have been there to break her fall. Refusing to pay the $3,000, Lee said: "I have lived in that building for over ten years, and I know very well there was no parking space on that street."

MAN MISTOOK WIFE FOR MONKEY

A Malaysian man shot his wife dead in 2004 after he mistook her for a monkey picking fruit behind their house.

UNDERTAKERS STRANDED AFTER POLICE TOW AWAY HEARSE

Two German undertakers were left stranded on the street with a coffin for two hours after over-zealous traffic police towed away their illegally parked hearse. The vehicle was parked in the city of Wiesbaden while the undertakers were collecting a corpse. Police said they did not realize it was a hearse.

PREACHER DROWNS TRYING TO WALK ON WATER

Franck Kabele, an evangelist preacher in Libreville, Gabon, told his congregation in 2006 that if he had enough faith, he could walk on water just like Jesus. One eyewitness said: "He took his congregation to the beach saying he would walk across the Komo estuary, which takes 20 minutes by boat. He walked into the water, which soon passed over his head, and he never came back."

CLUB MANAGER DIED HAVING SEX ON PIANO

Jimmy "the Beard" Ferrozzo, the 40-year-old assistant manager of the Condor Club, a topless bar in San Francisco, was crushed to death in 1983 while having sex with an exotic dancer on a piano. Ferrozzo and 23-year-old Teresa Hill were enjoying an after-hours romp on the Steinway baby grand when one of the pair inadvertently flipped the switch to the motorized winch that raised the instrument back up to the ceiling. Firefighters arrived several hours later to find Ferrozzo fatally sandwiched between the piano and the ceiling with Miss Hill still trapped beneath him, naked and hysterical. Only the cushioning effect of her erstwhile lover's body had saved her life.

BACK FROM DEAD BUT SHUNNED BY FIANCÉE

In 1993, Sipho Mdletshe was formally declared dead following a traffic accident in Johannesburg, South Africa. But after spending two days in a metal box in a mortuary, his cries alerted staff who rescued him. However his fiancée, who was also involved in the crash, didn't believe his story and flatly refused to see him because she believed he was a zombie who had come back from the dead to haunt her.

ROID-RAGE WIFE SHOOTS ABSENT HUSBAND

Bedridden on her stomach while recovering from haemorrhoid surgery, a Brooklyn woman took exception to her husband packing cans of beer and going off with his buddies on a six-hour fishing expedition. So when he finally arrived back home, she shot him dead. A police investigator said:

"She felt that her husband didn't demonstrate that he cared for her on that particular day."

PSYCHIC FAILS TO SEE LAMPPOST

A psychic who attempted to demonstrate her gift by driving a car blindfold in Perth, Australia, was killed when she crashed into a lamppost.

REVENGE OF THE BEES

Irritated by a bees' nest in their Los Angeles shed, Ani Saduki and his brother decided to remove it with explosives – the equivalent of a half-stick of dynamite. The resulting blast blew out surrounding windows and badly cut Ani. Deciding that he needed stitches in his wounds, the brothers headed for hospital but while walking towards their car, Ani was stung three times by the surviving bees. Unbeknown to either brother, Ani was allergic to bee venom and died on the way to hospital.

DIVORCEE ADVERTISES FOR SOMEONE TO SHARE A GRAVE

In 1994, Donal Bredin-Smith, a chiropodist from County Clare, Ireland, bought a double burial plot for himself and his wife, but they subsequently divorced. So four years later the 65-year-old took out an advertisement in the local paper looking for someone to share the grave. It read: "Spacious room for two occupants. Present owner seeks one female gravemate. First one in takes bottom berth. Garlic eaters and smokers need not apply." However he was inundated with applicants wanting to share his bed instead. He lamented: "They wanted to have a pre-grave relationship."

ONE-HUNDRED-YEAR-OLD MAN DIES SECONDS AFTER READING QUEEN'S TELEGRAM

At his retirement home in Dulwich, London, in 2000, Bob Talley read his 100th birthday telegram from the Queen, proudly announced, "Yes, I made it," then promptly died. His niece said: "He knew he had reached 100 and I think he relaxed and just let go." Buckingham Palace said it was happy that Mr Talley had received and read the congratulatory telegram but was sorry to hear that he had died so shortly afterwards.

FICKLE FINGER OF FATE FOR TEENAGE BIKER

In Kameoka, Japan, in 2002, police in cars were pursuing a teenage motorcyclist who kept riding through red lights. Unable to keep up with him through the narrow streets, they were eventually forced to abandon the chase, whereupon, sensing victory, he turned around to give them the finger. In doing so, he took his eyes off the road just long enough to avoid seeing a taxi ahead. The bike ploughed into the cab, killing the teenage rider instantly.

SURPRISE PARCEL WAS DAD'S BODY

When a large parcel was delivered to the Severin, Romania, home of Aurelia Cenusa in 2006, she thought it might be a prize from the lottery competition she had entered a few weeks earlier. Instead she opened it to find a banana crate containing the bones of her dead father. The body was sent to her in the post because the cemetery in which he had been buried for 16 years had been sold to developers.

WORKER BURIED UNDER AN AVALANCHE OF NUTS

Willie Murphy was buried alive under an avalanche of peanuts while working at a Georgia, US, processing plant in 1993.

MOURNERS SHOCKED BY PHONE RINGING IN COFFIN

Mourners at a chapel of rest in Belgium were horrified when a cell phone started ringing inside the coffin. Since the deceased had been badly mutilated in a road accident, the undertaker suggested that relatives say their farewells with the body already in the coffin. But as they tearfully gathered around the coffin to pay their last respects, a phone was heard ringing inside. Some family members were so startled that they ran out, while the embarrassed undertaker had to reopen the coffin to empty the dead man's pockets.

A BRIDGE TOO FAR FOR AUTO PRESIDENT

Mike Stewart, President of the Auto Convoy Company, Dallas, Texas, was killed instantly in 1983 when a flatbed truck unsuccessfully attempted to pass under a low-level bridge. At the time Mr Stewart had been standing on the back of the truck presenting a piece to camera for a TV item about the dangers of low-level bridges.

SISTERS KEEP DEAD MOTHER IN FRIDGE FOR TEN YEARS

In 2007 it was revealed that two sisters had been keeping their dead mother in an undertaker's fridge for ten years so that they could visit her at weekends. Unable to bear burying mum Annie after she died in 1997, Josephine and Valmai Lamas spent more than $25,000 to keep her in cold storage at a London funeral parlour and made weekly visits to sit with her in the parlour's chapel.

WORKER DIES IN VAT OF HOT CHOCOLATE

A temporary worker at a Camden, New Jersey, cocoa company died in 2009 after falling into an eight-foot-deep vat of hot chocolate. Vincent Smith II was pouring solid chocolate pieces into the vat for melting when he slipped and fell into the boiling chocolate. He was killed not by drowning but by being hit on the head by the paddle-like mechanism used to stir the chocolate.

FARMER KILLED BY SHEEP AND MOTORBIKE

To feed her flock of sheep at her farm in Durham in 1999, 67-year-old Betty Stubbs loaded a bale of hay on to the back of a motorbike and rode out to the field. The sheep were clearly hungry as 40 of them immediately rushed at the hay, knocking Betty over the edge of a cliff and down a 100-foot quarry. She survived the fall, only to be killed when the motorbike, which was also sent over the cliff in the stampede, came crashing down on top of her.

EMERGENCY TOILET BREAK PROVES FATAL

Stuck in stationary Florida traffic after visiting a Pompano Beach bar, Shawn Motero was desperate for a toilet break. Unable to wait a moment longer, he climbed from his car, jumped over a low roadside concrete wall – and fell 65 feet to his death. Pointing out that at the time of the fatality the car had been on an overpass above railroad lines, a police spokesman said: "He probably thought there was a road, but there wasn't." The dead man's mother revealed: "Shawn didn't do a whole lot for a living. He got along on his charm."

FAILED SUICIDE SUES ROPE MANUFACTURER

Victor Dodoi's attempt to hang himself in 2003 ended in failure when the rope broke and brought part of the ceiling down on his head. The Romanian promptly announced that he was suing the rope manufacturer on the grounds that he was now even more miserable than he had been before.

MAN IS KILLED BY LAVA LAMP

Philip Quinn, 24, died in 2004 after heating a lava lamp on the stove at his home in Kent, Washington State. The lamp became so hot that it suddenly exploded and sprayed shards of glass, one of which fatally punctured his heart. Police found no evidence of drug or alcohol use and suggested that the deceased had simply wanted to know what a really hot lava lamp would look like. "It wasn't bubbling fast enough for him," said his mother. "Philip had been a kid who tinkered with things ever since he was little."

CHEF FATALLY STABBED BY SPAGHETTI

CHEF JUAN RUIZ was stabbed through the heart with uncooked spaghetti stands when 150 miles per hour winds hit his restaurant in Mexico City. ●

FUNERAL ADDICT HAS A HOBBY TO DIE FOR

For over 25 years, Luis Squarisi has attended every single funeral in his home town of Batatais, Brazil, and even quit his job to feed his addiction. He explained: "The first thing I do every morning is to turn on the radio to find out if anyone has died. If I don't hear anything on the radio, I call the hospitals and the local funeral home." Whilst acknowledging that Mr Squarisi had an unusual hobby, a spokesman for the funeral home said: "We don't want him to go to therapy. Everyone expects to see him at the funerals. If he stopped coming, a lot of people would be disappointed."

BIRTHDAY CELEBRATION TURNS TO TRAGEDY

When Basilio Re turned 100 in 1996, nearly everyone in his Italian village turned out to help him celebrate. But a sudden gust of wind blew off his hat and as he chased it, he slipped, fell, hit his head and was killed.

PHONE CALL PROVES FATAL

Ken Barger of Newton, North Carolina, accidentally shot himself dead in 1992 while answering the phone in the middle of the night. He reached out to pick up the phone beside his bed but, half asleep, grabbed his .38 Smith and Wesson special instead. The gun went off when he pulled it to his ear.

SPITTING CONTEST ENDS IN DEATH

A 29-year-old Swiss man died in 2008 when he fell from a hotel balcony during a spitting match with a friend. He took a run-up from inside the room so that he could spit further, but lost his balance and fell 20 feet to the street below.

MIDGET WRESTLERS FATALLY DRUGGED BY BOGUS WHORES

Two professional midget wrestlers were found dead in a low-rent Mexico City hotel room in 2009 after it was claimed that they had been fatally drugged by two female robbers posing as prostitutes to attract victims. Police said 36-year-old twin brothers Alberto and Alejandro Pérez Jiménez had picked up the two women after filming a TV show but had their drinks spiked before being robbed. It is thought their 4-foot 1-inch frames made them more vulnerable to the drugs. Officers arrested a 65-year-old woman, accusing her and an accomplice known as "The Fat One" of spiking the wrestlers' drinks with eye drops.

FIVE SHOTS TO HEAD BUT SUICIDE BID FAILS

Determined to commit suicide, an 84-year-old Argentine man shot himself five times in the head and once in the stomach – but still survived. Police attributed his failure to the fact that the gun and ammunition he used were extremely old.

MAN BURNS TO DEATH AFTER FART

A man from Kansas died in a fire that apparently started when he struck a match to burn off the smell of a fart. A heavy smoker, he was found badly charred and fully dressed, sitting in an empty bathtub. Investigators initially suspected suicide until his wife pointed out that he often struck matches after passing gas and that the fire which killed him had started around the crotch area.

"DEAD MAN" ANGRY AT POOR FUNERAL TURNOUT

A man who faked his own death to see how many people would attend his funeral was furious when only his mother bothered to turn up. Amir Vehabovic, 45, paid for a fake death certificate and bribed undertakers to deliver an empty coffin. He then watched proceedings from behind bushes in the Bosnian town of Gradiska.

WIFE REACTS BADLY TO BEING TICKLED

A Vietnamese man crept up on his wife and playfully tickled her while she was chopping firewood. She responded by hurling the axe at him with such force that it nearly decapitated him. He died shortly afterwards as a result of his injuries. When police arrested the 62-year-old wife, she told them: "I hate being tickled."

PRISONER CHOKES TO DEATH ON BIBLE

A Canadian prisoner choked to death after attempting to swallow a pocket-sized Gideons' Bible. Staff at the Metro East Detention Centre in Toronto found 22-year-old Franco Brun in his cell with the New Testament wedged in his throat. The coroner said he believed the deceased was trying to purge himself of the devil by consuming religion.

MAN DIES WHILE WAITING IN LINE TO PROVE HE IS ALIVE

To crack down on cheats who were receiving pensions issued in the name of dead people, Colombian authorities introduced a "survival certificate" which claimants had to produce in order to continue drawing their monthly pension. When the measure was first introduced in 1999, thousands of elderly people joined long lines to obtain their certificate, but for one man the bureaucracy proved too much. Eighty-seven-year-old Arturo Suspe died of a heart attack in a local government office in Bogota as he waited patiently in line to collect the all-important certificate to prove that he was still alive.

WOMAN DIES WHILE STUCK IN LOVER'S CHIMNEY

A woman's decomposing body was found wedged inside the chimney of her lover's house in 2010 after she had tried to sneak into the property. Refused entry to the building in Bakersfield, California, 49-year-old Dr Jacquelyn Kotarac, who had what was described as an "on-off" relationship with the householder, William Moodie, scaled a ladder to the roof, removed the chimney cap and slid down the flue, planning to emerge in his living-room. But in the meantime her sometime lover had, according to police, left the house "to avoid a confrontation". Dr Kotarac's body was discovered three days later, about two feet above the fireplace, by a house-sitter who noticed "an odour and fluids" coming from that area. Mr Moodie said of the dead doctor: "She made an unbelievable error in judgement and nobody understands why."

BAD ROUND ENDS WITH GOLFER DROWNING

After missing yet another short putt on the final hole of a disappointing round at Lyon in 1995, elderly French golfer Jean Potevan was so angry that he hurled his golf bag into a lake. Having relieved his frustration, he prepared to drive home – only to remember that his car keys were in the bag. So he dived into the lake fully clothed, but drowned after becoming entangled in weeds. According to another player, his last words were: "I'm going back for the keys, but I'm leaving the clubs down there!"

DECEASED'S ASHES FORM TOWN'S MAIN STREET

As town manager of Erie, Colorado, Leon Wurl had campaigned long and hard to pave the network of streets that make up the old town. So when he died in 1999, his widow commemorated his work by pouring some of his ashes into the asphalt mix that became the new Main Street. She said: "He liked the smell of asphalt, so by God, he can smell it forever."

VIETNAM'S ELECTRIC MAN IS ELECTROCUTED

A Vietnamese man who had appeared on national television to demonstrate his amazing ability to resist electric shocks was electrocuted in 2006 while repairing a generator without first cutting the power supply. Paying tribute to Nguyen Van Hung, who was better known by his nickname "Hung Electric", a local official said: "When alive, he used to demonstrate at our office how he would insert two fingers into the electric plughole without problems."

UNDERTAKER ATTACKED BY CORPSE

New York undertaker Richard Blake was attacked by the corpse he was embalming. The body suddenly jerked into life, breaking Blake's ribs before suffering a massive heart attack and dying again.

TV VIEWER DIES LAUGHING

Alex Mitchell, a 50-year-old bricklayer from King's Lynn, Norfolk, died of heart failure brought on by uncontrollable laughter while watching a 1975 episode of the BBC comedy series *The Goodies*, in which a kilt-wearing Scotsman used a set of bagpipes to defend himself against an aggressor armed with a black pudding. Mr Mitchell's widow later wrote to The Goodies – alias Bill Oddie, Graeme Garden and Tim Brooke-Taylor – and thanked them for making her husband's final minutes so happy.

MAN FINDS THAT LIONESS DOESN'T BELIEVE IN GOD

Shouting "God will save me if he exists", a man lowered himself by a rope into the big cats' enclosure at Kiev Zoo, Ukraine, in 2006. He then took off his shoes and went over to the lions, whereupon a lioness knocked him down and severed his carotid artery, killing him instantly.

DRIVER DIES IN BID TO RESCUE HAT

Jason Jinks was driving near Slidell, Louisiana, one night in 1997 when a gust of wind caused his hat to fly out of the window. He immediately stopped the car, opened the driver's side door, leaned out and reversed at 30 miles per hour in the dark. When he spotted the errant hat, he slammed on the brakes – but the jolt threw him out of the open door and he landed on his head, sustaining fatal injuries. Two passengers in the car stated that Jinks had been drinking whiskey and taking pills.

TRAIN CRUSHES COUPLE HAVING SEX ON TRACK

A couple who were having sex on a railway track in Mpumalanga Province, South Africa, in 2008 were killed by a goods train after ignoring shouts from the driver to move. A police spokesman said: "The driver yelled at them as he pulled the train into the disused station but they continued with their business." The man died at the scene and the woman died later in hospital.

MAN DROPS DEAD IN OWN GRAVE

Sixty-three-year-old Giovanni Greco was so keen to ensure that his future resting place would be a perfect fit that he paid regular visits to check that the builders were constructing the tomb to his exact specifications. One day in 2002, he was making his customary trip to the construction site at Lascari, Sicily, when he climbed a ladder to get a better view of the work in progress. Alas, he slipped, fell, hit his head on a marble step and dropped dead into his own grave.

THIEF KILLED BY HOT DOG

Robert Puelo entered a 7-Eleven store in St Louis, Missouri, in 1994 and started shouting and cursing. When an employee threatened to call the police, Puelo grabbed a hot dog, stuffed it defiantly down his throat and walked out without paying. The police discovered him outside the store unconscious and turning purple. He choked to death before he could be saved.

SUICIDAL WIFE LANDS ON HUSBAND

After discovering that her husband had been unfaithful, Czech housewife Vera Czermak decided to end her life by throwing herself from her third floor balcony in Prague. By chance she landed on her husband who was walking directly below. The blow killed him while she escaped unhurt.

ESCAPE BID FOILED BY CROCODILE

A 28-year-old Panamanian was eaten by a crocodile as he swam across a river after escaping from prison in 2002. Oswaldo Martinez was being held in custody in Costa Rica on a murder charge but then he escaped and tried to re-enter his home country by swimming across the reptile-infested River Terraba.

CHILDREN'S ENTERTAINER KILLED BY INFLATABLE ELEPHANT

A CHILDREN'S ENTERTAINER was killed while driving to a party in Los Angeles when his trademark 20-foot-high, blow-up elephant – Colonel Jumbo – suddenly inflated in the car. Marlon Pistol was driving along the highway at 90 miles per hour with a deflated Colonel Jumbo lying on the back seat. For some unknown reason, the self-inflating pachyderm then sprang to life and within moments had filled the interior of the vehicle, causing Pistol to lose control and smash into a wall. One eyewitness reported: "A car sped past me with an elephant at the wheel." ●

SINS PROVE DEADLY TO CLERGYMAN

To add impact to his 1998 sermon about the seven deadly sins, Jacksonville, Florida, clergyman Melvyn Nurse used a .357 Magnum revolver loaded with just one blank, the remaining chambers being empty. He proceeded to illustrate each of the sins by playing Russian roulette, spinning the chamber and holding the gun to his head. After one spin, the gun fired and the cardboard wadding in the blank pierced his temple, causing fatal brain injuries. He had not realized that even blanks can be dangerous when fired from close range.

DEAD MAN TESTIFIES IN COURT

At a pre-trial hearing for a slander lawsuit in Payson, Arizona, in 1996, Judge Michael Flournoy permitted testimony from a man who had been dead for 500 years. As the courtroom lights were dimmed, Trina Kamp, of the Church of the Immortal Consciousness, contacted its spiritual leader, Dr Pahlvon Duran, from the witness stand so that he could tell the court why a local couple's attack on the church was wrong.

LAWYER DIES WHILE TESTING WINDOWS

Canadian lawyer Garry Hoy fell 24 storeys to his death in 1993 while demonstrating the safety of an office block's windows. Showing visiting law students around Toronto's Dominion Bank Tower, he decided to illustrate the strength of the windows by barging into a pane with his shoulder. The first time he threw himself at the window it held, but the second time it gave way and Hoy ended up in the courtyard below. He was described by the head of his legal firm as "one of the best and brightest" members.

WOULD-BE SUICIDE FAINTS BEFORE SHE CAN JUMP

A depressed Turkish woman who decided to end it all by jumping from a cliff was spared by the heatwave which swept through the country in 2000. Hulya Kirklar stood on top of the cliff near Antalya in temperatures of 111 degrees Fahrenheit for three hours ready to hurl herself to her death while police pleaded with her not to jump. But she was finally overcome by the extreme heat and fainted, collapsing on the edge of the precipice. When she came to, her first words were: "Aren't I dead?"

HOPELESS HITMAN SUFFERS HEART ATTACK

In an apparent attempt to kill her, a gunman dressed all in black and wearing a black wig and false moustache reportedly fired a number of shots at Rita Quam in Edwards, Colorado, in 1997. Each shot missed, and when his gun then jammed, he tried beating her on the head with large rocks. Quam managed to survive the assault, and when a deputy arrived, the assailant collapsed, wheezing in the thin mountain air, and his disguise fell off. Then he had a heart attack and died. His intended victim recognized him as Arthur Smith, a retired Chicago police officer.

WIDOW HAS HUSBAND'S ASHES SEWN INTO BREAST IMPLANTS

Sandi Canesco, a young Sydney widow, had the ashes of her late husband sewn into her breast implants in 2003. After husband Dustin was killed in a car accident, she took the unusual measure so that he would always remain close to her heart.

HUSBAND WHO LIVED IN TREE FALLS TO HIS DEATH

Convinced that his wife was being unfaithful, a 35-year-old man in Madhya Pradesh, India, vowed to live in a tree for the rest of his life. He stayed up there for eight months in 1997 before suddenly falling to his death.

PRIEST AND MISTRESS APPEAR NAKED IN FRONT OF COFFIN

A Romanian funeral procession turned to farce in 2001 when a priest and his mistress were thrown naked out of a house in front of the coffin. Less than three weeks after marrying a young couple in the village of Independenta, the 35-year-old Orthodox priest began an affair with the bride. However when her husband came home unexpectedly and caught them in the act, he threw them out the front door without their clothes and straight into the path of a passing funeral procession.

MAN CHOKES TO DEATH ON LIVE FISH

A 45-year-old man from Viburnum, Missouri, was drinking with his fishing buddies when he choked to death after trying to swallow a live, five-inch-long perch. According to one of the friends, the man's last words were: "Hey, watch this!"

WOMAN TURNS UP AT OWN FUNERAL

A 20-year-old Argentine woman who went missing following a New Year's party in 2006 turned up at her own funeral after her mother wrongly declared her dead. Angela Saraiva had only been gone for 20 hours but her anxious mother mistakenly identified a dead body as being that of her daughter and the funeral was in full swing by the time Angela resurfaced.

WALLET RETRIEVED AT A PRICE

A Milwaukee family literally found themselves out of pocket in 1996. A few days after his burial, relatives of Robert Senz demanded that the funeral home dig up the body because the deceased's wallet was missing. Sure enough, the wallet containing $64 was found in his pocket. Seven months later the funeral home sent the family a reburial bill for $2,149.

LAST TANGO IN LISBON

Portuguese dance teacher Alberto Fargo tangoed to his death straight out of a fifth-floor Lisbon window in 1998. Police said Fargo was showing his dance class how to keep their heads high by looking at the ceiling, as a result of which he had failed to notice that the window was open.

MAN REACHES 100 FAILED SUICIDE ATTEMPTS LANDMARK

In 2006, Mr Shi, a middle-aged man from Ningho, China, was rescued from hanging himself on a tree – at least the 100th time that he had been saved from committing suicide over the previous three years. His troubles had begun in 2003 when his wife divorced him and he decided that without her, life was meaningless.

HUNGRY BURGLAR COOKS DINNER AND SELF

Breaking into a restaurant and cooking himself a meal, a burglar accidentally set fire to the building and himself. Police said 57-year-old Robert H. Davis broke into the Gilleylen Dairy Bar in Amory, Georgia, but while attempting to cook with the restaurant's equipment he caused a blaze in which he sustained fatal burns.

WINS BET, LOSES LIFE

Sylvester Briddell Jr, 26, of Selbyville, Delaware, was killed in 1997 after winning a bet with friends who said that he wouldn't put a revolver loaded with four bullets into his mouth and pull the trigger.

RUSSIAN DIES AFTER VIAGRA-FUELLED ORGY

A Moscow mechanic died in 2009 after guzzling a bottle of Viagra pills to win a bet that he could maintain an erection throughout a 12-hour orgy. Sergey Tuganov, 28, had been bet the equivalent of $5,000 by two female colleagues that he would not be able to satisfy them non-stop for half a day. But just minutes after winning the wager, he suffered a fatal heart attack.

FISH SUFFOCATES SWIMMER

A 17-year-old boy died of suffocation while swimming in Cambodia in 2003 after a fish he caught jumped from his hands and lodged in his throat. Lim Vanthan caught an eight-inch kantrob fish, but it leaped into his mouth, where it stuck fast on account of the barbs running down its back.

SUICIDE PACT ENDS IN DISAPPOINTMENT

A Canadian couple's suicide pact failed miserably because the weapon they used was nearly as old as they were. Harold Pinna, 89, and his 92-year-old wife decided to end it all with a .22 calibre pistol that hadn't been fired in 60 years. Mr Pinna shot his wife in the head, but the rusty bullet ricocheted off a hair curler and she suffered only a mild scalp laceration. He then put the gun to his right ear and fired again, but the shot was so weak that the bullet lodged in his ear, whereupon the dazed couple decided to hand themselves over to the police.

WORKER RECEIVES NASTY SHOCK

A 23-year-old construction worker was electrocuted in New Berlinville, Pennsylvania, in 2008 when he ignored colleagues' warnings and placed electric clips on his chest piercings.

BODY FALLS FROM HEARSE

When an undertaker pulled up outside a chapel of rest in Chatham, Kent, he was horrified to find the hearse doors open – and the body that he had been transporting lying in the road half a mile back. The driver was charged with having an insecure load.

THREE KILLED AFTER SAWING THROUGH BOMB

Stumbling across an old Vietnam War shell in 2009 near Ho Chi Minh City, a father, his teenage son and a friend decided to saw through it so that they could sell the metal. Alas in the course of the exercise the 105-milimetre artillery shell exploded, killing all three.

GUEST DROWNS AT LIFEGUARDS' PARTY

In 1985, New Orleans lifeguards threw a party to celebrate a season without anybody drowning. As the party came to an end, one of the guests was found dead at the bottom of the pool.

MAN FOUND DEAD WITH TAMPONS UP HIS NOSE

A chronic snorer, Londoner Mark Gleeson tried to cure the problem in 1996 by stuffing two of his girlfriend's tampons up his nose – one in each nostril. He suffocated as he slept.

TWO KILLED, ONE INJURED IN PIG SLAUGHTER

Two Hungarian farmers were killed and one was seriously injured while attempting to slaughter a pig with a homemade stun gun in 2001. When one of the men was electrocuted trying to stun the pig with the faulty equipment, the shock of his death caused the pig's owner to suffer a fatal heart attack. Witnessing the carnage, a third man was injured when he pulled the stun gun plug from a socket to disable it. The pig survived.

WOMAN DRIVER HAS DEAD MOTHER AS PASSENGER

Eager to avoid undertaker's fees for transporting a body 1,000 miles from Colorado to Oregon, a woman drove there with the corpse of her 91-year-old mother sitting beside her, dressed in a pair of pyjamas.

MAN ELECTROCUTED AFTER PEEING ON RAIL TRACK

A Polish tourist died in 2008 after being electrocuted when he urinated on a train track at a London station. The 41-year-old was killed after walking on to the track at Vauxhall, a station which had no public toilets at the time. The victim – a teacher – had travelled to Britain to improve his English.

WOLF IMPRESSION WAS TOO LIFELIKE

A man renowned for his ability to mimic the cry of a wolf in order to lure other wolves out into the open for hunting was shot dead in Greece by fellow hunters who mistook him for the real thing.

WITCHDOCTOR'S BULLETPROOF POTION NEEDS NEW RECIPE

A Ghanaian man was shot dead by a fellow villager in 2001 while testing a magic spell designed to make him bulletproof. Aleobiga Aberima, 23, and some 15 other men from Lambu village had asked a local witchdoctor to make them invincible to bullets. After smearing his body with a concoction of prescribed herbs every day for two weeks, Aberima nobly volunteered to test the spell's effectiveness by agreeing to be shot. Accordingly, one of the group fetched a rifle and aimed it at Aberima who died instantly from a single gunshot wound. The others promptly rounded on the witchdoctor, handing out a severe beating and presumably demanding their money back.

INVENTOR BURIED IN TUBE OF PRINGLES

The man who invented the Pringles tube was so proud of its ingenious design that he was buried in one. Before his death in 2008, Fredric J. Baur asked that part of his ashes be placed in a Pringles tube and interred in a grave in his home city of Cincinnati, Ohio.

BUNGEE JUMPER FATALLY MISCALCULATES LENGTH OF CORD

Eager to participate in the bungee jumping craze that was sweeping the US in 1997, 22-year-old fast-food worker Eric Barcia decided to make his own apparatus. Having constructed a cord by taping straps together, he wrapped one end of the cord around his foot and tied the other end to a railroad trestle on a bridge near Springfield, Virginia. He then jumped from the bridge but was killed after hitting the pavement 70 feet below at full speed. A police spokesman explained: "The length of the cord that he had assembled was greater than the distance between the trestle and the ground." Barcia's grandmother was mystified, pointing out: "He was very smart in school."

COUPLE LURED BY FUNERAL FOOD

An elderly New Zealand couple attended strangers' funerals five times a week over a period of 17 years purely for the free food and drink.

7

SPORTS CRAZY

ENGLAND FANS STRANDED IN ONE-WAY STREET

Two English soccer fans who travelled to Cologne, Germany, for a match in 2006 lost their car after thinking they had parked it on a road called "One-Way Street". So as not to forget where they had left their vehicle, the pair looked for a street sign and wrote down "Einbahn Strasse" in the belief that it was the name of the road . . . blissfully unaware that it means "One-Way Street" in German. It was only when they returned to the area after the match that they discovered that every other street in the inner city had a sign saying "Einbahn Strasse". With the help of German police, they managed to track down their car several hours later.

CALLERS GET SEX LINE INSTEAD OF GOLF LINE

Callers to a freephone number advertising a US golf tournament in 2001 were surprised to hear a sultry female voice telling them they had "come to the right place for nasty talk with big-busted girls". A one-digit error published in 100,000 brochures for the Tournament of Roses in Pasadena, California, led callers to a sex line instead of the golf line.

REFEREE SENDS OFF WHISTLING PARROT

The referee of an important soccer cup tie was forced to send off a parrot after it caused chaos and confusion by repeatedly imitating his whistle. Accompanied by his owner Irene Kerrigan, the green parrot named Me-Tu sat in his cage watching from the touchline as Hatfield Town played Hertford Heath in the quarter-final of the Hertfordshire Senior Centenary Trophy in 2009 before 150 spectators. Me-Tu behaved himself for the first half but ten minutes after the restart, he began distracting the players by whistling just like referee Gary Bailey. After numerous stoppages, the match was halted and Mr Bailey told the woman and parrot to leave the pitch-side. Afterwards he said: "I've never known anything like it in my football career. It was a big game and there were quite a lot of people there. This woman was standing right by the touchline and suddenly unveiled a big cage with this big green parrot in it. I didn't mind at first, but then every time I blew my whistle, the bird made exactly the same sound. The players all stopped, so I had to ask her to move the parrot. It was bizarre. Looking back, I should have made far more of it and got out my red card to show to the parrot."

FORGOT TO TAKE OFF SHIRT BEFORE IRONING IT

Atlanta Braves' baseball team pitcher John Smoltz scalded himself in the act of ironing a shirt – while he was wearing it.

FOOTBALLER SACKED FOR PLAYING WITH HIMSELF

A Turkish soccer club sacked its French star Pascal Nourma after he put his hands down his shorts to celebrate scoring a goal. He said the gesture was a "private sign of joy".

GREYHOUND WORE CONTACT LENSES

A British woman who owned a short-sighted greyhound that kept finishing second in races because it needed another dog to follow turned it into a winner by having the animal fitted with contact lenses. The Manchester eye specialist who fitted the lenses said: "The greyhound was severely short-sighted and always came second because it followed the dog in front. With the lenses, it could see the hare and began to win." The owner didn't want the dog's name revealed because she feared bookmakers would slash its odds in future races.

PLAYER TRANSFERRED FOR SAUSAGES

A Romanian soccer player was transferred in 2006 for a fee of 15 kilos of pork sausages. After signing defender Marius Cioara from UT Arad, Fourth Division club Regal Hornia revealed: "We gave up the team's sausage allowance for a week to secure him." But the day after details of the deal were leaked to the media, Cioara dramatically announced that he was quitting football and going to work on a farm in Spain because he was fed up with the sausage taunts. Regal Hornia said they were asking for the return of their sausage meat.

SPIDER NIGHTMARE SIDELINES BASEBALL STAR

Toronto Blue Jays' baseball player Glenallen Hill sustained serious cuts after falling out of bed and crashing into a glass table . . . while having a nightmare about his body being covered in spiders.

ATHLETE STUMBLES OVER POTTED PLANT

Sweden's Svante Rasmusson seemed assured of the gold medal in the modern pentathlon at the 1984 Los Angeles Olympics when he pulled clear in the final event, the 4,000 metres cross country. But just 20 yards from the finish he stumbled over a potted plant, placed there by the organizers to brighten up the course, and by the time he had got to his feet he had been passed by Italy's Daniele Masala.

SOCCER PLAYERS PUT CONDOMS ON THEIR FEET

In 2008, it was revealed that impoverished soccer players in Cape Town, South Africa, were putting condoms on their feet to help their socks stay up during matches. Bandilo Nginingini, a 20-year-old player for Young Cosmos FC, admitted that he regularly went to a shop to buy four condoms before weekend matches. He said: "I wish that we could get proper soccer kit support so that we can stop this and let the condoms be used for their real purpose."

SENT OFF FOR FLIRTING WITH REFEREE

An East German junior soccer player was sent off for flirting with the referee. The official, 20-year-old Marita Rall, ordered him off when he tried to arrange a date with her while the match was in progress.

ROOFTOP PROTEST ALERTS EX-WIFE

When Ronald Stach staged a 14-day sit-in on the roof of a Baltimore, Maryland, bar in 2007 to protest about the dismal performance of the Baltimore Ravens football team, he inadvertently opened a can of worms.

For the publicity he attracted alerted his former wife to his whereabouts and enabled her to renew her long campaign for $40,000 in child support. Shortly afterwards a second woman came forward, claiming Stach also owed her $12,000 in back child support.

DEAD PLAYER IS BOOKED FOR DIVING

A footballer booked for diving by a no-nonsense referee had in fact dropped dead of a heart attack. Goran Tunjic, a 32-year-old defender playing for the Croatian side Mladost, collapsed and fell to the ground after being tackled during a 2010 match against Hrvatski Sokola. The referee, who had warned the teams before kick-off that he would not tolerate any play-acting, promptly marched across the pitch to the prone player and waved a yellow card at him. He quickly realized his error and summoned medical help but it proved to no avail.

BOYS' TEAM HIT BY OWN GULL

The outcome of a boys' soccer match in Manchester in 1999 was changed when a wayward shot was deflected into the net off a seagull. Stalybridge Celtic Colts were only leading Hollingsworth Juniors 2-1 when their 13-year-old striker Danny Worthington tried a hopeful shot from 25 yards. The ball was sailing way over the crossbar until it hit the passing seagull on the head, spun over the Hollingsworth goalkeeper and into the net. Hollingsworth were so demoralized by the freak goal that they went on to lose 7-1.

OLYMPIC LUGER BREAKS TOOTH ON MEDAL

David Moeller, Germany's silver medallist in the luge at the 2010 Winter Olympics, had to make an unscheduled trip to the dentist after breaking his front tooth while taking a celebratory bite into the medal. He said: "The photographers wanted us to bite into our medals at the presentation ceremony, and a corner of my front tooth broke off."

GOLFER HITS 42-MILE DRIVE

An unnamed member of the John O'Gaunt Golf Club at Sutton, Bedfordshire, produced what must surely be the longest drive in the history of British golf – one of 42 miles. His tee shot sailed out of bounds and instead of landing on the green, it landed on the greens – or to be precise a box of cabbages being transported on a passing vegetable truck. The truck was on its way to London's Covent Garden market and when the cabbages were unloaded there, the golf ball fell out.

DEATH ANNOUNCEMENT PROVES PREMATURE

More than 2,000 soccer fans held a minute's silence for one of their favourite former players, only to discover that he was still alive and well. Tommy Farrer had starred for County Durham amateur team Bishop Auckland in its glory years after the Second World War but in 2009 word reached the club that the old stalwart had died at the age of 86. The sad details were noted accordingly in the match day programme and a minute's silence was held before the team's next game. The club also arranged for a tribute to appear in a local newspaper. Bishop Auckland chairman Terry Jackson then telephoned Farrer's "widow" Gladys at the family home in Maidstone, Kent, to offer the club's condolences, but she told him she could pass them on to her husband himself, adding: "He will be back in a minute. He's only popped out to get a paper."

PRIDE COMES BEFORE A FALL

Australian motorcyclist Kevin Magee was delighted to have finished fourth in the 500cc United States Grand Prix at Laguna Seca, California, in 1989. But while waving to the crowds on his lap of honour, he fell off his machine and broke a leg.

BASEBALL PLAYER TRADED FOR TEN BATS

Minor league baseball player John Odom moved from the Calgary Vipers to the Laredo Broncos in 2008 for the price of ten bats. The 34-inch maple bats retail at $69 each, discounted to $65.50 for purchases of six or more, making Odom's value as a player a paltry $655. Nevertheless he insisted that he was not offended by the cut-price deal.

SOCCER STAR'S GRANNIES COME BACK TO HAUNT HIM

When Manchester City and Republic of Ireland footballer Stephen Ireland pulled out of a 2007 international match because his maternal grandmother had died, he received widespread sympathy. The Football Association of Ireland spent $100,000 hiring a private jet to fly him home from Slovakia so that he could attend the funeral of Patricia Tallon. However the news came as a shock to Mrs Tallon herself, who was alive and well and living in Cork. After the FAI discovered the truth, Ireland said that in his grief he had accidentally given the wrong name and that it was actually his paternal grandmother, Brenda Kitchener, who had died. So the association put out a new press release clarifying the situation, only for Mrs Kitchener's family to react angrily. For she, too, was alive and well. Eventually Ireland was forced to admit that neither of his grannies had died and the real reason he had wanted to come home was to be with his girlfriend.

WRONG CALL COSTS $1.5 MILLION

With contract negotiations between the two parties having stalled, McLaren Formula One boss Ron Dennis suggested to his Brazilian driver Ayrton Senna that they settle the matter on the toss of a coin. Senna called wrong – and lost $1.5 million.

STUDENT SUES SCHOOL OVER EXPOSED GENITALS

A New Jersey student sued the local board of education, his teachers, five of his fellow students and the printing company after the 2001 Colts Neck High School yearbook showed him in action in his basketball uniform with part of his genitals visible. Claiming that the photo had caused him "psychological harm", Tyler Bennett said: "I was shocked, embarrassed and upset. I remember a student taunting me and asking: 'How's it hanging?'"

PLAYER KILLED DURING GAME OF BOULES

In what is thought to be the first death in the sport's 100-year history, a Frenchman was killed after being hit on the head with a metal ball during a game of boules. Franck Hourcade, 39, was bending down to examine the jack in the course of a game at Adé in 2008 when another player threw his heavy steel ball towards it. Despite the sport's genteel image, the French authorities have been concerned by a worrying rise in incidents of "bouliganisme" – physical and verbal abuse caused by prize money, alcohol and generally uncivil behaviour.

FAKE TAN PUTS PLAYER OUT FOR NINE GAMES

Baltimore Orioles baseball player Marty Cordova missed nine games in 2002 after burning his face on a sun bed at a California tanning salon. Doctors ordered him to stay out of direct sunlight until his wounds started to heal.

JOCKEY SWITCHES RIDES IN MID-RACE

Confusion reigned in a 2009 steeplechase in New Zealand after five of the six runners fell, two jockeys broke collarbones, a horse was treated for stress and one jockey started on one horse and finished on another. Stewards took more than 30 minutes to unravel the events surrounding the race at the Canterbury Jockey Club meeting before declaring Nana the winner by an extraordinary 128 lengths. Three horses fell at the last fence, including Mala Strana who was battling for second place at the time. Mala Strana's jockey, George Strickland, inexplicably remounted Ice Pack, which had fallen earlier in the race, and claimed fourth place but was eventually disqualified. Steward Stewart Ching described Strickland's swap as "a bit weird", adding: "It was one of the more bizarre races I have had to deal with."

FEMALE FAN FLASHES BOOBS TO PUT OFF PENALTY TAKER

After the 2003 Somerset Morland Challenge Cup final between soccer teams Wookey FC and Norton Hill Rangers ended in a 0-0 draw, the ensuing penalty shootout was decided in the most bizarre manner. As the first Norton Hill player ran up to take his kick, Wookey fan Cheryl Laws, positioning herself behind the goal, lifted her top to expose her breasts, whereupon the distracted player ballooned the ball into the car park. The miss decided the match as Wookey went on to win the shootout 3-2. Losing captain Lee Baverstock said: "I couldn't believe it when she started flashing. It definitely got to the lads. With all that flesh on show they couldn't concentrate."

JOCKEY HEAD-BUTTS HORSE

Jockey Paul O'Neill received a one-day ban in 2006 for head-butting his horse after it threw him off before a race. O'Neill lowered his crash-helmeted forehead onto the nose of City Affair before a two-mile hurdle race at Stratford. Apologizing for his aberration, O'Neill said: "When I got to the start he headed straight for a car with me, stopped five feet from the car, whipped round and dropped me. I landed on my feet, but awkwardly for my knee. I was a little bit angry."

GOALKEEPER IS SHOWN YELLOW CARD FOR RESCUING CAT

When a cat wandered on to the pitch during a 2009 Croatian First Division soccer match in Sibenik, Medjimurje Cakovec goalkeeper Ivan Banovic picked up the animal and deposited it in a safe place near a scoreboard. However the referee took a dim view of his action and promptly issued him with a yellow card for leaving the pitch without permission. The referee was roundly booed by spectators for the rest of the match.

CHAMPION ANGLER USED PRE-CAUGHT FISH

A professional fisherman was disqualified from a major tournament in 2005 and banned from future events after being found guilty of cheating by using pre-caught fish. Competing in the Red River Bassmaster Central Open in Louisiana, Paul Tormanen, from Lees Summit, Missouri, tied bass that he had already caught to a tree stump before the event. However a fellow competitor spotted the hoard and persuaded officials to mark the fish. When Tormanen then presented one of the marked fish at the weigh-in, his sharp practice was exposed.

ANGRY NASCAR FAN SENDS TV STATION HALF A MILLION EMAILS

When Fox Entertainment aired a Boston Red Sox baseball game instead of the NASCAR race he had been eagerly anticipating, Michael Melo, of Billerica, Massachusetts, voiced his displeasure by sitting down at his computer and devising a programme calculated to bombard the Fox network with emails. Over a few days in late April and early May 2001, Fox received more than 530,000 emails from Melo, forcing the company to shut down part of its website. Melo's lawyer explained: "He was just very upset that the Red Sox would pre-empt NASCAR."

SOCCER FAN WATCHES MATCH THROUGH HOUSE FIRE

A Beijing soccer fan refused to let the small matter of his house burning down spoil his enjoyment of a 2006 World Cup match between France and Spain. After their home was completely gutted in the blaze, the man's wife told reporters: "When the neighbours shouted 'Fire!', I took my little baby and ran out in my nightclothes. My husband paid no attention to the danger, just grabbed the television and put it under his arm. After getting out of the house, he then set about finding an electric socket to plug it in and continue watching his game."

PLAYER SENT OFF AFTER THREE SECONDS

Soccer player David Pratt lived up to his name over Christmas 2008 by managing to get himself sent off after just three seconds of a match. The 21-year-old Chippenham Town striker received the world's fastest-ever red card for a lunge at Bashley's Christopher Knowles straight from the kick-off of their British Gas Business Premier League fixture in Hampshire. The Chippenham secretary said: "You could normally not meet a milder man than David, but he lost it on this occasion."

BOWLER DIES AFTER PERFECT GAME

A ten-pin bowler collapsed and died in 2008 after recording his first perfect score. Don Doane, 62, belonged to the same Ravenna, Michigan, bowling team for 45 years and finally managed to rack up the maximum 300. But as he was high-fiving his teammates, he suffered a fatal heart attack.

COUPLE LOSE DESPITE BETTING ON EVERY GREYHOUND

A couple who went greyhound racing managed to lose $20,000 despite betting on every dog in every race. The pair travelled hundreds of miles from the south coast of England to Sheffield's Owlerton Stadium in 2009 in the hope of scooping the $150,000 jackpot. Carrying $70,000 in cash in a supermarket carrier bag, they devised what they thought was a foolproof plan by placing bets to cover every possible placing of all six dogs in all six races. However they had not reckoned on two other punters also backing all six winners, as a result of which the jackpot was split three ways and they finished $20,000 out of pocket.

PIGEON DROPPING HITS HURDLER IN THE EYE

Boyd Gittins was eliminated from the 1968 US Olympic 400-metres hurdles trials when a pigeon dropping landed on his eye and dislodged his contact lens just as he was about to jump the first hurdle.

PLAYER KNOCKED OUT – THEN AMBULANCE CRASHES

Universidad de Chile soccer striker Juan Manuel Olivera was knocked out during a 2009 match in Rancagua, but shortly after he regained consciousness the ambulance taking him to a Santiago hospital crashed. The team doctor described it as "a tragicomic situation".

HEAD TENNIS PRANK PROVES A KNOCKOUT

Croatian tennis player Goran Ivanisevic needed stitches when he tried to head the ball over the net, only to bang heads with his doubles partner Mark Philippoussis, who was himself concussed.

DRUNK CHESS PLAYER FALLS ASLEEP AT BOARD

A chess grandmaster lost a game in a 2009 international tournament after turning up drunk and falling asleep in his chair. Frenchman Vladislav Tkachiev – ranked number 58 in the world – was already in an inebriated state when he arrived for his match against India's Praveen Kumar in Calcutta. He could hardly sit in his chair and after just 11 moves he dozed off, his head resting on the table. When officials were unable to rouse him, Tkachiev forfeited the match on the grounds that he was unable to complete his moves within the stipulated time of 1 hour 30 minutes.

"FATHER KILLS SON FOR BLOCKING FOOTBALL GAME"

According to newspaper reports, a 60-year-old man from St Louis, Missouri, was watching a football game in 1997 between Missouri Tigers and the Colorado State Rams when his 26-year-old son "deliberately stood in front of the TV". Reacting angrily, the father fired at him with a pistol and when the shot missed, the son grabbed the gun and began hammering his father over the head with it. So the father went to a closet and grabbed a shotgun. This time he hit the target, killing his son. The Rams won 35-23.

BASEBALL UMPIRE EJECTS ENTIRE CROWD

An umpire emptied the stands at a high school baseball game in 2009, ejecting the entire crowd of more than 100 for being unruly. Don Briggs took the drastic action during a game between Winfield-Mount Union and West Burlington in Iowa because he claimed fans were yelling and arguing. The unrest began when Winfield-Mount Union coach Scott McCarty came out to argue a call. Briggs then decided to throw everyone out and even called for police backup. There were no arrests and the police said they saw nothing out of the ordinary. Nevertheless the game was delayed for 40 minutes and was only resumed on condition that nobody present said anything negative about the umpiring. Afterwards both managers accused Briggs of overreacting.

GOLFER HITS TEE SHOT UP SHEEP'S BUTT

PLAYING AT Southerndown Golf Club, near Porthcawl, Wales, in 1995, Peter Croke was amazed to see his tee shot disappear up the butt of a passing sheep. Seemingly unruffled by the incident, the animal walked on for a short while before shaking the ball free. The good news for Croke was that his ball was now 30 yards nearer the hole. ●

FILLY BUSTER: RACEHORSE IS A HERMAPHRODITE

Following an impressive win in a race at Bankstown, Australian mare Tuscan Abbe was tested on suspicion of doping – but the tests showed that the horse is actually male, at least some of the time. For although Tuscan Abbe was found to possess the Y chromosome of a stallion and produced a large amount of testosterone, when she was re-tested shortly afterwards the results were negative. Two weeks later, however, the same tests showed her testosterone levels going "through the roof" again. Bewildered trainer Les Kosklin wasn't sure whether to race her as a mare or a stallion in future.

GOALKEEPER DROPS AWARD

Voted Leicester City's 1995–96 Player of the Year for his safe hands, soccer goalkeeper Kevin Poole was presented with a cut-glass rose bowl . . . which he promptly dropped.

GOLFER AIMS FOR THE CUP

During a 1973 US tour event, American golfer Hale Irwin saw his shot land in a spectator's bra. Rather than retrieve the ball personally from its unusual lie, Irwin graciously allowed the lady to do it herself.

RUGBY PLAYER CRIES AFTER HANDBAG ATTACK

When a brawl broke out in a Christchurch, New Zealand, bar in 2006, Wellington Hurricanes player Chris Masoe had to be restrained by his captain, Tana Umaga, who smacked him so hard with a woman's handbag that Masoe was left in tears.

DEFENDANT PLEADS GUILTY IN ORDER TO SEE SUPER BOWL

Appearing in a Texas court on murder charges, football fan Robert William Greer Jr agreed to plead guilty if he was allowed to remain in the county jail until the end of the month because he thought he would have a better chance of watching the 1999 Super Bowl on TV there than in the state prison. Accordingly the District Judge sentenced Greer to 18 years – but asked the county sheriff to delay his transfer to prison until after the big game.

BOXER KNOCKED OUT BY TV CAMERAMAN

When boxer Adolpho Washington was being treated for a cut eye before the final round of his WBA light-heavyweight title bout against Virgil Hill in Fargo, North Dakota, in 1993, a TV cameraman crowded into his corner to get a close-up of the wound. In doing so, he accidentally hit Washington's eye with the camera, causing it to bleed profusely and forcing him to retire.

SINGER MAKES ANTHEM BLUNDER

The British singer who sang the Croatian national anthem before the 2007 soccer international between England and Croatia at Wembley accidentally sang "My penis is a mountain." Tony Henry was performing the anthem in Croatian but instead of singing "mila kuda si planina" ("You know my dear how we love your mountains"), his words came out as "mila kura si planina" ("My dear, my penis is a mountain").

YACHT COMES UNDER FRIENDLY FIRE

To mark her progress in the 1974 Round the World Yacht Race, the *Adventurer* was given a nine-gun salute by HMS *Endurance* as she rounded Cape Horn. Unfortunately the sixth shot hit the *Adventurer*, severely denting her chances of adding to her victory in the previous leg of the race.

BOY WEARS SAME FOOTBALL JERSEY FOR 1,581 DAYS

A young American football fan from Ridgefield, Connecticut, wore his favourite player's jersey for 1,581 consecutive days – nearly four and a half years. Green Bay Packers fan David Witthoft was given the Brett Favre jersey for Christmas 2003 and wore it every day until his 12th birthday on 23 April 2008.

MARATHON RUNNER FINDS STADIUM LOCKED

Trailing almost 39 minutes behind the previous finisher in the marathon at the 1979 Pan American Games at San Juan, Puerto Rico, plucky Wallace Williams of the Virgin Islands approached the stadium expecting a sympathetic round of applause from the spectators, only to find that the place was locked. Everybody had forgotten about him and gone home.

REFEREE DROPS SHORTS DURING WOMEN'S MATCH

A referee who dropped his shorts during a women's rugby match in 2007 was suspended for 18 weeks. The Rugby Football Union for Women said Robert Tustin bared his bottom in the closing stages of a match in Peterborough. Amanda Walker, captain of opponents Thetford, said: "We were waiting to restart after Peterborough scored when the referee walked off the pitch and took his boots off. He then walked back on to the pitch and pulled his shorts down."

"WIFE OFFERED BASEBALL CARDS TO HITMEN"

Georgina Thompson, 37, was charged in Wellington, Kansas, in 1992 for allegedly offering two men her common-law husband's prized collection of baseball cards in return for them murdering him. Instead the pair reported her to the police and handed over the down payment she had made of ten of the cards. Referring to the unusual payment, the deputy sheriff remarked: "That's about as mean as a wife can get. The only thing lower would have been if she offered his hunting and fishing gear."

RACING PIGEON FLIES 500 MILES AND IS EATEN BY CAT

After beating 1,000 rivals in a gruelling 500-mile race, Percy the racing pigeon flopped down exhausted in his loft in Sheffield, South Yorkshire . . . and was promptly eaten by the neighbourhood cat. To add insult to injury, the 90-minute delay in finding his remains and handing his identification tag to the judges relegated Percy from first to third place.

SUMO WRESTLER FORFEITS MATCH OVER EXPOSED MANHOOD

Japanese Sumo wrestler Asanokiri lost a match and his dignity after his loin cloth fell off, exposing his manhood on national television. He automatically forfeited the 2000 bout under an obscure rule that penalizes a wrestler for allowing his privates to be exposed by not wrapping his mawashi belt tightly enough. The mawashi belts are about 25 feet long and are wrapped tightly several times around the wrestlers' massive bodies. Asanokiri had been involved in a closely-fought contest with Chiyohakuho but it was stopped immediately when a Sumo elder sitting ringside spotted the offending member and invoked the exposure rule. It was the first time since the rule was introduced in 1917 that a wrestler had lost a match in that way. A shame-faced Asanokiri said afterwards: "I tied my mawashi the way I always do, but today it just came loose."

JOCKEYS DODGE FLYING UMBRELLA

Jockeys in a 2006 race at Ellis Park, Kentucky, had to steer their mounts to avoid a large flying umbrella which blew across the course after being lifted off a picnic table in strong winds.

POLICE GAS THEMSELVES WHILE QUELLING RIOT

Trying to break up a fracas at the end of a soccer match in Nairobi, Kenya, in 1987 between Gor Mahia and AFC Leopards, police officers were overcome by their own tear gas, as a result of which they were unable to arrest anyone.

CATCHER INJURES SHOULDER IN PILLOW MANOEUVRE

Detroit Tigers baseball catcher Brandon Inge had to be rested from the team in 2008 after injuring his shoulder while pushing a pillow under the head of his sleeping three-year-old son.

HOCKEY STREAKER KNOCKS HIMSELF OUT COLD

Wearing nothing but a pair of red socks, 21-year-old student Tim Hurlbut climbed over the glass at a 2002 hockey game between Calgary Flames and visitors Boston Bruins and prepared to streak across the ice to win a $200 bet. Unfortunately his landing was less than perfect, as a result of which he fell backward, hit the back of his head on the ice and knocked himself out. The game was delayed for six minutes while staff treated the unconscious streaker and eventually carted him off on a stretcher.

GOLFER COMPLETES ROUND IN ONE SHOT

Eighteen-handicap golfer Neville Rowlandson claimed to have completed a round in just one stroke after his wayward tee shot at the first dropped into the 18th hole. Playing in a monthly competition at Felixstowe Golf Club, Suffolk, in 1996, the 56-year-old lorry driver saw his drive at the par-four opening hole hit a yellow wooden marker sign ten yards in front of the tee, ricochet away at an angle and drop into the hole on the adjacent 18th green. He said afterwards: "I wanted to draw the ball down the right-hand side of the fairway with my new driver. I was a bit upset when it hit the marker."

DEATH BOOSTS BOXER'S RANKING

Darrin Morris of Detroit moved up from 11th to fifth in the World Boxing Organization's super-middleweight division in 2001 – despite having been dead for four months. His last fight was in July 1999.

SHORT-SIGHTED MARATHON RUNNERS LOSE THEIR WAY

Two veteran runners competing in a 50-mile circular race around Rotherham, Yorkshire, in 2002 made an unscheduled 20-mile detour into Nottinghamshire because they forgot their glasses. Les Huxley, 57, and Barry Bedford, 61, couldn't read the route map or see the race signposts, as a result of which they got lost for 18 hours. With the other 140 runners long finished and asleep in bed, the hapless duo eventually crossed the line at 1.30 a.m. – but only after phoning the race organizer to come and get them.

SOCCER PLAYER KILLS PIGEON WITH BALL

Playing for Argentine club San Lorenzo against Tigre in 2008, Gastón Aguirre was left mortified after his shot struck a pigeon and killed it. Despite his side's 2-1 victory, the 27-year-old central defender was full of remorse after accidentally ending the life of one of the birds that was hunting for seed on the pitch. "I kicked the ball and the poor pigeon," he said afterwards, adding: "Now I will be remembered as the pigeon killer."

DEAD JOCKEY WINS RACE

Frank Hayes is almost certainly the only jockey in history to ride a winner while dead. In 1923, Hayes was a 35-year-old stable lad who pleaded with the owner of a horse named Sweet Kiss to let him ride the confirmed loser in a steeplechase at Belmont Park, New York. The owner relented and with the 20-1 outsider in a clear lead ten yards from the finish, Hayes became so excited that he suffered a heart attack. He managed to stay on the horse as it passed the winning post but when friends and connections rushed over to congratulate him, they found him slumped forward, dead in the saddle. After that, no other jockey wanted to ride Sweet Kiss.

MANAGER SACKED AFTER TEN MINUTES

Leroy Rosenior was appointed manager of struggling English soccer club Torquay United in 2007 – and then sacked ten minutes later. The Devon club unveiled him at a press conference which finished at 3.30 p.m. on 21 May and at 3.40 p.m. he was told that the club had been sold to a consortium and that he was out of a job. Rosenior commented: "For it to happen so soon after I finished the press conference was a bit of a shock. Obviously they thought I had done a fantastic job in those ten minutes and let me go."

MEDAL HOPES CRUSHED BY GARBAGE MEN

Having arrived in Canada to prepare for the 1976 Montreal Olympics, the Czech cycling team's medal hopes suffered a setback when all their wheels and spare tyres were inadvertently picked up by garbage collectors and crushed.

RALLY DRIVER CRASHES NEAR FINISH

After driving 3,000 miles across Europe in the 2000 Gumball Rally, Germany's Georg Etterer crashed his Mercedes just 100 yards from the finish in Hampshire because he momentarily forgot that the English drive on the left-hand side of the road.

PLAYER STABS HIMSELF WHILE OPENING DVD

San Diego Padres' baseball player Adam Eaton was rushed to hospital in 2001 after accidentally stabbing himself in the stomach with a knife while trying to unwrap a DVD. Even Eaton described his action as "boneheaded".

SOCCER FAN IN GORILLA SUIT IS UNMASKED

A teenage Middlesbrough Football Club fan decided to get round a court curfew by disguising himself in a gorilla suit for a 1992 League Cup replay against Peterborough United. But when his team scored the only goal of the game, he forgot himself, threw the gorilla head into the air in celebration and was subsequently recognized by a police officer watching highlights of the game on TV at home later that evening.

JOCKEY HIDES MOUNT IN THE FOG

Jockey Sylvester Carmouche was banned from riding in Louisiana for ten years after being found guilty of hiding in dense fog to win a mile race at Delta Downs in 1990. Riding the 23-1 outsider Landing Officer, Carmouche bolted home by 24 lengths but it transpired that he had dropped his horse out of the race shortly after the start, hidden in thick fog, and then rejoined the pack as they completed the circuit of the oval track. Suspicions were aroused when two jockeys in the race reported that no horse passed them at any time, to which Carmouche replied brazenly: "They never noticed me."

GOLFER IS KNOCKED OUT BY HIS OWN BACKSWING

Halfway through his backswing while driving off at the 17th hole at Lyme Regis Golf Club, Dorset, 69-year-old Derek Gatley received a nasty blow when the steel shaft of his club snapped, hit him on the back of the head and knocked him out cold. When he came round, Mr Gatley admitted: "It was the first thing I had hit all day."

WOMAN REFEREE ALLOWS BALL-BOY'S GOAL

A female referee in Brazil was suspended in 2006 after allowing a vital last-minute goal that was tapped into the net by a ball-boy. His side trailing 0-1 to visitors Atletico Sorocaba, a Santacruzense player tried a speculative shot in the 89th minute. The ball drifted harmlessly wide but then the ball boy brought it back onto the pitch and instead of returning it to the goalkeeper, he tapped it over the line and into the net. Referee Silvia Regina de Oliveira awarded the goal despite furious Sorocaba protests and the 1-1 result stood. She said later that she had based her decision on the word of her linesman, adding ruefully: "I should have trusted my own vision."

GREYHOUND RESPONDS TO OWNER'S CHEERING

A family who went to cheer on their pet greyhound in a race in Ireland in the early 1980s may have been better advised to stay away. For as the dog rounded the final bend, right in touch with the leaders, it recognized the voices of encouragement coming from the side of the track, whereupon it pulled itself up and, tail wagging, trotted over to the fence to greet its owners.

PLAYER LOSES FINGER IN GOAL CELEBRATION

Playing in the Swiss Soccer League in 2004, Servette midfielder Paulo Diogo scored a goal against Schaffhausen and promptly jumped into the crowd to celebrate. In doing so, however, he caught his wedding ring on a fence and tore off the top half of his finger. He was then booked by the referee for excessive celebration.

JOYOUS WELSH FAN HACKS OFF HIS OWN TESTICLES

WHEN THE WELSH rugby team beat England in 2005, 31-year-old Geoffrey Huish was so delighted that he celebrated by chopping off his own testicles. After taking ten minutes to perform the operation using a pair of blunt wire cutters, he put the severed parts in a blue plastic bag and staggered to a social club near his home in Senghenydd to show fellow Welsh fans his handiwork. There he collapsed with blood pouring from his groin as horrified drinkers put his testicles in a pint glass of ice. They were handed to paramedics who rushed him to hospital, but surgeons were unable to reattach them. Huish said: "I'd told my pal I'd cut off my balls if we won. So I started hacking away at my tackle. There was quite a lot of pain, but I just kept going. I cut my penis as well. There was a lot of blood but not as much as you would expect." Huish, who spent several months in a psychiatric unit afterwards, added: "I think about what happened every day and still haven't come up with a good reason why. I can't have kids now, but I still want a family. Maybe I'll adopt." ●

SOCCER STREAKER STRIPS OFF IN COURT

A 60-year-old German man, who was appealing against a conviction for running onto the pitch naked during a girls' soccer match and striking a range of "body builder poses", didn't help his case when he stripped off again in court. A spokesman for the court in Duisburg said: "It appears he sees it as art and views himself as a living work of art."

MORE HOOKERS THAN USUAL ON GOLF COURSE

Six people were arrested at a golf tournament in California after police discovered that tents set up around the course were occupied by prostitutes and that the players were allowed to visit them during their round.

TRAINER KNOCKS HIMSELF OUT WITH CHLOROFORM

During the 1930 Soccer World Cup semi-final between Argentina and the United States, the American team trainer, Jock Coll, ran on to the pitch to treat an injured player. Still fuming over a disputed Argentine goal, Coll threw down his medical bag in a temper tantrum, but in doing so he broke a bottle of chloroform, accidentally anaesthetized himself and had to be carried off by his own team.

RUGBY PLAYER FINDS TOOTH STUCK IN HEAD

An Australian Rugby League player competed for more than three months with an opponent's tooth buried in his head. Ben Czislowski, a prop forward with Brisbane team Wynnum, was involved in a violent clash of heads with Tweed Heads forward Matt Austin in early April 2007, a collision that left Czislowski needing stitches above his left eye and saw Austin lose several teeth and also suffer a broken jaw. In July, Czislowski complained of an eye infection and shooting pains – and a doctor discovered one of Austin's teeth embedded in the player's skull.

REFEREE SENDS HIMSELF OFF

English soccer referee Melvin Sylvester sent himself off after losing his temper and attacking a player who had jostled him. The 42-year-old was refereeing a 1998 Andover and District Sunday League match between Southampton Arms and Hurstbourne Tarrant British Legion when a player pushed him from behind and swore at him. Sylvester responded by punching the player several times, giving him a black eye, which required treatment from the trainer. After the other players had intervened to calm him down, Sylvester pulled out his red card and sent himself off, handing over control of the game to a spectator. He was subsequently fined and banned for six weeks by the Hampshire Football Association.

FANS THROW PIG'S HEAD AT PORTUGUESE INTERNATIONAL

In 2002 former Barcelona soccer star Luis Figo returned to the city's Nou Camp Stadium as a player with their bitter rivals Real Madrid. As the Portuguese international went to take a corner, angry Barcelona fans pelted him with all manner of objects including a pig's head.

FISHERMEN CATCH NOTHING BUT A COLD

The National Ambulance Servicemen's Angling Championships, staged at Kidderminster in 1972, proved something of a disappointment. After spending five hours on a canal side, pitting their wits man against fish, the 200 paramedics had not managed to catch a single fish. It was only then that a passer-by casually informed them that all the fish had been moved to other waters three weeks earlier.

SVEN LOOKALIKE BAFFLES MEXICANS

Mexican soccer officials and newspaper reporters were fooled by an English actor posing as Swedish manager Sven-Goran Eriksson. Derek Williams, who has earned his living as a Sven lookalike since the Swede's colourful reign as England manager, travelled in 2008 to Mexico, where Eriksson had recently taken over as national coach. Wearing Eriksson's trademark spectacles and with a pair of leggy brunettes on each arm, Williams settled into the dugout at the Estadio Universitario in Mexico City and started talking tactics with Ricardo Ferreti, the Brazilian manager of the Pumas, a championship winning team. "He explained to me that he was looking at players for his first squad selection for Mexico," said Ferreti, "and I believed him." The fake Sven then went on to conduct an impromptu press conference in the car park with reporters. After those present finally realized they had been duped, Ferreti said: "To tell the truth, I liked the joke." The national federation was less amused, however, and warned all clubs in the country's top league that there was a Sven impostor on the loose. Denouncing Williams for "irresponsibly exploiting his likeness to the national coach," it warned clubs "not to let yourselves be surprised by this individual".

GOLFER HAS TO BE RESCUED FROM BUNKER

Playing at Rose Bay, New South Wales, 14-stone golfer D.J. Bayly-MacArthur was dismayed to see his ball land in a bunker. However that was only the start of his problems because heavy rain had turned the sand in the bunker to quicksand so that when the burly MacArthur set foot in the trap, he found himself sinking fast. The sand was up to his armpits before his cries for help brought a timely rescue.

DEAD MAN PICKS GRAND NATIONAL WINNER

A family from Middlesbrough won £20,000 ($30,000) on the 2009 Grand National – thanks to a dead gambler's last bet. Shortly before his death, Danny Shea persuaded his wife Pat to put £200 on 100-1 outsider Mon Mome. She thought it was a waste of money but humoured him in his dying days by placing the bet. On her way to visit his grave to thank him for the winning tip, she said: "We could not believe it. He was generally pretty useless at picking winners."

TEAM'S RUDE SHIRTS ARE BANNED

An Essex soccer team was banned from taking the field with shirts bearing the slogan "The Referee's a W*nker". Players at Stambridge United got the strip in 2006 in a sponsorship deal with Chris Turner, author of a book of football chants. Although a red card was discreetly placed over the "a" in the last word, the Baliston Essex Olympian League deemed the shirts offensive.

BASEBALL PLAYER INJURED WHILE EATING DONUT

Baseball player Kevin Mitchell's catalogue of injuries includes straining a ribcage muscle while vomiting, and showing up late for spring training following emergency dental work needed after eating a chocolate donut.

While playing for Cincinnati Reds in 1994 he asked the trainer for eyewash but someone had put rubbing alcohol in the eyewash bottle, leaving Mitchell with burns on his eye. His teammate Hal Morris commented wryly: "It's always Kevin..."

GOLFERS LET PARACHUTIST PLAY THROUGH

Golfers at a course in Steinbach, Manitoba, were obliged to let a parachutist play through. Play was held up for 25 minutes after the female skydiver from Winnipeg dropped unexpectedly from the sky and landed on the 10th fairway. She had missed her intended landing site – a mile away – because her main chute had failed.

REFEREE PULLS RED LACY KNICKERS FROM POCKET

A BRAZILIAN soccer referee was left with a red face after pulling a pair of red lacy knickers from his pocket instead of a red card during a match in 2004. Carlos Jose Figueira Ferro was trying to send off a player during an amateur match in Anama but was so embarrassed by his gaffe that he ended the match 20 minutes early. His wife, who was watching the match, did see red, however, and was reported to be starting divorce proceedings. ●

JOCKEY WINS FIRST RACE AFTER 28 YEARS

In 2008, the man unkindly dubbed "British horse racing's worst jockey" finally won his first race – after 28 years of trying. Famed for usually coming last, 44-year-old amateur Anthony Knott stunned the racing world by riding the 7-1 shot Wise Men Say to victory at Wincanton. But even then Knott, whose previous best finish was fifth in a career stretching back to 1980, nearly blew it by jubilantly standing up in the saddle approaching the finishing line and the loss of impetus almost saw him overtaken by another horse. He explained: "I had no intention of doing that but the vicar and all my friends from my village of Sturminster Newton came running from the bar and there was a tremendous roar. You wave to people when you pass them in our village and I was just doing that. I simply forgot I was in a race." Perhaps wisely, he decided to end his riding career on that high. His wife Sarah said: "I'm just pleased he finally won and didn't hurt himself."

FOOTBALLER BOOKED FOR BREAKING WIND

A player at an amateur soccer match in Manchester was shown a yellow card in 2009 for distracting an opposition penalty taker by breaking wind. The referee decided the Chorlton Villa player made the noise deliberately and booked him for "ungentlemanly conduct". The spot-kick was saved but the referee ordered it to be retaken. The second kick was successful but International Manchester still lost 6-4 even though Chorlton Villa finished with only eight men after having three players sent off.

ROMANIAN CLUB APPOINTS BABY AS MANAGER

Aurel Rusu, president of Romanian soccer club Sadcom FC, was so dismayed because his team were languishing in the country's bottom division that in 1997 he appointed his son Lucian as the new manager. Lucian was six months old.

CROATIAN FOOTBALLER WINS FLOCK OF SHEEP

Ivica Supe, a footballer with Croatian Third Division team Zagora FC, turned up for training one day in 2007 to find 16 sheep waiting for him. He had been unaware of a deal made by the club's sponsor, local shepherd Josko Bralic, who had promised a sheep for every goal scored by a defender.

BOXER KO'S HIMSELF BEFORE BOUT

Preparing for his bout in the New York Golden Gloves Championships in 1992, boxer Daniel Caruso was psyching himself up by pounding his gloves into his face prior to the introductions. Unfortunately he overdid it and scored a direct hit with one punch, breaking and bloodying his own nose. Doctors examining him ruled that he was unfit to box.

MISPRINT INVITES BOWLERS TO DEFECATE ON GREEN

Advertising a forthcoming lawn bowls tournament, the English magazine *Where And When In East Anglia* grandly announced: "Men's and Ladies' Singles, Pairs and Triples as well as Mixed Pairs are invited to the Yarmouth Bowling Green to compete for £5,000 ($10,000) of prize money at the Great Yarmouth Open Bowels Festival."

RACE STARTER SHOOTS HIMSELF

A school's athletics competition in West London was halted temporarily after the race starter accidentally shot himself in the leg with the starting pistol.

COW WREAKS HAVOC ON GOLF COURSE

Playing the 10th hole at Guernsey Golf Club, amateur S.C. King saw his ball land safely on the fairway while his partner, R.W. Clark, disappeared into deep rough. After helping Clark to locate his ball, King returned to his own – and found it being eaten by a cow. The following day, the pair played the course again and were on the lookout for a hungry cow when they reached the 10th hole. This time it was King who drifted into the rough while Clark hit the fairway. Remembering the events of the previous day, Clark took the precaution of placing a protective woollen hat over his ball before setting off to find his partner's drive. On his return, Clark discovered that the cow had eaten his hat.

INTERNATIONAL HOCKEY TEAM LOSES 82-0

Bulgaria crashed 82-0 to Slovakia in a woman's ice hockey qualifying match for the 2010 Winter Olympics. Conceding a goal on average every 44 seconds in the Latvian town of Liepaja, the Bulgarians trailed 7-0 after five minutes, 19-0 after ten, and 31-0 after the first period. Bulgaria has only

37 registered female players and had lost its previous matches 30-1 to Croatia and 41-0 to Italy.

ANGRY MOTHER CHARGED WITH HURLING PIZZA AT UMPIRE

Furious after her son's team Concord lost a closely fought Little League baseball game in New Hampshire, Sherri Ferns, who had been working in the concession stand during the game, was charged with throwing a slice of pizza at one of the umpires.

GREYHOUNDS CONFUSED BY STRAY CAT

A black cat found its way on to Belfast greyhound track in the middle of a race in 1995. The dogs immediately focused on the cat rather than the hare but while the frightened feline managed to escape over a fence, the distracted greyhounds piled into each other and ended up in an unsightly heap on the track. The race was abandoned.

HOCKEY FANS UPSET OVER 12-YEAR-OLD RERUN

Bryan Allison suffered multiple injuries in 2001 when he plunged to the ground in the act of throwing a 25-inch TV set off the second-floor porch of his home in Niagara Falls, New York. He and his brother had been watching a video rerun of a 1989 hockey playoff game and decided to wreck the TV when they became upset about the result.

PLAYER SCORES WINNING GOAL WITH BROKEN FOOT

As his team strove desperately for victory in the last five minutes of a match, an injured soccer player threw down his crutches, ripped off his cast and hobbled on to score the winning goal with his broken right foot. Expected to be out of action for another month, Ian Williams was only on the substitutes' bench to make up the numbers for Welsh village side Pontlliw against local rivals Pontarddulais Town, but with the teams drawing 1-1 in the 85th minute, he begged the coach to send him on. No sooner had he entered the battle than Williams lashed the ball into the net with that broken foot – and almost immediately limped off in agony. Speaking after Pontlliw's 2-1 victory in 2008, Williams said: "When the ball hit the back of the net I couldn't believe it, but it hurt really bad the minute I struck it. I threw up pretty much straight away and had to be substituted a couple of minutes later. It was good to score the winning goal, but next time I think I'll wait until my foot's properly healed."

"DRUNK" HIGH JUMPER FLOPS OUT OF COMPETITION

Russian high jumper Ivan Ukhov was kicked out of a 2008 competition in Lausanne, Switzerland, amid suspicions that the 22-year-old former European Junior Champion was drunk. He was seen acting erratically during a series of failed attempts to clear the modest opening height. Unsteady on his feet, he had to hold onto a hurdle while struggling out of his tracksuit bottoms and then experienced difficulty tying his shoelaces. After pushing away a concerned official, he strolled towards the bar, hardly took off and collapsed on his back on the mat. At that point, officials at the Athletissima Grand Prix meeting asked him to stop competing. His fellow high jumpers later said that Ukhov had been drinking vodka and Red Bull during the competition. His manager, Paul Voronkov, said: "There's no denying that Ivan was drunk but he had a fight with his girlfriend and was also upset at failing to qualify for the Beijing Olympics."

HOMING PIGEON ENDS UP 5,000 MILES OFF COURSE

A homing pigeon taking part in a 600-mile race from Bourges, northern France, to Northumberland, England, in 2006 got hopelessly lost and ended up 5,000 miles away on a Caribbean island. Owner John Stewart believes Judy must have hitched a ride on a ship at least part of the way to the Dutch West Indies.

TEAM SELECTS DEAD PLAYER

Canadian Football League team Montreal Alouettes picked James Eggink in the 1996 draft – unaware that he had been dead for months. "I'm upset and embarrassed as an owner," said Montreal boss Jim Speros. "The research process can be very difficult."

BOXER FLOORS HIMSELF IN SORRY DEBUT

Rookie US boxer Harvey Gartley suffered the embarrassment of knocking himself out in his very first fight. Pitted against Dennis Outlette in a regional heat of the 1977 Saginaw Golden Gloves Championships in Michigan, Gartley sized up his opponent for the opening 47 seconds during which time neither man threw a punch. With the spectators growing restless, Gartley suddenly launched a wild swing in the vague direction of Outlette, missed by a mile, collapsed in a heap on the canvas and was counted out.

UNFORTUNATE MISPRINT CHANGES THE SENTIMENT

Previewing the 1954 Curtis Cup match against the United States at Ardmore, Pennsylvania, the women's golf magazine *Fairway & Hazard* concluded with a patriotic message for Baba Beck, captain of the Great Britain & Ireland team. It should have read: "And so, Mrs Beck, Good Luck and bring back to Britain that coveted Trophy." However, a typographical error meant that the final sentence began: "And sod Mrs Beck . . ."

WORLD'S SLOWEST RACEHORSE IS RETIRED

In his six-race career between May 2005 and December 2006, on English grass and all-weather tracks, over distances from five to ten furlongs, African Blues beat just two out of 68 horses. The only race in which he did not finish last was when, having been sent off at a price of 150-1, he finished 15th out of 17 runners at Leicester, 37 lengths behind the winner. Not surprisingly he was given the lowest handicap rating in Britain and was described by the punters' bible *Timeform* as "virtually unrideable". He was born with a silver spoon in his mouth but with lead weights in his hooves. His sire, College Chapel, was one of the leading sprinters of the early 1990s, while his dam, Pearl Dawn, was a prolific winner in England and Ireland. Born at stud in Newmarket in 2003, African Blues inherited all of their looks but none of their speed. Trained by Mark Hoad at Lewes, Sussex, he was sent off at 66-1 on his debut at Folkestone and lived down to expectations by veering right as he came out of the stalls and virtually refusing to race before being pulled up. A distant last in his next two races, he hinted at improvement in his fourth race at Brighton – at least in the eyes of his adoring owner, Jackie Taylor. "I thought he ran well that day," she said, seemingly oblivious to the fact that he fully justified his odds of 100-1 by trailing in last of 13, beaten by a staggering 65 lengths. After his sixth flop, African Blues was finally put out of his misery and retired. "I still believe he was better than he showed," insists Taylor. "I'm not sure whether he didn't want to race, or couldn't."

RUGBY TEAM CONCEDES 194 POINTS

Coventry Saracens rugby union team were thrashed 194-3 by Alcester in 2009 after taking the field with only eight players because of selection problems. Alcester ran in 32 tries and afterwards praised Coventry for their sporting spirit. Nevertheless Alcester's total was still well short of the score set by French Third Division side Lavardac against Vergt in 1984. Vergt were crushed 350-0, conceding no fewer than 66 tries, which were then valued at only four points each. However it seems that Vergt offered only minimal resistance to Lavardac in protest at having four players suspended. The previous week Vergt had been hammered 236-0 by Gujan Mestras in similar circumstances.

RUSSIAN WEIGHTLIFTER BREAKS SNATCH RECORD

A Russian woman set a new world record in 2009 by lifting a 14-kilogram glass ball with her vagina. Tatiata Kozhevnikova had been practising the little-known sport of vagina lifting for 15 years before becoming a world beater. Revealing how she first got into it she said: "After I had a child, my intimate muscles got unbelievably weak. I read books and learned that ancient women used to deal with this problem using wooden balls. I looked around, saw a glass ball and inserted it in my vagina. It took me ages to get it out!" For the uninitiated she went on to explain how the sport works. "You insert one of the balls in your vagina, and it has a string attached to it with a little hook at the very end. You fix a second ball onto this hook."

BAND LEADER ARRESTED AFTER FOOTBALL CLASH

A band leader was arrested in 2007 for refusing to stop playing at the end of an American football game between two rival high schools in Newport News, Virginia. Previous meetings between Phoebus and Hampton had ended in violent clashes between fans, so the police were anxious to get the 10,000 spectators out of the stadium quickly and efficiently, but officers were unable to communicate with each other over their walkie-talkies because of the noise from the rival school's marching band. The police said they asked the Hampton band director four times to stop playing and when he apparently failed to obey the request they arrested him on a charge of obstruction and hauled him away in handcuffs in front of his mystified musicians.

COUNTING LAPS NOT SO SIMPLE FOR SIMON

Spanish motorcycle rider Julian Simon threw away victory in the 2009 125cc Catalunya Grand Prix by celebrating his success a lap too soon. He was leading comfortably but as his trackside crew held out a sign indicating one lap to go, Simon, thinking the race was over, suddenly eased up on the gas and raised his hand in triumph. As he did so, a group of riders sped past him and his crew frantically waved for him to keep racing. A lap later, Simon trailed in a miserable fourth. "I should have known better," he admitted, "when I didn't see the chequered flag as I crossed the line."

TEMPER TANTRUM RESULTS IN HEAD WOUND

Russian tennis player Mikhail Youzhny was so upset with his play against Nicolas Almagro at the 2008 Sony Ericsson Open in Miami that he whacked himself on the head three times with his racket. Following the outburst, he needed a timeout because he had cracked his head open. Appropriately the incident occurred on April Fools' Day.

8

BAFFLED BY TECHNOLOGY

CITY THREATENS TO BAN "DANGEROUS" WATER

In 2004, an advisor to the Californian city of Aliso Viejo stumbled across a spoof scientific website that warned of the dangers of dihydrogen monoxide – a colourless, odourless substance known to be used as an industrial solvent and coolant, in nuclear plants, and even by a number of terrorist organizations. The site went on to warn the public about indicators of an overdose of dihydrogen monoxide – including neausea, vomiting, a bloated feeling and excessive urination – and added that dihydrogen monoxide can be deadly if accidentally inhaled. The advisor relayed these disturbing findings to the city council, blissfully unaware that dihydrogen monoxide was better known as H_2O or water. The city council was so concerned about the potentially dangerous properties of dihydrogen monoxide that it considered banning foam cups after learning that the chemical was used in their production. It went so far as to announce that foam cups were made with a substance that could "threaten human health and safety". When the hoax was finally revealed, there were red faces all round. "It's embarrassing," admitted the city manager. "We had a paralegal who did bad research."

THIEF HIDES PHONE UP HER BUTT

Romanian police caught a female cell phone thief by dialling the stolen phone – and hearing it ringing from her butt. Police in Iasi stopped the 24-year-old woman as she tried to get off a bus in 2005 after other passengers said they saw her steal a cell phone. But after a search failed to find the phone, police decided to call the number and heard a muffled ring tone coming from under the woman's dress. She was taken to a local police station where a strip search revealed she had hidden it up her bottom. A doctor extracted the phone and after being sprayed with disinfectant, it was handed back to its owner.

GPS SYSTEM STEERS MOTORIST INTO SUPERMARKET

An American tourist's trip through Bavaria in 2003 ended with an unexpected visit to the supermarket when his car's navigation system led him straight through the store's doors. The car only came to a stop when it crashed into a row of shelves. The driver, who was celebrating his 68th birthday, told police in Schwarzenbach that he had relied solely on the automatic navigation system as he did not know the area. He added that he hadn't noticed the doors of the supermarket looming before him until he had crashed through them.

TEXAS TOWN IS SOLD ON EBAY

The small, uninhabited town of Albert, Texas, was sold on eBay for $3 million in 2007. The online advert, which also offered the successful bidder the title of Mayor of Albert, boasted that the town was known for its "German heritage and laid-back attitude" and that its amenities included a schoolhouse, dance hall, bar, and tractor shed.

INTERNET LOVE SOURED BY BODY IN FREEZER

Yorkshireman Trevor Tasker announced that he had given up using the Internet after discovering that his new love was a pensioner with a corpse in the freezer. Tasker flew from England to South Carolina to meet Wynema Faye Shumate who had pretended to be in her 30s in the online chat room but was really 65. She had hooked him with sexy talk and by sending him a semi-naked photo taken 30 years earlier. Tasker's shock at the airport turned to horror when he learned that Shumate had put her dead housemate Jim O'Neil in the freezer after first chopping off one of his legs with an axe so that the door would shut properly. She had kept O'Neil, who had died of natural causes, in the freezer for a year while she lived in his house and spent his money. In 2001, Shumate pleaded guilty to fraud and the unlawful removal of a dead body and was sentenced to a year in prison. Back home in Selby, Tasker vowed: "I'll never log on again.

When I saw her picture I thought "Wow!" But when she met me at the airport I almost had a heart attack."

CELL PHONE FOUND INSIDE FISH

A businessman who lost his cell phone on a Sussex beach was amazed when it turned up a week later – in the belly of a giant cod. Andrew Cheatle thought he had seen the last of his phone after it slipped from his pocket and was swept out to sea but a week later he was shopping for a new phone with girlfriend Rita Smith when her mobile went off. "She said my old mobile number was calling her phone and when she answered it, she said some guy was going on about my phone and a cod. I thought he was winding me up but he assured me he had caught a cod that morning and was gutting it for his fish stall and that my Nokia was inside it." When Cheatle got his phone back from fisherman Glen Kerley, he found that it was still in good working order – if a bit smelly.

HI-TECH TOILET SWALLOWS WOMAN

A 51-year-old woman was subjected to a harrowing two-hour ordeal when she was imprisoned in a hi-tech public toilet. Maureen Shotton was captured by the maverick cyberloo during a shopping trip to Newcastle-upon-Tyne in 2001. The toilet, which boasted state-of-the-art electronic auto-flush and door sensors, steadfastly refused to release her and resisted all attempts of passers-by to force the door. She was finally freed when firefighters ripped the roof off the toilet.

JEALOUS HUSBAND ACCUSED OF SHOOTING WIFE'S COMPUTER

A man was accused of shooting his wife's computer after he caught her chatting to other men on MySpace. Jason Griffith, 23, of Scranton, Pennsylvania, allegedly fired a single bullet into her computer tower after an argument in the early hours of one morning in June 2007.

WOMAN INVENTS RAPID ORGASM GADGET

By connecting a sex toy to a vacuum cleaner, a Utah mother-of-three invented a device that can produce an orgasm in just ten seconds. Joanne

Drysdale was cleaning her carpets when she came up with the idea for Vortex Vibrations. She saw how a piece of rubber that had caught in the nozzle of her vacuum cleaner was gently resonating in the air flow. She said she also experienced a soft stimulation to her fingertips as she tried to remove the rubber. At the time she had not had sex for 15 years.

"ALIEN" SIGNALS CAME FROM MICROWAVE

Astronomers using a radio telescope at an Australian university believed they had discovered sensational evidence of alien life when they picked up a distinctive signal every evening around dinner time. They later realized that the signal was coming from the microwave oven downstairs.

GREAT WHITE EATS ANTI-SHARK DEVICE

An electronic device designed to ward sharks away from surfers failed so spectacularly during a trial off South Africa that it was eaten by a great white.

FUGITIVE FOUND THROUGH UPDATED FACEBOOK STATUS

After pleading guilty to assault as the result of a bar fight in Lockport, New York, Chris Crego failed to show up for sentencing. Police officers tracked him down six months later via his Facebook page which helpfully listed his address, the name of the Indiana tattoo parlour where he worked and even his working hours.

PAGERS ALARM BUSINESSMAN

A Ukrainian businessman who bought a pager for each member of his staff as a New Year's gift was so shocked when all 50 went off simultaneously on the back seat that he crashed his car into a lamp post. He was returning from the pager shop when the accident happened. After assessing the damage to his car, he looked to see what important message the pagers had to impart. It read: "Congratulations on a successful purchase!"

INVENTOR CONVERTS DEAD CATS INTO DIESEL

A German inventor has come up with a method of making cheap diesel fuel from dead cats. Dr Christian Koch says the corpse of an adult cat can produce 2.5 litres of fuel, which means that around 20 cats are needed for a full tank.

US DESIGNER INVENTS FAKE TESTICLES FOR CASTRATED DOGS

US DOG LOVERS are paying $400 on prosthetic testicles for their castrated pets. Invented by Gregg Miller, of Independence, Missouri, in 1992, "Neuticles" are implanted in the dogs' scrotums to make them appear "anatomically intact" and thereby avoid hurting the animals' male pride. Over 230,000 dogs — mostly owned by men — have been fitted with the fake testicles. ●

MAN SHOOTS SLOW-FLUSHING TOILET

Angry with a slow-flushing toilet at a restaurant, Raymond Cruz, from Schererville, Indiana, took out his gun and blew it to pieces in 1999.

VIGILANTE ROBOT PROWLS STREETS OF ATLANTA

Plagued by crime, an Atlanta, Georgia, bar owner has built a water pistol-wielding robot to patrol the streets. Rufus Terrill has devised the Bum Bot, a talking security guard with bright red lights, a spotlight, video camera and a water cannon on a spinning turret. Terrill claims that since its introduction in September 2007, the Bum Bot has already made his neighbourhood a safer place, although some residents said they found the red box with the menacing voice somewhat intimidating.

AUTHOR'S 13 YEARS OF WORK IS REDUCED TO SHREDS

At the end of 13 years writing a weighty tome about the Swedish economy, business consultant Ulf af Trolle finally took his 250-page manuscript to be copied. Alas it took only seconds for his life's work to be reduced to 50,000 strips of paper when an employee confused the copier with the shredder.

SLEEPING WOMAN SENDS EMAILS

In the first recorded case of its kind, a 44-year-old woman logged on to the Internet and sent three emails while sleepwalking. Researchers from the University of Toledo, Ohio, reported how, after going to bed at 10 p.m., the woman got up two hours later while still asleep. She then sleepwalked to the next room, turned on the computer, connected to the Internet, logged on to her email account by typing her username and password, and composed and sent three emails, asking friends over for drinks and caviar. It was only when a would-be guest phoned the next day to accept, that the woman realized what she had done.

MAN SELLS IMAGINARY FRIEND

A Welshman sold his imaginary friend for a reported $3,100 on eBay in 2007 after attracting 31 bids. His sales pitch read: "My imaginary friend Jon Malipieman is getting too old for me now. I am now 27 and I feel I am growing out of him. He is very friendly. Along with him, I will send you what he likes and dislikes, his favourite things to do and his personal self-portrait."

GERMAN INVENTION BARKS TOILET TRAINING ORDERS

In 2004, a German inventor came up with a device that berates men if they try to use the toilet standing up. It tells them: "Put the seat back down right away, you are definitely not to pee standing up."

VISITORS TO CRAWLEY RECEIVE RUDE WELCOME

Commuters driving to work in Crawley, West Sussex, were greeted by an obscene message one morning in 2006 after computer hackers had gained remote access to the council's digital roadside signs. Instead of giving information about parking availability in the town, the signs told visitors to "Fuck Off". A council spokesman said: "The hackers gained access to our computer at 6.45 a.m., but the first we knew of it was a phone call from a member of the public two hours later. Why they picked on Crawley, I have no idea. We apologize for any offence, but I think people realize this was not the work of the council."

CHEATING HUSBAND ACCIDENTALLY CALLS WIFE DURING SEX ROMP

An adulterous Finn pressed all the wrong buttons as he made love in a car, unwittingly prompting his cell phone to call home just in time for his wife to hear his mistress moan, "I love you". When her husband later arrived home, the wife attacked him with an axe.

CALIFORNIAN SHOOTS RELUCTANT LAWNMOWER

Francis Karnes of Sacramento, California, was charged with reckless endangerment after he pulled a gun and shot his lawnmower when it wouldn't start.

WOMAN TRIES TO PATENT HERSELF

Donna Rawlinson MacLean, a poet and casino waitress from Bristol, England, filed an application to patent herself in 2000. She insisted that she met all the requirements for a patent, including being useful and novel. She said: "It has taken me 30 years of hard labour for me to discover and invent myself, and now I wish to protect my invention from unauthorized exploitation, genetic or otherwise."

JUDGE JAILS HIS OWN STENOGRAPHER

A judge in Fort Lauderdale, Florida, jailed his own court stenographer in 2007 for working too slowly. Circuit Judge Charles Greene sent Ann Margaret Smith to prison for contempt of court because she had failed to finish a typescript needed for an appeal hearing.

HOTEL COUNTS COST OF ONE-CENT ROOM ERROR

A four-star hotel near Venice was left counting the cost in 2009 after its website mistakenly offered a romantic weekend in the Italian city for one cent. A night at the 151-room Crowne Plaza in Quarto D'Altino, 15 miles from Venice, usually costs up to $190. The cut-price offer, an error by the hotel group's head office in Atlanta, Georgia, only appeared for one night but in that short time the Crowne Plaza received bookings for the equivalent of 1,400 room nights. Sales manager Fulvio Danesin said the hotel, which was honouring the reservations, stood to lose over $100,000.

FRUSTRATED WIFE BECOMES COMPUTER HACKER

A woman became so angry at her husband chatting online to women until four o'clock in the morning that she literally became a computer hacker. The aptly named Kelli Michetti, of Grafton, Ohio, decided to put a stop to his antics by severing the computer's power cable with a meat cleaver. When that didn't work, she used the same implement to hack into his computer, bludgeoning the monitor while he tried to fend her off. She was fined $200 for domestic violence and resisting arrest.

AMERICA LAUNCHES ROBOT GIRLFRIEND

The world's first robot girlfriend was launched in Las Vegas in 2010 – a life-size rubber doll who can have sex with her owner and talk about football. The 5-foot 7-inch, dark-haired robot comes complete with artificial intelligence, flesh-like synthetic skin and five contrasting personalities. Wild Wendy is outgoing and adventurous, Frigid Farrah is reserved and shy, Mature Martha is matriarchal and caring, a young unnamed doll has a naïve personality, and S & M Susan caters for more adventurous types. Combined with her laptop, the doll costs up to $9,000 and is described by her inventor, New Jersey-based Douglas Hines, as "ready for action". He said the aim was to make the doll someone to whom the owner could talk and relate. "She can carry out simple conversations and knows exactly what you like. If you like football, she likes football. She can't vacuum, she can't cook but she can do almost anything else – if you know what I mean."

SATNAV DIRECTS WOMAN DRIVER ONTO RAILWAY TRACK

A 52-year-old driver ended up on a railway line in 2007 after following directions from her car's satellite navigation system. She was waiting at a level crossing in Pevensey, East Sussex, when the device told her to turn left, whereupon she drove her Ford Fiesta on to the track, blocking two lines. The woman explained to police that she turned on to the track "because my satnav device told me to".

HIDDEN SPY CAMERA TAKEN TO GARBAGE DUMP

A $20,000 spy camera that was concealed in a garbage bag with the intention of catching illegal tippers was accidentally thrown out by council workers. The expensive hi-tech camera was cunningly placed inside a black bag beside a notorious fly-tipping site in Chichester, West Sussex, but the disguise was so good that council workers took it to the dump in the belief that it was genuine garbage.

RESTING TRADER TRIGGERS BOND VALUE PLUNGE

A sudden nosedive in the value of French ten-year bond futures was sparked on 23 July 1998 by a London bank trader leaning absent-mindedly on his computer keyboard. In doing so, he accidentally pressed the "Instant Sell" button for a prolonged period.

ACTRESS CHARGED WITH HOLDING TECH SUPPORT MAN HOSTAGE

A Canadian actress/playwright was charged with holding a technical support man hostage after losing her Internet connection. With a deadline looming, Carol Sinclair, from Halifax, Nova Scotia, lost her connection with ISP Aliant and spent several frustrating days trying to get someone to fix the problem. "I was polite the first 20 times," she said. "But each one gave me the same routine: 'Is the modem connected? Are the lights blipping?' And then each one would say: 'It should be working. The problem must be with your computer.' I was a little stressed. I had six days to do a month's work." Eventually she resorted to impersonating a man's voice and got a repairman – 21-year-old David Scott – sent out the next day. When he said he couldn't fix the problem either, Sinclair allegedly told him that he was not leaving until her Internet was working and that she was taking him hostage. According to police, he made his getaway by claiming he needed to fetch a disk from his truck and then driving off. Denying the charges, Sinclair said: "He is a huge, strapping young man; I'm a Buddhist, a wimp, a pacifist."

"PRAYING" COUPLE WERE RECHARGING CELL PHONE

For more than a month in 2002, priests at a church in Milan observed a South American couple sitting attentively in front of a statue of the Virgin Mary for an hour at a time. Naturally the priests assumed the devout pair were seeking spiritual guidance until a cleaner noticed an electricity cable poking out from behind the statue. It turned out the couple had been recharging their cell phone from the electricity socket used to light up the statue.

WOMAN WINS ONLINE AUCTION TO SLAP STRANGER WITH FISH

British student Lucy Berry paid over $300 in 2006 for the privilege of slapping a complete stranger around the face with a wet fish. Inspired by the *Monty Python* fish-slapping dance, Ben Fillmore staged an auction on eBay to raise money for charity. As the successful bidder, 23-year-old Ms Berry was allowed to nominate the type of fish used in the slapping and chose two rainbow trout. Afterwards she described the experience as "extremely satisfying".

COMPUTER ORDERS CENTENARIAN TO START SCHOOL

A 105-year-old retired Swiss teacher was ordered to attend elementary school in 1998 after a computer cut a century off his age. The mix-up occurred because a list of residents in Echallens contained only the last two digits of their birth dates and so the pensioner, along with 65 five-year-olds in the town, received a letter telling him to start school. An apologetic town hall secretary said afterwards: "We have changed the computer programme in question."

MAGISTRATE'S MUSICAL TIE GOES OFF DURING SENTENCING

Just as he was passing sentence on an offender at court in Luton, Bedfordshire, in December 2000, magistrate Hector Graham's musical tie – an early Christmas present from his wife – launched into an impromptu version of "Santa Claus is Coming to Town". The red-faced magistrate explained that he did not know how to turn the tie off, which was unfortunate as it then went into two more Christmas songs, concluding with "We Wish You a Merry Christmas".

GIRL PUTS "MOANING" GRANDMOTHER ON EBAY

Ten-year-old Zoe Pemberton, from Clacton, Essex, put her "moaning" grandmother up for sale on eBay – and was offered $3,000 for her before the auction was halted. Zoe described grandma Marion Goodall as "rare and annoying and moaning a lot".

SUICIDE CALLERS ARE ASKED TO BE PATIENT

Nine out of ten Chinese people who called into a suicide prevention hotline during 2004 were greeted by an engaged signal.

GIRL, 3, BUYS $12,000 DIGGER ON THE INTERNET

While her parents were asleep, a three-year-old New Zealand girl bought a mechanical digger for $12,000 on an Internet auction site. Pipi Quinlan, from Auckland, logged onto the family computer and found the Trade Me auction site that her mother had been using earlier. She then submitted what turned out to be a winning bid for a giant earthmoving digger. The first her parents knew about the transaction was when they received a series of emails from Trade Me. Mother Sarah sighed: "Pipi doesn't even like tractors."

CONCERNED FATHER SELLS HAUNTED RUBBER DUCK

A supposedly possessed rubber duck was sold on eBay for $107.50 in 2004 after a man heard his 18-month-old son telling scary stories about fights he'd had with the duck. He also said the child had been bitten by the rubber duck.

WOMAN INVENTS COMPUTER BEAVER

Los Angeles artist and inventor Kasey McMahon has combined IT and taxidermy to create a computer housed in a dead beaver. She said: "I started thinking about the most ridiculous thing to put a computer into and decided it had to be a beaver."

PENSIONER CONFUSED BY ELECTRIC TOOTHBRUSH

An Isle of Wight pensioner who dialled the emergency services to report that someone was drilling a hole in the wall of her house had been confused by the noise of her electric toothbrush.

SCIENTISTS UNRAVEL MYSTERIES OF KNOTS

In a detailed 2007 paper, two scientists from the Department of Physics at the University of California in San Diego provided mathematical proof that hair, string or anything else of the kind will inevitably become tangled in knots – a process termed "spontaneous knotting of an agitated string". Dorian M. Rayner and Douglas E. Smith conducted 3,415 trials analyzing 120 different types of knot.

WORKER DIES IN QUEST FOR BETTER RECEPTION

Unable to get any reception on his cell phone, a 46-year-old construction worker in Custer County, South Dakota, persuaded his colleagues to raise him in a boom, 30 feet off the ground. But the boom's truck tipped over backwards, hurling the man to his death.

GERMANS KEEP WARM WITH INCONTINENCE PADS

An enterprising German power-plant chief discovered an alternative, environmentally friendly source of energy in the form of incontinence pads. Thomas Lesche, director of a Bremen incinerator plant, announced in 2003 that he had signed a pioneering deal with a local retirement home to buy up to 100 tons of used pads and soiled tissues each year. "The pollution emissions with used pads are far lower than with oil or coal," he said, adding proudly: "I do not know of any other plant in Europe that turns incontinence pads into energy."

WOMAN BLAMES GADGET FOR EXCESSIVE CLAPPING

In 1993, a New York appeals court rejected a claim brought by housewife Edna Hobbs against San Francisco company Joseph Enterprises, manufacturer of The Clapper, a sound-activated electrical switch. The complainant said that in trying to switch on the gadget, she had clapped her hands until they bled. The judge ruled that she hadn't adjusted the sensitivity controls properly.

"ALIEN" TRANSMISSION TURNS OUT TO BE RANDY RAM

For several days British intelligence analysts were mystified by strange high-frequency noises coming from one of their stations in Yorkshire. Staff at the Government Communications Headquarters said the 2003 transmission was unlike anything they had encountered before, leading them to believe it could be coming from spies or even aliens. Intriguingly, the signal only occurred during the day, and only Scarborough aerials could pick it up. Finally after extensive investigation, it was discovered that a ram in the Scarborough area had been rubbing its horns against the aerial masts in between servicing some local ewes. A GCHQ spokesman said: "It's possible the ram was attracted to the mast which may have given off some kind of tingling sensation, but it was probably just a post to rub against."

SPELL-CHECK CHANGES YEARBOOK NAMES

A computer spell-checker ran amok in 2008, giving several students at Middleton Area High School, Pennsylvania, interesting new names in the yearbook. As a result Max Zupanovic was listed as Max Supernova, Kathy Carbaugh appeared as Kathy Airbag and Alessandra Ippolito became Alexandria Impolite.

REAL WORM CAUSES COMPUTER TO CRASH

When Mark Taylor's computer crashed, he feared he had a worm virus in the system, but a technician who was called out to investigate discovered that the problem was caused by an actual earthworm. The five-inch worm had crawled through an air vent of the house in Yeovil, Somerset, and wrapped itself around the laptop's internal fan. By the time the worm was found, it had been burned to a frazzle by the overheating workings of the computer. Taylor said: "I couldn't help thinking that people get computer worms all the time, but not real life ones. So at least I was different."

PORN-SURFING CLERGYMAN QUITS THE CHURCH

A Swedish clergyman resigned after picking up a virus from a hardcore porn website – and crippling the entire church computer network. Father Gunnar Svensson, from Strangnas, was exposed when technicians trying to repair the breakdown discovered he had filled the hard drive of the computer with thousands of visits to extreme pornography sites. A Church of Sweden member said: "He'd picked up a lethal computer virus which then infected every other PC linked to the same system. Then they found thousands of visits to very unpleasant websites."

DEVICE TRAPS CHEATING WIVES

In 2001, Romanian inventor Vasile Prisca developed a cell phone to help married men trap unfaithful wives by sending a text message whenever anyone heavier than the wife got into the marital bed. Prisca even had the benefit of first-hand testimony to prove that his invention worked. He explained proudly: "I caught my wife in bed with my neighbour by using the device."

SATNAV SENDS TRUCK DRIVER TO WRONG COUNTRY

A Syrian truck driver transporting luxury cars from Turkey to Gibraltar on the southern tip of Spain was sent on a 1,600-mile detour to England by his satellite navigation system. Birdwatchers at Gibraltar Point in Lincolnshire looked on in astonishment as Necdet Bakimci tried to steer his 32-tonne truck down a narrow country lane towards the North Sea. When questioned by onlookers, he explained in broken English that he was looking for Gibraltar. It is thought the confusion arose because his device had Gibraltar listed as UK territory and so directed him towards Britain.

CRYONICS FOUNDERS CREMATED AFTER FREEZER MISHAP

Two French founders of the cryonics movement – whose members are frozen after death in the hope that modern science might one day revive them – had their dreams shattered in 2006 when they had to be cremated following a freezer mishap. Raymond Martinot, who died in 2002, firmly believed that if he was frozen, scientists would be able to bring him back to life by 2050. Accordingly the bodies of Dr Martinot and his wife Monique, who had died in 1984, were carefully stored in a freezer in their Loire Valley chateau . . . until their son Rémy discovered that the freezer had broken down and was left with no choice but to have his pioneering parents cremated instead.

9

LAW AND DISORDER

SUSPECT APPREHENDED AFTER FALSE LEG FALLS OFF

A man who allegedly tried to steal a cash machine was captured after his prosthetic leg fell off during the getaway. Gregory Daniels, 48, was arrested on suspicion of burglary at Pomona Ranch Market, California. As police officers pursued the getaway truck into a cul-de-sac, one man jumped from the truck and ran away but as Daniels hit the ground his artificial leg fell off. The police sergeant stated: "Daniels was on the ground near the vehicle in an attempt to flee from officers. However, he was unsuccessful as his prosthetic leg fell off."

BANANA ROBBER TRIES TO EAT HIS WEAPON

A teenage robbery suspect who was overpowered as he tried to hold up a North Carolina store with a banana tried in vain to eat the incriminating weapon before police arrived. Forsyth County police said 17-year-old John Szwalla held the banana under his shirt when he entered the store in 2009, saying he had a gun and demanding money. But the store owner and a customer jumped Szwalla and held him until deputies turned up. While they waited, Szwalla allegedly ate the banana but was unable to swallow the peel, which was subsequently photographed by the police as evidence. He was charged with attempted armed robbery and faced a possible additional count of destroying evidence.

CARDBOARD CUTOUT KEEPS 30 POLICE OFFICERS AT BAY

Armed police finally ended a 90-minute siege at a bank in New Jersey, only to discover that they had been involved in a tense stand-off with a cardboard cutout. Thirty officers – including SWAT team members from three different towns – raced to the PNC Bank in Montgomery Township after an alarm went off one evening in November 2008. They arrived to find the blinds drawn but, seeing the silhouette of a person in the window of the bank, they immediately sealed off the area and evacuated nearby buildings. For the next hour and a half, trained negotiators used bullhorns and telephones in a series of fruitless attempts to make contact with the shadowy figure. Fearing that time was running out, they eventually decided to send in the crack SWAT team . . . who discovered that the suspected bank robber was merely a life-sized female cardboard cutout that had previously been used in a bank promotion.

POST OFFICE ROBBERS MISTAKE FRIDGE FOR SAFE

A gang of three robbers who travelled some 200 miles from Manchester to Taunton, Somerset, to commit a Post Office robbery stole only $4,000 of the $116,000 on the premises because they mistook a fridge for a safe. The trio were masked and armed with hammers as they burst in and vaulted the counter. After scooping bank notes from an open cash drawer, one of the robbers, pointing at a fridge, ordered the postmaster to open the safe. "It isn't a safe, it's a fridge," said the postmaster. Confused, the gang ran off with their meagre haul and were arrested soon afterwards.

BOGUS LAWYERS BLOW THEIR COVER

Two bogus lawyers representing an assault suspect in a South African court in 2002 neglected to brush up on the basics. Their cover was blown when they called the magistrate "Your Majesty" instead of "Your honour" and when one of them asked what the term "previous convictions" meant. They were promptly arrested and instructed to find genuine lawyers to represent them at their own trial.

ARMED ROBBER ASKS FOR HUG

An armed robber held up a barbecue dinner party in Washington, DC, in 2007 before suddenly changing his mind and asking for a hug instead. The hooded man crept in through an open gate, put a handgun to the head of a 14-year-old guest and demanded money, but when one of the other guests coolly offered him a glass of wine, the robber readily accepted. After also taking a bite of cheese, the robber tucked the gun into his pants, apologized for the intrusion and asked for a group hug. He then walked off, wine glass in hand. Describing the case as "unusual", a police spokeswoman said of the hug: "They should have squeezed him and held onto him for us."

SUSPECT APPEARS IN COURT DRESSED AS A COW

A woman from Middletown, Ohio, was charged in 2008 with chasing children around a theme park, urinating on a neighbour's front garden and blocking traffic – all while wearing a cow costume. Michelle Allen, 32, had been hired to wear the outfit to advertise a haunted trail at the theme park but she left the job to embark on a two-day drinking binge. Arrested for causing chaos in the streets, she had to have her police photo taken while still wearing the bovine costume as she had no change of clothes. Detained in custody, she showed few signs of remorse and instead shouted at other inmates to "suck my udders". She even had to go to court wearing the cow outfit, prompting Judge Mark Wall to comment: "We get people dressed in various attire when they're in court. But this was a first, someone dressed as a cow."

PASSERS-BY ARE MUGGED BY WINNIE THE POOH

Two people in Tokyo were attacked and robbed in 2008 by a man dressed as Winnie the Pooh, because they had stared at his costume. Masayuki Ishikawa was hanging around on a street corner dressed as the honey-loving bear, accompanied by two friends dressed as a mouse and a panther, when he apparently took offence at two passers-by staring at him. Police said that the bear, mouse and panther then beat up the victims and stole $160 from them. The trio had apparently dressed as animals because they had run out of clean clothes.

ESCAPED PRISONER TRIES TO GET CREDIT FOR TIME ON THE RUN

A man who escaped from prison and was recaptured after nearly ten years on the run asked to be released immediately on the grounds that his original sentence would already have been completed. Timothy Marshall was convicted in 1985 of trafficking cocaine and was sentenced to 15 years in jail, but two years later he escaped and remained at large until 1997 when he was put back behind bars. Representing himself, Marshall complained that the state of Florida was wrongfully refusing to give him credit for the nine years, four months that he remained at large following his escape. Unsurprisingly perhaps, Judge Gary M. Farmer denied Marshall's request, adding: "This petition may take the prize for chutzpah."

ITALIAN ROBBER TAKES SHOP DUMMY HOSTAGE

A crook in Rome was arrested after taking a shop dummy hostage. The gun-wielding robber threatened to shoot the mannequin if the police tried to stop his getaway. A police spokesman said: "He was either blind as a bat, dumb or both."

HOPELESS THIEF STEALS BAGS OF DOG POOP

A thief in Frisco, Texas, stole two sealed plastic bags from a parked pickup truck, only to find that they contained 25 pounds of dog poop. Clearly the thief was expecting the contents to be considerably more valuable – even though the side of the truck was clearly marked with the words "We scoop poop." The owner of the pet waste-removal company smiled: "I sure wish I could have been there when he opened the bags."

FLEEING SHOPLIFTER FORGETS SON

A shoplifter planning a quick getaway from a Dutch supermarket after stealing a packet of meat left behind a crucial piece of evidence – his 12-year-old son. In his haste to get to his car, the thief forgot all about the boy who happily furnished police with his father's details.

LOBSTER THIEF TAKES HUMAN EYES BY MISTAKE

A thief who stole a plastic foam package from a bus station in Boston, Massachusetts, in 2000 thinking it contained lobsters got the shock of his life when he opened it and found that instead it housed two human corneas. The suspect was arrested in possession of his haul, which, packed in ice, had been donated ready for transplant. Detective Jeff Megin said: "I think it was just a crime of opportunity. I don't believe he's involved in any type of stolen human body part ring. He thought they were lobsters."

SCHOOLBOYS MAKE UNIFORM ERROR

A group of six Australian schoolboys from Toowoomba, Queensland, went to great lengths to produce fake driving licences of impressive quality to enable them to obtain underage entry into pubs and clubs. Sadly they forgot to change out of their school uniforms for the photos.

ROBBER THREATENS STORE STAFF WITH GOOSE

A man walked into a doughnut shop in Toronto, Canada, in 1997 holding a Canada goose and yelling: "Give me some money or I'll kill the goose!" A bird-loving customer went to a bank machine, drew out some cash and handed it over to the robber who immediately freed the goose and fled.

POLICE IN DARK AFTER LAMP POSTS STOLEN

Police in Egypt were hoping to shed light on the theft of 400 street lamps worth almost one million dollars. The lamp posts were stolen from a motorway outside the city of Alexandria where they were waiting to be installed.

ESCAPED CONVICTS EVADE POLICE BY DRESSING AS SHEEP

According to reports from Argentina, two convicts who escaped from jail in 2010 pulled the wool over the eyes of the police by disguising themselves as sheep. Maximiliano Pereyra and Ariel Diaz, who were serving time for robbery, are said to have dressed in full sheepskin fleeces with realistic looking heads and hidden in fields among flocks of genuine sheep. Although local people reported seeing the pair running through the fields at night, the disguises, stolen from a ranch, were good enough to fool the 300 officers who were searching for the fugitives. One farmworker said: "They were wearing grey clothes but had full sheepskins, including the sheep heads, over their heads and backs." A police spokesman lamented that identifying the two among thousands of other sheep was "almost impossible".

DEAD MEN DON'T COUNT

Ticketed for driving alone in the carpool lane, an Orange County, California, man protested that the four frozen cadavers in the mortuary van he was driving should count. However the judge ruled that passengers had to be alive to qualify.

ALL THAT GLITTERS IS NOT BRIGHT

In the act of robbing a store, a thief in Germany had a can of glitter sprayed into his face by a clerk and in the confusion left his wallet behind as he fled. He was later arrested for attempted robbery when he walked into a police station, still covered in glitter spray, to report that his wallet had been stolen.

ROBBER RETURNS FOR COFFEE

A man was arrested for robbing a Starbucks in Boulder, Colorado – when he returned two days later for a coffee. He was wearing the same distinctive outfit of yellow gloves, red backpack and wire-rimmed glasses that he allegedly wore during the 2008 robbery.

CRIMINALS LURED OUT OF HIDING BY PARTY INVITE

Police in Kimberley, South Africa, came up with a novel idea to flush out their most wanted criminals in 2005 – by inviting them to a party. They sent a VIP party invite, complete with the promise of celebrity guests, entertainment from a local DJ and a guaranteed prize, to the last known addresses of nearly 200 offenders. The party plan – dubbed Operation Nice Surprise – was enough to tempt 20 seasoned criminals who were stunned to be arrested as soon as the prizes had been handed out.

ROBBERY SUSPECT OBJECTS TO VICTIM'S DESCRIPTION

A convenience store clerk in Des Moines, Iowa, received unexpected assistance as he tried to tell police about the man who had just robbed the place. "He's about five foot ten," Harpal Singh told police over the phone. At that moment the suspect, returning to the scene of the crime, spoke up to correct him, saying: "I'm six-two." "About six-two," Singh clarified to the police, "and about 38 years old." "I'm 34," protested the suspect who then asked for the return of his wallet, which he had dropped in the store while making his escape with a haul of cigarettes. Seconds later, a deputy sheriff arrived and arrested 34-year-old, 6-foot 2-inch Steven Hebron on a charge of second-degree robbery.

BROKEN LEG SLOWS ROBBER'S ESCAPE

Police in Brockton, Massachusetts, charged a man with holding up a coffee shop in 2001 and then fleeing with the cash register. Two customers gave chase and quickly caught him, because he was slowed not only by the weight of the register but also by the plaster cast he was wearing as the result of a broken leg.

NEVADA COP ARRESTS WIFE

An off-duty sheriff's deputy from Elko County, Nevada, was arrested for drink driving in 2007 after being pulled over by her husband, also a sheriff's deputy. Mike Moore stopped wife Charlotte for a traffic violation and then called for back-up after she allegedly drove off without giving a breath test.

JUDGE CONSULTED IMAGINARY MYSTIC DWARVES

A Filipino judge who said he regularly consulted three invisible mystic dwarves was forced to quit his job in 2006. Florentino Floro said he possessed psychic vision, had the power to be in two places at the same time, and conducted healing sessions in his chambers during breaks with the help of the trio of dwarves – Armand, Luis and Angel. He also proclaimed himself to be the angel of death. The Supreme Court ruled that Floro was mentally unfit to continue as a judge, adding that it was concerned that dalliance with dwarves might gradually erode the public's confidence in the judiciary.

BURGLAR LEAVES BEHIND X-RAYS

A burglar who stole over $30,000 from a pensioner in Berlin, Germany, was arrested shortly afterwards because he had left his hospital X-rays in her apartment.

BANK ROBBER HAS "ONE OF THOSE DAYS"

Having already served a 20-year sentence for a bank robbery he committed in 1963, Edward Blaine might have been expected to take great care to ensure that any future heists went according to plan. But police said the 61-year-old suffered renewed anguish in 2003 after robbing a bank in Port Royal, Virginia. They claimed that as he fled, he dropped $100 bills in his wake and then on reaching his getaway car, he realized that he had left his keys inside. So he grabbed a large lump of wood to smash the window, but merely succeeded in drawing attention to himself. The owner and employer of an auto body shop where he had parked the car – blocking one of the bays – immediately gave chase as Blaine abandoned the vehicle and tried to escape on foot. When the two men caught him, Blaine allegedly attempted to shoot them but couldn't get his gun out of his coat and shot himself in the leg. For good measure, one of the men then also shot Blaine, hitting him in the same leg. "He had one of those days," said a police detective.

CAT BANNED FROM VISITING BUDDHIST PRISONER

A Buddhist bank robber had a request for his cat to visit him in jail turned down by a German court in 2009 despite his plea that it is the reincarnation of his mother. Peter Keonig, who was serving five years for armed robberies, demanded that his cat Gisela be allowed to visit him in jail "because she is my dead mum". He went on: "I know it is my mummy. She looks after me just the way she did. I need to see her like other prisoners see their wives and children." The court was not impressed, ruling: "The accused has not been able to furnish proof that his deceased mother has been reborn in a cat." However it did say that he would be allowed to write to the cat.

DRUNKEN JUDGE CALLS LAWYER A "FUCKWIT"

A drunken judge was thrown out of a courtroom in 2007 after she forcibly kissed a solicitor and swore at a prosecuting lawyer. Esther Cunningham, from Grantham, Lincolnshire, drank brandy before appearing in court as a solicitor to represent her cousin in a dangerous dog case, but decidedly the worse for wear, she told an usher to "fuck off" and called the Crown Prosecution Service lawyer "a fuckwit". She was suspended for six months after the Solicitors' Disciplinary Tribunal heard that she had also been drunk when teaching students on a legal course.

OFFICERS PROBE PRISONER'S RECTAL STASH

Determined to get to the bottom of how a prisoner managed to smuggle a whole array of goods into jail in 2010, police in Wenatchee, Washington State, found that he had hidden them up his rectum. Although an initial strip search revealed nothing, when a prison official later discovered a plastic bag and duct tape in the toilet, the prisoner was quizzed again and eventually handed over the contraband. It consisted of a cigarette lighter, cigarette papers, a bag of tobacco the size of a golf ball, a bottle of tattoo ink, eight tattoo needles, a small bag of what was thought to be marijuana, and an inch-long smoking pipe. A Wenatchee Police Department spokesman said: "We were all wondering: 'How do you put all that up there?' The tobacco was pretty impressive; it was a good ounce."

MUGGER LICKS VICTIM'S TOES BEFORE MAKING GETAWAY

A mugger in St Paul, Minnesota, paused to lick his victim's toes before making his escape. After robbing the 24-year-old woman of her keys and phone, Carlton Davis removed her shoes and licked her toes before fleeing. He was arrested four blocks away and put on probation for five years.

MAN TRIES TO ROB BANK WITH SPOON

A **MAN BURST** into a bank in Lublin, Poland, in 2009 brandishing a spoon and shouting: "This is a stick up." Staff and customers instinctively threw themselves to the floor until they realized his only weapon was an item of stainless steel cutlery. The robber was thus forced to flee empty-handed with the laughter of his intended victims ringing in his ears. ●

MAN ROBS POST OFFICE WEARING CHICKEN SUIT

A man tried to rob a Post Office in Kalmar, Sweden, in 1998 dressed in a chicken suit. Police said the robber, disguised in a yellow chicken outfit and brandishing a baseball bat, fled empty-handed but only after smashing windows and terrifying the female cashier. A police spokesman said: "She's now psychologically disturbed by the event and undergoing treatment."

"BURGLAR CHOSE BLIND MAN AS LOOKOUT"

According to police, when Kenneth Bartelson needed a reliable lookout while he burgled an apartment in Pawtucket, Rhode Island, he chose his legally blind brother. Eugene Allen could only see shadows and black and white, and not only did he fail to spot the arrival of police officers but he also confided details of the crime to the victims' neighbour, thinking it was Bartelson.

HANDCUFFED ESCAPEES SMASH INTO LAMPPOST

In a scene straight out of a Laurel and Hardy movie, two prisoners who were handcuffed together as they fled from a courthouse made the mistake of running to opposite sides of a lamppost, as a result of which they slammed into each other and fell to the ground. Regan Reti and Tiranara White made their unsuccessful bid for freedom from Hastings District Court on New Zealand's North Island in 2009, seemingly forgetting that they were joined at the wrist. They were re-captured by jailers as they struggled to their feet after their encounter with the lamppost.

EYEGLASSES OBSESSIVE CHARGED WITH OPTICIAN ROBBERIES

A man charged with a series of armed robberies on opticians in Milwaukee, Wisconsin, told police that he committed the crimes because he really likes eyeglasses. Detectives said Jerry Lowery would demand that opticians fill bags with designer glasses frames from the likes of Prada and Gucci. He would then wear the frames, look at himself in the mirror, and then either sell them, give them away or throw them out. He never tried to steal money from the opticians. Lowery reportedly turned himself in to police in 2009 after his latest robbery ended in failure when the optician punched him in the face. He told officers that he'd had issues with glasses for 15 years.

SPEEDING DRIVERS MADE TO HOP LIKE FROGS

Truck drivers caught speeding in an Indian state in 2005 were made to hop like frogs while chanting the name of their favourite political leader. Instead of taking offenders to court, police in Bihar made drivers sit on their haunches, hold their ears and hop for almost half a mile.

FORGETFUL THIEVES WRECK ESCAPE ROUTE

Industrial thieves broke into a plant in Canasta, Washington State, by crossing a metal catwalk. They then blew it up, forgetting that it was their only means of escape.

ARMED ROBBER ABANDONS HEIST FOR CUP OF TEA

When a robber wearing a Spiderman mask burst into a supermarket in Cesky Tesin in the Czech Republic, pulled out a gun and demanded money, he was taken aback by the reaction of 59-year-old shop assistant Marketa Vachova. For she decided that, beneath the mask, he was "a nice young man" and set about talking him out of the raid. She said: "I asked him why he was doing this and we got talking. There was no one else in the shop so I guess he relaxed a bit, and in the end he apologized. I said if he wanted he could come and talk to me and have a cup of tea and slice of homemade cake to talk about his problems. He agreed and then walked off."

BREATHING CORPSE ALERTS POLICE

A burglar who broke into a funeral home in the Spanish town of Burjassot tried to fool police by playing dead, only to be given away by two things. First, he was wearing scruffy clothes instead of the Sunday best that is traditional for the dearly departed, and second he was breathing heavily.

TEEN ARRESTED FOR TOSSING DEAD FISH AT PASSING CAR

A 15-year-old boy was charged with disorderly conduct after throwing a dead fish onto the windshield of a passing car on a remote stretch of road in New Jersey. Police said: "It's not immediately clear how the motorist reacted when the flying fish bounced across his car, but it's a safe bet that his first words were not 'Holy mackerel!'"

UNDERPANTS IN MISTAKEN IDENTITY CLAIM

After Leonard Hodge, of Madison, Wisconsin, was arrested in 1996 for failing to carry a driving licence, police officers found cocaine in his underwear during a routine search. By way of defence, Hodge claimed that the underpants he was wearing weren't his.

STREAKERS CATCH A COLD

Three men who streaked through a restaurant in Washington, DC, were left shivering in a car park in temperatures of minus seven degrees Fahrenheit. In their absence, a thief had stolen their car, which contained all their clothes.

GERMAN POLICE IN BROTHEL BRAWL

Three off-duty German police officers were arrested in 2009 for being involved in a fight in a Frankfurt brothel. The trio, who were detained after an argument with the brothel's bouncers turned violent, had ended up in the city's red-light district after an office party.

JUDGE SUES DRY CLEANER FOR $67 MILLION OVER LOST PANTS

Claiming that a pair of his suit trousers had gone missing from a Washington, DC, dry cleaner, Judge Roy L. Pearson sued Custom Cleaners for $67 million in 2005. Even though, as part of a $1,100 suit, the pants were worth just $395, Pearson sued Soo and Jin Chung for each day that the pants were missing, because their store promised "same-day service". The cleaners, who denied losing the pants, were so intimidated by the judge's lawsuit that they offered him $12,000 but he rejected the offer, although he did reduce his demands to a more reasonable $54 million. Insisting that it was not merely a case about a pair of suit pants but about the cleaner's claim of "satisfaction guaranteed" that hung in the store window, Pearson took the case to trial in 2007. There, he tearfully testified about the mental anguish he had suffered over the loss of the pants, which he had altered after gaining weight while unemployed prior to becoming an administrative judge. Not only did he lose the case, but a panel recommended against giving him a ten-year term on the bench, noting a lack of "judicial temperament". As one commentator observed: "Kissing his $100,512 salary goodbye, Pearson not only lost his pants, but his shirt."

ROBBER BURNS FACE IN BALACLAVA PALAVER

Bursting into a gas station in Foster, Rhode Island, two armed robbers sprayed a clerk in the face with pepper gas and snatched $157 from the cash register. Only then did they remember to put on ski masks, although one forgot to take the cigarette out of his mouth first and burned his face. The pair were easily identified on the store's security camera.

CUSTOMS OFFICERS SEIZE CIGARETTES FILLED WITH RABBIT POOP

Customs officials in Spain confiscated more than $1.5 million worth of counterfeit cigarettes that had been filled with rabbit droppings instead of tobacco. The fake cigarettes – due to be sold on the black market as famous brands – were discovered after British holidaymakers in the Canary Islands smelled a rat whenever they lit up. Following the arrest of a dozen smugglers, a customs official in Tenerife said: "The cigarettes stank. They smell just as you'd imagine burning poop to smell."

FAKE APE STEALS FAKE BANANAS

A thief wearing an ape costume burst into a petrol station in Fond du Lac, Wisconsin, in 2009 and stole a bunch of Styrofoam bananas that were on display. Police revealed that it was the third time in two nights that someone wearing an ape costume had tried to steal bananas.

HALFWITS CALL TAXI AS THEIR GETAWAY VEHICLE

Two New Zealand burglars broke into a tobacconist's shop in 2001 and then called for a taxi to collect them. Unfortunately they rather drew attention to themselves by waiting outside the shop they had just robbed, their arms laden with cigarettes and tobacco, while waiting for the taxi to arrive. After the taxi driver had alerted the police, the judge at their trial called it "the most spectacularly incompetent burglary I have heard of". Even one of the culprits was forced to concur. "The judge is not wrong in saying we are halfwits. We must be the most useless and stupid burglars New Zealand has ever had."

"DOZY VISITOR REVEALED HIDDEN DRUGS"

Having gone to the sheriff's station at LaPorte, Indiana, to bail out a friend, Edward Green ended up being arrested himself. Told to take a seat while officers sorted out the paperwork, Green promptly fell asleep, snoring loudly with his mouth open. When a deputy went to wake him, he said he couldn't help noticing several small plastic bags inside Green's gaping mouth. The bags were found to contain cocaine and Green was arrested on a count of possession.

JUDGE SACKED OVER BUM RAP

A Mexican judge was fired in 2010 for trying to punish a teenage graffiti artist by spray-painting his buttocks. Instead of imposing a standard fine, the civilian judge ordered the young artist to pull down his pants before attempting to spray his buttocks with the same paint the boy had used during his crimes.

MAN RILED BY MARS BARS AND NEW JERSEY

Thomas Mitchell was convicted of shooting his girlfriend three times in 1999 because he thought she was going to say "New Jersey". His trial at Galveston, Texas, heard that Mitchell suffered from an irrational hatred of the sound of certain words, including "Mars Bars", "Wisconsin", "Snickers" and "New Jersey". To avoid speaking those words out loud during the trial, witnesses were supplied with flashcards. At a pre-trial hearing, Mitchell had reportedly screamed and sworn on catching sight of the "Snickers" card.

ITALIAN ROBBERS ARGUE OVER THEIR ROLES

Three men in Italy planned to rob a postal worker in 2002 using a toy gun. But they were apprehended after they attracted attention by getting into a fight with each other on the street because none of them wanted to be the lookout man.

DEFENDANT APPEARS IN COURT "BUTT NAKED"

When defendant Jeremiah Johnson appeared in court in Polk County, Florida, in 1994, he showed up wearing a pair of shorts. The bailiff informed him that shorts were inappropriate attire to wear before the judge, so Johnson walked out, took them off and returned butt naked. The judge was not amused and gave him 179 days in jail for contempt of court.

DEFENDANT INCRIMINATES HIMSELF

At Dennis Newton's trial for armed robbery in Oklahoma City in 1985, the District Attorney asked the supervisor of the store that had been robbed to identify the culprit in court. When she pointed to the defendant, Newton leaped to his feet, accused the witness of lying and screamed: "I should have blown your fucking head off!" Following a moment of stunned silence, he added as an afterthought: "If I'd been the one that was there." He was jailed for 30 years.

TEXAN PRISONERS PRETTY IN PINK

In a bid to deter repeat offenders, a Texan prison was painted pink and inmates were forced to wear pink jumpsuits and pink slippers. Sheriff Clint Low reported that re-offending was down by 70 per cent at Mason County Jail since he introduced the colour change – because no prisoner wants to be seen in pink.

DRUGS RAID OFFICERS GET STUCK IN ELEVATOR

To launch a surprise drugs raid on a high-rise flat in Coventry, England, nine police officers climbed into the apartment block's elevator . . . and failed to see the notice that read: "Maximum Load 8 Persons." Unable to take the extra weight, the elevator broke down and the clueless cops were trapped inside for 45 minutes until a resident, hearing their pleas for help, volunteered to fetch the police. "We *are* the bloody police," came a cry from inside the elevator. "Get the fire brigade!"

"HOOKER" IS CHIEF INSPECTOR IN DRAG

Italian vice police arrested a high-heeled blonde soliciting in a Milan street in 1996, only to discover that "she" was their own male chief inspector in drag.

CANADIAN CROOKS MAKE MAMMOTH ERROR

Two Canadian burglars didn't think things through properly when they tried to sell a prehistoric mammoth tusk to the company that had supplied it in the first place. The thieves stole the 30,000-year-old ivory tusk from a gallery in Banff, Alberta, and then took it to experts in Calgary, demanding $40,000 for the relic and claiming that they had inherited it. However they chose the very dealership that had sold the tusk to the gallery. As one detective on the case noted: "These guys were very, very stupid. I mean, a piece like this isn't jewellery. It's very hard to sell."

ELDERLY SUSPECT GIVES OFFICER A NASTY SUCK

Trying to resist arrest after allegedly stealing a shirt from a shop in Braunschweig, Germany, in 2006, a 70-year-old shoplifting suspect went to bite a police officer, only to realize that he had left his false teeth at home. Instead he was only able to leave a wet mark from his gums on the officer's arms.

POLICE DRAG MAN FROM TOILET WASTE TANK

A 45-year-old man was arrested in 2005 after a teenage girl saw him staring up at her from a cesspit below a toilet seat at a beauty spot in Albany, New Hampshire. Firefighters had to hose down the man, who was wearing waders, before police handcuffed him.

CAR THIEF FOILED BY LACK OF ENGINE

A man broke into a Volkswagen car at a garage in Langenzenn, Germany, in 2008 and spent half an hour trying to hotwire the vehicle without realizing the engine had been removed for repairs.

ROBBER LOCKS HIMSELF IN TRUNK OF GETAWAY CAR

Wanting to make a quick change of clothing after pulling off a bank robbery in Hermiston, Oregon, a man climbed into the trunk of his getaway car . . . but accidentally locked himself in. Forty minutes later, a police officer was walking through a parking lot two blocks from the bank when he heard pounding from inside a car trunk and a voice pleading for help. He opened the trunk and promptly arrested the occupant. As a detective on the case noted: "Having carried out the robbery, the guy was probably hoping that his cries for help would be answered by someone other than a police officer."

BURGLAR COLLARED BY OWN DOG

A burglar was arrested after he left his pet dog at the scene of a crime – and it led police straight to him. Accompanied by his dog Roxy, Stephen Wilson broke into a house in Dewsbury, West Yorkshire, in 2002 but when owners Derek and Rita Lewis returned unexpectedly, he abandoned the dog and escaped through a window. When police officers arrived, they put Roxy on a lead and the dog took them to Wilson's home 200 yards down the road. After Wilson was jailed for 21 months, Mr Lewis said: "He should have left the dog at home. It wasn't his best friend that night."

ROBBER MAKES CATALOGUE OF ERRORS

A crook who decided to rob a Port St Lucie, Florida, houseowner at 1 a.m. one night in 2001 devised what he thought was a foolproof plan: he would gain entry by asking if he could use the phone and then he would surprise the occupant. His first mistake was to choose the home of retired Sheriff C.L. Norvell. Once inside he stuck to his plan and, in order to appear plausible, made the phone call. His second mistake was to call his own home. Then it was time for the robbery, only for the master criminal to run off as soon as Sheriff Norvell pulled out his gun. However any hopes he had of evading justice were wrecked when his girlfriend, who had answered his call to home, rang back, using the number that she saw on the caller ID box, thereby kindly providing Sheriff Norvell with the would-be robber's home telephone number.

SUSPECT CLAIMS ALIENS DROPPED HIM AT BURGLED HOUSE

Charged with burgling a house in Des Moines, Iowa, in 2000, Brian Waddington came up with an ingenious alibi – he said aliens must have picked him up 170 miles away in Davenport and dropped him off at the stranger's house. Although the case against Waddington appeared strong, detectives were taking no chances. One said: "I can assure you that if we do find any aliens, we'll drop the charges."

OFFICER RESCUED AFTER BURGLARY FIASCO

A police officer had to be rescued by an Oxford University porter after he climbed into a locked compound at Trinity College to confront a burglar he saw illuminated by the moonlight. To add to the officer's woes, the "burglar" turned out to be a statue.

ESCAPED PRISONER FLAGS DOWN POLICE BUS

After making a daring break for freedom from a police cell in Belo Horizonte, Brazil, in 2002, Sergio Vilas Boas flagged down a bus, only to find that it was full of policemen who had been sent out to look for him.

THIEF STEALS LOBSTER FROM AQUARIUM

A man was arrested in 1994 after being seen walking out of an aquarium at Seaside, Oregon, with a 25-pound lobster named Victor under his arm. The aquarium manager gave chase and eventually caught the culprit. "It wasn't too difficult to spot the guy," he said. "He was the only person about with a lobster under his arm."

TRAFFIC LIGHT THIEVES CAUGHT RED-HANDED

Two men were arrested in Buenos Aires in 2005 for stealing traffic lights from one of the Argentinean capital's busiest junctions. On further investigation police officers found another four sets of traffic lights that the pair had stolen from other streets. A police spokesman said: "We still haven't really understood why they wanted all those traffic lights."

INCRIMINATING DNA ADDS INSULT TO INJURY

Charles Edward Jones robbed a Miami bank in 2002 but it all went wrong for him as he made his getaway. First, in stuffing his gun into his waistband, he succeeded in shooting himself in the pants and then he was hit by a school lunch van, the impact knocking two gold teeth from his mouth. The DNA from these teeth led to his subsequent conviction.

"ITALIAN KIDNAPPED EX-GIRLFRIEND FOR HOUSEWORK"

A 43-year-old man was accused of kidnapping his ex-girlfriend in 2008, just so that she could iron his clothes and wash his dishes. He allegedly dragged her out of a bar in Genoa, Italy, shoved her into a car and drove her to his home, where he made her do housework.

MECHANICAL IGNORANCE PROVES DOWNFALL

A 45-year-old woman was arrested in San Antonio, Texas, after a mechanic informed the police that 18 packages of marijuana were hidden in the engine compartment of the car that she had brought in for an oil change. She told the police that she didn't realize the mechanic would have to raise the hood in order to change the oil.

MAN CUTS OFF FINGER IN DEBT PROTEST

In despair after a judge ruled that he would have to sell part of his farm to settle an outstanding debt, Portuguese businessman Orico Silva cut off one of his fingers in court with a butcher's knife. Retrieving documents from his briefcase, Silva noticed the knife he had recently bought and decided to slice off his index finger, using a court desk as a chopping board. He then proceeded to cut the finger into three pieces. He said afterwards: "My intention was to tear up all the case papers and splatter them with blood so I could prevent the expropriation order for my land."

CONFUSED ROBBER THREATENS TO SHOOT HIMSELF

A MAN IN HIS forties tried to rob a group of people in Ogden, Utah, in 2001 by pointing a handgun at himself and threatening to shoot unless they handed over their vehicles. Not surprisingly, nobody complied. ●

STORE ROBBER WEARS BEER BOX ON HEAD

A man who robbed a convenience store in Lincoln, Nebraska, in 2009 chose an unconventional disguise – he put a 12-pack beer box over his head. He escaped with around $50 worth of cigarettes, dropping the beer box as he made his getaway.

GRAND THEFT AUTO SUSPECT ARRESTED PLAYING "GRAND THEFT AUTO"

Sheriff's deputies in Florida found a suspected car thief playing the "Grand Theft Auto" video game – and they subsequently charged him with exactly that. After a stolen Dodge Durango was spotted outside a Haines City house in 2010, deputies found a man inside, playing the popular game. He was charged with grand theft auto, burglary and drug possession.

CLOWN CRASHES INTO POLICE CAR

The golden rule for avoiding arrest by the police is not to draw attention to yourself. A drink-driving suspect in Vancouver, British Columbia, spectacularly failed in this respect by crashing into a police car after driving erratically the wrong way down the road . . . while wearing a clown suit. Although nobody was injured in the collision, police confirmed that the clown "will have some explaining to do in court".

GUNMAN DEMANDS CASH – AND A WHOPPER WITH CHEESE

A masked gunman held up a Manchester, Connecticut, burger bar in 2001 and ordered the manager to open the safe. After grabbing the cash, the hungry bandit ordered the cook at gunpoint to make him a Whopper with cheese. "That was, 'To go,'" noted the detective in charge of the hunt for the robber.

FARE DODGER SLAPS POLICE OFFICER WITH UNDERPANTS

After being caught hiding in a train toilet to avoid paying for a ticket, a German man was taken to the nearest police station where he suddenly tore off his pants and started hitting an officer in the face with his underpants.

ONE-LEGGED SUSPECT CAUGHT WITH ONE STOLEN SHOE

After only one shoe was stolen from a store in the Belgian town of Maldegem in 2009, police quickly deduced that the thief was likely to be an amputee. Acting on a witness description, officers quickly arrested a one-legged Russian asylum seeker. The shoe was also recovered.

CAR THIEF CALLS POLICE TO ESCAPE IRATE OWNER

With an angry owner in hot pursuit, a Norwegian car thief decided that he would be safer in jail, and called the police from the stolen vehicle so that they could arrest him. The owner of the stolen Opel Kadett had spotted his car while driving through Porsgrunn in 1997 and, after an unsuccessful attempt to reclaim it at traffic lights, had chased the vehicle for 15 miles before the thief surrendered to police. "I guess I looked pretty furious," said the owner, "but I didn't want to lose the car."

GUNMAN PAYS FOR OUT-OF-DATE INFORMATION

A gunman burst into a district water office in Nicholasville, Kentucky, in 2009 and demanded money. When an employee replied that the office didn't have money, the gunman snapped: "I know you have money. It's a bank!" The employee then pointed out that it was no longer a bank (the building had previously been a branch of Farmers Bank), at which the disappointed robber put away his gun and walked out with nothing.

FRAUDSTERS LET DOWN BY CAR WITH NO ENGINE

Intent on claiming on their car insurance, two men towed their damaged vehicle to the middle of a street in Puzhany, Russia, in 2003 before calling the police to report that it had been involved in an accident. The fraudsters hoped the police would simply accept their version of events but the plan was wrecked when officers opened the hood of the car and "found an empty space instead of an engine".

BLUNDERING BURGLAR HAS NIGHT TO FORGET

A burglar who broke into a wood sales company in Bremen, Germany, one night in 2003 experienced a catalogue of misfortune, largely of his own creation. First he smashed open a coffee vending machine in the hope of snatching the coins inside, to discover that the machine only accepted tokens – a fact that was written in large letters on the front of the machine. Then he stole a cell phone, which only worked in the grounds of the company, and a cordless screwdriver – but he forgot the batteries and the charger. Finally the intruder drank a can of Coca-Cola that had been standing in one of the offices and was 12 months past its sell-by date. Speculating that the culprit should be easy to find, a police spokesman said: "He's the one who is stranded with a load of useless junk, looks tired, is sick to his stomach, and is probably the laughing stock of all his mates."

ROBBER TRICKED BY AGE QUERY

Holding up a Colorado Springs corner store, an armed robber ordered the clerk to fill a bag with cash. He then spotted a bottle of whiskey on a shelf and told him to put that in the bag too, but the clerk refused because he didn't think the robber was 21. To prove that he was, the robber obligingly showed the clerk his driving licence – bearing his full name and address. He was arrested two hours later.

THIEF BURIED IN AVALANCHE OF PEAS

A teenage thief who forced open the doors of an industrial container in Ashburton, New Zealand, was immediately buried up to his waist in an avalanche of peas. Police and ambulance men were called to the scene and had to use a forklift truck to free him.

WOMAN HANDCUFFED FOR OVERDUE LIBRARY BOOKS

An American woman was arrested and handcuffed in 2008 for having two library books overdue. Heidi Dalibor, from Grafton, Wisconsin, was frogmarched from her home and taken to the local police station where she was fingerprinted and photographed. The incident cost her $30 for the overdue paperbacks – and it cost her mother $170 bail money to free her.

FOILED ROBBERS END UP IN TEARS

A pair of bank robbers in Wroclaw, Poland, ended up crying and choking after they tried to use pepper spray on a cashier in front of an air conditioning unit blowing out warm air. The unit blew the spray back over the robbers who, coughing and spluttering, staggered out of the bank empty-handed.

ROBBER CALLS GUILTY ACCOMPLICE AS CHARACTER WITNESS

Acting as his own lawyer in an Austin, Texas, federal court in 2004, robbery suspect Adam Martin inexplicably called his brother Michael as a character witness – even though Michael had already pleaded guilty to being Adam's partner on four robberies. So when Adam asked his brother if he had ever committed any crimes, Michael replied instantly: "Yeah. You were with me on four different bank robberies, Adam. You know that." Adam was sentenced to life imprisonment.

THIEVES SNATCH REPLICA BISON TESTICLES

To add a little colour to the 2001 World Athletics Championships in Edmonton, Alberta, statues of brightly painted ornamental bison were erected at key locations around the city. However in a bizarre five-day crime spree, at least 20 of the fibreglass bison had their testicles severed. Two men were later found in possession of one pair of imitation genital glands, but the other thefts were thought to have been copycat crimes. A police spokesman admitted that he was at a loss to explain why anyone would want to steal the testicles of a replica bison.

SUSPECT FINGERED BY DETACHED DIGIT

After losing his middle finger, Victor Arreola headed for the Scripps Hospital in Chula Vista, California. When police arrived at the hospital they brought with them a finger and asked Arreola to identify it. "Yeah, that's my finger," he said, whereupon an officer told him he was under arrest for carjacking, the finger having been severed when the driver of a van slammed the door on the would-be robber's hand. Arreola thought about this for a minute, asked to take another look and decided that, no, it didn't look like his finger after all!

"LONELY MAN BUGGED PHONE OPERATORS"

Takahiro Fujinuma, 37, from Tokyo was charged in 2008 with making at least 2,600 calls – and maybe as many as 10,0000 – to Directory Inquiries.

Police said he made 200 calls a night, during which he would whisper "darling" to the female operators and beg them not to hang up on him, but the real thrill was when they became annoyed with him. He told detectives: "I would go into ecstasy when a lady scolded me." He was said to be lonely.

ROBBER BEMUSED BY McDONALD'S MENU

A man entered a McDonald's restaurant in Sydney at 8.50 one morning in 2000, produced a gun and demanded money. However the cashier said she couldn't open the till without a food order. So the robber ordered a Big Mac, but was told by the cashier that they weren't available until 10.30 because only the breakfast menu was on offer at that time. Frustrated, the gunman gave up and walked out.

MARTIAN SUES OVER DEATH PLOT

Renee Joly, 34, sued the Canadian Defence Minister, Citibank and various drug store chains, claiming that the defendants were trying to murder him because he was a Martian. The judge ruled that the plaintiff, not being human, had no status in court and ordered that he be detained in a mental hospital.

JUDGE GIVES CHASE IN VAIN

When he saw Douglas Murphy running out of a Richland County, Ohio, courthouse in 1994, Municipal Judge Donald Hoover immediately threw off his robe and gave chase. A number of police officers joined in and 20 minutes later they found Murphy cowering behind a bush. It was then that they learned that Murphy wasn't a fugitive at all – he had been freed from court on bond and had simply wanted to make a quick exit.

GANG MURDERED PEOPLE TO SELL THEIR BODY FAT

Three men arrested in a remote jungle area of Peru in 2009 confessed to killing people and extracting their body fat to sell to international cosmetic companies for anti-wrinkle treatments. Colonel Jorge Mejia, chief of Peru's anti-kidnapping police, said the men had admitted to the murders of five people – and to draining the corpses afterwards. Describing the grisly method of fat extraction, Col. Mejia said the gang would cut off victims' heads and limbs, take out the organs and then hang the torsos above candles to heat the flesh, allowing the fat to drip into tubs below. It was then apparently sold on to intermediaries in Lima before heading to cosmetic and pharmaceutical companies in Europe. At the scene of the arrest, officers found human remains and two bottles of fat. The captured men revealed that one litre of human fat could sell for $15,000.

INCRIMINATING PHOTOS LEAD TO GANG'S DOWNFALL

After he and five others burgled a Tesco store in Greater Manchester, Roland Tough took photos of the raid to show their friends in jail how well they were doing. His mistake was to drop the roll of film off at the very same Tesco two weeks later, where employees recognized some of the stolen items. When Tough returned to collect his prints, police were waiting to arrest him. He was sentenced to six years, giving him ample time to tell his friends in person how he was doing.

STORE ROBBED BY MEN IN THONGS

Two men who held up a convenience store in Arvada, Colorado, in 2008 wore women's thongs as masks. One wore a green thong while the other opted for blue – but the skimpy panties left most of their faces visible, and the robbers were duly sentenced to 12 and 4 years respectively.

OFFICER MISHEARS RADIO INSTRUCTION

A female police officer on her way to investigate a burglary in Scarborough, Yorkshire, misheard a radio briefing about a missing fax and arrested a passer-by carrying a saxophone.

ROBBER GETS HIS TIMING WRONG

Aaron Bell, 19, robbed a KFC outlet in Philadelphia in 2002 – the same store where he had worked for the previous two years. Despite this, he opted against wearing a mask or any other form of disguise with the result that the employees on duty recognized him immediately. He was also forced to leave empty-handed because his inside knowledge had evidently not extended to remembering that the store's safe was time-locked at 9 p.m. – 15 minutes before his raid. Nevertheless he hid from the police for two days before, on the third day, bizarrely reporting for work at KFC and acting as if nothing had happened. The manager quickly called the police.

MIGRANT SNEAKS INTO UK IN BUS FULL OF BORDER AGENTS

An illegal immigrant crept into the UK in 2009 by smuggling himself aboard a bus containing at least 20 British Border Agency staff, whose job it is to keep illegal immigrants out. The man hid in a small space between the bus's chassis and fuel tank as it crossed the English Channel from France. When the bus arrived in England, he jumped from his hiding place and ran off.

BURGLAR SUES OVER MOCK VALENTINE'S CARD

In 2002, Sussex police sent out ten lipstick-marked Valentine's cards to known criminals. The poem inside, which was meant to act as a warning, read:

"Will you be my Valentine?
I'm hoping we can meet.
We have a cosy cell,
Prepared here at John Street.
Just continue with your lawbreaking
And we can guarantee
A ride in a police car
And a lack of liberty."

But serial burglar Gary Williams decided to sue the force after his girlfriend, thinking the card was from another woman, hurled an ashtray at him. Williams claimed the card was malicious and had caused him distress.

ROBBER ASKS FOR DIRECTIONS TO BANK

A Boston, Massachusetts, bank robber went into a copy shop by mistake in 2004 and passed his holdup note across the counter. Told that he was in a copy shop, not a bank, he asked where the nearest bank was and headed there after being given directions.

DRIVER CLAIMS DOGS WERE IN CONTROL OF CAR

Arrested after his car lurched forward, nearly hitting the police officer who had pulled him over for speeding, an Adelaide man claimed unsuccessfully in court in Australia in 2002 that it was actually his two dogs who were driving the car at the time of the near-miss. He said one dog was pressing the gas pedal while the other dog simultaneously pushed the vehicle into gear.

DRUG SQUAD RAIDS OWN OFFICES

Anti-drug authorities in Mexico raided their own offices and found 1,000 pounds of marijuana. Nine staff were arrested.

PRISONER FREED BECAUSE KOSHER MEALS ARE TOO EXPENSIVE

Although he had been sentenced to 11 months in prison for writing a bad cheque, Neil H. Lederman was released after just three weeks in 1998 because Fairfax County, Virginia, prison officials couldn't afford his kosher meals. The 43-year-old Orthodox Jew was placed on home detention instead to save the extra $70 a day that his special meals were costing.

KIDNAPPER DEMANDED RANSOM FOR FALSE TEETH

Debra Letourneau claimed that Gary Lee McMurray, of Keokee, Virginia, phoned her in 2003 to tell her that if she ever wanted to see her upper plate of false teeth in one piece again, she would have to pay a ransom of $20. He allegedly said that if she did not pay up, he would stamp on the dentures. Instead she called the police and McMurray was arrested but she later decided against pressing charges. She was just happy to have got her teeth back.

GANG RECRUITS GETAWAY DRIVER WITH NO ARMS

A gang that pulled off a $250,000 jewellery raid in Essex escaped in a car driven by a teenager with no arms. As police gave chase, the thieves' getaway was hindered by the fact that the other gang members had to help the driver change gear. Even so, he managed to drive for 30 miles at speeds of up to 100 miles per hour before crashing.

ROBBER FORGETS TO PLUG IN WEAPON

A 20-year-old woman was arrested in Lake City, Florida, after attempting to rob a motel. Her chosen weapon for the raid was an electric chainsaw, which was not plugged in.

REDNECK JURORS WERE NEARLY ALL RELATED

The entire 86-member jury pool for a criminal trial in Centreville, Tennessee (population 16,000) had to be dismissed in 1996 because, according to the prosecutor, too many members of the pool were related to each other.

NOTHING GOES RIGHT FOR FEMALE ROBBER

From the moment a female robber armed with a crowbar burst into a West Midlands newsagent's in 2000, things started to go wrong. She began by threatening the sales clerk but in the ensuing struggle she accidentally hit herself on the head with the crowbar. Then she managed to cut herself with the hook end of the weapon and her shirt got caught on something and was ripped off. Realizing it wasn't her day (the Post Office inside the shop, which was her intended target, was closed) she fled the scene with a male accomplice. Appealing for witnesses, a police spokesman said: "There must be someone out there who is aware of a couple running away from the premises, the female bloodstained with just her bra on."

WHEELCHAIR CLAIMANT JAILED AFTER JOGGING BOAST

Over a period of years, John Moses, of Haswell, County Durham, picked up around $120,000 in disabilities benefits by claiming to be confined to a wheelchair. But in 2002, the 51-year-old was charged with deception after filing a claim with his insurance company stating that his car had been stolen while he was out jogging, an activity which, he went on to say, he did three times a week. Moses, who compounded the error by later chasing the insurance investigator around the house, was jailed for 18 months.

FRAUD SUSPECT CLAIMS PLAN WAS DOG'S IDEA

Robert Meier, of Tampa, Florida, was charged with theft and forgery after marrying his comatose girlfriend, Constance Sewell, hours before she died and then allegedly charging $20,000 to her credit cards by forging her name on the receipts. In mitigation, Meier maintained it wasn't his idea. A police officer explained: "He said he was sitting on the couch when Ms Sewell's dog told him she would want him to go on living, have a better life, and it would be OK to use her credit cards."

THIEVES STEAL GIANT SPONGEBOB SQUAREPANTS

Thieves in Lewiston, Idaho, stole a 14-foot inflatable SpongeBob SquarePants replica from the roof of a Burger King restaurant. The blowup SpongeBob had adorned the roof of the restaurant for about a month in 2009 before its tethers were cut. Police said the inflatable icon was worth around $600 but doubted whether it would be easy to sell.

THIEVES STEAL 756 SHOES – ALL FOR RIGHT FEET

Thieves broke into a shop in Medellin, Colombia, in 1999 and made off with men's and women's shoes valued at $16,583. Unfortunately they had failed to notice that the 756 shoes were all for right feet, the matching left shoes having been safely locked away in a storeroom. The store owner groaned: "My merchandise is now completely useless. Who is going to buy a shoe for just one foot?"

BANK ROBBER LOSES THE WAY

After robbing Oregon's Klameth First Bank in 2003, a robber was caught by police while running around the street asking passers-by if they knew the quickest way out of town. Unfortunately for him, among those he asked was the bank manager's son.

OVERWEIGHT COPS ARE ORDERED TO CLIMB VOLCANO

Overweight Filipino police officers were ordered to climb the 4,740-foot-high Mount Pinatubo volcano once a month as part of a strenuous physical fitness campaign. Under the 2000 initiative all male officers with waists in excess of 34 inches (29 inches for women) were instructed to make the six-hour climb and to take part in a tough aerobics regime. A police department spokesman explained: "Our men say they are in shape, but it is the wrong shape."

JUDGE FIRED FOR SIGNING DOCUMENTS AS "SNOW WHITE"

Judge Richard "Deacon" Jones was removed from office in Nebraska for signing official court documents with names such as "Snow White" and "A. Hitler" and setting nonsensical bail amounts of "a zillion pengos". He also set off a firecracker in the office of a fellow judge after an argument.

SUSPECT SAID SHOES HE WAS WEARING WEREN'T HIS

Customs officers at Tokyo's Narita Airport became suspicious of a five-foot six-inch man who was wearing inordinately large shoes. So they asked him to remove them and inside they found 350 grams of heroin. Protesting his innocence, the suspect said he had no idea what was inside the shoes, adding: "I was asked by a Thai man to wear the shoes at Bangkok airport."

ROBBER FOILED BY PAPER BAG SHORTAGE

Not wanting to draw attention to himself, a bank robber in Portland, Oregon, handed the cashier a note ordering her to put all the money in a paper bag. She read the note, wrote at the bottom, "I don't have a paper bag", and handed it back to the robber. With no Plan B springing to mind, he fled empty-handed.

BLIND MAN BANNED FROM SAYING "PHLEGM"

A blind man's obsession with groping women while talking about phlegm saw a court in Kingston, Surrey, ban him from ever using the word. Neil Middlehurst, 49, would ask women for help crossing the road and then touch their breasts while talking about sore throats and phlegm. In 2004 he was jailed for 16 months, banned from saying "phlegm" and told that in future he must only touch women on the shoulder when they help him across the road.

MAN DISGUISED AS TREE ROBS BANK BRANCH

A robber held up a bank in Manchester, New Hampshire, in 2007 while disguised as a tree. He entered the bank with branches and leaves taped to his body but unfortunately for him CCTV cameras penetrated the foliage and he was arrested shortly afterwards.

ROBBER BUSTED FOR STILL CARRYING AROUND HOLD-UP NOTE

When a Gulfport, Mississippi, man was stopped by police for urinating in public, a search at the station revealed that he was still carrying in his pocket the hold-up note from a bank robbery the previous day. In addition to disorderly conduct, he was therefore charged with robbery. A Gulfport police spokesman commented: "We're fortunate that some of these crooks aren't too intelligent."

SANTA'S STOLEN GROTTO

A 49-year-old woman caught stealing Christmas decorations in a Swiss village was found to have a huge cache of them at her home, including illuminated reindeer, miniature Santas and plastic snowmen.

JURORS STRUGGLE TO FOLLOW MURDER TRIAL

A 1978 murder trial in Manitoba had been under way for two days when one juror confessed that he was completely deaf and had no idea what was going on. The judge, Mr Justice Solomon, asked him whether he had heard any evidence at all, and when there was no reply to the question, he dismissed him. Then a second juror, a fluent French speaker, revealed that he didn't understand a word of English and expressed considerable surprise that he was attending a murder trial. Proceedings were finally abandoned when a third juror said that he, too, spoke no English and, for good measure, was almost as deaf as the first man. The judge ordered a retrial.

PARTY REVELLER MAKES GETAWAY ON MILK FLOAT

When police raided a party in England, a drunken Matthew North jumped on a milk float to make his getaway. He put his foot on the gas and zoomed off at . . . seven miles per hour. Three policemen quickly overtook him by walking. It emerged that North already had a ban for driving a steamroller while drunk.

PRISONER SUES OVER ESCAPE INJURY

Scott Gomez Jr sued jail officials in Pueblo County, Colorado, alleging that they failed to take adequate measures to prevent him escaping. Gomez was seriously injured in 2007 when he fell 40 foot while scaling a wall in his second escape attempt. After his first attempt he had apparently told the sheriff how poor security was but claimed that no improvements had been made.

MAN THREATENS TO BLOW UP RESTAURANT WITH SAUSAGES

A robber threatened to blow up a restaurant in Benxi, China, with sausages, disguised as explosives, strapped to his body. After eating a meal at the restaurant, the 23-year-old man grabbed the owner's daughter, put a knife to her neck and demanded money from the till. He was quickly overpowered but when police officers arrived, he jumped to his feet and revealed his "explosive" belt. Bomb disposal experts were called . . . and instantly spotted that the explosives were actually sausages. The man said he staged the robbery because he was depressed after splitting up with his girlfriend. He told police that he had been "inspired" by the shape of the sausages.

POLICE DOG ATTACKS OFFICER INSTEAD OF ROBBER

After an armed robber shot police dog handler Katie Johnson in the leg, she set her dog on him, believing that he would save the day. But instead of jumping on the robber, the Alsatian bit her on the arm, allowing the gunman and his accomplice to escape from the scene in Preston, Lancashire. WPC Johnson had only been paired with the dog for three weeks and bore no grudges. Appropriately the dog's name was Chaos.

ROBBER'S CUNNING PLAN SEES HIM CAUGHT IN THE ACT

A Winnipeg man who wanted to rob a store without having to worry that the police would catch him in the act hatched a cunning plan which ensured that the police did catch him in the act. Just before entering the store in 2002, he called 911 from a phone booth across the street to report a fictitious shooting at another location, in the hope that this diversionary tactic would keep police well away. But as soon as they found that it was a false call, the police obtained the address of the phone booth and arrived just in time to catch the surprised robber brandishing a knife and taking money from the cashier.

MAN CONCLUDES INSANITY DEFENCE BY HOOTING "CUCKOO"

A Florida man accused of aggravated battery concluded his insanity defence by loudly hooting "cuckoo, cuckoo", then dropping his pants and mooning the jury. Following the outburst, Cornell Jackson was dragged from the courtroom by bailiffs and Bay County sheriff's deputies. The jury took just 30 minutes to find him guilty.

MAN PESTERED FIREMEN ABOUT THEIR UNDERPANTS

A **HONG KONG** man telephoned Chai Wan fire station repeatedly over a period of five years, each time asking if the fire officer who answered the call had "put on his underpants". Police eventually tracked down the pest, and in 2002 a 45-year-old was fined for making offensive telephone calls. His motive remained unclear. ●

WOMAN TRIES TO SMUGGLE COCAINE UNDER WIG

A British woman was arrested in Norway in 2008 after customs officers found a kilo of cocaine hidden under her wig. An officer at Vaernes airport thought the woman had rather a lot of hair and a closer examination revealed the bag of cocaine glued to her head.

POLICE CALL UP WRONG NUMBER

Paul Goldsmythe was quietly watching a late-night movie on TV when he received a phone call from the police to say there were armed officers surrounding his house. He was then told to walk out into the street in

Christchurch, New Zealand, with his arms in the air and with no weapons. Alarmed by the order, he nevertheless did as he was told, but when he stepped outside nobody was there. So he went back in. That was when the police negotiator still on the other end of the phone realized he must have called the wrong number. In fact the police were surrounding a different address half a mile away. Accepting a police apology, Mr Goldsmythe said: "I was pretty hysterical because I couldn't understand why somebody would be out front with a gun. I'm not a gang member or a drug dealer. I'm a repossession agent."

FARMER ATTENDS COURT CAKED IN MANURE

A farmer charged with careless driving in a tractor after injuring a neighbour and leading police on a 12 miles per hour chase down Devon country lanes, appeared in court in 2003 caked in manure from head to toe. Anthony Boundy went straight from tending his cows to Exeter magistrates' court, where the stench was so bad that choking staff had to throw open windows. One onlooker said: "Everything about him was brown."

THIEF MAKES CLEAN GETAWAY

A burglar broke into a house in Wichita, Kansas, just so that he could do his laundry. Disturbed by the lady of the house, he fled wearing his boxer shorts. She found the laundry room in a mess and his jeans and belt in her washing machine.

ROBBER FINISHES RAID $5 WORSE OFF

A man walked into a store in Louisiana, put a $20 bill on the counter and asked for change. When the store clerk opened the cash drawer, the man pulled a gun and snatched the contents of the drawer – $15. He then ran out, leaving his $20 bill on the counter, and thus finished the raid $5 out of pocket.

BURGLAR ASKS POLICE FOR HELP WITH BREAK-IN

After failing to break down the door of a Wisconsin church with a metal shovel, a 24-year-old man called the police for assistance. He told them he was having difficulty breaking into the church and hoped they might be able to help. When officers arrived, they found him under the influence of marijuana.

ROBBER MAKES FATAL MOVE

A pair of Michigan robbers entered a record store in a state of high agitation. Nervously waving his gun, the first robber yelled: "Nobody move!" When his accomplice moved, the first bandit shot him.

ESCAPED CONVICT CHOOSES LEPRECHAUN DISGUISE

A man who escaped from a Waco, Texas, jail in 2003 was worried that his orange prison uniform might attract attention. So he broke into a university theatre department and decided that he would blend better into the crowds by wearing a leprechaun outfit.

COPS IN SHOOTOUT WITH EACH OTHER

Shortly after two Seattle police officers pursuing a stolen patrol car lost sight of the vehicle, they spotted another police cruiser and mistook it for the stolen one. When they then rammed it, the lone officer inside thought he was being attacked and opened fire. In the ensuing mayhem, the three police officers in the two police cars fired more than 20 rounds at each other before belatedly realizing that they were all on the same side of the law. Luckily every shot missed its target.

CAREER CRIMINAL SUES FOR STATE PENSION

Having spent 30 years in jail for 19 different crimes, Austria's Ernst Walter Stummer sued the state claiming it should pay him a pension as a career criminal.

BEER THIEVES HOLD DRIVER'S HAIRPIECE HOSTAGE

Making their getaway after stealing cases of beer from a San Francisco store in 2000, two thieves hijacked a taxi and forced the driver to take them to their destination by ripping off his hairpiece and holding it hostage.

STORE WORKERS MISTAKE DRUNK FOR ROBBER

Shop assistants at a convenience store in Waterloo, Iowa, that had been robbed twice in the previous two months mistook a drunken customer for a robber and threw a bag of money at him. When the 32-year-old man started rambling incoherently about the earlier raids and put his hand in his pocket, the workers were convinced that he was about to hold them up. So they grabbed money out of the cash register, stuffed it into a bag and threw it at him. The drunk totally ignored it and staggered out of the shop. Police later found him standing in the street near the store with watery eyes and slurred speech.

FLEEING THIEF SMASHES HIS HAUL

A thief fled from the Yanmonoki Museum in central Japan in 1998 with a 600-year-old Chinese platter dating from the Ming dynasty and worth an estimated $500,000. But as he made his escape, he dropped the priceless platter in the road, causing it to shatter into hundreds of pieces.

BUNGLING BANK ROBBER LOSES HOSTAGES

A Los Angeles bank robber took hostages during a bungled raid in 2002 but surrendered when it dawned on him that, one by one, all the captives had escaped through the front door or the bathroom window. A LAPD sergeant said: "He was on the phone, kind of looked around, and realized he had no hostages."

BURGLAR SCARED OFF BY MAN DRESSED AS THOR

A homeowner scared away a burglar by running at him while dressed as the mighty Norse god Thor. The terrified intruder leaped from a first-floor window to escape builder Torvald Alexander, who was dressed as the Norse god of thunder in a red cape and silver helmet and breastplate. Mr Alexander, who had just returned from a New Year's Eve party when he discovered the man in his Edinburgh home, said: "We were both startled but then the instant reaction was that I ran at him and he just jumped straight out of the window. He may have thought the property was empty and almost certainly would not have expected to meet a strong builder, especially one dressed in tinfoil and silver."

THIEVES SNATCH THE WRONG KIND OF CHIPS

Thinking they had intercepted a stash of valuable casino gambling chips, two Las Vegas hijackers ordered the driver of a truck marked "Vegas Chips" to surrender his load at knifepoint. It was only later that they discovered the vehicle was full of potato snacks instead.

PSYCHIATRIST SHOOTS PATIENT

DR OSCAR DOMINGUEZ, a 45-year-old psychiatrist in Sao Paulo, Brazil, became so fed up with listening to a female patient telling him about her sex life that he pulled a gun and shot her dead. He told the court: "I couldn't take those nutcases any more." ●

PRISONER SUES HIMSELF FOR HIS FAILINGS

Robert Lee Brock, who was serving 23 years in jail in Chesapeake, Virginia, admitted that it was his own fault that he got drunk and committed a string of offences. So he sued himself for $5 million for violating his own religious beliefs about alcohol. However, since he was unable to work and was a ward of the state, he argued that the state should pay the $5 million. Conceding that Brock had "presented an innovative approach to civil rights litigation," Judge Rebecca Smith nevertheless dismissed his claim as "ludicrous".

SUDOKU FANATICS HALT DRUGS TRIAL

A major Australian drugs trial that had lasted over three months and cost nearly $1 million was scrapped in 2008 after a number of the jurors were found to have been playing Sudoku during the courtroom evidence. The judge in Sydney became suspicious after some of the jurors were seen writing their "notes" vertically instead of horizontally. The solicitor representing one of the accused said: "We actually thought they were quite a diligent jury. The judge had made many comments about how they were taking copious amounts of notes." One juror claimed the number game helped focus the mind.

DRUGS SUSPECT WAS AERATING HIS PIRANHA

In 1992, Sheriff Bill Wiester announced that he had arrested a man sitting in a car in Moses Lake, Washington, who was bobbing his head up and down in a manner that suggested he was doing drugs. On closer inspection, however, it emerged that the man had a straw in his mouth and was blowing bubbles into a fishbowl he was holding in his lap in order to aerate the water for his pet piranha.

ROBBERS FLEE AFTER BEING PELTED WITH CHEESE

A German supermarket cashier foiled three armed robbers by pelting them with cheese. The masked gunmen burst into the store at Berlin-Wilmersdorf and demanded the daily takings but clerk Martina Bolle flatly refused to hand over any money. Instead she grabbed packs of cheese from the delicatessen counter and began throwing them at the gunmen, forcing them to flee empty-handed. A witness said: "She hit one of them smack in the face with a very ripe gorgonzola, which must have been like getting a dose of natural CS gas."

PARKING FINE PAYMENT LEADS TO DRUGS BUST

A Pennsylvania man went to court in 2002 to pay an overdue parking ticket, but, for reasons best known to himself, took with him 46 packets of crack cocaine and two bags of marijuana, one of which, according to police, fell incriminatingly from his pocket as he was paying his fine.

MAN REMOVED FRIEND'S BREAST IMPLANTS IN TEMPER

Leonard Ruckman, 40, was arrested in Stotts City, Missouri, in 1996 and charged with assault outside a bar following an altercation over car keys. In a fit of anger, he allegedly slashed open a female acquaintance's breast and removed her implants.

MUGGER LEAVES HIS FALSE EAR AT SCENE OF CRIME

James Cottrell, of Runcorn, Cheshire, left behind incriminating evidence – his false ear – when he snatched a woman driver's bag. After attacking his victim with a hammer, he grabbed the bag while she sat in her car, but when a plastic ear was found at the scene, police quickly arrested Cottrell who they said was known to them. He was sentenced to nine years at his 2001 trial, after which officers said that his ear would be returned to him when it was no longer needed as evidence.

COUNTERFEITER FORGETS TO DO BOTH SIDES OF DOLLAR BILLS

Police offers reported that a Paramount, California, counterfeiter had done a thoroughly professional job creating the forged notes which he handed over to a store owner. In fact they said the only clue they had that the cash might not be genuine was that he had forgotten to print both sides of the dollar bills.

THIEF RETURNS TO SHOP TO COMPLAIN ABOUT BEING OVERCHARGED

A man who bought two mobile phones on a stolen credit card was arrested by waiting police after returning to a Singapore store to complain that he had been overcharged. The man had escaped on a motorcycle after snatching a woman's handbag containing several credit cards, a cell phone and cash. He promptly bought two phones for $2,160, using one of the stolen credit cards, but by the time he went back to complain about the price, the alert store owner had summoned the police.

STAR-STRUCK FELONS TAKE POLICE BAIT

More than 50 wanted criminals responded to a 1997 invitation to work as extras in an upcoming Robert DeNiro movie being filmed in Boston, Massachusetts – unaware that the invitation was from police officers who were waiting to arrest them. As she and other fugitives from the law were led away in handcuffs, one woman angrily complained that she had taken a day off work.

BANK ROBBER TRIES TO PAY OFF OVERDRAFT

An armed robber was arrested after he held up a bank – and then returned minutes later to pay off his overdraft. Wearing a balaclava and brandishing a shotgun, the man held up the Kredi Bank in Nova Varos, Serbia, in 2009 before running out with $50,000 in cash. Staff were still recovering from the shock when the same man, this time without his balaclava, walked back in to settle his overdraft. Keen-eyed tellers recognized the distinctive trainers he had been wearing and alerted the police. A police spokesman said: "The man had been wearing bright red trainers and everyone remembered them distinctly when they saw him run out of the bank. They could not believe their eyes when they saw a man wearing the same shoes come back in, and they kept him in the bank talking about his overdraft while our officers arrived."

FAKE COP STOPS REAL DETECTIVE FOR SPEEDING

James Winton, from Barrie, Ontario, specialized in impersonating a police officer . . . until one day in 2003 he had the bad luck to pull over a real Canadian detective for speeding. His bluff was called when Constable Jarrod Hunter demanded to see his police badge. Winton replied unconvincingly that he had left it at home. He was jailed for six months.

CLEANER HITS GUNMAN WITH MOP FOR WALKING ON WET FLOOR

Furious at seeing a man march across the Romanian shop floor she had just washed, cleaner Florica Dumitru instinctively lashed out at him with her mop – unaware that he was an armed robber. She continued battering him even after he had fired a shot at her, although fortunately he missed because of the soap in his eyes. Acknowledging afterwards that she hadn't known he was a thief with a gun, the 42-year-old cleaner barked: "It would have made no difference. Nobody walks on my wet floor."

MAN DRINKS PETROL AND SHOUTS AT CARS

A 35-year-old man was charged with disorderly conduct in Milford, Massachusetts, in 2008 after running into the street and screaming at passing cars. A witness said the man had earlier been seen getting down on his hands and knees and lapping spilt petrol from the ground at a gas station.

SANTA ARRESTED FOR BRAWLING IN STREET

Children watched tearfully as Santa Claus was led away in handcuffs by police following a street brawl in Great Yarmouth, Norfolk. The Santa in question – a street trader – had been involved in a fight with a member of the public who objected to him selling $1.50 presents from his sack. "It was extremely upsetting for the children to see Santa being nicked and handcuffed," said police sergeant Steve Parsons. "A lot of them thought he was going to be put in jail so he would not be around to bring them presents on Christmas Day. We handcuffed him because he was being quite aggressive and had to be controlled. He was certainly not being very jolly on this occasion." Santa was later released after being cautioned for a public order offence.

BANK ROBBER FORGETS TO CUT EYE HOLES IN MASK

Pulling a mask down over his face as he burst into a bank in Giessen, Germany, a robber suddenly realized to his horror that he had forgotten to cut any eye holes in the mask. After stumbling aimlessly around the bank, bumping into customers and crashing into walls, he finally fumbled his way to the counter where, in order to demand money, he decided to remove the mask and look straight into the bank's security camera. Unsurprisingly he was arrested shortly afterwards.

BURGLAR LANDS IN CACTUS PLANT WHILE MAKING GETAWAY

When choosing to burgle a house in Anaheim, California, a man made the mistake of picking the home of police officer Luis Gasca. Thinking the burglar had a gun, Gasca fired at him, whereupon the intruder panicked, ran outside and fell into a large cactus plant. After managing to extricate himself from the cactus, he tried to jump a fence but slipped and impaled himself on a wrought iron spike. He was arrested in some discomfort at a nearby hospital.

JUDGE SIGNS EXECUTION ORDER WITH HAPPY FACE

A lawyer representing a death row prisoner protested in 1993 after Texas judge Charles J. Hearn signed his client's execution order with a little "happy face" symbol. The judge insisted he meant no disrespect when he sent the order to Robert Drew, who had been convicted of the 1983 murder of an Alabama teenager. "It's just become part of my signature," said the judge who also put the happy face on his driving licence, checks and other courtroom documents. "It's that simple. I'm a happy person." But Drew's lawyer, William M. Kunstler, complained: "It's like he's saying, 'Have a nice death.' Obviously a man with this lack of sensitivity should not have been presiding at a capital murder trial."

DRUGS SMUGGLER GIVES COPS EASY CLUE

An Italian drugs smuggler tried hiding 400 grams of cocaine inside a shampoo bottle. But the police quickly decided that the contents of the bottle might be worth checking because the man carrying it was completely bald.

ARMED SHRUBBERY AT FLORIDA STORE

A man tried to rob a store in DeLand, Florida, in 2008 armed only with a palm frond. He threatened to stab the clerk with the frond if he didn't hand over cash, but the clerk chased him out of the shop with a bar stool.

TEENAGE ROBBER UNDONE BY POOR HANDWRITING

A teenage girl bank robber bungled a raid in Rochester, New York, in 2002 because the teller was unable to read the writing on her holdup note. So the indecipherable note had to be passed to another teller and by the time the girl was handed a bag of money, the bank was closing and other employees were locking the doors. The girl robber ended up trapped in the foyer, where police soon arrested her.

DRUG DEALER GATECRASHES POLICE PARTY

A man was arrested in Ashland, Massachusetts, in 2003 after spontaneously deciding to gatecrash a party at a private home that he happened to be driving past. He thought the party would be a good place to find customers for his drug operation and was understandably dismayed when it turned out to be a gathering of off-duty police officers.

BANK ROBBER DEMANDS MONEY FROM HIS OWN ACCOUNT

Brandishing a rifle, a former Russian army colonel took a woman hostage at a bank in Moscow in 1999 and demanded money from his own account.

The gunman, who released the hostage after being promised funds, said he needed the money to pay for an operation for his wife. A number of Russian banks had stopped depositors gaining access to their accounts in the wake of the previous year's financial crisis.

THIEF DEPOSITS HAUL WITH VICTIM

Three days after stealing a collection of valuable coins, a thief in Germany took them to the bank for safe keeping – and delivered them into the hands of the man he had robbed. The thief received the shock of his life to find that his victim worked at that same bank.

GAS STATION ROBBERS RUN OUT OF GAS

Two men who robbed a gas station in Kirkwood, New York State, in 2009 were caught because they forgot to fill up their getaway car with petrol while doing so. Officers said they found the pair a mile away at the side of the road with their car which had run out of fuel.

SHOPLIFTER RETURNS TO STORE TO EXCHANGE STOLEN JEANS

In 2002, a Dutch woman stole a pair of jeans from a store, the theft being captured by its surveillance cameras. Dissatisfied with her day's work, she later rang the store to ask if they would exchange the jeans for a larger size. When she duly returned, she seemed surprised to find the police waiting for her.

PHOTO ALBUM BORES BURGLAR TO SLEEP

A burglar was arrested in San Francisco in 2004 after his 73-year-old victim insisted on showing him her family photo album. The man was so bored by page after page of family snaps that he eventually fell asleep, enabling the woman to call the police.

POLICE FIND $50,000 IN TRAVELLER'S STOMACH

When police officers at Bogota airport, Colombia, X-rayed a nervous-looking passenger about to board a 2004 flight for Lima, Peru, they discovered $47,500 stashed away in his stomach. The photo showed dozens of latex-wrapped packets inside the man's stomach prompting police to assume it was drugs, but when he duly passed the packages from his body, they were found to contain cash. Col. Jorge Luis Vargas, the head of Bogota's airport police, commented: "We find drugs inside the stomachs of smugglers all the time, but this is the first time we've ever found dollars."

THIEF HIDES STOLEN CHICKEN IN UNDERPANTS

A shoplifter in Lowestoft, Suffolk, was caught after trying to hide a cooked chicken in his underpants. When apprehended he offered to put the chicken back on the supermarket shelf.

UNLUCKY HOOKER HITS ON COP

Reno, Nevada, homicide detective David Jenkins was sitting in his unmarked car with the police radio on when a 19-year-old woman jumped in and propositioned him for sex. When he produced his badge and arrested her, she complained: "You wear glasses, and I didn't think police could wear them."

DEFENDANT APPEALS AGAINST "TOO LENIENT" SENTENCE

An Austrian businessman accused of maltreating his wife rejected the court's fine of $1,200 and demanded instead that he be jailed for a year. The case arose from a domestic argument in 2000. When the wife said she wanted a divorce, her husband dragged her in front of a crucifix and shouted: "You will be chastised, woman – you will burn! Our marriage is consecrated before God – you will not end it!" Although he denied physically attacking her, he still thought the sentence was too lenient. While the public prosecutor was left baffled by the unusual request, the wife simply remarked of her husband: "He's gone crazy."

BANK ROBBER MAKES GETAWAY IN ELECTRIC WHEELCHAIR

A man in his sixties armed with a handgun robbed a bank in Palo Alto, California, in 2008 and then made a low-speed getaway in an electric wheelchair.

PARKING TICKET PROVES COSTLY FOR IRATE CANADIAN

Heading back to his car, a Canadian man was livid to see a police officer writing out a parking ticket. In a violent rage, he kicked the officer's car, causing $1,000 worth of damage. As a result he was arrested and, on being searched, was found to be carrying marijuana. So he was charged with that offence, too. After all that, it transpired that the parking ticket wasn't even for his car.

MAN SUES HIMSELF FOR MAKING HIS LIFE HELL

A man suffering from multiple personality disorder filed a $250,000 lawsuit against himself for making his life a living hell. Tax accountant Randy Burcheon, of Belton, Texas, apparently has six personalities, five of which are "kind, considerate people". But, said Burcheon's attorney, "the sixth – an unemployed, alcoholic bully known as Larry – is constantly causing trouble and destroying anything good that happens in my client's life. This has been going on for more than ten years, and it's time for it to stop." According to Burcheon, Larry's misdemeanours have included sexually harassing his girlfriend, yelling obscenities at his supervisor during an important business meeting, running up thousands of dollars in charges on his credit card at liquor stores and strip joints, subscribing to dozens of German porn magazines, and writing threatening letters to the President of the United States, which resulted in an angry visit from the Secret Service. Larry countered that the allegations were false and hired his own lawyer to defend him in court. "Randy's lying through his teeth," said Larry. "I never did any of those things he's accusing me of. Personally, I think he's dragging me to court simply because his girlfriend finds me more attractive than him. He's just plain jealous." All five of Randy's good personalities declared that they were willing to testify against Larry, who, in the event of defeat, would have had to pay any settlement out of his own insurance policy as Burcheon was not a wealthy man. Nervous insurance agents were said to be hoping the case would get thrown out of court.

BANK ROBBER WITH DYE-STAINED HANDS WAVES TO POLICE

A suspect was literally caught red-handed after robbing a bank in Wilmington, Delaware. Police said that as Cawayne Brown made his getaway from the bank, a packet of dye hidden in the cash exploded, staining his skin fluorescent orange. A few minutes after the robbery, a man waved a friendly greeting to a passing police patrol car, the occupants of which couldn't help noticing that the man's hands were bright orange. After

Brown was charged with robbery, a police spokesman said: "If he had gone about his business, the cop car would have gone right past him."

SUSPECTED GNOME RUSTLER ARRESTED

A 53-year-old man was arrested in Brittany, France, in 2008 on suspicion of a crime spree that involved stealing ornamental gnomes from other people's gardens. French police reportedly found 170 gnomes at his address.

JUDGE ORDERS VOCAL DEFENDANT TO HAVE MOUTH TAPED

Following a series of interruptions, an Idaho judge lost patience with a defendant's disruptive behaviour and ordered court officials to tape the man's mouth shut. Judge Peter D. McDermott took the drastic action during a 2009 probation violation hearing for former mental patient Nicklas Frasure. After one verbal outburst too many, the judge told bailiffs to silence Frasure, which they did by means of a strip of duct tape. By way of mitigation, Frasure's lawyer informed the judge: "He's obviously not mentally competent." As he was led out of the courtroom at the end of the hearing, Frasure offered to arm-wrestle the bailiffs.

SOLE BLACK MAN IN IDENTITY PARADE ACQUITTED

A Nigerian convicted of assault in Spain was acquitted in 2009 when he was found to have been the only black man in an identity parade presented as key evidence in the case. Spanish authorities conceded that the identity parade had been "badly assembled".

HUNGRY SHOPLIFTER TARGETS STORE

When a woman was caught shoplifting from a store in Ottawa, Canada, in 1999, hidden under her dress were three whole chickens, a pork roast, a beef roast and a duck.

GREEDY ROBBER PAYS THE PRICE

A man who robbed a Post Office in Stockholm, Sweden, in 2002 demanded both a bag of cash and a sizeable deposit into his bank account, the number of which he obligingly handed to the clerk.

DRUG SUSPECT TRIES TO FOOL POLICE WITH FAKE PENIS

A HEROIN ADDICT on probation for burglary tried to pull a fast one on police officers by using a fake penis to provide urine for a drug test. A Bexar County, Texas, probation department technician who was watching the 37-year-old man give the urine sample realized something was amiss because the bleached-pink penis was a different colour to the man's skin. "There were too many telltale signs," said a department colleague. "He had this eight-inch penis in his hand squeezing urine out of it. He fumbled with it, it fell out of his shorts, and he caught it before it hit the ground. But the urine was discharging from all different angles like water shooting from a sprinkler – and it was cold from having been in a refrigerator. The whole thing was crazy." ●

LOVESICK ARSONIST STARTS FIRE TO APPEAR BEFORE JUDGE

A lonely Austrian photographer became so infatuated with a female judge that he continued committing crimes just so that he could appear before her again. He had first met the judge in court after being charged with setting fire to his Vienna apartment following a drunken binge. She ordered him to be released on bail but he then began bombarding her with requests for dinner. When these failed, the frustrated Romeo started another blaze and ended up being jailed for two years. He explained: "She showed no interest and would not even speak to me, so I started the fire so I could see her again, even though it would be in court rather than during a candlelit dinner."

FLORIDA COPS CAUGHT PLAYING Wii DURING DRUG RAID

While raiding the Florida home of a convicted drug dealer who was already in custody, police officers were caught on camera playing a Nintendo Wii bowling game. One was seen jumping up and down excitedly in celebration while another detective was filmed taking several breaks from cataloguing evidence so that she could bowl frames. The officers were unaware that a surveillance camera had been set up in the house before the raid.

BURGLARS FIND THEY ARE MARKED MEN

Before trying to break into an apartment in Carroll, Iowa, in 2009, a pair of burglars decided to disguise themselves by drawing masks on their faces with a black marker pen. Unfortunately for them, they chose a permanent marker, which meant that police, alerted by a witness to the attempted break-in, had little trouble identifying them a few blocks away. The local police chief said: "Guilt was written all over their faces."

VANDAL IN HOLE LOT OF TROUBLE

A Sunderland man had to be rescued by fire crews in 1994 after using a manhole cover to smash a shop window, then stepping back and falling down the hole.

SUSPECT DONS WOMEN'S CLOTHES AND GIVES POLICE THE SLIP

Stopped by police on suspicion of drink-driving in Knoxville, Tennessee, a 19-year-old man ran to a nearby house and changed into women's clothing. He was arrested two hours later while walking down the street wearing women's shoes, pants and jacket.

CREATURE OF HABIT PROVES EASY TO CATCH

On four consecutive days, a man robbed the same Mexico City pastry shop at 8 a.m., each day holding up an employee at knifepoint before escaping with a chocolate cake. After successful raids on the Friday, Saturday, Sunday and Monday, the robber with the sweet tooth was apparently surprised to find police officers waiting for him when he burst into the shop at 8 a.m. on the Tuesday.

MAN IN PYJAMAS ROBS OHIO BANK

A man who robbed a bank in Bexley, Ohio, in 1999 chose an unusual disguise: he wore pyjamas. The thief walked into the National City Bank just before noon dressed in a blue and white zipper jacket, a black cap, blue and white checked pyjamas and bedroom slippers that were open at the heels. A detective on the case speculated: "Maybe he overslept."

DIRTY PHONE CALLER DIALS POLICE CHIEF BY MISTAKE

John Mullen Jr, of Lakewood, Ohio, decided to phone a sex chat line in 2003, but misdialled and unfortunately selected the number of Capt. Guy Turner of the Westlake, Ohio, Police Department. To make matters worse, after talking dirty for 20 minutes, Mullen fell fast asleep while still holding the phone, giving the police plenty of time to trace the call.

ROBBER HIDES LOOT UP BUTT

A New Zealand bank robber who stashed the proceeds of a heist up his back passage was caught out by "rustling sounds from his bottom area". The 36-year-old man was arrested soon after the raid but told police that he had handed the cash to an accomplice. However he was given away by the rustling noises and on closer inspection officers noted that "a roll of cash was found protruding from his anus". The recovered bills were destroyed.

MAN SUES BOOK OVER "MOST LAWSUITS" CLAIM

An American named in *The Guinness Book of World Records* as the world's most litigious man announced in 2009 that he was suing them over the claim. Jonathan Lee Riches is believed to have filed over 4,000 lawsuits against various people, entities, objects and concepts, including Britney Spears, the Eiffel Tower, Google, the Roman Empire, Che Guevara, the Magna Carta, Emilio Estevez and Plato.

FLEA OUTBREAK HALTS FRAUD TRIAL

Judge Graham Hume Jones discharged the jury and ordered the retrial of a 1994 fraud case at Exeter Crown Court, Devon, after two jurors complained that one of their colleagues was infested with fleas.

MEN ARE ROBBED AFTER LICKING WOMEN'S BREASTS

Three young Colombian women encouraged men to lick their drug-coated breasts and then made off with their valuables. The trio dissolved powerful narcotic pills in water and rubbed it into their breasts before striking seductive roadside poses near bars and restaurants in wealthy districts of Bogota. When motorists were persuaded to stop and lick the women's breasts, they quickly lost consciousness, coming round hours later to find they had lost their wallets and sometimes their cars but with no recollection of what had happened.

GUNMAN ALARMED BY MICROWAVE OVENS

A gunman raiding a Portland, Oregon, branch of Burger King in 1998 panicked when he heard the timers on the microwave ovens. Thinking they were security alarms going off, he fled from the store empty-handed.

THIEF ROBS WOMAN OF DEAD DOG

A distraction thief who targeted a female passenger at a London Tube station ran off with her suitcase . . . unaware that it contained nothing but a dead dog. The woman was taking a friend's recently deceased dog to a vet for disposal, but when her car broke down, she was forced to catch the Tube. She was struggling with the heavy hound at Victoria Station until a polite well-dressed man offered to help her carry the case up an escalator. At the top, he gave her a bag weighted with stones as a distraction and then fled with her case. One witness said: "The guy was a pro. But I would have liked to have been there when he opened the suitcase."

BY HOOK OR BY CROOK

A 36-year-old man who robbed an Ontario discount store in 1996 was swiftly apprehended, principally because he had made no attempt to conceal the metal hook which he used in place of a hand.

JUDGE DISMISSES SENATOR'S LAWSUIT AGAINST GOD

In 2007, Nebraska State Senator Ernie Chambers filed a lawsuit seeking a permanent injunction against God. He said God had inspired fear and caused "widespread death, destruction and terrorization of millions upon millions of the Earth's inhabitants". However Douglas County District Court Judge Marlon Polk threw out the lawsuit on the grounds that the Almighty could not be properly served the writ because he had an unlisted home address. Unbowed, Chambers said: "The court itself acknowledges the existence of God. A consequence of that acknowledgement is a recognition of God's omniscience. Since God knows everything, God has notice of this lawsuit."

WOMAN MAKES 7,177 EMERGENCY PHONE CALLS

Japanese police arrested a 38-year-old woman on charges of making 7,177 emergency phone calls over a one-month period between September and October 2008. The woman bombarded the police with calls because an officer had not taken her earlier assault complaint seriously. A police spokesman revealed that she would often shout "drop dead" – or words to that effect – down the line and added: "She apparently had a grudge against police officials."

BANK ROBBER LEAVES TELLTALE NOTE

A bank robber in Jacksonville, Florida, made the mistake of writing the demand note on the back of a police report of his previous arrest.

ROBBER DISGUISES HIMSELF AS CARPET

A Polish crook thought he had found a novel way of evading capture – by disguising himself as a carpet. After robbing a cosmetics store in 2009, the man rolled himself up in a giant rug and propped himself against a balcony while police officers searched his aunt's apartment in Warsaw. He was only found after a two-hour search when a frustrated detective went out onto the balcony for a cigarette and noticed that the carpet was trembling.

COPS LOSE GUNS ON WAY TO SAFETY CLASS

Two Raleigh, North Carolina, police officers lost an MP-5 machine gun and a handgun in 2002 while they were on their way to teach a gun safety class. They apparently put the guns, which were stored inside a bag, in the bed of their pickup truck but lost them when they fell out as they were driving along the highway.

PHARMACY THIEF FALLS ASLEEP ON THE JOB

Before robbing a pharmacy in Amman, Jordan, in 2001, a thief took three sleeping tablets to steady his nerves. Unfortunately the dosage was so strong that he fell asleep inside the pharmacy and was apprehended there by employees the following morning.

ITALIAN COURT BANS CROTCH-GRABBING

In 2008, the Italian Supreme Court clamped down on men touching their genitals in public. An ancient Italian superstition that is believed to ward off evil, crotch-grabbing is traditionally practised by men if passed by a hearse or when discussing illness. However the court ruled that a 42-year-old man from Como had flouted the law by "ostentatiously touching his genitals through his clothing". His lawyers claimed he had a "compulsive, involuntary movement" because of uncomfortable overalls but the judges ruled that he had offended public decency and advised that if men felt they needed to fondle their genitals, they should wait until they were in the privacy of their own home.

BASKETBALL TICKETS PROVE BURGLARS' DOWNFALL

Breaking into a North Carolina house in 2002, two burglars stole, amongst other things, tickets for a forthcoming basketball game. Police had the simple task of arresting the pair when they sat in the corresponding seats at the game.

ROBBER TRIPS UP ON ITALIAN JOB

No sooner had he burst into a Milan bank than an Italian robber tripped over a doormat and went flying. As he did so, his mask slipped and his gun went off. Quickly regaining his composure, he rushed towards the cashier, only to lose his footing again on the slippery floor, causing him to drop his gun. Deciding to abandon the heist, he ran out of the bank and straight into the arms of a police officer who had just written him a ticket for parking his getaway car in a prohibited place.

ONE-LEGGED DRIVER OUTRUNS POLICE

Police officers in Pasco County, Florida, were embarrassed in 2007 when a driver with no arms and just one leg lost them in a high-speed car chase – for the second time. Michael Wiley, who has overcome three amputations and taught himself to drive with stumps, led the police on an eight-minute chase before shaking off his pursuers. In 1998, he had led deputies on a 120-miles-per-hour chase down Interstate 125. His attorney explained that Wiley starts the car with his toes, shifts gear with his knee and steers with the stump of his left arm. He turns on the lights with his teeth. According to state records, Wiley's other crimes include stealing a car, attacking his wife (headfirst) and kicking a state trooper – with his only leg.

FAMILY FORGOT TO FREE PRISONER FOR 9 YEARS

An innocent man spent 14 years in prison in India because nobody, not even his family, bothered to tell him or the jail authorities that he was free to go. Pratap Nayak, from New Delhi, was just 13 when he was found guilty of murder in 1989 and sentenced to life imprisonment, but five years later the Orissa High Court quashed the conviction and ordered his release. However neither the court nor Nayak's own family thought to inform the prison, as a result of which he was left languishing in jail for another nine years until a local lawyer stumbled upon his case and secured his eventual release in 2003. Nayak was subsequently awarded $20,000 compensation.

SUSPECT USES CLONING AS A CREATIVE DEFENCE

An Ottawa, Ohio, man accused of killing a 15-year-old boy said that it was his clone who was the murderer. The suspect claimed the US Army had cloned him three times.

JUROR'S COUGH SENDS DEFENDANT TO JAIL

Defendant Alan Rashid almost ended up serving a prison sentence after a juror chose the wrong moment to cough. The cough came just as the jury foreman announced a verdict of not guilty in Rashid's 1999 trial at Cardiff Crown Court, but Judge Michael Gibbon only heard the word "guilty" and promptly sentenced Rashid to two years in jail. It was only when one inquisitive juror asked an usher why Rashid was going to jail after being found innocent that the mistake was uncovered and the jury was herded back into court to repeat its verdict.

HOUSEOWNER FINDS BURGLAR COVERED IN BARBECUE SAUCE

Hearing strange whistling sounds in the middle of the night, an Appleton, Wisconsin, man grabbed his shotgun and went down to the basement of his house to investigate. There he found an intruder covered head to toe in barbecue sauce. When police arrived, the burglar told them the barbecue sauce was urban camouflage because he wanted to hide from the government.

THIEVES STEAL BRIDGE

Scrap metal thieves in Russia managed to steal a 200-tonne steel bridge in 2008 without anyone noticing. The 38-foot-long structure vanished overnight from its site in Khabarovsk.

HEAVY HAUL GOES UP IN FLAMES

A gang of determined thieves in Australia pulled an ATM from a store, only to find that it was too heavy to lift onto their pickup truck. So they attached a chain to the machine and towed it behind the truck through four suburbs. Unfortunately for them, the friction caused by dragging it along the streets caused it to overheat dramatically and before they had a chance to open it, the machine went up in flames, along with the cash inside it.

SUSPECT PAYS PRICE FOR PLAYING WITH HANDCUFFS

Sean Barry, a 23-year-old waiter from Phoenix, Arizona, learned two important lessons about handcuffs in 1999. First, don't play with handcuffs unless you have the key. Second, if you don't have the key, call a locksmith rather than the local police – especially if you are a wanted man. Officers had gone to Barry's home in response to his distress call about not being able to free himself from the handcuffs, but on making a routine computer check into his background, they found an outstanding arrest warrant for failing to appear in court on a charge of driving on a suspended licence. Consequently he was taken into custody – still wearing the handcuffs. A police spokesman said: "We did eventually take them off like he asked, but by then he was in jail."

BRITISH TOURISTS STEAL FUCKING SIGNS

BRITISH TOURISTS angered the residents of a quiet Austrian village by constantly stealing their signs. The residents of Fucking, near Salzburg, failed to see the funny side when their village signs were snatched by tourists armed with screwdrivers. So they set the signs in concrete but that has not stopped the British seeking other memorabilia from the village. Local guesthouse proprietor Augustina Lindlbauer revealed: "Just this morning I had to tell an English lady who stopped by that there were no Fucking postcards." ●

CANADIAN ASKS FOR DISCOUNT ON JAIL SENTENCE

A Canadian man, facing seven years in jail for robbing a Champlain, New York, bank in 2002, argued that he should receive a discount on his jail sentence to allow for his country's weaker exchange rate against the US dollar. Robert Moisescu insisted that because, at prevailing exchange rates, the Canadian dollar was worth only 62 per cent of its American counterpart, the conversion should also apply to prison time, meaning that he ought to serve just four years. "Seven years Canadian is worth four years American," he told the court optimistically.

DUCT TAPE BANDIT KEPT UNDER WRAPS

A 25-year-old man was sentenced to ten years in prison for robbing a liquor store with his head swathed in duct tape. Kasey Kazee entered the Ashland, Kentucky, store in 2007 with his entire head, except for openings at his eyes and mouth, wrapped in duct tape. After threatening a female clerk and snatching money from the cash register, he was tackled in the parking lot by another employee and held until police arrived. "The duct tape proved easy to remove," said the Ashland Police Department. "He had perspired so much it nearly fell off."

WOULD-BE BURGLAR HIDES HIMSELF IN PARCEL

A young Colombian thief hatched an ingenious way of breaking into a wealthy Medellin home in 2004 – by hiding himself in a large parcel delivered to that address. However the planned burglary went wrong when suspicious guards at the condominium called in bomb disposal experts. Unable to breathe inside the package and fearing that he was about to be detonated, the occupant began screaming for help and tried to punch his way out. Police unpacked the parcel to find a gasping 24-year-old man, along with a knife, a gun, ropes and a ski mask.

NEIGHBOUR KILLED FOR WATERING LAWN

A man in Sydney, Australia, was charged with beating a neighbour to death in 2007 because the neighbour was watering his lawn, thereby violating the city's water restrictions.

PRISONER DEMANDS RIGHT TO WORSHIP NORDIC GODS

A prisoner has filed a lawsuit against the Utah Department of Corrections, accusing it of denying him his right to practise an ancient Nordic religion that worships gods such as Odin and Thor. Michael Polk, who is serving time for aggravated assault and robbery, claims to have been a member of the Asatru faith since 2005, and in order to practise it he says he needs numerous items including a Thor's Hammer, a prayer cloth, a mead horn for drinking wassail, a drum made of wood and boar skin, a rune staff and a sword. In his lawsuit, Polk said he had asked the prison chaplain for the items but had been denied them.

SMUGGLER LEAVES HEROIN TRAIL AT AIRPORT

A Colombian smuggler, who tried to hide heroin from customs officers in 2002 by starching it into his clothes, used so much – over two pounds of the drug – that his clothes appeared unnaturally stiff, smelled of vinegar, and he left a trail of white powder behind him as he walked through the airport.

IRATE DEFENDANT SMEARS HIS LAWYER IN FAECES

The defendant in a 2009 San Diego robbery trial was so unhappy with the performance of his lawyer that he produced a plastic bag with faecal matter and smeared it on Deputy Alternate Public Defender Jeffrey Martin's hair and face. Weusi McGowan then hurled the bag at the jury. The prosecutor revealed that McGowan had wiped human faeces on himself in the past.

ILL-PLANNED INSURANCE SCAM

A British woman was intent on claiming insurance money for the theft of her expensive ski pants in Erpendorf, Austria, in 2003. So she marched down to the police station to report them stolen, forgetting that she was still wearing them.

STORE THIEVES FORGET THE BUTTER

Two Brazilian store thieves, who stole bread, milk, soft drinks, biscuits, chocolates and some $10 in cash from a shop in 2002, returned five minutes later because they had forgotten to steal some butter. Unfortunately for the pair, the police were there at the time investigating the first robbery.

BRAWLING GRANDMOTHERS DRAGGED APART IN STORE

Two grandmothers on mobility scooters had to be separated by staff after getting into a fight at a supermarket in Crawley, West Sussex. The warring women, who were friends, apparently fell out over money and started trading blows and, according to a shelf-stacker who witnessed the fracas, "ramming each other like dodgems".

WARDEN LOSES PRISON KEYS

A warden at Westville Correctional Facility, the largest prison in Indiana, misplaced two master keys to the prison in 2002, requiring the 2,559 inmates to suffer restricted movement within its walls for eight days and the state to spend $53,000 replacing all the locks. The warden's wife later found the keys at home while she was cleaning.

BANK STAFF IGNORE ROBBER AT WRONG WINDOW

Wearing a balaclava and brandishing a pistol, a man burst into a bank in Feldmoching, Germany, and demanded cash – but the staff refused to answer his demands because he was standing at the wrong window. He fled empty-handed complaining about the appalling service in the bank.

SNAP-HAPPY BURGLARS LEAVE VITAL EVIDENCE

Two burglars who broke into a home in Cumberland County, Pennsylvania, in 2004 helped police catch them by taking photos of each other with a camera which they then left behind in their stolen getaway vehicle.

MEN GO BANANAS IN COSTA RICA

Two men caught with $372,000 in cash in a briefcase near the Costa Rica–Panama border in 2008 told police that the money was simply to enable them to buy some bananas. Bananas cost $1.65 a pound in Costa Rica.

JUDGE BITES DEFENDANT ON NOSE

After defendant Bill Witten had sworn at him for refusing to reduce his bail on a charge of grand larceny, Judge Joseph Troisi, of St Mary's, West Virginia, took off his robes, stepped down from the bench and bit him on the nose. Judge Troisi resigned from the bench shortly after the 1997 incident. He was said to have had a history of courtroom outbursts.

THIEVES TRY TO SQUEEZE COW INTO CAR

Thieves in Malaysia tried to steal a cow by stuffing it into the back seat of a saloon car. Villagers spotted the would-be rustlers and gave chase, whereupon the driver lost control, crashed into a tree and ran off.

BODY LOTION THIEF FAILS TO MAKE CLEAN GETAWAY

A shoplifter who hoped to make a clean getaway with 75 bottles of body lotion stuffed down his pants was easily caught by store detectives because his five-gallon haul made it virtually impossible for him to run. After a store clerk had spotted him feeding bottles of lotion through the zip in his pants, the suspect was apprehended following a brief chase at a shopping mall in Springfield,

Massachusetts. Officers were then unable to fit him into their patrol car because his pants were bursting at the seams and he could not bend over. Sgt John Delaney said the man's legs were "extremely chafed" when he was taken into custody and added: "He needed the use of some of the stolen items."

SATANIC INTRUDER FORGETS WORDS OF CHANT

In 1993, an 18-year-old man held a woman captive in her home in Hawaii and began uttering a satanic chant. Halfway through the chant, however, he forgot the words and told the woman that he was going to the public library to look them up. While he was away she managed to break free and call the police who arrested him in the "Occult" section.

SECURITY CAMERA SHOPS INEPT THIEF

A woman from Conklin, New York, let herself into the store where she worked while it was closed and then went up to the security camera, turned it off and stole $4,700. It would have been the perfect robbery had police not found the tape in the security system showing the woman letting herself into the store where she worked while it was closed and then going up to the security camera and turning it off.

ARMED POLICE RAID COWBOY PARTY

Armed police officers swooped on a Wild West fancy dress party in Castle Donington, Leicestershire, in 2009 after receiving a report of people walking around with guns. Roy and Val Worthington held the party at a local pub to celebrate renewing their wedding vows and had previously informed the police that they and around 80 of their friends would be sporting Stetson hats and toy guns for the occasion.

FORGETFUL TV BURGLARS GO BACK FOR THE REMOTES

Two men were arrested for burglary in 2001 after unwisely returning to the house in Tallahassee, Florida, from where they had stolen two TV sets a short while earlier. By the time they returned to the scene of the crime, police officers were already there. The reason the burglars went back was because they had forgotten to steal the remotes for the TVs.

POLICE SEARCH FOR MISSING CONES

Police in Scarborough, Yorkshire, announced that they were declaring an amnesty in 2004 in the hope of recovering their traffic cones. They had just three left from an original allocation of 300 in 1999. Chief Inspector Ken Gill said: "It seems people love to hoard them."

PRISONER RELEASED EARLY BECAUSE TOO FAT FOR CELL

Prison authorities in Canada were forced to release a 450-pound drug gang member less than halfway through a five-year sentence because he was too fat for his cell. Michel Lapointe – known as Big Mike – could not fit on his chair in his Montreal cell and his body hung over six inches on either side of his prison bed.

STAFF ATTACH ELECTRONIC TAG TO PRISONER'S FALSE LEG

A British prisoner was able to dodge a curfew after staff attached an electronic tag, which was supposed to monitor his movements, to his artificial leg. Tony Higgins, who was on home release from a jail in Redditch, Worcestershire, got round the 7 p.m. to 7 a.m. curfew simply by taking off his false leg. As a result he was able to go to the pub unmonitored for two weeks. When prison staff were alerted to their blunder, they transferred the device to his other leg.

TENNESSEE COURT GETS "JURY POOL FROM HELL"

A group of prospective jurors summoned to listen to a case of Tennessee trailer park violence in 2005 was described by defence attorney Leslie Ballin as the "jury pool from hell". Immediately after jury selection began, one man stood up to announce: "I'm on morphine and I'm higher than a kite." When the prosecutor then asked if anyone had ever been convicted of a crime, another would-be juror revealed that he had once been arrested and taken to a mental hospital after almost killing his nephew. He said he had been provoked because his nephew refused to come out from under the bed. Then another potential juror disclosed that he had alcohol problems and had been arrested for soliciting sex from an undercover police officer.

"I should have known something was up," he added. "She had all her teeth." A fourth man said it probably wasn't a good idea if he served on the jury either because "in my neighbourhood, everyone knows that if you get Mr Ballin (as your lawyer) you're probably guilty". He was not chosen. For the record, Mr Ballin's client was found not guilty of hitting her brother's girlfriend in the face with a brick.

DRIVER CHARGED WITH FARTING ON POLICE OFFICER

Arrested for drink driving at South Charleston, West Virginia, in 2008, Jose Cruz was escorted to the police station to have his fingerprints taken. There, police claimed that Cruz passed gas and fanned it toward an officer, an action that led to an additional charge of battery, although this was subsequently dropped. Those present remarked that the odour was very strong while Cruz claimed that his request to use a washroom had been denied.

SMALL-TIME CROOKS HIT SWEDEN

Thieves have been robbing long-distance coaches in Sweden by sneaking dwarves into the luggage holds inside sports bags. Once the holds are closed, the little people climb out of their hiding places and rifle through the belongings of unsuspecting travellers. They then take their loot back to their sports bag, climb back inside and wait to be collected by another gang member when the coach reaches its destination. A Stockholm Police spokesman confirmed: "We are looking at our records to identify criminals of limited stature."

THIEVES SNATCH BULL SEMEN

A farmer in Smithburg, Maryland, returned to his property in 2005 to discover that a 70-pound tank filled with bull semen had been opened and the carefully collected sperm of nearly 50 bulls – valued at $75,000 – was missing. A police spokesman said the raid took a lot of spunk.

GERIATRIC BURGLARS CAUGHT IN THE ACT

Two 78-year-old burglars were caught red-handed in Sao Paulo, Brazil, when the homeowners returned unexpectedly. The one inside the house was too deaf to hear the warning of his accomplice outside, and the lookout was not fit enough to escape.

FLORIDA COP FIRED OVER FREE COFFEE DEMANDS

A Florida police officer was fired in 2008 over accusations that he threatened to take his time in responding to emergency call-outs unless he received free coffee. An internal investigation heard that Lt Major Garvin, a 15-year veteran of the Daytona Beach Police, called in at his local Starbucks up to six times a night and would always barge to the front of the queue to demand his complimentary coffee laced with white chocolate mocha syrup. However when denied free coffee by the store's new management, he allegedly told them: "I've been coming here for years and I've been getting whatever I want. I'm the difference between you getting a two-minute response time – if you needed a little help – or a 15-minute response time." Garvin emphatically denied the accusations but failed a lie-detector test.

NERVOUS THIEF TRAPPED BY HIS OWN VOMIT

A young Australian robber who was so nervous during a hold-up that he was physically sick was incriminated by his own vomit. The 20-year-old lost his nerve when his accomplice unexpectedly produced a gun during the raid on an Adelaide post office. He was traced by DNA from the pool of sick.

STOREKEEPER FIGHTS OFF ROBBER WITH SALAMI

When a man tried to rob a Miami delicatessen in 1995, the store owner broke the thief's nose with a blow from a giant salami. Fleeing from the store and clutching his nose in agony, the robber hid in the trunk of a car, which, unfortunately for him, belonged to a police undercover surveillance team. It was five days before the police heard his despairing whimpers.

FEMALE ROBBER RECOGNIZED BY HER BIG BUTT

A female bank robber was caught as she tried to raid the same German bank twice – when a witness identified her by her large butt. Following a $24,000 armed robbery in Norf, witnesses described the raider as a woman with a "very large" backside and "powerful thighs". Three weeks later, one witness found himself standing behind what he believed to be the same bottom as they queued at the same bank. He called the police who arrested her and found a ski mask and handgun in her jacket. One bank worker recounted: "He said he recognized her bottom straight away – he'd never forget something that big."

PRISONER DEMANDS REDUCED SENTENCE OVER BLAND FOOD

A Chinese criminal demanded that his sentence should be reduced because he was unhappy with the prison food. Law Kwok-hing, who was serving 20 months in a Hong Kong jail for theft, said he was struggling to adjust to life in prison because he couldn't get spicy food behind bars. He complained: "I am a native of Hunan and I like spicy food, but there is no spicy food here." Unsurprisingly the court threw out his appeal.

FRAUDSTER FORGETS TO REMOVE CLOTHING LABELS

Arrested for selling counterfeit designer clothing in Iowa in 2003, a Winona, Minnesota, man claimed the garments were originals manufactured by Tommy Hilfiger, Nike and Ralph Lauren. Unfortunately he had forgotten to remove the "Fruit of the Loom" tags from the clothes before selling them.

FLEEING SUSPECT TRIPS OVER HIS OWN PANTS

Spotted by police taking a pee in public in 2002, a Tallahassee, Florida, man hastily pulled up his pants, pushed the cigarette he was smoking into his pocket and ran off. His escape bid was slowed when his pants ignited, leaving behind a trail of smoke and ashes, and it finally came to an end when his pants fell down around his ankles and tripped him up.

BUNGLING COPS ARREST EACH OTHER

After two robbers raided a liquor store in Berlin in 2009, German police officers succeeded only in arresting each other while allowing the thieves to get away. The robbers threatened a female employee with a machete but when she opened the till and handed over the cash, the shop's silent alarm was activated. Plain-clothes policemen arrived at the shop within minutes but ended up being arrested when uniformed officers stormed in seconds later. The shop manager said: "We all thought the uniformed police had caught the crooks, and when the plain-clothes cops tried to tell them who they were, they were told to keep quiet. It was only when one of the uniformed officers recognized one of the plain-clothes cops that they realized what had happened. They knew they had made fools of themselves and that the real thieves were long gone."

INEPT CROOKS STEAL WRONG KIND OF DOUGH

An Australian "Bonnie and Clyde" were jailed in 2007 for a failed heist which left one of them with a bag of bread rolls and the other with a bullet in the left leg. Benjamin Jorgensen and Donna Hayes targeted the manager of a Melbourne restaurant but when Jorgensen grabbed what he thought was a bag of money, he found that it contained just bread. To make matters worse, his shotgun went off accidentally, putting his accomplice in hospital for a month. The judge described the two, who had expected to steal takings of $26,000, as a "pair of fools".

COP PULLS OVER WOMAN DRIVER TO ASK FOR DATE

A part-time Pennsylvania police officer was jailed for 30 days in 2007 for pulling over a woman driver while he was off duty – just so that he could give her his phone number. Steven Klinger used red and blue lights mounted on the dashboard of his pickup truck to pull over a woman in Berwick. She became suspicious when he began asking her if she was married or had a boyfriend.

CAR THIEF DETAILED CRIMES TO PROVE INNOCENCE

A Romanian car thief kept a detailed notebook of all his thefts, including licence plate numbers and date and time stolen, so that he could prove he was innocent of any theft of which he was wrongly accused. He presented the notebook as evidence at court in 2002 to prove to the judge that he was guilty of only four of the five car thefts with which he was charged.

WOMAN THOUGHT POLICE PURSUERS WERE AN ESCORT

A Glenburn, Maine, woman led police on a high speed chase in 2002, reaching speeds of 80 miles per hour in a 25 miles per hour zone. When she was finally pulled over, she said she hadn't stopped because she thought her police pursuers were merely providing an escort for her as she took her niece to hospital.

ONE-LEGGED MUGGER SENT TO JAIL

A one-legged man in a wheelchair who tried to rob two men in the street was jailed for five years in 2007. Heroin addict Mark Milverton, 27, wheeled up to his victims in Weston-super-Mare, Somerset, and threatened to stab them if they did not hand over 20 pence (50 cents). The intended victims simply ran off.

JUDGE'S MESSAGE SPARKS MEDICAL ALERT

The clerk of the court sprang into action after reading a scrawled message from Denver County, Colorado, Judge Claudia Jordan: "Blind on the right side. May be falling. Please call someone." The clerk immediately phoned 911 and informed the judge that paramedics were on the way, whereupon Jordan let out an anguished cry and pointed to the sagging venetian blinds on the right side of the courtroom. When stretcher-toting paramedics entered the courtroom a few minutes later, the judge interrupted the drink-driving case she was presiding over to assure people that she was fine and that all she had wanted was a maintenance man.

BANK ROBBER DRAWS GUN – ON PIECE OF PAPER

A MAN WHO robbed a bank in Durham, North Carolina, in 1998 drew a small handgun on the corner of the note he passed to the teller. The illustrated note said "This is a robbery", and although no real weapon was seen, the teller played safe and handed over the money. "It was a very good drawing," she told police. "Very artistic." ●

GIRLFRIEND BLOWS ROBBER'S STORY

A man made the fatal mistake of failing to brief his girlfriend properly after robbing a store in Kansas in 1992. The robber had worn a cap and when police officers asked their prime suspect whether he owned such a cap, he answered no, at which point his girlfriend interrupted helpfully: "Yes you do. It's in the closet."

MAN RETURNS FROM HOLIDAY TO FIND HOUSE STOLEN

A Russian man returned from holiday in 2008 to find his entire two-storey house had been stolen by a neighbour. Yuri Konstantinov, from Astrakhan, came back from visiting relatives to discover that his house had been dismantled brick by brick, leaving only the foundations. The neighbour had taken the house apart and sold everything, including the bricks and window frames and all the contents, right down to the kitchen sink.

SURPRISE FOR SIEGE POLICE

Police in Oakland, California, spent two hours trying to flush out a gunman who had apparently barricaded himself inside his own home. After firing ten tear gas canisters into the property, officers realized the man was standing in line next to them, shouting: "Please come out and give yourself up."

THIEF STEALS DIFFERENT-SIZED SHOES FROM STORE

A bungling German thief stole a pair of shoes in two different sizes and was caught when he went back to the store two days later to fix his mistake . . . wearing a jacket that he had also stolen in the same raid. The store owner in Bielefeld spotted the man trying to switch shoes and recognized him as the shoplifter because the white shoes and sports jacket he was wearing were only available in that shop. A police spokesman said: "You have to wonder why he went back into the shop in the stolen get-up."

STORE ROBBER WEARS HAT WITH HIS NAME ON IT

James Newsome might have got away with robbing a Fort Smith, Arkansas, convenience store – if only he hadn't worn an orange hard hat with his name on it. The store clerk remembered Newsome's name on the hard hat and spelled it for police. The hat was later recovered from a trash bin at the company where Newsome used to work. Before Newsome was sentenced to ten years for aggravated robbery, the prosecutor pondered: "Could he have been smarter about the way he tried to cover things up? Yes he could have."

MAN IN RABBIT COSTUME ARRESTED FOR ARMED ROBBERY

A man dressed in a giant blue rabbit costume – and his shotgun-wielding accomplice – were arrested following a failed armed robbery in Farsta, Sweden. The pair tried to force their way through the security doors of a currency exchange office, but quick-thinking staff managed to shut the second of the two doors in their face, forcing the gunman to flee and the bunny to hop it. Two suspects were arrested shortly afterwards.

BURGLAR LEFT HANGING UPSIDE DOWN IN WINDOW

Burglar John Pearce thought nothing of turning his victims' homes upside down, but the shoe was on the other foot in 2008 when the house he had broken into turned *him* upside down. Attempting a daylight raid on a house in Dartford, Kent, he smashed the upper pane of the front window with a hammer, only to get the lace of one of his training shoes caught in the window frame as he tried to climb through. Unable to extricate himself, he was left hanging upside down in the window for more than an hour as a crowd of 30 neighbours and passers-by assembled to heap ridicule on him. When the house owner, Paul Ives, eventually arrived home from work, Pearce tried to claim that he had spotted someone else raiding the house and had selflessly attempted to catch the burglar, getting stuck in the process. However his chances of being believed were not helped by the fact that he still had the hammer in his hand. After calling the police and paramedics to put Pearce out of his misery, Mr Ives said: "He was screaming at us to get him down and we were all saying, 'I don't think so.'"

SUSPECTS IN HOT WATER OVER ATM THEFT

Columbus, Ohio, police arrested two men at five o'clock one morning in 1996 and charged them with tearing an ATM out of a bank's wall and attempting to carry it away in the trunk of their car. When questioned about the incident, the suspects tried to convince officers that the ATM was a washing machine.

FAKE ID WRECKS WOMAN'S SCAM

A Dorchester, Massachusetts, woman tried to obtain credit in 2002 by using a stolen driving licence and a stolen credit card for ID. However her plan failed primarily because, while she was black, the picture on the driving licence she produced was that of a white woman.

ROBBER IN DRAG IS $5 WORSE OFF AFTER BUNGLED RAID

An armed robber in drag made such a mess of a restaurant hold-up that he finished up $5 out of pocket. Dressed as a woman in a blonde wig, pink top and sunglasses, the raider walked into a café in New Orleans. He ordered two doughnuts but after handing over a $5 bill to pay for them, he suddenly produced a handgun from his bag and pointed it at the girl sales clerk. When she instinctively screamed, he ran off – without taking any money or his doughnuts. A worker behind the counter said she could tell straight away it was a man rather than a woman, adding: "It was kind of weird."

THIEVES STEAL HAUL OF FAULTY GOODS

A gang of determined thieves smashed their way into a warehouse near Swansea, Wales, in 2002 and made off with a haul of TV sets, video recorders and DVD players – unaware that the goods were all faulty as the warehouse was used specifically to store items that were being returned to the manufacturers.

FUGITIVE THREATENS TO SUE OVER POLICE INCOMPETENCE

On the run from police in the winter of 2002, Harvey Taylor hid in woods near Mattawamkeag, Maine, for three nights, during which time he contracted severe frostbite and lost several toes. When he was finally captured, he announced his intention to sue Maine police for not arresting him quickly enough.

THIEVES STEAL ROLLERCOASTER

Thieves in Bischofsheim, Germany, stole an entire rollercoaster in 2006. The 20-ton big dipper was on its way to a local funfair when it was stolen from a truck. "We have no idea what the thieves could possibly want with it," said the police.

MAN LASHES OUT WITH ANGER MANAGEMENT FOLDER

After harassing and punching an innocent 59-year-old woman at a bus stop in Minnesota, Justin John Boudin then attacked an elderly man who tried to intervene, hitting him with a blue folder. As he ran off Boudin dropped the folder, which was found to contain his anger management homework. The 27-year-old had been on his way to his anger control class when he lost his temper.

THIEVES STEAL BIKER'S FALSE HAND

A motorcyclist who lost his right-arm following a head-on crash with a bus in Bristol, England, in 2007, had his prosthetic hand stolen while he was visiting his girlfriend. Jack Baker parked his Suzuki outside his girlfriend's home and left the $800 hand gripped on the handlebars, but to his amazement when he returned to the machine the hand had vanished. "It was the first time I had left my hand on the bike," said the 19-year-old ruefully. "I thought I was only going to be ten minutes, but I ended up staying for two hours. It's frustrating because my hand's no good to anyone else."

SUSPECT HAD BAG OF POT STUCK TO FOREHEAD

Police in Lebanon, Pennsylvania, nabbed a real pothead in 2009 when an officer spotted a man inside a convenience store with a small plastic bag of marijuana stuck to his forehead. They said the man had earlier been seen peering inside his baseball cap, but when he looked up again the bag was stuck to his head. The officer peeled the bag off and placed him under arrest. Police confirmed that the sweatband of a baseball cap is a popular hiding place for drugs.

ROBBER ASKS FOR GUN BACK

A Chilean man bungled a 2002 store robbery when the shop owner grabbed his gun. The raider ran off, went home, showered, changed into smart clothes and returned to the store later that day to ask politely if he could have his gun back.

COPS TARGET *NEWSDAY* TRUCKS IN REVENGE MISSION?

The day after *Newsday* published an exposé on police staffing and wasteful spending, more than a dozen of its trucks were issued with tickets by Nassau Highway Patrol officers. The newspaper said its fleet usually received one ticket every few months, so suspicions were aroused in April 2000 when its delivery vehicles were the target of 14 out of the 15 tickets issued on the Long Island Expressway over a period of a few hours. The police dismissed the figures as "coincidence".

ROWDY NUNS ARRESTED

A group of 17 Orthodox nuns were arrested in Romania in 2008 for creating a public nuisance during a procession in Iasi for the naming of a new bishop. As well as their unruly behaviour, the nuns also received a caution for calling the arresting police officers "sons of Judas".

FORGER IS LET DOWN BY SPELLING

A Jacksonville, Florida, woman was arrested in 2002 as she tried to cash a forged $498.35 cheque drawn on the Frist Unoin bank.

ROBBER THROWS TANTRUM DURING RAID

A robber wearing a werewolf mask held up a Subway sandwich shop in Pittsburgh, Pennsylvania, in 2007, claiming that he had a gun hidden under a paper bag. But the two employees on duty were unimpressed and refused to hand over any money, whereupon the robber threw a tantrum. Petulantly ripping off his mask, he stormed out of the shop, complaining: "I can't believe you won't listen to a man with a mask and a gun!"

FORGER FAILS TO CASH IN ON COMPANY NAME

An optimistic 18-year-old dockworker at Roadway Express in Dallas, Texas, tried to cash a cheque made out to the company. He went to the bank and produced photo ID giving his name as Mr Roadway V. Express. After appearing to accede to the request, the bank manager said: "OK, Mr Express, I'll be right back." Instead he called the police who arrested "Mr Express" for forgery.

JAMAICAN POLICE HUNT STOLEN BEACH

Police in Jamaica were investigating the theft of an entire beach in 2008. An estimated 500 truck-loads of white sand were stolen from a planned resort at Coral Springs, forcing developers at the resort to put their plans on hold. With rivals in the tourism sector the chief suspects – because a good beach is a major asset to hotels – police carried out forensic tests on other beaches along the coast to see if any of them contained the stolen sand.

GRAVEDIGGER STEALS BODY PARTS TO MAKE ASHTRAY

Gravedigger Keith Chartrand pleaded guilty in 2007 to stealing human body parts – a skull and a leg bone – from a cemetery in Fitchburg, Massachusetts, and taking them home to make an ashtray and a pipe respectively. Commenting after the hearing, the cemetery superintendent said that although Chartrand was a "good worker", he would not be returning to his job there.

CITY PANICS OVER PENIS THEFTS

Panic spread through the Congolese city of Kinshasa in 2008 after sorcerers were accused of using black magic to steal or shrink men's penises. Victims claimed that sorcerers simply touched them to make their genitals shrink or disappear and would then try to extort cash from them with the promise of a cure. The topic soon dominated radio call-in shows, with listeners advised to beware of fellow passengers in communal taxis wearing gold rings. "I'm tempted to say it's one huge joke," said Kinshasa's chief of police, "but when you try to tell the victims that their penises are still there, they tell you that it's become tiny or that they've become impotent. I say, 'How do you know if you haven't gone home and tried it?'"

TYPO VIGILANTE CORRECTS UNGRAMMATICAL SIGNS

A self-styled typo vigilante toured the United States in spring 2008, wiping out grammatical errors on government and private signs. Jeff Deck persuaded a coffee shop clerk to remove an unwanted "e" from "Sweedish" and was given permission to correct a Hollywood "stationary" store's display to "stationery". But there was no goodwill when he was convicted of defacing a 60-year-old hand-painted sign at Grand Canyon National Park. Deck and an accomplice,

Benjamin Herson, used a marker to cover an erroneous apostrophe, put the apostrophe in its correct place with white-out, and added a comma. The pair were banned from national parks for a year.

MAN TRICKS WOMEN INTO TAKING OFF THEIR TIGHTS

A 40-year-old security guard from Teignmouth, Devon, was convicted of deception in 2006 after fabricating stories about car repairs in order to trick women into taking off their tights. Glyn Hatcher told the women he needed their tights to repair his fan belt, claiming that he was too embarrassed to buy them from a shop. He was finally caught after approaching the same two women twice.

SAFE ROBBER SAYS HE'LL CALL BACK

When an armed robber burst into a Chicago shop early one morning in 2008 and demanded the money from the safe, the staff told him there wasn't much cash at that time and in any case they didn't know the combination. Unfazed, the bandit gave them his phone number and told them to call him when the owner arrived. Receiving the call, the robber returned around noon . . . to find that police officers were also waiting. One of the shop workers said: "He told us to call him back when the owner returned with the money and he was going to come back and rob him." Police Lt Scott Schwieger added: "No one could make this up."

MAN STOLE 1,613 ITEMS OF LADIES' UNDERWEAR

Garth Flaherty of Pullman, Washington State, was sentenced to 45 days in prison after a police raid caught him in possession of 1,613 pairs of panties, bras and assorted women's underwear. His haul of nicked knickers weighed 93 pounds and filled five garbage bags.

ROBBER ASKS CASHIER FOR DATE

A Romeo robber in Genoa, Italy, was caught after he returned to the post office he had held up the previous day and asked the cashier for a date. The robber had forced 21-year-old Lucia Marcelo to hand over money at gunpoint but could not get her out of his head and revisited the scene of the crime the next day armed with a big bunch of flowers and an apology and asked her out. But she didn't fall for his charms and while keeping him talking, she activated a silent alarm connected to the police station.

FAMILY MOVES AFTER GUARD DOG STOLEN

A family in Wigan, Lancashire, decided to move after being burgled on 20 separate occasions. The last straw was when their guard dog was stolen.

CARJACKER WAS HARDENED CRIMINAL

Fleeing from the scene of a failed carjacking in Reno, Nevada, a male suspect ran into a building, only to become stuck in a freshly poured concrete floor.

BOY ASSAULTED WITH HEDGEHOG

A New Zealand man was fined in 2008 for assaulting a 15-year-old boy with a hedgehog. William Singalargh picked up the animal and threw it at the boy from a distance of 15 feet, causing a large red welt and several puncture marks on his leg. A police sergeant revealed that Singalargh had been arrested after the incident in the North Island town of Whakatane and been "charged with assault with a weapon – namely the hedgehog".

THIEF HAS IDENTITY CRISIS

With a haul of stolen security cameras, a thief in Garden Grove, California, was worried that police might be looking for his distinctive white Mitsubishi pickup truck having spotted it on surveillance video. So he decided to switch vehicles – and made the police's job a whole lot easier by stealing another white Mitsubishi pickup truck

BURGLAR ASKS VICTIMS FOR HELP WITH STEREO

A burglar in New Mexico was arrested after he telephoned the homeowners to ask how the stereo system he had recently stolen from them worked.

ROBBER CONVICTED BY SILLY WALK

An armed robber who was part of a gang that targeted jewellers' shops in and around London was convicted in 2000 because of his odd way of walking. John Saunders, from Bradford, West Yorkshire, could not disguise his bandy legs and rolling walk, described by one detective as "like an old outlaw who has left his horse behind". The prosecution called a podiatrist, an expert in the science of lower body movement, who told the jury that less than five per cent of the population had the same distinctive legs and bow-legged gait as Saunders.

MAN SMEARS BUTT IMPRINT ON WINDOWS

A 35-year-old man used lotion or petroleum jelly to make greasy imprints of his naked behind on windows of stores, churches and schools in Valentine, Nebraska. Dubbed the "Butt Bandit", Thomas Larvie targeted at least eight buildings in 2007 before finally being caught in the act. Police remained baffled by his motive, as no theft was ever involved.

KFC CUSTOMER TAKES THE BISCUIT

An employee at a Kentucky Fried Chicken store in Mill Valley, California, ran a lucrative sideline handing out marijuana with the food to people who knew that the secret pass phrase to obtain drugs was to ask for "extra biscuits". The scheme fell to pieces the first time a customer actually wanted extra biscuits.

GHOST HELPS ACQUIT MURDER SUSPECT

Two letters that were apparently dictated by a ghost helped acquit a Brazilian woman of murdering her lover in 2003. The letters, written by a medium who claimed to be in contact with the victim, were used as evidence in the trial of Iara Marques Barcelos. The medium claimed the spirit had revealed that Barcelos was innocent.

FAKE BREAST CLUE IN HUNT FOR CROSS-DRESSING THIEF

In 2008, police in Port St Lucie, Florida, were on the lookout for a cross-dressing man who snatched a 74-year-old woman's purse. Their main clue was a condom filled with water that the suspect left behind at the scene of the crime and which he had been using as a fake breast. A witness told officers the thief was wearing a short denim skirt and black tube top, and that he fled in a silver car with two other male cross-dressers.

HYPNOTIST HITS MOLDOVAN BANKS

A string of banks in Moldova were robbed by a hypnotist who put cashiers into a trance before making them hand over thousands of dollars. He would then bring them back out of the trance, leaving them with no memory of giving him the cash.

MAN HIDES IN TOILETS TO COLLECT WOMEN'S URINE

A 22-year-old man from Houma, Louisiana, was arrested in possession of four plastic bags containing women's urine. Police said his *modus operandi* was to disable the flush mechanism of a ladies' toilet in a department store after lining the bottom of the bowl with plastic. He would then come out of hiding from a neighbouring stall immediately after a woman used the toilet and collect her urine, which he would proceed to label with appropriate descriptions such as "old woman". According to reports, the police had yet to establish a motive.

CROOK BEGS FOR JAIL RETURN

An Italian crook begged to go back to jail in 2008 to escape from his nagging wife. Prison bosses in Naples had freed Luigi Folliero to serve the second year of his two-year sentence for theft under house arrest but after just two days he fled back to Ponte San Leonardo jail and pleaded to be allowed to return to his old cell because he couldn't stand being at home with his wife.

BURGLAR IN SPICE AND SAUSAGE ATTACK

A burglar broke into the home of two farmworkers in Fresno, California, and woke them by rubbing spices on one and hitting the other with an eight-inch sausage. A 22-year-old man was arrested after being found hiding in a field wearing only a T-shirt, boxers and socks.

BLIND MAN TRIED TO ROB BANK

When a 48-year-old man, obviously blind, shuffled into a bank in Memphis, Tennessee, he accepted the guard's kind offer to escort him to the cash teller's window. There, according to police, the man, who was unarmed, slipped a note to the teller. At first she thought his blindness might be an act but when she waved her hand in the air and he didn't react, she mouthed to the guard: "It's a robbery." She handed the man some cash, at which point it suddenly dawned on the guard that he was standing by while the bank was being robbed by a blind man. So he stepped in and apprehended the suspect as he was going out of the door. The police said the man was apparently surprised to be caught.

GUARDS ARE DISTRACTED BY RABBIT

When five guards spotted a rabbit raiding the vegetable garden at Kotido prison in Uganda in 2002, they instinctively gave chase. In their absence, 31 prisoners seized the opportunity to escape. The rabbit also made a clean getaway.

SUSPECTS MAKE UNWITTING CONFESSION

Two men appeared in court in Amarillo, Texas, in 2003 on a charge of beating and robbing a woman. When the District Attorney asked the victim, "And are the two perpetrators of this terrible crime present in the courtroom today?" both defendants raised their hands and said: "Here, your honour." The pair were convicted.

ARMED ROBBER IS ALL FINGERS AND THUMBS

A man was arrested in Modesto, California, in 2002 after trying to hold up a bank without a weapon. He used a thumb and a finger to simulate a gun but forgot to keep his hand in his pocket during the raid.

MAN DEMANDS TO BE KICKED IN THE GROIN

On at least seven occasions over a two-month period in 2007, Jarrett Loft of Guelph, Ontario, approached women in the street and asked to be kicked in the groin. After being sentenced to 60 days in prison, Loft, 28, said he was simply curious. One victim, saying that she feared what Loft might do if she refused, kicked him several times between the legs, after which he thanked her and rode off on his bicycle.

10

THE WORLD OF POLITICS

DEAD MAN WINS ELECTION

A candidate won election to a North Carolina county board in 2006 – despite having been dead for a month. Sam Duncan polled 12,000 votes more than his opponents to gain election to Union County's Soil and Water Conservation Board. County officials knew of Duncan's death before the election, but nobody had informed the voters.

FEUDING MAYORS DECLARE STREET ONE-WAY IN OPPOSITE DIRECTIONS

Rival mayors from neighbouring suburbs of northwest Paris caused traffic mayhem in 2009 by declaring the same road one-way – but in opposite directions. First, Patrick Balkany, the Conservative mayor of Levallois-Perret, made the D909 road one-way through his district to reduce the amount of commuter traffic. This angered Gilles Catoire, Socialist mayor of neighbouring Clichy-la-Garenne, who complained that the measure increased congestion in his area. So he declared his section of the D909 one-way, but in the opposite direction. With contradictory road signs in place, the inevitable result was gridlock and road rage, and municipal and national police were called in to divert traffic away from the area. Central government eventually stepped in to resolve the feud and ordered Clichy to re-establish two-way traffic on its part of the road.

CANDIDATE BEGS PEOPLE NOT TO VOTE FOR HIM

For weeks, Doug Couvertier did his utmost to persuade people in the small Florida town of Southwest Ranches to vote him onto the city council at the 2000 election. He campaigned door-to-door, advertised heavily and sent out hundreds of letters in search of votes. But he then discovered that under a Miami-Dade County charter, if he were elected to office, he would have to quit his job as a fire chief. Horrified at the prospect of losing his job and with officials ruling that it was too late to remove his name from the ballot, 54-year-old Couvertier abruptly changed his message to the voters and began begging them *not* to vote for him. He called newspapers, friends and neighbours and told them that he would resign immediately if elected. He was therefore hugely relieved when he polled just 74 of the 1,700 votes cast.

ROWDY PARTY NEARLY TRIGGERS RUSSIAN NAVAL ATTACK

A noisy wedding party almost sparked a Russian naval attack in 2008 after guests fired pistols and flare guns into the air on Georgia's disputed Abkhazian coast. Believing it was coming under fire from Georgian forces, a Russian amphibious assault warship radioed for permission to open fire on the aggressors. But just as the engines of the *Azov* had been fired up to head for deeper water and her guns' optimum range, her crew was informed that the "attack" was just a traditional Georgian wedding party. "Nerves are very frayed in this part of the world," admitted a Georgian official. "We are now working to calm down our wedding celebrations in future."

ESTONIA INTRODUCES FART TAX ON CATTLE

The Estonian government announced in 2008 that it was slapping a flatulence tax on farmers to compensate the country for the methane gas produced by cows. A single cow produces an average 350 litres of methane and 1,500 litres of carbon dioxide a day from flatulence and burping. Cattle are said to be responsible for up to 25 per cent of all methane gas emissions in Estonia.

"BIGGEST DICK" REJECTED AS SAUDI ARABIA AMBASSADOR

A leading Pakistani diplomat who was nominated in 2010 for the post of his country's ambassador to Saudi Arabia had his application rejected because his name translates into Arabic as "Biggest Dick". Akbar Zib had previously been rejected for similar posts in two other Arabic-speaking nations, United Arab Emirates and Bahrain, due to the unfortunate translation of his name.

BEER-LOVING GOAT IS TOWN MAYOR

The Texan border town of Lajitas traditionally has a goat as its mayor. Back in the 1980s Tommy Steele, a visitor from Houston, was named mayor of Lajitas – a decision which irked local man Bill Ivey who said that someone living in Houston was no more suitable to be mayor than his goat. Subsequently Ivey put forward his goat, Clay Henry, for election and it won a landslide victory. He has since been succeeded by two more four-legged, bearded mayors, Clay Henry II and Clay Henry III. The latter holds court at the town bar where he drinks his favourite bottled beer, having overcome a health scare a few years ago when he was castrated in revenge for drinking a patron's beer. The mayor's testicles were apparently found in the fridge of a hotel mini-bar. It means that when the next election comes around, Clay Henry III has a little less to lose than his opponents.

POLITICIAN HAS HER LEGS STRETCHED

An Australian politician had her legs surgically stretched so that she could become three inches taller and be taken seriously. Hajnal Ban, a councillor in Logan City, Queensland, had feared that her height of 5 foot 1 inch would damage her credibility. So she paid a Russian clinic over $35,000 to break both her legs in four places and stretch them slowly on a daily basis. Despite enduring nine months of excruciating pain, she insisted the surgery had been worthwhile, adding: "But I don't want to be remembered solely as the girl who got her legs lengthened."

TOWN DECIDES ELECTION WITH DECK OF CARDS

An Arizona town turned back the clock to the days of the Wild West in 2009 by deciding a deadlocked election with a deck of playing cards. Thomas McGuire and Adam Trenk each polled 660 votes in an election for a seat on the Cave Creek council, but a recount was considered too expensive. Instead town leaders invoked a 1925 statute that calls for such eventualities to be settled by a game of chance – in this instance drawing from a deck of cards. Under the watchful eye of the town's judge, McGuire drew the six of hearts, only to be outgunned by his younger rival who drew the king of hearts. The victorious Trenk said: "In an ideal world we'd have had another run-off, but this is what the state legislature mandates. I'm happy with the result. A king of hearts is pretty good." McGuire, who moved to the town in 1999 from New York, said he immediately knew Cave Creek was different when he went into a bar and found a horse inside.

COUNCIL FORGETS TO ORDER BOOKS FOR NEW LIBRARY

South Gloucestershire Council had to inform residents of Emerson Green, Bristol, that the new $2.5 million local library could not open as planned in 2003 because the council had forgotten to order any books for it.

MAN HELD AFTER SNATCHING MP'S WIG

A man was detained in Taiwan in 2008 after snatching the wig of a member of parliament who had complained about former president Chen Shui-bian's release from jail on charges of forgery and money laundering. A supporter of the president grabbed Chiu Yi's toupee, exposing a mostly bald head, according to media reports. Chiu himself said of the incident: "It felt like someone pulled my pants down in public." The wig snatcher was later released on bail as police officials struggled to find a name for his crime.

TICKING GIFTS DISRUPT STAR TREK CONVENTION

When Illinois attorney-general Jim Ryan shipped a box of clocks as gifts to delegates at the Republican National Convention in Philadelphia in 2000, he took the precaution of warning the hotel of their impending arrival. Nevertheless a vigilant hotel employee heard the ticking package, alerted the police and the building was quickly evacuated, the guests including a group of *Star Trek* fans attending a convention in full costume.

FRENCH POLITICIAN CONFUSES ORAL SEX WITH INFLATION

Glamorous French politician Rachida Dati had to issue a public apology in 2010 after confusing oral sex with inflation during a radio interview.

Asked by the national Europe 1 station about overseas investment funds profiteering during a period of economic uncertainty, the 44-year-old former justice minister replied: "I see some of them looking for returns of 20 or 25 per cent, at a time when fellatio is almost non-existent." Apologizing for mixing up the French words *fellation* ("oral sex") and *inflation* ("inflation"), she said: "This kind of thing happens if you speak too quickly on this kind of programme. It is unfortunate that this is the only political message that has been received on such a serious subject."

PROMISE OF BETTER WEATHER SEES CANDIDATE ELECTED

Danish comedian Jacob Haugaard was elected to parliament in 1994 on the back of a manifesto that promised better weather and better Christmas presents. The founder of the Union of Conscientiously Work-Shy Elements, Haugaard stood in Aarhus where he polled an impressive 23,253 votes and ended up serving four years in the Danish parliament. Among his other vote-winning promises were tail winds on all cycle paths and more bread for the ducks in the parks.

NEW MAYOR PROMISES TO RIP OFF VOTERS

A CROATIAN politician swept to power in 2009 after promising voters that he would rip them off at every opportunity. Josko Risa was elected mayor of Prolozac on the back of his campaign slogan: "All for me – nothing for you." Risa explained: "I just told them the truth." ●

DOG IS REGISTERED TO VOTE

A New Zealand man managed to register his dog to vote in the country's general election. Peter Rhodes sent his Jack Russell terrier Toby's application form to the electoral authorities, signed with a paw print and listing the occupation as rodent exterminator. The dog was duly registered as Toby Russell Rhodes in the Otago constituency and sent a voter's card but he made no attempt to vote in the polls. Mr Rhodes said he had registered his dog as a protest against bureaucracy.

POLITICIAN SNIFFS FEMALE COLLEAGUE'S CHAIR

Troy Buswell, the leader of the West Australian Liberal Party, admitted in 2008 to sniffing the chair that a female colleague had been sitting on in his office. The woman said she had just finished an interview in December 2005 "and when I got back I walked into the room to pick up my notepad from the desk and Buswell started grabbing the chairs going, 'Aaahww, which one did you sit in? I'll be able to tell.' And then he picked them up and started sniffing them and groaning and making sexually satisfying noises." Buswell had previously confessed to snapping the bra of a party staffer. His deputy described him as a "rough diamond with a robust sense of humour".

MAYOR CREATES STATE OF PANIC

With time to kill on a quiet afternoon, Mayor Jim Baca of Albuquerque, New Mexico, decided to test the panic button which, he had been assured, would bring security guards rushing to his office in a matter of seconds. Having pressed the button, he waited . . . and waited. After 15 minutes and no sign of anyone racing to his aid, he gave up and prepared to go home. As he stepped out into the corridor he bumped into the security staff, all of whom were frantically searching for the key to his office.

COUNCIL PAINTS WARNING SIGNS OUTSIDE CLOSED SCHOOL

Aberdeen City Council in Scotland ordered workers to paint yellow zigzag "school keep clear" signs on the tarmac outside a nursery school in 2009 – forgetting that the school had actually been shut for more than ten years. The workmen carrying out the job failed to notice that the building was boarded up and the grounds overgrown. In a separate embarrassment, the council destroyed its own new hospital markings in the belief that they were the work of vandals. The council ordered workmen to destroy the pavement signs – a blue circle with a white cross in the middle – believing them to be a student prank, but was forced to spend more money spraying new signs back onto the pavement after realizing that the markings were part of its own initiative.

PM'S UNDERWEAR-STEALING PAST IS REVEALED

In 2008, the Prime Minister of Australia was exposed as the descendant of a child underwear thief and a convict exiled from England for stealing a bag of sugar. Investigation into Kevin Rudd's family tree showed that his fifth great-grandmother, Mary Wade, was sent to Australia at the age of 12 for stealing another girl's dress and underwear. On the other side of the family, Rudd's fourth great-grandfather, Thomas Rudd, was deported to Australia in 1801 to serve seven years for "unlawfully acquiring a bag of sugar". Thomas Rudd later married another convict, Mary Cable, who had been exiled for stealing cloth.

PRESIDENTIAL CANDIDATE CLAIMS NEGATIVE ENERGY LOST HIM ELECTION

Mircea Geoana knew exactly why he had lost the 2009 Romanian presidential election – he had been subjected to attacks of negative energy by aides of President Traian Basescu during a crucial debate. The former Foreign Minister said he had seen "people with paranormal abilities" in the conference room where the debate took place, adding that he had previously seen the same people at the presidential palace. "My husband was very badly attacked," claimed Mihaela Geoana. "He couldn't concentrate." Earlier a Geoana aide had accused Basescu of dressing in purple on Thursdays to increase his chance of victory.

COUNCIL BLINDED BY WINDOW GLARE

When a worker complained in 2001 that sunlight coming through a window caused glare on his computer screen, Burgess Hill Town Council in Sussex sprang into action. They held six months of discussion, three meetings, sought out several contractors, produced a detailed six-page report, and considered five possible solutions – including spending up to $10,000 to put computer-controlled screens on the outside of the window or coating the window in reflective film – until the Town Clerk decided simply to move the desk away from the window.

FLORIDA CALLS FOR BAN ON ORNAMENTAL BULL BALLS

A Florida senator championed a 2008 bill to ban ornamental metal replicas of bull testicles from the rear end of trucks. The dangling replica testicles have become trendy bumper ornaments in the state but Senator Carey Baker labelled them obscene and proposed a $60 fine for any drivers displaying them.

BRIDGE COLLAPSES DURING ITS BIRTHDAY PARTY

A civic ceremony to mark the 200th anniversary of a famous wooden bridge in Montreux, Switzerland, in 1995 came to an abrupt end when the bridge collapsed, throwing spectators into the river.

TRAFFIC JAM SURVEY CAUSES TRAFFIC JAM

When council officials wielding clipboards stopped motorists in Poole, Dorset, to conduct a survey into traffic congestion in 2006, they merely succeeded in creating a two-mile tailback of morning rush-hour traffic. Hundreds of people were late for work by at least half an hour as Poole Borough Council officials pulled drivers over to the side of the road to answer a questionnaire. In response to frustrated motorists' claims that the timing of the survey was "ridiculous", the council's transport boss explained: "We were aiming to understand drivers' problems and reduce traffic congestion. It was not possible to give advance warning as drivers might have taken alternative routes."

PM LOSES SEAT OVER PAPERWORK BLUNDER

The Prime Minister of the tiny Pacific nation of Vanuatu lost his Parliamentary seat in 2009 because he forgot to hand in a note explaining that he would be away on business. Under the terms of the constitution, Edward Natapei forfeited his seat because he had missed three consecutive sittings without notifying the speaker. In fact he had been attending a Commonwealth summit in Trinidad and Tobago. A Vanuatu political commentator remarked: "It's truly unbelievable something as basic as that could have been overlooked. It's a massive oversight by the Prime Minister's people. All they had to do was give notice he was away on official business."

MAYOR KEEPS PROMISE TO WALK NAKED DOWN THE STREET

When Jim Whitaker, mayor of North Platte, Nebraska, promised to walk naked down the street in 1998 if $5,000 could be raised for an animal welfare society, he was besieged with angry calls telling him he should be ashamed of himself. But Mayor Whitaker remained true to his word and, with the money raised, he walked down the street . . . fully clothed alongside a dog called Naked.

VOTERS BARE THEIR FEELINGS AT ITALIAN POLL

Some 30 people wore nothing but their underwear when they turned up to vote in Italy's 2000 regional elections. They opted for the minimalist look to enter the polling station in Agrate Conturbia, west of Milan, as a protest against noise caused by planes at nearby Malpensa airport.

VISITING LEADER GREETS PM'S CHAUFFEUR BY MISTAKE

Arriving at London's Heathrow Airport in the early 1970s for a state visit, Yugoslav leader Marshal Tito walked straight past British Prime Minister Edward Heath, who had his arm outstretched in welcome, and shook hands instead with Heath's baffled chauffeur.

SHORT PEOPLE ORDERED TO STAND BEHIND SARKOZY

Twenty short people were brought in by bus to stand behind French President Nicolas Sarkozy while he delivered a televised speech from a Normandy auto technology plant. The workers – all under Sarkozy's height of 5 foot 5 inch – were chosen specially in order to make the diminutive President look taller. Sarkozy, who is extremely sensitive about his height, did not want a repeat of a previous incident when he was caught standing on a footstool while delivering a speech alongside Gordon Brown and Barack Obama.

INQUIRY LAUNCHED INTO COUNCILLOR WHO MADE SHEEP NOISE

An English council was left feeling decidedly sheepish in 2006 after spending $15,000 on an investigation to discover the identity of the councillor who "baaed" like a sheep at a planning meeting. Havering Council in Essex took 12 months to compile a 300-page report into the bizarre incident, which occurred during an application to build a mobile home on a farm where rare sheep are bred. When a male councillor impersonated a sheep, another councillor was so outraged that he filed an official complaint which in turn led to the inquiry. But by the time the report appeared, the chief suspect was no longer a councillor and therefore could not be punished.

PRESIDENT'S MEN ROBBED WHILE TAKING A SWIM

When President Clinton decided to go for a swim at Daytona Beach, Florida, in 1996, the three Secret Service agents who were assigned to protect him had no choice but to follow him into the sea. The agents returned to shore to find that their Secret Service badges, wallets, credit cards, hotel room keys, jewellery and clothes had all been stolen.

MAYOR FINES MEN WHO HAVE FUN ON A THURSDAY

Javier Checa, mayor of the Spanish town of Torredonjimeno (population 14,000), declared Thursdays to be "ladies' night" in 2003 and vowed that he would fine any man found out and about on the town's streets. In a measure designed to encourage men to stay at home one night a week and do the chores, all males discovered in a bar on a Thursday evening were liable to a $5 fine. Unsurprisingly the men of Torredonjimeno were less than ecstatic about the proposal.

GOVERNMENT MINISTER IS SCULPTED IN DUNG

In a conservation protest a New Zealand artist sculpted the head of the country's environment minister out of cow dung. Sam Mahon created the dung likeness of government minister Nick Smith because he was upset about plans to dam a river on the South Island. Mahon put his sculpture up for sale on the Internet but said that if he couldn't sell it, he would simply regrind it and spread it on the garden.

BIRTHDAY PARTY FOR POTHOLE

Residents in Bromsgrove, Worcestershire, threw a birthday party in 2001 for a 30-yard long pothole after the council left it unrepaired for a year.

CANDIDATE ROBBED AFTER PRAISING LOW CRIME RATE

During a 1998 TV appearance, congressional candidate Hale McGee maintained that his Ontario, California, district did not have a crime problem. Shortly after leaving the studio, McGee and his campaign manager were robbed at gunpoint when they stopped at a gas station.

MAYOR CALLS FOR "UGLY" WOMEN TO POPULATE TOWN

The mayor of an Australian town where men outnumber women five to one has urged the country's "ugly ducklings" to move there in order to improve the ratio and find lasting happiness. John Molony, Mayor of Mount Isa, Queensland, said the mining town – population 21,421 in 2006 – was in desperate need of young women, even ugly ones. "We should find out where there are beauty-disadvantaged women and ask them to proceed to Mount Isa," he said, adding: "Quite often you will see walking down the street a lass who is not so attractive with a wide smile on her face. Whether it is the recollection of something previous or anticipation for the next evening, there is a degree of happiness. Beauty is only skin deep. Isn't there a fairy tale about an ugly duckling that evolves into a beautiful swan? So a move to Mount Isa is perhaps an opportunity for some lonely women."

CHANCELLOR PRAISES OUTPUT OF CLOSED FACTORIES

Addressing an audience in Consett, County Durham, in 1995, former Conservative Chancellor of the Exchequer Ken Clarke said: "At Consett, you have got one of the best steelworks in Europe. It doesn't employ as many people as it used to because it is so modern." The steelworks had closed in 1980. He went on: "Consett is also one of the major centres for disposable baby nappies." That factory had closed in 1991.

CIVIC PRIDE TAKES A BLOW

When a fierce storm hit Alma, Arkansas, in May 2008, residents rushed to take refuge in the prestigious new community shelter which the town had just built. However as the winds howled, the 20 people who showed up had to take their chances and sprawl on the ground because the shelter was locked and the deputy who had the key was busy on a call.

CAR PARK SPLIT BY COUNCIL WRANGLE

Motorists using a town centre car park in Wales were faced with the prospect of having to pay at one end but not the other because two separate councils each owned half. Powys County Council wanted to charge for its half of the car park but Llanfyllin Town Council planned to keep its side free. "I've never come across anything more ludicrous in my whole life," said Peter Lewis, a member of both the town and county council. "It will be massively confusing. Will they paint a big red line down the middle of the car park?"

MAYOR BURSTS INTO SONG TO BOOST CITY'S FINANCES

In a bid to ease the economic crisis gripping the Ukrainian city of Kiev in 2009, its mayor, Leonid Chernovetskiy, released an album of himself singing "heartbreaking 1980s love songs". Promising that all profits from sales of the album would go into the city's coffers, the mayor boasted: "I sing very well. I don't think anyone sings as well as me apart from, maybe, God." Not everyone was convinced. One elderly woman he serenaded on the street outside city hall fainted after he launched into a Ukrainian love song called "My Lovely".

COUNCIL SCHEME FAILS TO SCARE OFF SEAGULLS

A local council plan to scare off seagulls from the North Yorkshire seaside village of Staithes in 1995 backfired spectacularly. The council hoped that by playing a high-pitched recording of a bird in distress, other seagulls would take flight but instead the wailing sound attracted hundreds of gulls who swooped in to see what was wrong. As the screeching black cloud descended on Staithes, tourists dived for cover and residents prepared for a major clean-up.

SWAZILAND SPEAKER RESIGNS OVER THEFT OF KING'S DUNG

Mgabhi Dlamini, speaker of Swaziland's House of Assembly, was forced to step down in 2000 for taking cow dung from the yard of King Mswathi

III. After a man was spotted gathering dung from the royal cattle enclosure, he led soldiers to a car containing the parliamentary speaker. It was claimed that the dung, possibly imbued with special powers because it came from the king's property, was taken for use in witchcraft and that Dlamini had somehow hoped it would enhance his political standing. Instead it landed him in a heap of trouble.

POLITICAL SPEECH INTERRUPTED BY FLYING PENIS

When arch Kremlin critic Garry Kasparov delivered an address at a 2008 Moscow rally designed to unite opposition political forces, his speech was interrupted by a helicopter rotor-assisted flying penis. The radio-controlled chopper buzzed around for about 20 seconds before one of the former chess champion's minders battered it to the floor. The prank was said to have been staged by a group of pro-Kremlin Young Russia activists.

STUDENT BUSTED FOR TRYING TO SELL VOTE ONLINE

A University of Minnesota student tried to sell his vote for the 2008 US Presidential election on eBay. Max P. Sanders, who asked for a minimum of $10, claimed it was a joke but was nevertheless prosecuted under an 1893 law banning the sale of votes.

NO NEWTS IS BAD NEWS FOR UK COUNCIL

Leicestershire County Council spent $2 million protecting a colony of rare newts on a road construction site, only to discover that none actually lived there. Acting on a report from environmental experts which said that great crested newts – a protected species – inhabited the area, the council delayed the building of the Earl Shilton bypass for three months and spent hundreds of thousands of pounds on special newt-fencing and traps so that the rare amphibians could be moved when hibernation ended in spring. Workers were even required to inspect the traps twice a day once temperatures rose above 41 degrees Fahrenheit. However although the traps caught a number of ordinary newts, the great crested was conspicuous only by its absence. Council leader David Parsons said: "I'm not happy that we have gone a million pounds over on the bypass and then found no great crested newts. It is an awful lot of money."

POLITICIAN LOSES WATCH WHILE SHAKING HANDS

Running for vice-president of the Philippines in 1998, Senator Edgardo Angara was out shaking hands with voters in the build-up to the elections. However when he thrust his arms into the throng, one of the crowd swiftly removed the senator's watch from his wrist and fled.

WIDOW TAKES PARTNER'S ASHES TO COURT TO PROVE HE IS DEAD

A woman took her dead partner's ashes to court in 2006 after bureaucrats refused to accept that he was dead and summonsed him for non-payment of $1,200 council tax. Denise Moon told Stockton Borough Council that her partner Stuart McMillan had died the previous year, even sending his death certificate, but the council continued to demand money from him. The issue of the summons proved the last straw, so in order to convince the council that he really was dead, she went to Teesside Magistrates' Court with an urn containing his ashes. When asked by a court usher where Mr McMillan was, she nodded at the urn. The council apologized and said it was reviewing its procedures.

MONKEY URINATES ON ZAMBIAN PRESIDENT

A monkey urinated on Zambian President Rupiah Banda during a 2009 press conference outside his office. Looking up at a tree where the colony of monkeys had set up home, a startled Mr Banda told the culprit: "You have urinated on my jacket."

POLITICIAN WROTE NEWSPAPER LETTERS PRAISING HIMSELF

Paul Reitsma, a Liberal Party member of the British Columbia Legislative Assembly, was uncovered in 1998 as the author of at least ten letters written under bogus names to a Parksville newspaper, the contents of which extolled his virtues as a politician and slammed his rivals. The letter-writer's true identity was revealed after the suspicious newspaper hired a Royal Canadian Mounted Police handwriting expert to compare a sample of Reitsma's handwriting to that of letters submitted to the editor by a "Warren Betanko". In one letter Reitsma managed to misspell his own name and the word "hypocrisy". He was forced to resign when the deception became public.

MAYOR APPOINTS PARROT AS OFFICIAL SPOKESMAN

Irritated by what he considered to be pointless, time-wasting questions from inquisitive journalists, a mayor in Ecuador came up with a solution in 2005 by appointing a parrot as his official spokesman. Jaime Negot, Mayor of Guayaquil, confirmed that the parrot would be responsible for dealing with any "undesirable questions" from the media. The mayor went on: "Some people only talk nonsense to me, so the parrot will answer back in the same way."

VILLAGE RE-ELECTS DEAD MAYOR

The residents of a Romanian village knowingly voted in a dead man as their mayor because they preferred him to his living opponent. Neculai Ivascu defeated opponent Gheorghe Dobrescu by 23 votes in the 2008 election even though he had recently died from liver disease. One Ivascu supporter explained: "I knew he died, but I don't want change."

CANDIDATE RECEIVES NO VOTES

As a Conservative candidate standing in a Labour stronghold, 72-year-old Shirley Bowes did not hold out much hope of victory at the 2007 English local government elections. But she admitted to being a little disappointed after failing to pick up a single vote. She couldn't even vote for herself because she lived outside the New Trimdon and Trimdon Grange ward in County Durham.

CITY SEARCHES FOR LOST TIME CAPSULE

When the city of Elkhart, Indiana, voted in 2008 to open a time capsule that had been buried 50 years earlier, there was just one small problem – nobody seemed to know exactly where it was. Since no note of the capsule's whereabouts was made in council meetings of the time, the committee was forced to ransack people's memories. Several committee members seemed to think that the capsule was buried in a park, but it transpired that they were confusing it with another time capsule buried in the 1970s to commemorate the US bicentennial celebration. A local resident, present at the 1958 event, thought the capsule was buried on a street corner, but that stretch of sidewalk had just been replaced as part of a streetscaping project, so nobody was in a hurry to dig it up again. Meanwhile the city announced that it was planning to create a 2008 time capsule – and this time it was making a note of the precise location. One committee member remarked: "If there's intelligent life on this planet in 2058, they won't have to go through this same fiasco."

BIRMINGHAM IS RECYCLED TO ALABAMA

To celebrate the success of its recycling scheme, the city council of Birmingham, England, printed a congratulatory pamphlet featuring a picture of the city's skyline. Unfortunately the city skyline it chose was that of Birmingham, Alabama, over 4,000 miles away. The error was spotted when one of the 720,000 pamphlets was sent to a local man who also happened to be a frequent visitor to the US.

FOOT POWDER ELECTED MAYOR

Voters in the Ecuadorean town of Picoaza accidentally voted a foot deodorant as mayor. As election posters appeared in the region, the enterprising manufacturer of foot deodorant Pulvapies decided to cash in on the publicity by adding one of his own: "Vote for any candidate, but if you want well-being and hygiene, vote Pulvapies." Then on the eve of the election the company stepped up the campaign by distributing leaflets the same size and colour as the official voting papers and urging: "For Mayor: Honorable Pulvapies." In the ensuing confusion, the electorate cast more votes for Pulvapies than any other candidate, thus voting the deodorant into office. The rival candidates were distinctly unamused.

PRESIDENT PUTS FAITH IN TOILET PAPER MYSTIC

Lithuanian President Rolandas Paksas came under fire in 2008 for placing his faith in a mystic who wraps people in toilet paper to cure their ills. Lena Lolisvili claims to energize toilet paper, which she then wraps around her patients. She also says God tells her the future. The country's largest newspaper commented: "Lithuania risks becoming the laughing stock of the world."

FRENCH TOWN BANS PEOPLE FROM DYING

WITH NO MORE room in its small cemetery and with plans to build a new one having been turned down, the French Riviera resort of Le Lavandou (population 5,508) announced in 2000 that it was banning death for any of its residents who did not already have a burial plot. Mayor Gil Bernardi issued a municipal decree which declared: "It is forbidden to anyone who does not have a burial plot to die within town limits." The day after introducing the new rule, he was happy to report that nobody had yet broken it. ●

MAYOR'S PANTS FALL DOWN DURING LIBRARY VISIT

The Lord Mayor of Leicester felt obliged to apologize after his pants fell down in front of hundreds of schoolchildren during a 2010 visit to a local library. When Colin Hall stood up to thank the organizers of the event at Southfields Library, his pants dropped to his ankles in what was described by onlookers as a "Benny Hill moment". The mayor's wardrobe malfunction occurred because he had recently lost weight and was not wearing a belt. On his Twitter site, the 16-stone politician joked: "I was wondering how to publicize the progress of my diet. It looks like the issue has been resolved!"

MAYOR DEMANDS POLICE PROTECTION FOR TOILET VISITS

In the wake of an altercation with a city councillor, the mayor of Snellville, Georgia, requested a police escort for whenever he needed to go to the toilet. Jerry Oberholtzer said he no longer felt comfortable going to the toilet alone after a verbal bust-up with councillor Robert Jenkins in the gents at City Hall in 2008.

WELSH ROAD SIGN IS LOST IN TRANSLATION

Wanting to erect a sign barring heavy goods vehicles from a road, Swansea Council opted for a bilingual sign – in both English and Welsh. Accordingly, it contacted its in-house translation service by email so that the Welsh version could be printed below the English "No entry for heavy goods vehicles. Residential site only". However as the translator was not available, the council received an automated email reply in Welsh saying: "I am not in the office at the moment. Please send any work to be translated." Alas the council thought this was the translation, and put it on the sign, which meant that Welsh-speaking drivers were greeted with a road sign saying: "I am not in the office at the moment." This was not the first problem involving Welsh language signs. In 2006, cyclists between Cardiff and Penarth were left confused by a bilingual sign telling them "bladder inflammation upset" instead of "cyclists dismount". In the same year a sign for pedestrians in Cardiff reading "Look Right" in English was translated in Welsh as "Look Left".

ENTIRE TOWN FORGETS TO VOTE

Voter apathy in the small farming town of Pillsbury, North Dakota, was so great in 2008 that nobody bothered to turn up to vote in the June mayoral elections – not even the candidates. Incumbent mayor Darrel Brudevold said he had intended to vote but was busy tending to his crops on election day.

11

FLASHES OF INSPIRATION

MAN EATS UNDERWEAR TO BEAT BREATH TEST

When 18-year-old David Zurfluh of Stettler, Canada, was stopped by police for erratic driving, he chose an ingenious way of trying to beat the breathalyzer test – he started eating his own underwear. Sitting in the back of the patrol car he suddenly ripped the crotch out of his shorts and stuffed the fabric in his mouth before spitting it out in disgust. He had hoped that the cotton fabric would absorb the alcohol before he took the test.

DRUNK STUDENT SWALLOWS HOUSE KEY TO PARTY ON

When Chris Foster's friends told him he had drunk too much and they were taking him home from a party in the student halls at Bournemouth University, he decided the only way to stay was to swallow his door key so that he couldn't get into his house. Sobering up the next morning, the 18-year-old was unable to remember a thing. "I thought it was a bit of a wind-up when my friend said I had swallowed the key. But my throat started to feel very sore and my stomach didn't feel right, so they took me to hospital." There, X-rays revealed the presence of the key, and doctors simply told him to wait for nature to take its course. "Luckily I didn't need keyhole surgery," he added ruefully.

DRIVER SHOOTS CAR IN TEMPER TANTRUM

A 64-year-old man from Fort Lauderdale, Florida, was so annoyed when his car wouldn't start in 2005 that he shot it. An incensed John McGivney pulled out a gun and fired five rounds into the bonnet of his Chrysler. When startled neighbours asked what he was doing, McGivney replied:

"I'm putting my car out of its misery." Although he was arrested for discharging a firearm in public, he insisted he had no regrets, adding: "I think at one time or another every guy in the universe has wanted to do that to his car. It was worth every damn minute in that jail."

MAN CONFESSES TO MURDER TO GET LIFT HOME

A Romanian man confessed to a murder he didn't commit in 2007 simply because he wanted a lift home. Stranded in a village 100 miles from his home in Botosani and with no money, 23-year-old Marius Varzar told local police that he had killed one of his friends and was handing himself in. He was immediately arrested and driven to Botosani in a police van but it emerged that the alleged murder victim had died from natural causes, whereupon Varzar admitted that he had only been looking for a free ride home. He was duly handed a fine for wasting police time and to cover the cost of the transport.

WOMAN POSES AS DAUGHTER TO ENROL AT SCHOOL

A 33-year-old woman from Green Bay, Wisconsin, posed as her 15-year-old daughter to enrol at high school because she had always wanted to be a cheerleader. Wendy Brown used her daughter's ID to become a student at Ashwaubenon High School. She attended cheerleading practices, a party at the cheerleading coach's house and was given a cheerleader locker, apparently in a bid to fulfil a lifelong ambition, having missed out on such opportunities in her own childhood. The ruse was uncovered when Brown started skipping school. Teachers said that although the student appeared older than her classmates, she had a teenage-like demeanour. She was found not guilty of identity theft by reason of mental disease and was committed to a mental health facility for three years.

THIRSTY BUILDERS DRIVE EARTH DIGGER TO LIQUOR STORE

A pair of Polish builders left a $100,000 trail of destruction when they drove to a liquor store in a digger truck after running out of alcohol on their building site. Weaving the digger crazily across the street, Marek Cowalski and Tomasz Dzwonicki ploughed into parked cars, garden walls and fences and a set of traffic lights on their way to buy more drink for a birthday party on the building site in Glogow. On reaching their destination, they tried to reverse into a parking place outside the liquor store, but drove straight into the shop and got stuck. "They must have been over the moon as they had all the drink they could want," said a local shopkeeper. Fire crews eventually managed to free the pair who were left with the sobering prospect of up to five years in jail for their escapade.

"DRIVER CHANGED CLOTHES AT WHEEL, CAUSED PILE-UP"

South Carolina Highway Patrol officers said that 20-year-old Marie Butler caused a five-car pile-up on State Road 90 in 2002, sending three people to hospital, when she lost control of her car while changing clothes during her drive to work.

MAN CUTS HIS OWN CAR IN HALF TO DENY CLAMPERS

Builder Ian Taylor returned to his home in Tredworth, Gloucestershire, to find that his Ford Fiesta had been impounded for having no road tax despite the fact that it was actually off the road. But a zealous wheel-clamper spotted that two inches of the bumper were protruding from his drive and demanded the equivalent of $560 to release the vehicle. So when the clampers arrived to tow away the car two days later, Taylor grabbed their disc cutter, sliced the vehicle in half and invited them to take the rear section as that was the only part that was breaking the law. After the police refused to take any action against Taylor, the clampers reluctantly released the car and told him he could keep both halves. He had bought it for just $100 for his stepson and kept it off the road because it needed repairs. He admitted afterwards: "It was a drastic step but I had to make a point. These people are petty and won't listen to you."

PENSIONER BURNS DOWN HOUSE WHILE EVICTING RACCOONS

In an attempt to smoke out a nest of raccoons in his attic, Kansas City pensioner C.W. Roseburr succeeded in burning down his house instead. He went into the attic wielding a kerosene-soaked rag on a stick, but his actions led to the eaves catching fire. Afterwards a defiant Mr Roseburr exonerated himself of all blame, maintaining: "I set the raccoon on fire. He's the one that set the house on fire."

PASSENGER FOUND WEARING 100 ITEMS OF CLOTHING

A Kenyan air passenger flying home from China in 2007 was wearing more than 100 items of men's and women's clothing. Security staff at Guangzhou Baiyun International Airport became suspicious when they noticed him wearing a really thick suit on a hot summer's day, and when he opened it, they saw the clothing packed tight around his body. The man said he had bought the clothes in China for resale in Kenya and had decided to wear them to save the excess luggage fee.

INQUISITIVE MAN KNOCKED OUT BY BRICK CHALLENGE

One evening a man from Merced, California, decided to find out how high he could throw a brick. After a couple of trial runs, he threw the brick so high that he lost sight of it in the darkness and it came crashing down on the back of his head, knocking him unconscious.

HEAD LICE REMOVAL ENDS IN BLAZE

When Romanian Gheorghe Harlaucescu fell victim to head lice, he decided to kill them by massaging petrol into his scalp. Unfortunately he then chose to dry his head by putting it next to a wood-burning stove. The petrol ignited, leaving him with severe skin burns.

WIRE THIEF GETS UNEXPECTED SHOCK

A 41-year-old man ended up in hospital after his attempt to steal a roll of copper wire gave him a 27,000-volt electrical shock. The man was found wandering in a Surrey, British Columbia, railroad yard with second-degree burns but without his shoes, which had been blown off when he tried to disconnect the wire from a running generator.

BARMAN HIDES DAY'S TAKINGS IN HOT OVEN

When Norfolk, England, pub landlord Martin Talbot asked barman Luke Woolston to cash up and put the takings in a safe place, he expected him to choose a secure spot. So he was horrified to discover that the barman had put the £1,000 ($2,000) in a switched-on oven. Talbot said: "He's usually a sensible lad so I trusted him to cash up and conceal the takings away from prying eyes. I thought he was joking when he said he'd stuck the money in the oven. But when I got to the kitchen and smelt the burning, I realized he was being serious. I pulled out the plastic till drawer using oven gloves and stared at £1,000 ($2,000) of badly burnt notes. I didn't know whether to laugh or cry."

MAGNET MAN WAS ATTRACTED TO WOMEN

Armed with a magnet, a San Francisco man staked out body piercing parlours waiting for women to leave in the belief that his device would sexually stimulate them.

WIFE BREAKS INTO PRISON TO HAVE SEX WITH HUSBAND

Apparently unable to bear the torture of being apart, a wife broke into an English prison in 2007 so that she could have sex with her husband. She sneaked into Standford Hill open prison on the Isle of Sheppey in the early hours of the morning by climbing over a fence. Her husband, who was waiting for her, then took her to his cell where they enjoyed a passionate romp before she left again a short while later. However a guard spotted her as she was making her exit, mainly because she stood out as the only woman in an all-male jail. In the wake of the breach, her husband was transferred to a higher security prison.

WOMAN ORDERS EXTRA MILK TO SAVE BOYFRIEND'S JOB

A woman from Nanjing, China, ordered 3,000 barrels of milk over a three-month period because she was worried that her boyfriend – a regional sales manager for a dairy company – would be recalled to head office due to poor milk sales.

THWARTED BUYER SAWED HOUSE IN HALF

Police said Rodney Rogers was so angry at missing out on the chance to buy a house in Hillsboro, Ohio, in 2007 that he attempted to cut it in half with a power saw. Believing that he would be sold the house, which an acquaintance had constructed, Rogers apparently reacted badly when the friend changed his mind about selling. Highland County Sheriff Ronald Ward said Rogers made a lateral cut in the walls all the way round the house and that gravity was the only thing keeping the top half in place with the bottom half.

MAN CREATES BOMB HOAX TO SEE WOMEN NAKED

Choosing a day when it was used by women bathers only, a man made a hoax bomb call to a public spa in the Russian town of Ulyanovsk in 2003, hoping that when police came to evacuate the building, the women would rush out naked. He was therefore disappointed when all the women took the time and trouble to put their clothes on first.

PROTESTOR CHAINS HIMSELF TO WRONG BUILDING

A man protesting against the war in Iraq and President Bush's foreign policy spent hours chained to the wrong building in 2003. Jody Mason padlocked himself to the entrance of the Washington State Grange Building, thinking it was a sub-office of the US Department of Energy when in fact it was a benign, non-profit organization dedicated to helping people in rural areas. Even when Grange employees told him he was protesting outside the wrong address, Mason was unable to move as he had thrown away the key to the padlock. Police eventually had to free him with heavy-duty bolt cutters. Mason said he had looked up the address for the Department of Energy in the phone book.

DELIVERYMAN LIGHTS MATCH TO SEE INSIDE PARAFFIN TANK

Wanting to see how much paraffin was in a tank he was delivering in 2001, a Johannesburg trucker lit a match so that he could look inside. The answer was none – after he had struck the match. For the resulting explosion smashed the tank, spewed burning paraffin far and wide and left the inquisitive deliveryman and four others badly burned.

PASTOR CRASHES MOTORBIKE DURING SERVICE

A pastor in Kokomo, Indiana, brought a dirt bike onstage during a church service to demonstrate the concept of unity, but ended up in hospital with a broken wrist after losing control of the machine. Jeff Harlow, the senior pastor at Crossroads Community Church, plunged off the five-foot-high platform and into the first row of seats, which luckily were unoccupied. His wife Becky said: "He had this idea that he would bring this bike out onstage and show people how the rider would become one with the machine. He was going to just sit on it and drive it out. He was just walking the bike out onstage and somehow it got away from him. Although he broke his wrist, I think his pride was more bruised."

TRUCKER DRIVES 400 MILES WITH CARDBOARD WINDSHIELD

A Chinese trucker drove 400 miles in freezing conditions with a sheet of cardboard covering his broken windshield. Mr Li said that he hadn't had time to repair the damage because of his tight delivery schedule and so he decided to drive on by sticking his head out of the side window or, when his neck became sore and numb, by peering through small holes in the cardboard. When police eventually stopped him in Henan Province, his face was purple from the cold.

PRISONER PULLS OUT HIS EYE AND EATS IT

A Texas death row inmate with a history of mental problems pulled out his only good eye in 2009 and told authorities he had eaten it. Andre Thomas had plucked out his other eye in 2004 before his trial for murdering three members of his family.

CHESTNUT SELLER MAKES BOMB HOAX TO BOOST TRADE

An Austrian hot chestnut seller decided to drum up trade on a slow business day in 2002 by making an anonymous hoax call to say that a bomb had been planted near his outdoor cart. He hoped that people would stand around in the cold to watch the police activity and so buy chestnuts from him.

MAN TRAPPED IN TOILET USES HANDEL TO GET OUT

A pensioner trapped in a hospital toilet was freed after singing the opening verse of Handel's *Hallelujah* chorus. Eighty-year-old George Hudson, who sings in his local choir, was at the Kent and Sussex Hospital in Tunbridge Wells for a hip operation when he became stuck in the toilet. After three tugs of the emergency chord failed to produce a response from staff, he burst into his favourite song and was rescued immediately. He said: "I like to think it was because they didn't want to disturb the rest of the patients rather than a comment on my singing."

SMOKING LECTURE BURNS DOWN HOUSE

Angry that her new husband had fallen asleep the previous night while smoking a cigarette, in the process burning a small hole in the bed, a woman decided to show him the possible consequences of his reckless behaviour. So she put a lighted cigarette on the bed of their house in Columbia, Tennessee, and walked out. The house was destroyed by the resulting fire and she was charged with arson.

SPEEDING MOTORIST MOVES ROAD SIGNS TO PROVE INNOCENCE

Caught speeding twice in two days, John Hopwood, from Stockport, England, tried to deceive investigators by dismantling a road sign and erecting it at a different location. A day after a speed camera clocked him doing 48 miles per hour in a 40 miles per hour zone in Manchester, another camera spotted him travelling at 41 miles per hour in a 30 miles per hour area in nearby Rochdale. In an attempt to dodge a speeding ticket, Hopwood removed the 40 miles per hour sign in Manchester and drove it ten miles to Rochdale where he attached it to a lamppost and took a photo. He then sent two letters to the Central Ticketing Office, including pictures of the same sign in its two locations, to try to claim that he was barely over the speed limit both times. For good measure, he added how "angry, upset and shocked" he was at being branded a law-breaker. However his elaborate plan began to unravel when other motorists began querying the speed limit sign which had mysteriously appeared in Rochdale. By drafting in a facial mapping expert to study marks on the two signs, prosecuting lawyers were able to prove that they were one and the same. Sentencing Hopwood for attempting to pervert the course of justice, the judge told him: "This was a stupid act bound to fail."

THIEF WEARS WOMEN'S UNDERWEAR TO AVOID DETECTION

A man caught stealing from a store in Kiuzhou, China, was found to be wearing women's underwear. He told police that he was very superstitious and believed that if he wore lingerie, his crimes would go undetected.

DRUNK SHOOTS HIMSELF WHILE TRYING TO CURE ITCH

Drinking beer and playing poker until 3 a.m. in his home at Fort Worth, Texas, Jorge Espinal suddenly experienced an itch on his back. Since it was in a hard-to-reach location, he picked up the first thing that came to hand to use as a backscratcher – a loaded revolver. The gun went off and Espinal returned to the game with blood pouring from a wound to his back. But at least his itch was cured.

FAMILY SPRAY URINE ON LAMPPOSTS TO FIND LOST DOG

A family from Bristol tried to lure home their missing dog by spraying their own urine on lampposts and trees. The Baltesz family bottled their urine to scent-mark the streets where they lived in the hope that Simon the black labrador would recognize the familiar smell of his owners and return home.

MAN ASKS FOUR-YEAR-OLD TO DRIVE HIM TO POLICE STATION

After his driving licence had been confiscated by deputies, a man in Moulton, Alabama, needed to go to the sheriff's office to collect it. Not wanting to get into trouble for driving to the police station without a licence, he hit on the bright idea of getting his four-year-old nephew to drive him instead. This landed him with three new charges when deputies saw the boy drive into the parking lot.

FARMER BUILDS AMY WINEHOUSE SCARECROW

Desperate to find something scary enough to keep the pigeons off his sugar beet, Norfolk farmer Marlon Brooks decided to model his scarecrow on controversial singer Amy Winehouse. So he planted the lookalike – complete with her trademark beehive and tattoos and clutching a cigarette and a bottle of liquor – in the middle of his field . . . and waited for the reaction. He was soon able to report: "The pigeons are terrified. They're sitting up on the telephone wires too scared to come into the field. She's the best scarecrow we've ever had. In fact, I'd be happy to offer her a full-time job if she needs one when the singing is over."

ROMEO SERENADES GIRLFRIEND WITH AMBULANCE SIREN

A lovesick Italian man stole an ambulance so that he could serenade his girlfriend with its siren. Spotting the keys in the ignition, he drove the ambulance to her apartment near Ancona, switched on the siren and began singing romantic love songs. "I can't play an instrument," he told police officers, "and I wanted a memorable way to romance my girl."

CAR CRASH IS CAUSED BY DRIVER SHAVING BIKINI LINE

Florida police said a 2010 car crash in Key West was the result of the driver attempting to shave her bikini line while the vehicle was moving. They said the 37-year-old woman, who was on her way to meet her boyfriend, was attempting to shave her pubic hair while her ex-husband held the steering wheel, only for her car to crash into the back of a pickup truck.

MAN STYLES GIRLFRIEND'S HAIR WITH POWER DRILL

When they arrived home from an evening out in Edmonton, Alberta, in 2004, Janine Rose asked her boyfriend, Shee Chung Theng, to give her a massage and comb her hair. Leaving the bedroom to get some food, the boyfriend said he watched a TV commercial for a hair-styling device . . . which apparently inspired him to fit a Barbie brush to an electric power drill. As a result Rose woke up screaming and bleeding when the tool tore out a clump of her hair. Admitting that using the drill for hair-styling was a "ridiculous" idea, Shee was ordered to undergo counselling, complete 70 hours of community service and was banned from handling power tools for nine months.

MAN DESTROYS CAR WHILE TRYING TO WARM IT UP

When his car failed to start in 2001, a 78-year-old German man lit a fire under it to thaw it out – but could then only watch as it burst into flames, reducing the vehicle to a charred ruin. He had ignited a pile of paper towels in a metal box and placed them directly beneath the engine and the fuel tank.

SUSPECT IS RUN OVER BY HIDING PLACE

A suspect who fled from Phoenix, Arizona, police after his car was pulled over in 2009 decided to hide under a nearby removals truck. Unfortunately while officers were searching for him, the truck driver returned and drove off, running over the suspect in the process.

BAILIFF FLEES AMOROUS GRANNY

A 6-foot 6-inch bailiff sent to raid a home over an outstanding credit card bill fled back to his office after being showered with kisses by a 58-year-old grandmother. When Sandra Hertzog opened the door of the family house in Tetge, Germany, and saw the bailiff, she threw her arms around him and tried to reach up to kiss him on the lips. The terrified bailiff eventually managed to free himself from her grasp and rushed back to his base to report the incident to his superior. Hertzog protested: "I wasn't trying to scare him off. He just looked like such a hunk standing there I felt like giving him a kiss."

ACCUSED GOES TO COURT WITH CARDBOARD BOX ON HEAD

Not wanting a potential witness to recognize his client, Justin Kalich, prior to a 2006 preliminary hearing on charges relating to the theft of a reel of wire, attorney Jeff Leonard suggested that Kalich wear a cardboard box on his head. Thus Kalich sat wearing a blue and white box with two eyeholes while waiting outside the office of District Judge James Albert at the courthouse in Greensburg, Pennsylvania. However, after a meeting with the judge, Kalich agreed to pay for the wire, and the charges were dropped. Explaining his idea, Leonard said: "I'm trying to think outside of the box, so to speak."

DRUNK COMPLAINS THAT BED IS TOO HARD

Walking home after a heavy night's drinking, one Grant Shittit, of Timaru, New Zealand, decided to sleep it off on what he thought was a nice soft bed of moss. He lay down in it right up to his neck, only to discover when it was too late that it was actually a trench full of cement. He was stuck fast for three days until spotted by a passing motorist who mistook him for a hedgehog.

MAN TRIES TO DISGUISE HIMSELF AS FEMALE DUMMY

When tax inspectors raided a Buenos Aires textile sweatshop in 1994, everyone ran for the exits except one man who had the bright idea of posing as a female mannequin. Hurriedly slipping on a dress, he stood motionless in the hope that nobody would see through his cunning disguise. He might have got away with it but for the fact that he was still wearing a pair of big scruffy sandals.

SCHOOLBOY FAKES KIDNAPPING TO COVER FOR BAD REPORT

Rather than bring home a bad school report, an 11-year-old boy concocted a story about having been kidnapped by a gunman. He claimed a stranger in a red car grabbed him as he left school in Huntsville, Alabama, in 2009 and forced him into the vehicle. The boy said he managed to jump out of the car, leaving behind his school bag which contained his report, and ran to his grandparents' house. However police were suspicious that the boy had somehow been able to escape with his band instrument, but not his bag. The boy eventually confessed to making up the story to cover for his bad grades. The whereabouts of his school bag and report card remained uncertain.

SIX WOMEN TRAPPED IN TOILET WHILE TRYING TO SAVE MONEY

In an attempt to save money on toilet fees, six young women decided to squash themselves into the same public toilet in Hartlepool, England. Instead they became stuck there for nearly three hours before a passer-by heard their screams and alerted the fire brigade who freed them by cutting off the roof. A police spokesman said: "They were furious at being ignored but the sound of screams from public toilets in Hartlepool isn't uncommon."

STUDENT STARTS FIRE TO MEET WOMEN

A male student at the University of Central Florida decided that the best way to find true love was to set a couch on fire at the Academic Village

Dorms. He told police he hoped he would be able to meet women as the building was evacuated.

PRISON VISITOR GETS PISTOL STUCK IN RECTUM

Visiting an inmate at the high-security La Picota prison in Bogota, Colombia, a woman concealed an automatic pistol in her rectum. But once inside the prison she realized to her dismay that the gun was stuck fast. Complaining of acute stomach pains and claiming that she was pregnant, she was taken to hospital where doctors eventually found the source of her discomfort. The gun was removed from its hiding place and she was charged with possessing an illegal weapon.

ROMANIAN WIFE STRIPS OFF TO HELP HUSBAND

After her husband Valeriu was kicked unconscious by a horse, 25-year-old Ana-Maria Botea stood by the side of the road near Galati, Romania, desperately trying to flag down passing motorists to fetch help. After three hours not one car had stopped so, as a last resort, she decided to strip off. Immediately two men stopped to take a closer look and agreed to take her husband to hospital. From his sickbed Valeriu said: "I've got the cleverest – and best-looking – wife in the world."

RIVER CAR WASH PROVES COSTLY

When Stan Caddell wanted to wash his Chevrolet, he thought he would save money on a car wash by using the Mississippi River instead. So he carefully backed the car into a foot of water at Hannibal, Missouri, but no sooner had he climbed out to clean it than it floated away. Police eventually managed to retrieve the vehicle some distance downstream. An officer attending the incident confirmed that no action would be taken against Caddell because "you can't ticket a guy for being stupid".

MAN HAS FEET CUT OFF IN INSURANCE SCAM

Saddled with heavy debts, Chung Kyu-chil hit on a novel way of solving his problems: he took out two dozen insurance policies that would pay him up to $1.7 million if he became disabled and then he hired someone to hack off his feet. The 51-year-old grocer from Seoul, South Korea, initially told police that he awoke in his shop on the morning of 11 December 1998 after a heavy drinking session and found his feet missing. Unsurprisingly the police were somewhat sceptical and when the recently purchased insurance policies came to light, Chung confessed that he had hired a taxi driver, Kim Kui-yong, to sever his feet at the ankles and that he had agreed to pay him $41,600 if the scam proved successful. The taxi driver said he had cut off Chung's feet with an axe and dumped them in the Han River. Kim was arrested on assault charges but Chung escaped punishment because he never tried to collect the insurance.

LOVESICK WOMAN CALLS 911 TO MEET "CUTE COP"

After a sheriff's deputy called at her home in Aloha, Oregon, to investigate a neighbour's complaint, Lorna Dudash was so smitten that she rang 911 in the hope of getting a date with him. "He's the cutest cop I've seen in a long time," Dudash told the dispatcher. "I just want to know his name. I'm 45 years old and it doesn't come very often that a good man comes to your doorstep. I know this is absolutely not in any way, shape or form an emergency, but if you would give the officer my phone number and ask him to come back, would you mind?" The deputy did indeed return, but the only date Dudash got was a date in court as he arrested her for misusing the 911 system.

HORTICULTURAL SHOW CHEAT CAUGHT OUT BY PRICE TAG

An entrant in the North Otago, New Zealand, Horticultural Society's 2002 summer flower and plant show was disqualified when the judges spotted that his winning plant still bore the flower shop's price tag on the bottom of its pot.

BORED SOLDIER LIGHTS FIREWORK IN BUTT

Bored with a Sunderland fireworks display in 2006, a 22-year-old soldier decided to liven things up by setting off a firework between his buttocks. He dropped his pants and slipped a powerful Black Cat Thunderbolt between the cheeks of his backside. A friend then set the firework alight and the soldier bent over as his butt exploded in a shower of sparks. The impromptu display resulted in the soldier ending up in hospital with a scorched colon and other injuries.

MAN TRIES TO DEMOLISH HOUSE WITH PICKUP TRUCK

Fuelled by an 18-pack of beer, Dave Anthony decided to use his pickup truck to help demolish a friend's house in Kent, Washington State, in 2000. First, he knocked down the garage by ramming it with his truck. Buoyed by that success, he drove the truck onto the roof, whereupon the weakened structure started to buckle, leaving Anthony and his truck high and dry. A towing company was called out to bring the truck down but Anthony quickly sobered up when handed a bill for $695. When he couldn't pay it, the towing company impounded his truck.

ARRESTED MAN THROWS HIS INTERNAL ORGANS AT POLICE

WHILST BEING taken to a Michigan jail on a misdemeanour arrest warrant, a man broke his handcuffs, used them to slice open his own stomach and then tried to throw his internal organs at police and rescue workers. After seven officers had eventually managed to subdue the man and put him on a stretcher, a witness said: "The guy was spraying blood and reaching into his stomach, tugging on his organs in an attempt to get them out. It was real weird, even for Detroit." •

UNIVERSITY THROWS OUT PRICELESS LIZARD POOP

A university apologized to a graduate student after his unique collection of lizard excrement – collected over a period of seven years – was accidentally thrown away. Daniel Bennett had been studying the rare and reclusive butaan lizard in the Philippines and had built up a collection of faeces samples which were stored in England at Leeds University. But the 35-kilogram bag of precious poop was thrown out in 2009 during a clear-out. Bennett said: "To some people it might have been just a bag of lizard shit, but to me it represented seven years of painstaking work. Its loss has left me reeling and has altered the course of my life forever."

TRAPPED MOUSE BURNS DOWN HOUSE

Perhaps to teach a mouse a lesson, Ranvir Singh, from the Manipuri district of India, caught it in a trap, tied a kerosene-soaked rag to its tail and set fire to the rag. The mouse proceeded to run around Singh's house, setting everything on fire and destroying the property.

WOMAN TRAPPED UNDER CAR WHILE LOOKING FOR KEYS

A 91-year-old woman who crawled under her car to look for her keys was stuck beneath the vehicle for two days in 2008. Betty Borowski, from Milwaukee, Wisconsin, was only rescued when a mailman saw letters piling up on her doormat. Firefighters lifted the car and removed the pensioner, who was dehydrated and confused, having been pinned to the ground by the axle. "She was pretty wedged in there," said the local police chief. "It looks like she crawled under headfirst." Her keys were found in the car door.

DRUNKEN WOMAN FAILS WRITTEN DRIVING TEST

A Romanian woman was disqualified from her driving test after she failed a breathalyzer while taking the written section of the exam. Monika Cristescu, 20, from Arad, sank four gins to calm her nerves before the theory test, but when she started giggling loudly, shouting out the answers she was giving and telling the other candidates she was going to get every question right, a police officer walked over to her, immediately smelt alcohol and gave her a breath test. She was found to be double the drink-drive limit and was banned from taking the written paper until a date when she was sober. A police spokesman said: "Even though she was in a room and not actually on the road, she needed to learn that alcohol and driving don't mix."

DROWNING MAN ALERTS RESCUERS BY WAVING WOODEN LEG

A holidaymaker who fell into the sea from a small inflatable dinghy off the coast of Cornwall in 2009 was rescued by the crew of a passing boat after attracting their attention by waving his wooden leg.

TEACHER LIVENS UP LESSON BY STRIPPING OFF

Dana Gibson, 43, a substitute teacher at a Catholic high school in Santa Maria, California, was teaching Spanish one day in 2001 when a student complained that the lesson was boring. So Gibson took off her shirt to reveal a sports bra and continued with the lesson. After being fired from her job, she commented: "It didn't seem like a big deal, but maybe something's totally wrong with me."

CROOKED LAWYER IS NAMED WORLD'S UNLUCKIEST MAN

A British lawyer laid claim to the title of the world's unluckiest man after going on a spectacularly ill-fated gambling spree with tens of thousands of dollars stolen from a client. Edward Bentley, who practised as a solicitor in Yarm, Cleveland, ran up debts of over $45,000 when a stock market investment crashed. His solution was to steal around $100,000 from an account in the hope of breaking the bank in Monte Carlo with a single bet on the roulette wheel, but on arrival in Monaco he found that the casino's maximum stake on that kind of bet was $16,000. Undeterred, he flew back to London and decided to try his luck on the horses instead. He put $15,000 on a horse that was considered a certainty to win a race at Ayr at odds of 3-1. It fell. Sure his luck would change, he gambled the remaining money on the stock market by predicting a fall in futures prices. Instead they went up, leaving him with just $1,500 from his original stake. In desperation, he decided to take his own life and drove to Nottingham where he tried to gas himself in his car. The engine cut out. So he bought another second-hand car and drove to Scarborough, North Yorkshire, but his second attempt to kill himself was halted after police stopped him during a routine vehicle check. Bentley's only stroke of good fortune was finding a lenient judge who gave him a 15-month suspended sentence for theft. His own lawyer described the whole sorry saga as "more like a scene from a Peter Sellers farce".

DRIVER STOPS SOFA GETTING WET BUT CAUSES PILE-UP

A woman who suddenly drove her flat-bed truck under a bridge to protect her sofa when it started raining caused 24 vehicles behind her to crash. The woman swerved violently to get the truck under the overpass in Atlanta, Georgia, and planned to stay there until it stopped raining, but her action caused eight separate accidents which left 11 people with minor injuries. The woman's truck wasn't hit.

SEXUAL GRATIFICATION ENDS IN PAIN

A 51-year-old man from Long Branch, New Jersey, decided to seek sexual pleasure with his vacuum cleaner in 1998. However he didn't realize that the suction on the hand-held cleaner was created by a blade whirling just beneath the hose attachment and seconds after inserting himself into the vacuum, his pleasure was cut short when the blade lopped off a half-inch tip of his penis. He staggered to the phone and called the police but told them he had been stabbed in his sleep. When they pointed out the blood on the vacuum cleaner, he claimed not to remember the incident.

MAN THROWS SAVINGS OUT WITH GARBAGE

Worried that burglars might target his house while he and his wife were away on a 2007 business trip, a Mr Cui of Qingdao, China, decided to hide his savings of over $6,000 in the kitchen garbage bin for safe keeping. However on their return he forgot all about the secret stash and instinctively threw away the garbage because the bin was full. It was another two days before he suddenly remembered about the money – but by then it was too late; the garbage had been taken away. "Our last hope was the city garbage treatment centre," he wailed, "but the landfill was so vast that we knew our money was lost forever."

BURNING PASSION ENDS IN REJECTION

To prove his love for his girlfriend, 20-year-old Hannes Pisek made a giant heart out of 220 candles on the floor of his apartment in Hoenigsberg, Austria, in 2006. He then lit them and went to collect his sweetheart from work. But his hopes of a romantic evening were dashed when the flat caught fire in his absence. He not only lost his home but also his girlfriend who promptly dumped him and moved back in with her parents.

LAST CIGARETTE FOILS SUICIDE BID

Intending to commit suicide in his trailer home, a man in Tucson, Arizona, turned on the gas and settled down to die. Then, in a moment of impulse, he decided to light one last cigarette, and in doing so caused an explosion which saw him hospitalized with serious burns but still alive.

MAN MICROWAVES HIS OWN HAND

Believing he bore "the mark of the beast" – the number 666 – on one of his hands, a man cut off the offending hand with a circular saw, then cooked it in a microwave oven and called the police. The man, in his mid-20s, was calm when sheriff's deputies arrived at his home in Hayden, Idaho, although Capt. Ben Wolfinger said of the hand: "It had been somewhat cooked by the time the deputies arrived."

FARMER USED LIVE BOMB AS ANVIL

A live Second World War missile was destroyed in a controlled explosion by an army bomb squad in 2008 after a Romanian farmer was spotted using it as an anvil. The man had discovered the 122-millimetre calibre missile in his garden a few months earlier and had been using it for sharpening hoes and scythes.

WOMAN BITES DOG TO SAVE PET

A woman from Minneapolis, Minnesota, bit a pit bull terrier on the nose to save her pet labrador. Amy Rice first tried to prise the pit bull's jaws from her beloved Ella's throat and when that failed she bit the pit bull on the nose. "I broke the skin and had pit bull blood in my mouth," she said. "I knew what happened, and I knew that it wasn't good."

TRAIN MOONER DRAGGED HALF NAKED ALONG TRACKS

A German student mooning at railway staff in a departing train got his pants caught in a carriage door and ended up being dragged half naked for 200 metres along the station platform and onto the tracks. The 22-year-old had shoved his backside against the window of the train as a protest after staff had thrown him off at Lauenbrueck for travelling without a ticket.

MAN JAILED FOR SELLING OWN URINE

Kenneth Curtis of South Carolina was jailed for six months for selling his urine over the Internet to people facing drug tests at work. For $69 customers received Curtis's drug-free urine, a small pouch, tubing and a heating pack.

FARMER FORGOT TO TELL STAFF ABOUT BOOBY TRAP

A Hungarian farmer nearly killed one of his labourers after wiring his barn door to the mains to stop thieves stealing animal food at night. The labourer suffered a heart attack and severe burns from the electrical booby trap installed by farmer Laszlo Miklos to combat a series of thefts. Miklos said: "I have an electric fence around parts of my farm to stop the animals getting out and that gave me an idea that I could use electricity to stop the thieves getting in, but I forgot to tell my staff."

PRISONER TRIES TO HANG HIMSELF WITH DENTAL FLOSS

Prisoner Richard Barber tried to kill himself in his Iola, Kansas, jail cell in 1996 by wrapping dental floss that he had patiently collected around his neck and jumping off a ledge. But he succeeded only in cutting his neck. Ironically Barber was in jail for having killed a dentist.

PENSIONER DESTROYS ANTS AND APARTMENT BLOCK

A Polish pensioner destroyed an entire apartment block when he poured insecticide down a ventilation shaft to get rid of ants. Marcin Bartosz, 74, used gallons of insecticide but when it appeared to have no effect, he threw in a burning towel for good measure. The resultant explosion reduced the block of flats in Lubin to rubble and left him in hospital with third-degree burns.

POLICE SEE THROUGH INVISIBILITY SCAM

An Iranian paid a holy man the equivalent of over $1,000 to make him invisible. Convinced that he couldn't be seen, he then went into a Tehran bank and snatched a wad of banknotes. The first inkling he had that he had been duped was when police arrested him.

DRUNK TRIES TO REVIVE LONG-DEAD OPOSSUM

A 55-year-old Pennsylvania man was charged with public drunkenness in 2010 after he was seen attempting to give mouth-to-mouth resuscitation to a long-dead opossum he had found on a highway.

SHIT HITS THE FAN . . . LITERALLY

Appearing in court in Colombo, Sri Lanka, on theft charges in 1998, a defendant smuggled in a quantity of faeces in a plastic bag and hurled them at a police officer. However he missed and hit a spinning ceiling fan instead, thereby splattering everyone in the court.

NAKED MAN GETS TRAPPED IN CLOTHES DRYER

Following a drinking session with friends in 2009, Dave Chapman, from Waipopo, New Zealand, decided to change his clothes and started to look for a clean pair of underpants in his tumble dryer. Naked below the waist, he peered into the darkest recesses of the dryer in an attempt to find the elusive underpants, which he was certain were in there somewhere. To obtain a better look, he climbed in but although he managed to get his head and shoulders inside, he then succeeded in wedging his upper-torso in the door opening. To make matters worse, as he tried in vain to extricate himself, the dryer, which was hot from recent use, then fell to the floor on top of him. It took friends, ambulance staff, a police officer and two fire brigades to free him.

BOY CLEANS PUPPY BY FLUSHING IT DOWN LAVATORY

When his week-old cocker spaniel puppy got muddy after going on a walk, four-year-old Daniel Blair, of Northolt, Middlesex, thought the best way to wash him was to put him in the toilet and flush it. Luckily the dog survived being trapped in a waste pipe for almost four hours.

STUDENT BRINGS GRENADE TO SCHOOL

Four hundred children had to be evacuated from a school in Dennis, Massachusetts, in 2008 after an eight-year-old boy brought a Second World War hand grenade into class for a show-and-tell session.

MAN SHOOTS HIMSELF WHILE CHANGING WHEEL

A 66-year-old man had been repairing his Lincoln Continental outside his home in South Kitsap, Washington State, for two weeks in 2007 but was having problems removing one nut on the right rear wheel. Eventually in desperation and frustration he fetched his 12-gauge shotgun and decided to loosen the stiff nut by shooting it. However the blast peppered him with buckshot and he was rushed to hospital with random pellet injuries stretching from his chin to his feet. The man was said to have been perfectly sober at the time.

DALMATIAN LOVERS PAINT HOUSE IN SPOTS

After their beloved pet Dalmatian dog Bingo was run over by a car, Goran and Karmen Tomasic decided to commemorate him by painting the exterior of their house in Pribislavec, Croatia, white with black spots. "We have to admit that at first we were afraid of what the neighbours would say," said Goran, "but we loved Bingo so much we had to do it."

POLICE CHIEF STARTS FIRE TO IMPRESS EX-GIRLFRIEND

In 2002, John Tuchek, police chief of Lanesboro, Minnesota, deliberately started a fire behind a general store in the historic downtown area so that he could impress his former girlfriend, who lived above the store. He hoped that by saving her from the fire, he could win her back with his heroism. Alas the fire got out of hand, destroying two nineteenth-century buildings and taking 16 hours to bring under control. And Tuchek, who was by then the former police chief, ended up being sentenced to six years in prison for arson.

BOY ON TOILET SETS FIRE TO AEROSOL

A boy sitting on the toilet was blasted through the bathroom window after setting fire to an air freshener can. Thirteen-year-old Dennis Bueller, from Recklinghausen, Germany, had sprayed the smelly toilet with an aerosol but then decided to play with a lighter. "Suddenly there was this big orange flame," he recounted. "I woke up outside with my clothes burned off me and smelling like a barbecue." His father said: "He realizes he was a bit dim."

BUDDING ENTREPRENEUR TRIES TO SELL FOG

In 2002, Italian Giorgio Valentinuzzi came up with the idea of selling fog from his home village of Rivignano. He grabbed the fog in coffee tins which he then sealed and attempted to sell for $2.50 a time. He saw the business opportunity after being told that Rivignano's fog was the wettest in Italy.

PENSIONER CAUSES FIRE BY GRILLING SLIPPERS

A HAMPSHIRE pensioner nearly burned down her old folks' home in 2007 after putting her slippers under the grill to warm them up. After washing her slippers, 84-year-old Joan Hiscock placed them under the grill to dry but forgot all about them and they set fire to the oven. As the smoke triggered fire alarms, firefighters raced to the home in Stockbridge, evacuated the residents and, after bringing the blaze under control, found the smouldering slippers on the grill pan. A Hampshire Fire and Rescue Service spokesman said: "We told her it is all right to put kippers under the grill – but not slippers!" ●

WOMAN THROWS OUT MATTRESS CONTAINING $1M

Deciding to surprise her elderly mother with a new mattress, a woman in Tel Aviv, Israel, threw out the old one, only to discover that her mother had hidden her life savings inside – a cool $1 million. When she went to look for the mattress, it had already been collected by garbage men, prompting a frantic search of local landfill sites. One dump manager warned: "The mattress will be hard to find among the 2,500 tons of garbage that arrive at the site every day."

PIGEON TRIBUTE FAILS TO TAKE OFF

For a 9/11 memorial service in Jersey City, New Jersey, in 2002, organizers planned to release 80 white doves or homing pigeons in a symbolic gesture, the idea being that the birds would soar high in the sky and then return to the owner's roost. But all the professional birds had already been hired for use in other services that day, so the organizers decided instead to buy their 80 pigeons from Newark poultry market. The trouble was that the young market birds were bred for eating, not flying. Indeed, having spent much of their short lives squashed in small cages, most of them could barely fly at all. As a result, the ceremony turned into a blur of feathers and confusion. A number of the birds plunged into the Hudson River, while others smacked into plate-glass windows on office buildings or careered into the crowd, getting tangled up in people's hair. One sat on top of the hard hat of a construction worker whose company had helped clear ground zero. "I don't know how anyone could be so short-sighted, especially for 9/11," said a member of staff at a local bird hospital that was treating some of the injured pigeons. Amid the chaos, chief organizer Guy Catrillo searched hard and managed to find a positive. He said of the hapless birds: "Without a doubt it beats what could have happened to them. They were squab; they were soup birds. I like the idea that I helped these squab get another chance."

SUSPECT SEES THROUGH PC CUNNINGTON'S CUNNING PLAN

When police detectives in London were experiencing problems executing a search warrant on a house with a solid steel door, PC Dean Cunnington volunteered to borrow a postman's uniform and knock on the door in disguise. Hearing the knock, a voice inside the house called out: "Who is it?" "It's the police," replied PC Cunnington.

12

AT WORK AND PLAY

TEDDY BEAR KILLS 2,500 FISH AT MAINE FARM

About 2,500 rainbow trout died from lack of oxygen in a hatchery pool at Milford, Maine, in 2006 – and the culprit was a teddy bear. The child's bear, dressed in a yellow raincoat and matching hat, had somehow become lodged in a pipe that led fresh water to the pool. The deaths prompted the hatchery to post a warning notice to visitors: "RELEASE OF ANY TEDDY BEARS INTO THE FISH HATCHERY WATER IS NOT PERMITTED."

COUPLE RECEIVE RUDE MAILOUTS

Linda and Frederick Hinrichs failed a lawsuit in 1992 after a clerk at a motor dealership in Aurora, Colorado, put an abusive name on their ownership records, which were later used as the basis for mailouts. The couple said they subsequently received two mailouts from the Mazda Motor Company addressed to "Buttface Hinrichs".

LIFEGUARD RESCUES AIR MATTRESS INSTEAD OF WOMAN

When a woman toppled off an air mattress into the sea off Sydney's Bondi Beach in 2002 and began to drown, a lifeguard instantly sprang into action . . . but inadvertently rescued the mattress instead of her. The hapless lifeguard, who was subsequently sacked, explained that without his contact lenses his eyesight was so bad that he was unable to tell the difference between the woman and the mattress, especially as the latter "had all the bumps in the right places". Fortunately a passing motorboat driver rescued the drowning woman.

FLOOR COLLAPSES AT WEIGHT WATCHERS MEETING

The floor of a Weight Watchers clinic in Vaxjö, Sweden, collapsed beneath a group of 20 slimmers who had gathered to find out how many pounds they had shed. As the dieters lined up in 2010 for their weekly weigh-in, the floor started to rumble ominously before collapsing completely. One of the group compared the sensation to an earthquake. Happily the only things hurt were the dieters' feelings.

CROSS-DRESSING SCHOOL PRINCIPAL IS BUSTED AS HOOKER

Having apparently decided that his pay as principal of a West Virginia elementary school was insufficient, a 55-year-old man was accused of taking up a second job – as a prostitute. Police said that, sporting a black wig and lipstick, he tried to drum up business by undercutting the prices of the more traditional street-corner hookers. Unfortunately in interrupting one transaction, he allegedly offered oral sex to two undercover police officers.

SACKED EMPLOYEE DUMPS PORCUPINE DUNG OVER COLLEAGUES

Sacked for poor job performance, Empire, Michigan, postal worker James Beal returned to the office carrying three buckets filled with porcupine dung and worms, which he then threw over three of his colleagues. "It was in their pockets, it was in their shoes, they were covered from head to toe," said Assistant US Attorney Mark Cowtade. Sixty-two-year-old Beal, who was jailed for 18 months for the assault, admitted: "I let my anger with this sort of overrule my judgements."

CASINO EJECTS SMELLY POKER PLAYER

A Brooklyn gambler kicked up a stink in 2008 after being thrown out of a casino on account of his bad body odour. When Michael Wax went to the restroom at the casino in Atlantic City, New Jersey, a poker room manager followed him and informed him that his fellow players were complaining about his smell. Wax then tried to retake his seat at the table, but was ordered to leave. The 31-stone punter did not deny that he stank but said that he had been playing poker for 17 hours and had not had time to clean up.

130,000 INFLATABLE BREASTS LOST AT SEA

AN **AUSTRALIAN** men's magazine was at the centre of a storm in a D-cup after 130,000 inflatable breasts went missing en route from Beijing to Sydney. After launching a nationwide search, editor Santi Pintado was hugely relieved when the wayward breasts turned up a week later in Melbourne – just in time to be distributed free with the magazine's January 2009 issue. He said: "You'd think the Chinese economy was in enough trouble without misplacing 130,000 pairs of boobs." ●

EXOTIC DANCER PROTESTS OVER AGEISM SLUR

A 52-year-old exotic dancer from Toronto, Canada, complained that a local strip club violated her human rights for firing her because she was too old. Shirley Zegil said: "It's a human rights issue. It's discrimination. I'm fighting for the rights I'm supposed to have as a Canadian." A spokesman for the club said: "She was fired for being ugly. She's not only bad, but her body is too hairy. She looked like she was wearing somebody's toupee."

WORKER LOSES TWO FINGERS IN GUILLOTINE

In 2002, 25-year-old Keith Sanderson lost the tip of his thumb while operating a guillotine at a factory in Newcastle upon Tyne. Hearing his cry of pain, his supervisor ran over to ask what had happened, whereupon Keith demonstrated with his other hand . . . and severed half of his index finger. Surgeons managed to repair the thumb but were unable to save the other digit.

MAN SOLVES RUBIK'S CUBE AFTER 26 YEARS

In 2009, Graham Parker, from Portchester, Hampshire, proudly announced that he had finally solved his Rubik's Cube puzzle after 26 years of trying. He bought the toy in 1983 and had since spent more than 27,400 hours and endured countless sleepless nights endeavouring to find the solution. His long-suffering wife Jean said the cube had frequently put a strain on their marriage, causing blazing rows between them. She added that her husband was so obsessed with the cube that sometimes it felt as though there were three people in the marriage. A jubilant Mr Parker said: "I cannot tell you what a relief it was to finally solve it. It has driven me mad over the years – it felt like it had taken over my life. I have missed important events to stay in and solve it, and I would lay awake at night thinking about it. Friends have offered to solve it for me, and I know that you can find solutions on the web but I just had to do it for myself. I have had wrist and back problems from spending hours on it but it was all worth it. When I clicked that last bit into place and each face was a solid colour, I wept." Erik Akkersdijk of the Netherlands holds the record for the fastest solve of a Rubik's Cube with a time of 7.08 seconds.

FISH WERE DYING FOR A BEER

A worker at the Coors brewing plant in Golden, Colorado, turned the wrong valve in 1991 and sent over 150,000 gallons of beer into the adjacent Clear Creek, killing 3,000 fish.

PALLBEARER CRUSHED BY COFFIN AFTER FALLING INTO GRAVE

A pallbearer in San Antonio, Texas, was injured in 2008 after he fell into a grave and the coffin that he was helping to carry crashed down on top of him. Joseph Rivas said he stepped on a piece of Astroturf, which collapsed beneath him.

BUM RAP FOR ITALIAN PHOTOGRAPHER

A keen photographer was arrested in Venice in 2008 on suspicion of snapping more than 3,000 women's bottoms. Italian police became curious when they spotted the 38-year-old carrying a large bag as he followed miniskirted women through St Mark's Square. Whenever the women bent down, he appeared to be trying to angle the bag behind them. Police said he was filming through a small hole in the side of the bag and had kept his collection of butt images on a series of DVDs. He later admitted that he had been filming in and around the square for two years.

MISPRINT SCARES AIRLINE PASSENGERS

A proofreading error in an advertisement meant that Japan's JAS airline offered its English-speaking customers "non-stop fright" to Okinawa in 2002.

GREETER WEARS JUST A WAL-MART SACK

Dean Wooten, a 65-year-old Wal-Mart greeter from Muscatine, Iowa, was fired in 2005 for welcoming customers to the store with a computer-generated photograph of himself wearing nothing but a Wal-Mart sack. Wooten, who had worked for Wal-Mart for seven years, said: "A friend of mine got the photo of the body off the Internet, and he had a picture of me and he put my head on it. When I first saw it, I pretty near died laughing, and I thought the customers would find it amusing too." In fact, a number of them complained. Denying Wooten unemployment benefits, a judge ruled that "a reasonable person would know the act of showing a naked body wearing a Wal-Mart sack would not be good for the employer's business".

POLICE SWOOP ON GUN-RUNNING GERIATRICS

Police in Slovakia closed down a club for pensioners in 2001 after the members were discovered making machine guns, which they were selling on to criminals.

JOB APPLICANT IS RULED TOO INTELLIGENT TO JOIN POLICE

A college graduate who wanted to become a police officer was rejected because he scored too high on an intelligence test. Forty-nine-year-old Robert Jordan took the exam in 1996 and scored 33 points, the equivalent of an IQ of 125. But New London, Connecticut, police interviewed only candidates who scored between 20 and 27, reasoning that intelligent people would quickly become bored with police work.

SCIENTIST FAILS TO LAND STREET SWEEPING JOB

A jobless South Korean scientist with a doctorate in physics applied for a street sweeper's job at the height of the economic slump in 2009, only to fail the physical. Applicants for the job in Seoul had to carry two sandbags, each weighing 44 pounds, over their shoulders to simulate stacking garbage bags before running back and forth over 25 yards with another sandbag on their shoulder. But the 36-year-old scientist – one of 63 applicants for five vacancies – was three seconds too slow in the sprint.

HELPLINE PRIEST FALLS ASLEEP DURING SUICIDE CALL

A suicidal man who phoned a Swedish Samaritans-style helpline in 2010 was left in limbo when the priest at the other end fell asleep and started snoring down the line. Luckily the priest's response to his woes left the troubled man feeling angry rather than depressed, and he abandoned all thoughts of suicide.

FLAME-GRILLED BURGER BOSSES

A dozen Burger King bosses suffered first- or second-degree burns in Key Largo, Florida, in 2001 after walking over an 8-foot strip of white-hot coals as part of a team-building exercise. Surveying the line of wheelchair-bound employees at the airport the next day, one of the organizers remained unrepentant. "It made you feel a sense of empowerment and that you can accomplish anything."

BANK CUSTOMER RECEIVES 287 IDENTICAL LETTERS

John Tiemens, from Runcorn, Cheshire, received a staggering 287 letters confirming that he had cancelled his credit card – in the same post. "I hadn't a clue what was going on," he said after nearly falling over the mountain of mail on his doormat. "Then I picked up some of the letters and realized they were all identical." A spokesman for the company, Capital One, blamed a computer malfunction.

GUARD SAYS HE WENT NAKED TO TRAP STREAKER

Gary Aicard was arrested in 1997 after being seen running naked through the building at Lee's Summit, Missouri, where he was employed as a security guard. Over the previous few days, there had been several reports of sightings of a streaker in the building. When questioned by police, Aicard explained that he had stripped naked in an effort to befriend the real streaker so that he could catch him.

WOMAN, 33, POSES AS 13-YEAR-OLD BOY PUPIL

Staff at a school in Norway were alarmed to discover that the 13-year-old boy they had been teaching for the past three months was really a 33-year-old woman. "Adam" had enrolled at the Marienlyst School near Oslo in September 2007 but when he disappeared from a children's home in December of that year, police launched a nationwide search, which led them to reveal that he was, in fact, 5-foot 2-inch Czech national Barbora Skrlova, who had posed as a schoolboy by shaving her head and binding her breasts with tape. After Skrlova was deported back to the Czech Republic for psychiatric evaluation, the school principal commented: "We did react to Adam's behaviour, but children at that age can be so different."

PROFESSOR STUDIES WHY WOMEN FLASH BREASTS AT HOCKEY GAMES

In 2005, Professor Mary Valentich, of the University of Calgary's Faculty of Social Work, announced that she was going to conduct a study as to why women fans of the Calgary Flames had a tendency to flash their breasts at hockey games. She said she thought her study would shed light on current Canadian attitudes towards female nudity, adding: "There are gender role issues here. These women are doing something unconventional and yet they're using the traditional sexual route to express whatever they're expressing."

FRENCHMAN TAKES FIVE YEARS OFF WORK

In 2000, France's social services department finally realized that one of their civil servants in Cannes had not been into work for five years. Every morning the employee would ring in to head office and claim that he was on his way to one of the many other offices on his patch. But he never showed up. His deception was eventually uncovered when his bosses decided to post someone at the door of every office to see whether he put in an appearance.

CAMERAMAN'S BADGE SETS DOMINOES TOPPLING

In 1978, Bob Specas was preparing to break a world record by knocking down 100,000 dominoes at New York's Manhattan Centre. Specas had painstakingly positioned 97,499 over the course of several hours when a TV cameraman, on hand to capture the big moment, dropped his press badge and accidentally set off the whole wave of dominoes.

JOB INTERVIEW COMES 34 YEARS TOO LATE

After applying for a job with the Indian government in 1968, Navindra Nath Halder was called for an interview . . . in 2002. However by then he was 52 years old and the maximum age for a government job was 37. The country's labour minister admitted that it often took a long time for a person to be called for an interview.

SHOP ASSISTANT LOSES $2,700 BY MISREADING PRICE TAG

A set of Victorian military medals worth over $2,700 was sold for a fraction of the price in 2009 after a part-time shop assistant in Norwich, England, misread the £1,850 price tag as £18.50 ($30). The 13 medals, which date back to the 1890s, belonged to an antiques dealer who was on his lunch break at the time. When the error was pointed out to the assistant, she "went very white and got very upset".

SPELLING DVD HAS SPELLING ERROR ON COVER

The makers of a 2006 spelling game DVD fronted by Northern Irish TV presenter Eamonn Holmes had to scrap 10,000 copies after spelling his name as "Eamon" on the cover. The mistake was spotted by Holmes when DDS Media sent him one of the first DVDs to be pressed. He told them: "How can you expect people to buy this game when you've misspelt my name on the front!"

CIVIL SERVANT NEEDS 20 PEOPLE TO REPLACE HIM

An Indian government worker was considered so irreplaceable that when he eventually retired, it took 20 younger men to do his job. Described by his bosses as a human dynamo with a computer-like memory, Sachidanand

Maitra should have retired in 1989 but was granted 12 annual extensions while he trained 20 men to take over the job he had done for nearly 50 years. Bringing a lighter note to his retirement speech, his immediate superior said 70-year-old Mr Maitra possessed "an unmatched knowledge of the laws and by-laws of countless state government departments".

MOTHER CALLS POLICE TO STOP GAMER SON

Angela Mejia, from Roxbury, Massachusetts, called the police because she could not get her 14-year-old son to stop playing Grand Theft Auto on his Sony PlayStation. After ordering him to go to sleep hours earlier, she was so angry at finding him playing the game in his room at 2.30 a.m. that she summoned the police. Officers gently persuaded him to turn off the PlayStation and go to bed.

STUDENT WITH SMELLY FEET WINS RIGHT TO STUDY

Following a ten-year legal battle, a philosophy student with smelly feet has won the right to attend lectures at a Dutch university. Teunis Tenbrook was banned from Rotterdam's Erasmus University after complaints from professors and his fellow students that the stench from his feet made it impossible to study. But in 2009 a court ruled that having smelly feet is no cause for exclusion. The judge said: "Our considered opinion is that the professors and other students will just have to hold their noses and bear it."

TEACHERS PLAY TRUANT FOR 23 YEARS

The entire staff at a school in eastern India was fired in 2004 after their boss discovered that they hadn't been to work for 23 years. The 11 employees, including eight teachers, at the Rajendra Memorial High School in West Champaran only showed up for work twice a year on occasions of national importance. The scam eventually came to light when the local examination board chairman carried out a snap inspection – and also found that the names of most of the students enrolled in the school were fake.

COMPANIES SETTLE DISPUTE WITH ARM-WRESTLING CONTEST

Two New Zealand telecommunications companies locked in a $112,000 dispute reached an unusual out-of-court settlement in 2003 – a best-of-three arm-wrestling match between the rival chief executives. Defeated CEO David Ware said: "Sure, losing hurts, but not nearly as much as paying lawyers' bills."

ROAD SIGN SPELLS JUST ONE WORD CORRECTLY

A sign erected in 2009 on Interstate 39 near Rothschild and Schofield, Wisconsin, succeeded in spelling only one word correctly – "exit". The flawed sign read: "Exit 185 Buisness 51 Rothschield Schofeild."

LATVIAN TOURIST SLOGAN SENDS OUT THE WRONG MESSAGE

Embarrassed Latvian tourism chiefs were forced to scrap a 2009 campaign after their slogan to encourage visitors to the country, "Easy to go, hard to leave", was mistranslated as "Easy to go, hard to live". The $750,000 campaign had been intended to promote the cultural delights of the capital city, Riga, to English-speaking travellers but, as a tourist board spokesman admitted ruefully: "Apparently nobody checked it properly before the leaflets and posters went to the printers."

"FIREMAN STARTED BLAZES TO EARN OVERTIME"

A teenage Polish firefighter was accused in 2008 of deliberately starting a series of fires so that he could build up enough overtime to buy his girlfriend a birthday present. Pawol Leszek allegedly set fire to barns in the Studzianki area and then went to the local fire station where he earned $4 an hour as a voluntary firefighter.

ANTI-DRUGS MESSAGE FAILS TO MAKE ITS POINT

A company that sent a school in New York State a batch of pencils bearing an anti-drugs slogan had to recall them after one pupil spotted an elementary problem. The pencils carried the message "Too Cool To Do Drugs", but a ten-year-old at Ticonderoga School noticed that when the pencils were sharpened, the slogan turned into "Cool To Do Drugs", then simply "Do Drugs". "We're actually a little embarrassed that we didn't notice that sooner," said a company spokesperson, adding that the new batch of pencils would have the slogan written in the opposite direction.

SWEDISH COMMANDOS BLOW UP WRONG HOUSE

An elite Swedish commando force – considered to be the country's most deadly division – blew up the wrong house during a 2009 training exercise. The K3 unit were supposed to attack an unoccupied property in Rojdafors bought for that purpose by the military but instead they launched a terrifying night attack on another home 200 yards away, blowing out both front and back doors and every window before realizing their mistake. Fortunately the property owners were not at home at the time.

COLOURBLIND MAN DEMANDS RIGHT TO INSTALL TRAFFIC LIGHTS

Cleveland Merritt filed a federal lawsuit in 2001 against Palm Beach County, Florida, claiming it had violated the Americans with Disability Act when it fired him. The county had dismissed the traffic light installer because he was colourblind and couldn't distinguish between the red and the green wires.

COMPANY'S MAIL IS POSTED IN THE CHIMNEY

A postwoman was responsible for a fabric firm in South Normanton, Derbyshire, not receiving any mail for days on end in 2002. It transpired that she thought a hole in the office building's chimney stack was the company's letterbox and had been carefully depositing all the mail in the flue.

VALUABLE CHURCH ARTEFACTS SOLD OFF AS JUMBLE

Visitors to a church jumble sale in Wales in 2003 picked up a bargain when a gold chalice, silver goblet and ornate candlesticks – worth a combined $15,000 – were mistakenly sold for less than $15. The sacred ornaments were sold on the cheap after sale organizers mixed the items up with bric-a-brac in the church hall at Newquay, Cardiganshire.

MAN PAID FOR FIVE YEARS BY COMPANY HE DIDN'T WORK FOR

After accepting a job with Avaya Inc., a New Jersey-based telecommunications company, in 2002, Anthony Armatys subsequently changed his mind. However his change of heart failed to register with the firm's computer system, which never removed his name from the payroll, and over the next five years Avaya proceeded to pay him $470,000 – even though he had never done a day's work for them. The error was eventually spotted by Avaya's auditors, and 35-year-old Armatys duly pleaded guilty to theft.

LOST JOGGER STUCK IN SWAMP FOR FOUR DAYS

A jogger who took a wrong turn during his lunchtime run ended up stuck in a swamp for four days. Eddie Meadows, 62, left his desk at the University of Central Florida's research park every lunchtime to jog around the campus but one day in September 2006 he strayed into the bog, where he was eventually discovered by volunteer searcher Ron Eaglin "stuck like glue". Eaglin said: "I heard someone sloshing off in the woods and then I heard cries of help. I said: 'Are you looking for Eddie Meadows?' And he said: 'I AM Eddie Meadows!'"

SAFETY LEAFLET URGES: "TO ESCAPE FIRE, JUMP ON A DONKEY"

Scotland's fire services scrapped hundreds of leaflets in 2006 after an error in translation advised members of the public to jump on a donkey when fleeing a house fire. The leaflet, aimed at Urdu readers, urged that anyone leaving a burning building from a window should lower themselves onto cushions. However the authors got the Urdu word for "cushion" mixed up with another very similar Urdu word for "donkey".

OWL IMPERSONATORS WERE HOOTING AT EACH OTHER

Neighbours Fred Cornes and Neil Simmons, from Stokeinteignhead, Devon, spent a year hooting to owls every night from their respective gardens – unaware that they were actually hooting to each other. The truth only came to light when Kim Simmons told Wendy Cross about husband Neil's nocturnal owl watching and described how he got the birds to hoot back. "That's funny," said Wendy. "That's what Fred has been doing!" Neil said ruefully: "That's when the penny dropped. I felt such a twit."

BANK CUSTOMER DEPOSITS $1,413 IN SMALL CHANGE

Angry that his bank had previously refused to cash a cheque for $1,413 because it said it did not recognize his signature, a Brazilian customer marched into the same São Paulo branch of HSBC and deposited the amount in coins. Jose Luis Pereira da Silva rented a bus to transport the 34 friends he needed to accompany him on the mission because the bank imposed a limit to how much each person could deposit in change. It took staff three hours to count the coins which weighed a total of 121 pounds. Afterwards Mr da Silva celebrated by holding a barbecue for his friends.

TAXI DRIVER HAS THREE ACCIDENTS ON FIRST DAY

First-day nerves seemed to get the better of a New York taxi driver when he was involved in three separate accidents in quick succession. His licence was suspended only hours into the job after he rammed two parked cars, injured a pedestrian and left the scene of an accident. First he hit a parked car on Sixth Avenue and continued driving. A block away, he struck a 22-year-old pedestrian and again continued driving. Police finally caught up with him after he struck a second parked car and he was charged with leaving the scene of three accidents. The former restaurant worker had received his licence after 40 hours of training.

SAILORS MUST SHOUT "BANG" IN COST-CUTTING EXERCISE

In 2000, British Royal Navy recruits at a gunnery in Plymouth, Devon, were ordered not to fire expensive live shells during training exercises. Instead they were instructed to shout "Bang". The initiative was part of a Ministry of Defence plan to cut spending but sailors said it made a mockery of their training. One recruit said: "It's like being a kid again, playing cowboys and Indians in the school playground."

POLICE CANDIDATE HID WOOD IN HAIR TO PASS HEIGHT TEST

An Indian man was arrested on suspicion of hiding a block of wood in his hair to meet the minimum height requirement for joining the police. Gajendra Kharatmal had passed all the police exams in Mumbai but his application had been rejected because at 5 foot 1 inch he was two inches too short to join the force. So he tried again, and this time he measured an acceptable 5 foot 3 inches. One of the examiners said: "We were puzzled by this, so we asked him to stand there once again. The second time, we felt something hard hidden in his hair and discovered a piece of wood." His application was again turned down and he was arrested on charges of cheating.

TOKYO STORE SOLD FRESHLY USED WOMEN'S UNDERWEAR

At a store in an upmarket district of Tokyo, women would come in, undress, and sell the underwear that they had been wearing on the spot. Over a period of seven months, police said the shop owner sold 11 items from 4 women who had undressed for their customers. Officers finally put a stop to his business on the grounds that he did not possess a licence to sell second-hand goods.

IRATE FATHER SUES OVER SPELLING CONTEST

The father of the beaten finalist in a 1987 California spelling bee contest sued the event sponsor, the Ventura County *Star-Free Press*, claiming mental distress and seeking $2 million in damages. A state court judge and a court of appeals dismissed the lawsuit, ruling that the principal reason the plaintiff's son had lost the spelling bee was not because the contest was badly run but because he could not spell "iridescent".

TEACHER DISPLAYS PORN DURING SCHOOL EXAM

Seventeen students at Marlborough College, Wiltshire, were part way through a mock AS-level exam in 2002 when several looked up and noticed indecent pictures being relayed onto a large screen. The invigilator, maths teacher Richard Jowett, had apparently been looking at the material on his personal computer, forgetting that it was linked up to the monitor. The school's head teacher confirmed that during the exam Jowett had "used the computer and entered a website for 13 minutes containing still photographs of naked adult women".

COMPANY TRUCK ROLLS INTO RIVER DURING SAFETY MEETING

A concrete company's safety meeting was interrupted in 1998 when one of its unattended trucks rolled 50 yards across a street, over an embankment and plunged 20 feet into the Hudson River. The driver had left the vehicle at the rear of a business complex in Troy, New York State, while he unloaded a scale from the truckbed, but when he returned he saw to his horror that the truck had vanished. It was hauled out of the river two hours later. A company spokesman admitted: "It was unfortunate that this should happen while we were discussing safety in the workplace."

WORKER UNFAIRLY SACKED OVER FART ROW

Swede Goran Andervass was awarded $85,000 compensation in 2003 after a tribunal ruled that he was unfairly dismissed for telling off a co-worker for passing gas. The early-morning flatulence prompted an angry response from Andervass who was suspended and then made redundant after the farter complained to management. "My colleague was absolutely aware of the awful smell," said Andervass. "It was pure provocation." Commenting on the compensation award, the Swedish Work Environment Authority said: "If a fart is done on purpose when going into somebody's office, it is important that management takes the matter seriously."

ROYAL MAIL DELIVERS LETTER 89 YEARS LATE

A LETTER DATED 29 November 1919 was eventually delivered to Janet Barrett's guesthouse in Weymouth, Dorset, in December 2008 – 89 years late. A note from Royal Mail, apologizing for any delay, accompanied the delivery. ●

BUILDING EVACUATED IN SCARE OVER PRESENTATION DEVICE

Thousands of people were evacuated from an office complex in Columbus, Ohio, in 2009 after an employee spotted a black box with lights, wires and a timer in one of the conference rooms. Only after several of the evacuated employees had been overcome by summer heat in the parking lot did it emerge that the suspicious item was simply a device designed to keep presentations short. The lights warn a speaker when it is time to shut up.

MIAMI GETS PARKING METER FAIRY

Miami acquired its very own parking meter fairy in 2004 when 37-year-old actor Xavier Cortes donned a curly pink wig, lavender tutu and fake wings and roller skated around the city putting change into meters that were about to run out. He had answered an advertisement placed by Coconut Grove retailers and restaurateurs who feared that visitors to the district were being discouraged by parking tickets. The advertisement stated that the successful candidate would be "a colourful one-of-a-kind extrovert who looks good in tulle". Carrying a wand and armed with $40 in dimes, Cortes skated through the neighbourhood, leaving his calling card under windshield wipers: "You've just been saved by the Coconut Grove parking-meter fairy."

MAN COVERS HIMSELF IN EXCREMENT TO CLOSE BANK ACCOUNT

An angry bank customer in Thailand smeared himself in human excrement before walking into a branch to close his account. Chuay Kotchasit said the stench would be more bearable than the "stink of mismanagement" at the bank. He was thought to be upset after losing $9,000 on a savings investment.

HOTELIER GIVES SERVICE WITH A SNARL

A hotelier in Maine was so routinely abusive that in 1999 he was ordered by a court not to have any contact whatsoever with his guests. The court heard how 66-year-old Clifford Shattuck, who owned the Lighthouse Motel in Lincolnville, "repeatedly threatened his customers in a scary and unusual way". Fining him $15,000, Justice Donald Marden found that Shattuck was abusive towards people who asked to see rooms before they registered and towards those who used the motel driveway to turn around. It was not the first occasion that the hotelier had been in trouble. In 1994 he was fined for violating the civil rights of two Israeli tourists. They claimed Shattuck told them that Hitler "should have killed another six million Jews" and threw rocks at their car as they left.

SUSSEX PENSIONER KNITS BREASTS

Sussex octogenarian Audrey Horncastle has an unusual hobby – she knits woollen breasts. She gives them to her daughter, community nurse Rhona Emery, to help teach new mothers to breast feed. Mrs Horncastle, from Woodingdean, near Brighton, reckons she has knitted more than 100 breasts in three years. "I try to keep the basic fleshy tone," she said, "but sometimes people ask if I can put in a bit of colour as well just to make things a bit different. People do tend to give me a strange look when I tell them what I am knitting."

ROAD SIGN WORKERS FORGET TO USE SPELL-CHECK

California highway department employees, painting a large white warning sign on a road in 2002, made the mistake of doing so without first checking their spelling. The sign read "CRUVE".

FIRM CHOOSES NAME ON ITS DOORSTEP

Norwich Union, Britain's largest insurance firm, spent a year and $1.4 million on consultants, focus groups and research in 50 countries to come up with a new name. Eventually it chose Aviva, which just happened to be the same name as a small dress shop 300 yards from its head office. Although Norwich Union insisted that it hadn't seen the dress shop before thinking up the name, it seemed more than a coincidence to the shop's owner Annie Catlin. "I couldn't believe it," she said, adding that it had taken her ten minutes over a cup of coffee to think up the name Aviva, which is Hebrew for "joy of spring".

WOMAN RINGS UP $120,000 TAB ON PSYCHIC HOTLINE

Cheryl Burnham, a clerk at a Los Angeles juvenile facility, was sentenced to 30 days in jail in 1999 for ringing up a $120,000 tab on her employer to a psychic hotline. She placed a total of 2,500 calls on county telephones to the psychic hotline in the Dominican Republic. The district attorney's office commented: "Unfortunately the psychic failed to foresee the jail sentence."

FIRM HIRES WITCH TO HUNT BAD DEBTORS

A debt-collecting firm from Vilnius, Lithuania, hired local witch Vilija Lobaciuviene to hunt down companies and individuals who were failing to repay outstanding debts during the 2009 credit crunch. "There are certain people who are using this crisis situation and refuse to pay banks or other companies," said the firm's director before adding ominously: "Our new employee will help them to understand the situation, reconsider what is right and wrong and act accordingly." The country's media called the move a "return to the Dark Ages".

SACKED WORKER WREAKS TUNA REVENGE

Fired from Fanny's Cabaret strip club in Ottawa, Canada, a woman vowed to take revenge on her employers. She carried out her threat by leaving bags filled with tuna all over the club – on tables, chairs, next to walls and in coat and champagne rooms. A number of guests complained of burning eyes and upset stomachs.

GRANNIES BANNED OVER BINGO BRAWL

Two grandmothers were banned for life from a Bridgend, Wales, bingo hall in 2002 after brawling over a supposedly lucky chair. Security staff had to pull the women apart as 500 other players watched in astonishment. Sandra Fry was arrested for punching Lynn Want who was taken to hospital with a broken nose and two black eyes. "She called me names for months," protested Mrs Fry, "before I snapped and hit her. I didn't plan it – it was one punch. I don't know where it came from – I was just as shocked as she was."

MAN ATTENDS DENTAL APPOINTMENT NAKED

A man turned up five days late for a dental appointment in Stratford, Connecticut, in 2009 – with no clothes on. A horrified female receptionist screamed and the naked man ran out. She was later able to identify him by his blue eyes and deep tan.

CCTV OPERATION TRAPS THIEVING MOUSE

Following dozens of cash thefts from the offices of a company in Villach, Austria, management decided to install closed-circuit television in a bid to catch the thief. The camera revealed that the culprit was a mouse which had been using 50-euro notes to build its nest.

CAR COMPANY SENT LETTERS TO "PASSED AWAY"

A widow received three letters from a car rental company that were not only addressed to her dead husband but also included the words "passed away" in the address. Cynthia Haigh, of Brighouse, West Yorkshire, lost her husband on Christmas Day 2006, but despite informing the new owners at Polar Ford in Huddersfield of his death, they kept sending letters to him. In December 2007, a letter arrived at her home addressed to Mr David Haigh, Passed Away Died, Brighouse, West Yorkshire. Although the family contacted the company and received a letter of apology, two more letters, addressed the same way, arrived at her home the following February.

STOLEN CORPSE DRESSED AS DARTH VADER

Three students in New York were accused of taking a corpse from a crypt, dressing it up as *Star Wars* villain Darth Vader and taking it to a fancy dress party.

BALD MAN, 49, IS ASKED TO PROVE HE IS OVER 18

When balding 49-year-old Maurice Harris tried to buy a bag of party poppers at a Tesco supermarket in Bedworth, Warwickshire, in 2009, staff told him they needed proof that he was over 18 because the poppers were classed as explosives. He was finally sold them when a security guard he knew at the store vouched for him. Mr Harris said: "I'm 50 next month but I look older. I've hardly got a hair on my head."

DRACULA DESCENDANT ENCOURAGES BLOOD DONORS

The last surviving descendant of Count Dracula (also known as fifteenth-century Transylvanian nobleman Vlad the Impaler) was enlisted by Germany's Red Cross in 1999 to try to persuade people to become blood donors. Ottomar Rudolphe Vlad Dracul Prince Kretzulesco, who lived in the crumbling Castle Schenkendorf on the outskirts of Berlin, agreed to help the Red Cross after hearing a radio appeal for more donors. The count said he was happy to hold a blood donor session at the castle "although I will draw the line at letting them put up crosses".

CLEAN-UP COMPANY PAINTS GRAFFITI TO BOOST BUSINESS

A Swedish graffiti clean-up company admitted in 1998 that it painted graffiti on buildings in Oerebro after the number of contracts it received diminished drastically because local police had been so successful in apprehending taggers. "The police were too effective in the battle against graffiti," explained the clean-up company owner. "We were without work and started to paint graffiti ourselves. Otherwise we risked going bankrupt."

SPELLING MISTAKES DISCOVERED IN LAKE SIGNS

As the result of a six-year campaign by the local newspaper, embarrassed officials in Webster, Massachusetts, finally admitted in 2009 that some road signs pointing to Lake Chargoggagoggmanchauggagoggchaubunagungamaugg were spelt incorrectly. Errors in the 45-letter name – said to be the longest place name in the United States – included inserting an "o" for a "u" in the 20th letter and an "h" for an "n" at the 38th letter. Among the two dozen other rejected variations was a 49-letter version with extra "g"s. The local Chamber of Commerce said it would attempt to find out who originally painted the signs and get them to correct them. Unsurprisingly local residents refer to the location as "Webster Lake".

VISITORS RIOT ON DISCOVERING MERMAID WASN'T REAL

In a bid to boost visitor numbers to the city aquarium at East London, South Africa, in 1998, tourism director Craig Nancarrow hired 18-year-old aquarium guide Tessa du Toit to dress up as a mermaid. However when she refused to go into the water for fear that it would ruin her costume, some of the crowd of 350, lured by the promise of seeing a mermaid, reacted angrily and started throwing things at her. "They thought mermaids really existed," said du Toit, "and things got a bit out of hand when they discovered the truth."

WORKERS PAINT YELLOW LINES AROUND PARKED VAN

When Gordon Dickson parked his van in an Edinburgh street in 2002, it was in a perfectly legal place. However while he was away council workers started painting yellow lines around the van and stuck a $45 parking ticket on his windshield. The city council later quashed the fine.

"BOY STABBED FATHER IN ROW OVER VIDEO GAME TACTICS"

An Italian man who argued with his son over tactics on a Sony PlayStation soccer game was rushed to hospital after the boy allegedly stabbed him in the neck with a 15-inch kitchen knife. According to newspaper reports, the row broke out when the father offered his son Mario advice on how to improve his play on the video game FIFA 2009 – and then turned the TV off in response to the 16-year-old's reaction. Police said that the teenager then fetched a knife from the kitchen and stabbed his father in the neck before returning to clean the weapon at the kitchen sink in front of his watching mother and leaving it to dry on the draining-board. The mother said she had no idea what had happened until her husband stumbled into the room, clutching his throat. She said the game had been given to her son as a birthday present a few days earlier. "Mario is obsessed," she added. "He's forever playing on his PlayStation, and we bought him FIFA 2009 because we didn't want him playing violent games."

PRESERVATION GROUP TARGETS WRONG BOAT

For eight years a Tennessee preservation group called Raise the Gunboat campaigned tirelessly to raise enough money to bring up the *Tawah*, part of a Union fleet that was sunk in the Tennessee River in 1864. They had managed to collect $220,000 when they suddenly discovered to their horror that the wreck on the river bed was not the *Tawah* but a barge that may have been built as late as 1925. "They didn't have the right boat," sighed Memphis archaeologist Stephen James. "They're good guys, but they're not archaeologists."

FARMER ACCIDENTALLY ANAESTHETIZES HIMSELF

A Chinese farmer who was supposed to be anaesthetizing deer accidentally knocked himself out for 11 hours after the needle pierced his skin. Mr Liu was using a strong animal anaesthetic to tranquilize the deer at his farm in

Chongqing so that he could harvest their antlers for Chinese medicine. But after administering a shot to one deer, he noticed anaesthetic dripping from the needle and made the mistake of using his hand to wipe it dry. No sooner had the needle made contact with his skin than the hapless farmer was laid out cold. Doctors later said the anaesthetic was so powerful it could have knocked out an elephant in less than a minute.

NUDISTS SIGN BOOSTS SHOPKEEPER'S TRADE

Bernard Patenaude, proprietor of the Pomfret Spirit Shoppe, was certain that he would get much more passing trade if drivers on Route 169 between Pomfret and Woodstock, Connecticut, didn't race past so quickly. So he had a big sign painted: SLOW DOWN NUDISTS CROSSING AHEAD. The ruse worked a treat. Motorists slowed right down; some even turned round and crawled back. As a result, business at the Pomfret Spirit Shoppe was booming. However the state police took a dim view of the sign, and pointed out that there was a law against private citizens ordering motorists to slow down. Besides, they said, the sign was too close to the road. Proprietor Patenaude pondered his next move all winter. Finally he came up with a solution which he hoped would satisfy everyone – a new, bigger sign on Route 169 but set farther back from the road. It read: WATCH OUT NUDISTS CROSSING AHEAD.

DRIVERS FILL UP WHILE GAS STATION ATTENDANT SLEEPS

When motorists drove into a gas station in Tortosa, Spain, and saw that the attendant had fallen asleep, they decided to fill up their cars free of charge and hurriedly phoned their friends urging them to do the same. The fuelling frenzy finished $1,000 worth of gas later when police grew suspicious after noticing an unusually long line of cars in front of the station. A police spokesman said: "Our officers went in and woke the man but by then a lot of people had come and gone. It was their lucky day."

CONTRACTORS DEMOLISH WRONG HOUSE

A contractor hired to demolish a house in Texarkana, Arkansas, in 2001 accidentally knocked down the wrong one after a mix-up with city officials.

On learning of the error, the contractor explained: "We were sitting on the street and we made a call to City Hall. We asked them if we were at the right house. They asked us if there were trees covering it up, and we said yes. They said: 'Then you're at the right place.' Evidently there were two houses that were covered by trees." Authorities confirmed that they were expecting a claim for compensation from the house owner.

"MISTER SOFTEE TRIED TO KILL ME!"

LUIS AMARO, a 51-year-old part-time Mister Softee driver in Hartford, Connecticut, was accused in 2002 of charging out of his ice cream van and swinging a bat threateningly at 64-year-old Wilbur Troutman, who for months had led a crusade complaining about the company's noisy, repetitive jingles. One of Mr Troutman's fellow protesters said: "Every night, it's the same songs, over and over. It drives you crazy." For his part, Mr Troutman was surprised at the attention his campaign had attracted. "I'm well known, almost notorious, for being the anti-Softee man," he admitted. "Hey, we all have our 15 minutes. I was hoping it would be for something nobler." ●

CROATIAN SMURFS FEEL BLUE OVER RECORD

Eager to get the town's name into *The Guinness Book of World Records*, the people of Komin, Croatia, searched for easy targets on the Internet. Discovering that the record for the largest gathering of people dressed as Smurfs was a modest 290 by an American group, they launched a determined campaign, set a date for the record attempt and informed the press. When the time came, 395 Smurfs descended on Komin – men, women and children all painted blue from head to toe, and wearing white trousers and white floppy hats. But when they contacted Guinness to verify the record, they were told that it had all been a waste of time. The Internet site they had consulted was out of date: the previous year, students at Warwick University in England had managed to assemble 451 Smurfs, beating the Croatian effort by 56. A dejected Croat spokesman said: "We could easily have got more Smurfs, but we thought that over a hundred more than the American record we found on the Internet would be enough."

JOB APPLICATION UPSETS THE WELSH

An English student made the mistake of applying for a job at a Welsh tourist attraction using the email address "atleastimnotwelsh". James Kettle, a student at Pershore Agricultural College, Worcestershire, also managed to send his application to the wrong address. Instead of sending it to the National Botanic Garden of Wales, he sent it to Aberglasney Gardens, Carmarthenshire, where a manager wrote back to him: "It may be prudent to change your email address. It could have a detrimental effect on any career aspirations of working in Wales." Kettle admitted: "I feel a right fool. I set up the email at school because several Welsh kids were in my year. I forgot it was with my application."

WRONG MAN APPEARS ON NORWEGIAN STAMP

The Norwegian postal service printed 1.3 million postage stamps in 2002 . . . featuring a picture of the wrong man. It had intended to honour noted Norwegian soccer referee Lars Johan Hammer but unwittingly used a picture of little-known German referee Peter Hertel instead. The postal service had been sold a picture from the 1997 junior Norwegian Cup, in which both men were officiating, but chose the wrong ref. To make matters worse, the two men did not look remotely alike. A disappointed Hammer said: "I was really looking forward to it and had alerted all my relations to the big event. I don't have glasses or a beard and I must say I was stunned to see this strange referee on the stamps."

BUTCHER FIRED OVER SUGGESTIVE MEAT CUTS

Butcher Kenneth Black was fired from a South California supermarket after a female co-worker complained that he had intentionally cut meat to resemble female genitalia. Black said it was the first time he'd had a complaint about his meat in 20 years.

FIFTY-FOOT SIGN REMOVED IN EXCHANGE FOR SHOES

Seeing a 14-foot by 48-foot vinyl billboard sign that promised, "Bring in this ad and you'll get a free pair of shoes", three intrepid coupon clippers decided to do just that. They removed the 70-pound sign from its location next to an expressway in Scranton, Pennsylvania, and contacted Shoestrings to claim their free shoes. The general manager of Chancellor Media Group, which installed the sign, admired the trio's audacity and agreed to pay for three pairs of shoes in return for the undamaged sign. "How can I prosecute?" she said. "They did what we told them to do!" Shoestrings said they would be placing a disclaimer on their next billboard.

TOURISTS ACCIDENTICALLY LOCKED IN HISTORIC PRISON

A retired prison officer and his wife became a historic jail's first inmates in almost 100 years when they were accidentally locked inside by staff. Pensioners Norman and June Bradshaw were still looking around Ruthin Jail in Denbighsire, North Wales, in 2009 when staff closed up early and went home. Trapped in the souvenir shop, their cries for help were heard by a worker in a nearby building but she could not release them because she did not have the keys. They were eventually freed an hour later. Mr Bradshaw said: "I joined HM Prison Service in 1966 and retired in 2004. During all that time I was never locked inside a prison with no escape – that is until now. My sons and their wives all work for the prison service so it really is quite ironic."

ALLIGATOR PHOTOGRAPHER TAPES HIMSELF TO TREE

A man who got lost in a Florida swamp during a trip to photograph alligators had to be rescued by police after taping himself high up in a tree so that the reptiles couldn't attack him at night. Gemini Wink had taped himself to a branch so securely that sheriff's deputies had to climb 40 foot up the tree to free him.

CHIMP LANDS TOURISM JOB

A chimpanzee called Bobby has been appointed Tourism Promotions Inspector by the Polish town of Radkow on a salary of $140 a month. Bobby is taken around the regional capital Wroclaw with a sign on his back advertising the nearby Table Mountains range, which has a local beauty spot known as Monkey Rock.

NEWSPAPER PRINTS OWN NAME INCORRECTLY

A US newspaper made arguably the most embarrassing typographical error possible – it spelt its own name wrong, in the masthead on the front page. Readers of New Hampshire's *Valley News* who picked up the 21 July, 2008, edition were surprised to see the title across the top of the front page read "Valley Newss". The following day, the editor apologized for the blunder, saying: "Given that we routinely call on other institutions to hold themselves accountable for their mistakes, let us say for the record: We sure feel silly."

MARATHON WALK WRECKED BY THE FRENCH

A man who planned an epic two-and-a-half-year walk from Britain to India without spending any money only got as far as Calais before turning back. Mark Boyle set off on foot from Bristol in January 2008 with the intention of eventually reaching Gandhi's birthplace on the west coast of India, but he managed only 300 miles to the French port before giving up the trek because it was cold and the people there only spoke French! He quickly announced plans to walk around Britain instead.

EASTER BUNNY ARRESTED FOR BRAWLING IN MALL

The Easter Bunny was arrested for brawling with an assistant at a shopping mall in Madison, Wisconsin, in 2000. The 15-year-old girl playing the Easter

Bunny became involved in an altercation with her 20-year-old sidekick, which ended with punches being thrown and the Bunny falling over her own head.

STRIPPER ATTACKED AFTER TURNING UP TO WRONG VENUE

Carlo Pampini, a male stripper from Naples, Italy, arrived at a hotel suite to perform for a hen party in 1997. He stripped off and wedged a large sausage firmly between his buttocks, but when he invited a woman to remove it, he was whacked with a chair. When a dazed Pampini regained his senses, he realized that he had mixed up the room numbers and had in fact been entertaining a meeting of the Catholic Mothers Against Pornography Guild.

BUSINESS STUDENTS CHEATED IN ETHICS EXAM

Twenty-five San Diego State University business students were found guilty of cheating in an exam – on ethics. Ensnared in a trap set by a suspicious lecturer, about a third of those enrolled on the course were caught using answers that had been given to an earlier test. All were awarded failing grades for the course. One student sighed: "What did I learn from the course? You shouldn't cheat – unless there's absolutely no risk of getting caught."

AIRLINE HIRES BALD MEN AS WALKING BILLBOARDS

Air New Zealand announced in 2008 that it was looking for 50 bald passengers willing to act as "cranial billboards" bearing temporarily tattooed messages on their shiny pates to advertise new improved check-in services. The airline said it would pay $700 a head to volunteers. Its marketing manager Steve Bayliss said: "How better to tell our customers that Air New Zealand is going to do something about long check-in queues than through messaging they can read while standing in a queue themselves?"

SPURNED SALESWOMAN DEFECATES ON PORCH

A spurned cosmetics saleswoman took her revenge on a housewife who refused to answer the door of her Florida home in 2009 by defecating on her doorstep. The houseowner said she didn't answer the door because she didn't recognize the car outside, whereupon the saleswoman, apparently angered by the snub, decided to leave an unconventional calling card.

SCHOOL PRINCIPAL GETS HER ANSWERS WRONG

The principal of a school in Boerum Hill, New York, was accused of changing up to 119 answers on 14 competency tests in an attempt to improve students' marks. Officials said it was easy to tell what had been changed because she used a green eraser to remove the old answers whereas all the students had been given red erasers. Furthermore, nearly a quarter of her corrections were wrong.

LAZY STREET WORKERS PAINT WOBBLY LINES

Workmen painting double yellow "no parking" lines on a street in Huddersfield, West Yorkshire, in 2002 could not be bothered to move a solitary traffic cone that was in their way. So rather than stop their machine, they swerved around the cone, creating wobbly lines 18 inches into the road.

BUNGLING FRENCH ARMY SHELLS MARSEILLE

Hundreds of Marseille residents were evacuated in 2009 after the French Army conducted artillery practice in hot summer weather with the result that every shell landing on a hillside started a fire. As high winds fanned the flames towards the city suburbs, numerous buildings were destroyed, including a retirement home housing 120 pensioners. Thousands of acres of land were burnt to a cinder. Regional government prefect Michel Sappin branded the army "imbeciles".

TALKATIVE ACCOUNTANT THREATENED WITH JAIL

An accountant in Salem, Pennsylvania, was charged with defiant trespass in 2002 for talking too long at a public meeting – an offence that carried a possible two-year prison sentence. Jim Barbe, 60, committed the crime of speaking for 11 minutes, instead of the allotted five, at a meeting to discuss a new sewage disposal plan, but was spared jail when the case against him was eventually dropped.

MAN SETS UP NAKED DECORATING BUSINESS

In 2008, a Lincolnshire naturist launched Britain's first naked painting and decorating service. Nick Male advertises on naturist websites and eBay, claiming that having a naked decorator around the house oils the creative wheels and makes customers feel less inhibited. "Business is booming," he said, "and I work more now than when I left my clothes on. The service is a serious one though: I don't do titillation."

COUNTY ADVERTISES FOR KLINGON-SPEAKING APPLICANTS

A county advertising a job helping mental patients in Portland, Oregon, said it welcomed applicants who were fluent in Klingon, the fictitious language spoken by aliens in *Star Trek*. Multnomah County's purchasing administrator Franna Hathaway explained: "There are some cases where we've had mental health patients where this was all they would speak." However the county later admitted: "It was a mistake, and a result of an overzealous attempt to ensure that our safety-net systems can respond to all customers and clients."

WOMAN CALLS EMERGENCY SERVICES TO SOLVE CROSSWORD

A woman from Grevenbroich, Germany, called the country's emergency services in 2009 because she was stuck for the answer to a crossword clue. Petra Hirsch explained: "I had finished the crossword except for this one answer and I was totally stumped. I had looked all over the Internet and asked friends. It was really bothering me. The clue was for the full name of a police border protection unit, so I thought they would not mind helping and I called the hotline – but they were really rude. All I wanted was a bit of help and it would only have taken them a second to tell me the answer, but instead I got told to get off the line." A police spokesman said: "It is called an emergency number for a reason – to deal with emergencies. Crossword solutions are not an emergency."

LAWYER IS LISTED IN DIRECTORY UNDER "REPTILES"

Linda Ross, a family lawyer in Southern California, was dismayed to see that in a 2000 edition of Yellow Pages she was mistakenly listed under "Reptiles". She said she was worried the listing might confirm what people already believe about attorneys.

JEHOVAH'S WITNESS IS ATTACKED BY RAM

Visiting homes uninvited in 2003, a South Australian Jehovah's Witness ignored a "Private – Keep Out" sign on someone's property and was attacked by a ram. He sued his church over his injuries on the grounds that they had failed to advise him that "Private – Keep Out" meant that he should keep out.

CINDERELLA AND SNOW WHITE ARRESTED IN DISNEYLAND PROTEST

Cinderella, Snow White, Tinkerbell and other fairy tale characters were handcuffed, frisked and loaded into police vans following a protest at Disneyland, California, in 2008. The arrest of 32 protesters – many of whom were in costume – was part of a pay dispute among staff at three Disney-owned hotels in the area. The incident left tourists bewildered. One visitor from England said: "Nothing Disney could create could be more surreal than seeing Tinkerbell being handcuffed and bundled into a police van."

HERO WORKER HAS WAGES DOCKED

A baker who received a bravery award after tackling three robbers at the Canterbury, Kent, supermarket where he worked was then docked two weeks' wages for taking time off to recover from his injuries.

WOMEN HAVE CHESTS RUBBED WITH HAM AT PARTY

The Myrtle Beach Fire Department of South Carolina handed back a $2,400 donation in 2000 because the money had been collected at a party where women danced on stage while having their bare chests rubbed with a ham. The department, which wanted the money to buy a new truck, said it had not known what the party would involve.

SPANISH KING IS REPLACED BY HOMER SIMPSON ON COIN

A Spanish shopkeeper stumbled across a defaced euro coin where the head of King Juan Carlos had been transformed into that of Homer Simpson. Don Juan Carlos's regal half-profile topped by a full head of curls had morphed seamlessly into the pop-eyed, big-nosed, bald-headed features of Homer, complete with familiar five o'clock shadow. "The coin must have been done by a professional," said Jose Martinez who found it in the cash register of his shop in Aviles in 2008. "It's an impressive piece of work." Amid fears that the illegal defacement might be part of a republican conspiracy against the Spanish monarchy, thousands of *Simpsons* fans from across the globe bid over $30 for the coin.

APPLICANT CREATES SPARKS AT JOB INTERVIEW

An Australian man built up so much static electricity in his clothes when he walked that he burned carpets, melted plastic and sparked a mass evacuation. Frank Clewer, from Warrnambool, Victoria, was wearing a synthetic nylon jacket and a woollen shirt when he went for a job interview in 2005 but as he walked into the building, the carpet ignited from the 40,000 volts of static electricity that his clothes had created. "It sounded like a firecracker," he said, "and within about five minutes, the carpet started to erupt." Worried fire crews evacuated the building and cut its power supply in the belief that the scorch marks in the carpet had been caused by a power surge. When the culprit was finally uncovered, fire chiefs said the charge was almost high enough to cause spontaneous combustion. On leaving the building, Mr Clewer scorched a piece of plastic in his car.

BEWARE OF THE "BMUP"

In 2003, highway workers in Richmond, California, painted a warning sign in four-foot-high letters on the road. It read "BMUP". Appropriately while doing this, they had erected a sign saying "Slow Men Working".

FIREMAN RUNS SCARED FROM MICE

An Essex fireman faced the wrath of senior officers after fleeing his duty station when he saw two mice. The fireman locked up the Waltham Abbey station after spotting the mice in the kitchen and promptly drove back to headquarters, telling colleagues he was too frightened to stay on his own at night.

"VACUUM CLEANER SALESMAN CHASED AWAY WITH GUN"

Police said that Fred Banks, of West Haven, Connecticut, was so annoyed by the persistent attempts of salesman Ricardo Vasquez to sell Mrs Banks a vacuum cleaner that he chased Vasquez out of the house with a gun.

STUDENT GETS MARKS FOR SWEARING IN EXAM

A British student who wrote "Fuck off" as his answer to a GCSE English exam question in 2008 was given two marks just for spelling it correctly. He gave the four-letter answer when asked to "describe the room you are sitting in". Peter Buckroyd, chief examiner of English, said: "It does show some very basic skills we are looking for, like conveying some meaning and some spelling. He would have got even more marks if he had added an exclamation mark."

GERMAN MAGAZINE RUNS CHINESE BROTHEL AD BY MISTAKE

Seeking to illustrate a special report on China with Chinese characters, a respected German research institute mistakenly ran an advert for a Chinese brothel on its front page. The Max Planck Institute had bought the picture of Chinese characters in good faith from a photo agency and had it checked by a Chinese speaker, but when the piece appeared describing China as "a many-faceted, fascinating land", readers noticed that the text also included a reference to an advertisement for stripping housewives in a brothel.

MAN WAS SHOT AT FOR HARASSING FISH

Ut Van Ho of Ada, Oklahoma, was charged in 1992 with shooting at a 22-year-old man who was "harassing" his pet fish by shining a flashlight into the fish tank during an afternoon card game.

SHOP REFUSES TO MAKE BIRTHDAY CAKE FOR ADOLF HITLER

The American parents of a three-year-old boy named Adolf Hitler were fuming in 2008 after a shop refused to inscribe his name on a birthday cake. Heath and Deborah Campbell wanted to buy a cake inscribed "Happy Birthday Adolf Hitler" at a ShopRite supermarket near their home in Holland Township, New Jersey. The store decided the request was "inappropriate" and also refused to make a cake for Adolf's sister, Aryan Nation, who turned two in 2009. The Campbells, who said they named their son "Adolf Hitler" because nobody else would be using the name, apparently could not understand what all the fuss was about. "ShopRite can't even make a cake for a three-year-old," moaned Mrs Campbell. "That's sad. They're just names, you know. Yeah, the Nazis were bad people back then. But my kids are little. They're not going to grow up like that."

BANK APOLOGIZES FOR CALLING CUSTOMER "DICKHEAD"

A bank apologized to a customer after sending him a debit card bearing the name "Dick Head". Chris Lancaster of Tiptree, Essex, received a NatWest cash card in 2005 with the wording "Mr C. Lancaster Dick Head". The 18-year-old said: "I know I've been overdrawn a few times but I've done nothing to deserve this. The bank said it must have been a worker with a grudge."

BOTANISTS SLEEP ON RARE ORCHID

AFTER 15 YEARS of searching for an elusive orchid, corybus carseii, which only flowers for two days a year and was thought to be extinct, botanists Lionel Pucker and Tim Batty spent $25,000 on one final expedition to a remote corner of New Zealand's South Island. At the end of another six fruitless weeks, they decided to pack up and go home, only to discover as they took down their tent that a specimen was lying flattened beneath their groundsheet. Batty recalled: "We were lifting up our groundsheet when we spotted what looked like a pair of squashed lips. I said, 'Bollocks, it's the orchid!' Then we both started crying." Batty noted that the crushed plant was on Pucker's side of the tent and that it "didn't stand a chance because he's fat and rolls around in his sleep." ●

NEGLECTED LUNCH SENDS FIRE STATION UP IN FLAMES

Firemen in Florida returned from a 2004 blaze to find their station on fire. They had forgotten to turn off their lunch that was cooking on the gas oven.

NOBODY NOTICED WORKER DEAD AT DESK FOR FIVE DAYS

An employee at a New York publishing firm sat dead at his desk for five days in 2001 before anyone noticed that he had passed away. George Turklebaum, 51, who had been employed as a proofreader at the firm for 30 years, had suffered a heart attack in the open-plan office he shared with 23 other workers. He died on the Monday but it was not until the following Saturday morning that an office cleaner asked him why he was still working at the weekend. His boss said: "George was always the first guy in each morning and the last to leave at night, so no one found it unusual that he was in the same position all that time and didn't say anything. He was always absorbed in his work and kept much to himself." Ironically George was proofreading manuscripts of medical textbooks when he died.

BREAST IMPLANTS ARE TAX DEDUCTIBLE

A prostitute in Denmark was allowed to reclaim the cost of her breast implants – over $4,000 – as a tax allowance. The surgery was deemed to constitute a legitimate business development.

EVERYONE'S A WINNER IN SCRATCH CARD PRIZE DRAW

When a Roswell, New Mexico, car dealership hired a direct-mail marketing company to send out 50,000 scratch-off tickets to local residents in 2007, the idea was that just one ticket would be the $1,000 grand prize winner. But a typographical error meant that all 50,000 tickets were grand prize winners, as a result of which the Roswell Honda dealership was besieged by people claiming their cash.

POLICE ORDER COVER-UP

Police in Iasi, Romania, have ordered women to cover up after receiving saucy snapshots on identity card applications. Officers said some of the pictures were so revealing that it was impossible to tell whether the women were wearing any clothes. Police chief Viorel Scutaru complained: "We had many cases when ladies came wearing very sexy tops so that from the picture you believe she's naked. But this is official ID, so it should be decent."

EXPERTS SOLVE TOMATO MYSTERY

Puzzled by the lack of tomatoes on her plant, a 70-year-old British gardener took it along to a recording of the BBC radio series *Gardeners' Question Time*, where the experts informed her that it was actually a cannabis plant.

GYM TEACHER TAKES BRIBES FROM STUDENTS

A gym teacher at a school in Pensacola, Florida, was put on three years' probation in 2006 after pleading guilty to taking around $230 in bribes from six students so that they could skip his class. Terence Braxton collected $1 a day in return for allowing students to miss gym but the scam came to light when one of the students eventually told his parents.

HOTEL OWNER BANS ENTIRE TOWN

An Australian motel owner living in New Zealand became so angered by the "awful behaviour" of local people that in 2009 he banned all 16,000 residents of Wainuiomata from his establishment. Former Sydney resident Steve Donnelly claimed the North Island town of Wainuiomata was full of young "troublemakers" and "bad people" who regularly trashed his motel. He accused groups of youngsters from the town of engaging in vandalism, spitting, swearing and playing loud music at night. He said: "We have had about 100 people from there over the last couple of years – and maybe one that we liked." The ban provoked fury among New Zealanders. Trevor Mallard, an MP who was born and bred in Wainuiomata, said of the country's answer to Basil Fawlty: "I'm not surprised, he's Australian."

FAMILY TREE SEARCH PROVES IN VAIN

Ian Lewis from Lancashire devoted 20 years of his life to tracing his family tree back to the seventeenth century. Travelling the length and breadth of Britain, he spoke to more than 2,000 relatives and proudly announced his intention to write a book about how his great-grandfather had left to seek his fortune in Russia and how his grandfather had been expelled following the revolution. It was compelling stuff, but just as Mr Lewis was about to start work on his tome he discovered that he had been adopted when he was a month old and that his real name was David Thorton. He immediately resolved to begin his family research all over again.

PET SHOP ORDERS FISH, GETS COFFIN

Owing to a mix-up at Philadelphia Airport, a local pet shop that was expecting a shipment of tropical fish received a dead body instead. Shop owner Mark Arabia went out to the delivery man's vehicle to collect the $1,000 fish consignment but was stunned to be given a coffin containing the body of a 65-year-old man from San Diego, California. Mr Arabia said: "At first when I looked at the coffin, I thought to myself, 'Fish never come this way.'"

BANK BLOCKS PASSWORD PROTEST

Blaming Lloyds Bank for a holiday insurance muddle which left him with a $2,000 bill following a skiing accident, disgruntled computer consultant Steve Jetley, from Shrewsbury, changed his bank account password to "Lloyds is Pants". He said: "It was half joke, half protest, and Lloyds staff usually burst out laughing when I used it." But on calling the Lloyds TSB business centre in Birmingham in 2008, Mr Jetley was furious to discover that staff had changed his password to "No We Are Not". He immediately demanded it be re-set to "Lloyds is Rubbish". When told that was inappropriate, he tried "Barclays is Better", and when that, too, was rejected, he went for "Censorship", but was informed the word could only be six letters. Finally he suggested "Faeces", only to be advised that new rules meant the characters had to be numbers, not letters. While Lloyds were apologizing for the fact that a staff member had broken banking rules by changing a customer's password without consent, Mr Jetley was trying to think of a cunning new password that he could slip past the censors.

13

ROCKY RELATIONSHIPS

HUSBAND SURPRISED TO MEET WIFE IN BROTHEL

A Polish man received the shock of his life in 2008 when he visited a brothel and found his wife working there. She had told him that she was working at a store; his excuse for being present was not reported. The couple, who had been married for 14 years, announced they were divorcing.

MARRIAGE COUNSELLING SESSION ENDS IN GUNFIGHT

When Michael Martin arrived late, drinking a beer, for a marriage counselling session at their local church in Fresno, California, his wife Bonnie stormed off. Police said he responded by pulling out a gun and shooting at her. Wounded, she reached into her purse and pulled out her own gun to fire back. The gunfight continued into the church parking lot. Afterwards the Rev. Bud Searcy remarked: "It's a good thing that he had been drinking because he could have hit her more. He was a lousy shot."

HUSBAND PUTS NAGGING WIFE UP FOR SALE

Builder Gary Bates became so fed up with wife Donna's incessant nagging that he put her up for sale in a trade magazine. His advert in *Trade-It* read: "Nagging Wife. No Tax, No MOT. Very high maintenance – some rust." Mrs Bates, from Ebley, Gloucestershire, was put in the "Free to Collect" section of the magazine – the same section in which her husband advertised his fishing tackle. To his surprise, he was inundated with calls from men offering to take her off his hands. "I didn't think anyone would ring up," he said, "but I've had at least nine or ten people calling about her. It's gone mad. There was no one I knew – just people asking, 'Is she still available?'"

Meanwhile 40-year-old Mrs Bates protested: "I don't think I do nag him. He just doesn't do what I want him to, that's all."

"GIRLFRIEND LASHED OUT WITH PROSTHETIC LEG"

Greg Gale tried to escape his girlfriend's fury on two legs, only to be beaten with a third. Police said Tammy Johnson saw red and argued with Gale in Midland, Michigan, hitting him over the head with his spare prosthetic leg as he tried to flee the house.

PREGNANT WOMAN SENDS EX 10,783 TEXTS

Convinced that she was pregnant by her ex-boyfriend Timothy Mortimore, 23-year-old Lee Amor of Brixham, Devon, bombarded him with 10,783 abusive text and phone messages in just 65 days – an average of around one every eight minutes. It turned out that the father was someone else anyway.

BROTHERS' FEUD OVER MOTHER'S WELFARE

In Little Rock, Arkansas, in 1995, a 41-year-old man clubbed his 32-year-old brother with a handgun and fired two shots at him in a dispute over which of the two siblings would take their mother to her doctor's appointment.

ANGRY WIFE SMASHES UP WRONG CAR

Furious after a row with her husband, a German woman decided to smash up his Ford Fiesta, but after doing $1,300 worth of damage, she realized that she had attacked her neighbour's Opel Corsa by mistake.

MAN PLANS TO MARRY WOMAN WHO TORE OFF HIS TESTICLE

A Tennessee man announced his intention to marry the woman who was jailed for ripping off one of his testicles. In 2001, following a row about another woman, Aretha Oneal used her fingernails to rip off one of boyfriend Dennis Ross's testicles while he lay asleep on the bed. It was an act which might have put something of a strain on a lesser relationship but Ross simply drove himself to a Nashville hospital, where the testicle was successfully reattached, and resolutely refused to press charges. Nevertheless the state did prosecute Oneal who was sentenced to 81 days in prison, including compulsory attendance at anger management sessions. Awaiting her release, Ross remained a paragon of forgiveness. "I love that girl," he said. "That's my heart, my soul, and that's my better half. I can't wait to marry her."

ACCOUNTANT BITES OFF EX-LOVER'S EAR

When a female accountant bumped into her former boyfriend a few weeks after he had dumped her, a bitter argument broke out which ended with her biting off part of his ear and spitting it onto the floor. Louise Croxson lunged forward and sank her teeth into Andrew Robbins after a London pub night out with friends in 2007 descended into a drunken row. Ignoring his screams of agony, Croxson kept her jaw locked onto his earlobe until it was completely severed. She then spat the mangled piece of flesh onto the floor of the pub. The lobe was saved only because one of the bar staff picked it up and put it in an ice bucket so that surgeons could reattach it.

WOMAN KNOCKS OUT HUSBAND WITH POTATO

Police were called to a house in Nicholson, Georgia, in 2007 after a woman knocked out her husband with a potato. She hurled the potato after he had called her a rude name and it him square on the nose, knocking him out cold. He decided not to press charges.

VIRTUAL AFFAIR LEADS TO REAL DIVORCE FOR COUPLE

A woman filed for divorce in 2008 after discovering her husband had been cheating on her in an online fantasy adventure. Amy Taylor met husband Dave Pollard in an Internet chat room in 2003 and they later set up home in Newquay, Cornwall. Both joined Second Life, an online community where players adopt imaginary personas, called avatars. Taylor was represented in the game by a slim, dark-haired young woman with a penchant for cowboy outfits while Pollard appeared as a sharp-suited muscleman with long hair. In reality, he was plump and balding. They first wed in a virtual ceremony held in an exotic tropical setting before tying the knot for real at a register office, but the marriage ran into trouble after Taylor allegedly caught her husband's avatar having cyber sex with a virtual prostitute in 2007. She said she had fallen asleep and when she woke up, she saw the pair cavorting on the computer screen. She gave him another chance but the following year she caught his avatar cuddling a woman onscreen on a sofa. "It looked really affectionate," said Taylor. "He confessed he'd been talking to this woman player in America for one or two weeks, and said our marriage was over." According to reports, both quickly found new online lovers. Pollard's Second Life profile said he was virtually engaged again and could not wait to marry his new fiancée in real life while Taylor apparently hooked up with someone from another cyber-universe, World of Warcraft.

CHANCE MEETING SHATTERS COUPLE'S ALIBIS

A Romanian couple each had a lot of explaining to do after bumping into one another at a seaside resort while both were pretending to be somewhere else. Victor Dragomirescu and his wife Lucica were talking to each other on their cell phones on the beach at Mamaia on the Black Sea. Victor was complaining about how much work he had to do at his parents' house, many miles away, while Lucica was wailing that she was too ill to get out of bed at their home in Ploiesti. However their covers were blown when they realized they were standing next to each other. After the conversation had come to an abrupt end, the Dragomirescus conceded that a divorce was the most likely outcome.

"ITALIAN SHOT NEIGHBOUR'S UNDERWEAR"

A woman went to bring in her washing in Carnago, Italy, in 2008 . . . and found her underwear riddled with bullet holes. Police said her neighbour, 69-year-old Massimo Lazzaretti, had taken pot shots at her undies with his rifle after the pair had fallen out.

DIVORCING COUPLE SAW HOUSE IN HALF

A couple from Cambodia who decided to separate after nearly 40 years of married life avoided expensive lawyers' fees by sawing their house in half. Following their decision, the husband's friends helped him move his wife's belongings to one side of the property before using saws, hammers and chisels to cut the building in two. The wife stayed in the upright part while the husband carried away his half to erect in a field on the other side of Cheach village.

PILOT ARRESTED FOR STALKING EX-GIRLFRIEND WITH PLANE

In 2009, police arrested a pilot who they said stalked his ex-girlfriend by repeatedly flying his airplane low over her house. They said Tom Huey made a number of low passes in a Beech single-engine aircraft over a residential neighbourhood of Concord, California. The police department confirmed that it had been investigating reports of a low-flying plane in the area for more than a year. During that time flyers containing derogatory statements about the woman were dropped on lawns in the area – possibly by plane.

WIFE SHOT DEAD IN EGG DISPUTE

Walter Jeurgens, a 19-year-old from Germany, was exasperated at being served eggs at every meal by his young wife, Elfreide. He got so fed up with it that he left home but when he decided to return in 1990, Elfreide made the fatal mistake of frying him some eggs as a "welcome back" meal. He promptly shot her dead, telling investigators: "I used to like eggs."

HUSBAND JUMPS IN RIVER TO ESCAPE NAGGING WIFE

A Chinese lorry driver jumped into a fast-flowing river at night in 2009 because he was unable to put up with any more of his wife's nagging. Mr Zhou and his wife were travelling by ferry on the Yangtze River when he suddenly ran from his cabin, his hands covering his ears, shouting: "I can't stand it any longer." As his wife ran after him and continued to harangue him, he jumped overboard into the rushing river. Although the ship's crew rated his chances of survival as zero, he somehow managed to swim a mile to shore.

FLIRT LOSES FALSE TEETH DOWN WOMAN'S CLEAVAGE

A man who tried to chat up a woman in a German nightclub in 2003 accidentally dropped his false teeth down her cleavage. "I wasn't very interested in him," said 37-year-old shop assistant Tina Lange, who met the Romeo at a disco in Mannheim, "but when I was leaving he whispered in my ear, 'I hope we'll see each other again.' He then dropped something down my cleavage, which I thought was his phone number." Later in the evening when she went to fish the number from her breasts, she found that it was a plate of three of his false teeth, which had fallen from his mouth as he had leaned over to whisper.

HUSBAND'S TARZAN ACT PUTS HIM IN HOSPITAL

A 66-year-old Romanian man ended up in hospital in 2005 after he tried swinging from tree to tree to escape his wife and go drinking. Stefan Trisca had been locked in the bedroom of his Bacau home by his wife who was sick of him going drinking with his friends, but his Tarzan-style escape backfired when he slipped from a vine and fell 15 feet to the ground, breaking an arm, an ankle and a leg. He moaned: "Unfortunately it was more difficult than it looked in the Tarzan movies and I suppose I forgot to take into account that Tarzan was a lot younger."

JEALOUS WIFE SINKS TEETH INTO HUSBAND'S PENIS

A woman from Osorno, Chile, was arrested in 2007 after she tried to bite off her husband's penis in a jealous rage. A police spokesman commented: "She said this was the only way to teach her husband a lesson and that it was a proof of love. She is sure he will understand and forgive her."

HEARTLESS HUSBAND EYES UP NEW WIFE

After a Saudi woman donated an eye to restore her husband's sight, she lost him to another woman – because he couldn't stand having a one-eyed wife.

MARRIAGE FOUNDERS OVER 94-YEAR-OLD'S DEMANDS FOR SEX

A 94-year-old man appeared in court in the Italian town of Chieti in 2000 after his third wife, a 52-year-old woman he met through a marriage agency just five months earlier, had filed for divorce. Asked why he thought the marriage had broken down, the nonagenarian dynamo told the court that it was probably because he had wanted too much sex.

THREE WIVES GREET DOUBLE BIGAMIST IN HOSPITAL

Melvyn Reed's worst fears were realized when he woke up from a triple bypass heart operation in 2005 to find all three of his wives visiting him in hospital at the same time. The 59-year-old company director from Kettering, Northamptonshire, had tried to preserve his secret by staggering his spouses' visits but to his horror they turned up simultaneously. Reed was trying to pass off his third wife, Lyndsey, as a hospital visitor to his second, Denise, when his first and only legal wife, Jean, appeared. Sensing that something was amiss, the wives held a meeting in the parking lot and learned that they were all married to the same man. While wives two and three were said to be furious, wife one was reported to be standing by him.

MAN MAILS BLOODY COW'S HEAD TO WIFE'S LOVER

Learning that his wife was having an affair, Jason Michael Fife, of Pittsburgh, Pennsylvania, sent her lover a severed cow's head with a puncture wound in its skull. Police said he obtained the head from a butcher's shop, claiming that he wanted it for decoration, and then mailed it frozen so as not to alert parcel carriers to the contents. The box became bloody after sitting on the recipient's doorstep on a warm day in June 2006. After Fife was sentenced to probation and community service, his lawyer said: "My client did step over the line here, but one can certainly understand his frustration, given that the victim was carrying on an affair with my client's wife. But he now understands that in a civilized society a person cannot send a severed cow's head to anybody."

HUSBAND GETS FISHING ROD FIXED WHILE TAKING PREGNANT WIFE TO HOSPITAL

When his heavily pregnant wife began to have contractions in 2001, Steve Phillips wasted no time in driving her to hospital in Wolverhampton. However on the way he noticed a fishing tackle shop and thought it would be the perfect opportunity to make a quick stop to get his rod repaired. Leaving his wife outside in the car, it was 20 minutes before he returned – with a jar of maggots. Understandably Mrs Phillips, who had been in considerable pain during his lengthy absence, was furious and said later: "He put the maggots before our baby!" Her husband explained: "I knew that we would be busy after the birth and I needed the rod fixed first. The maggots were just an afterthought."

ANGRY HUSBAND ATE EX-WIFE'S PASSPORT AFTER ROW

Ivan Volokov, from Nizhny Novgorod, Russia, was arrested after he allegedly tore up ex-wife Anna's passport during a row and then ate all the pieces. A police spokesman said: "They had just got divorced but the couple remained living in the same flat. He wanted to destroy the passport as it was the woman's only official document which proved she had the right to stay living in the house."

MAN WITH TWO PENISES LOSES WIFE

A German man who persuaded doctors to give him a second penis lost his wife when he showed her the result. Michael Gruber lost his original penis in a motorbike accident but doctors built him a second one using a mixture of skin, bone and other tissue from his body. The replacement worked so well that he was even able to father a child with his wife Elena in 2004. However in his quest for perfection, Herr Gruber asked doctors to build him a better organ. This they did, but just in case the new transplant was not a success they temporarily left the old one in place, leaving him with two penises. When Gruber showed his wife his unique double penis, she packed her bags and walked out. From his hospital bed he sighed: "I've got two penises but no wife, but I am hoping that when I get rid of one of the penises I will get her back."

"URINATING SLEEPWALKER STABBED BY GIRLFRIEND"

A girlfriend allegedly stabbed her sleepwalking boyfriend after he urinated in the wardrobe of their home in Kansas City. Police officers said she woke at 1.30 a.m. to find her boyfriend, who had arrived home drunk several hours earlier, urinating in the closet. When he ignored her repeated attempts to wake him up, she reportedly stabbed him in the shoulder because she was afraid he might hit her in his somnolent state.

SUSPICIOUS GIRLFRIEND MAKES KISS OF DEATH

A woman killed her boyfriend in 2007 with a single kiss after she suspected that he might be seeing someone else. Xia Xinfeng and Mao Ansheng, from Maolou, China, had sworn an oath that if either were unfaithful, they would have to die. So when Xia saw him chatting with another woman, she immediately set about fulfilling her side of the bargain. Next day before they met, she filled a plastic pellet with rat poison, hid it under her tongue, and while they were kissing passionately, she eased it into his mouth. Failing to notice, Mao swallowed the pellet and died shortly afterwards.

MAN HANDS OVER WIFE TO PAY DEBT

WHEN JOZEF JUSTIEN Lostrie turned up on Emil Iancu's doorstep in Romania in 2006 to collect a $3,600 debt, Iancu had no money to pay the debt . . . but offered the creditor his wife Daniela instead.

Daniela claims the unusual deal has worked out well for her. "Before I had to clean the house and look after our three children on my own, while Emil did nothing, but now I'm treated like a guest and hardly have to raise a finger." ●

OCTOGENIARIANS DIVORCE OVER AFFAIR

A German woman of 83 divorced her 81-year-old husband in 2005 after 60 years of marriage because he was caught having sex with his mistress at work. Georg Meister met his lover, who is 30 years his junior, while doing voluntary work at an animal breeding centre. Their affair was exposed when they forgot to pull the curtains while having a "quickie" in one of the centre's offices.

ACCOUNTANT SUES AFTER BEING STOOD UP ON DATE

Stood up on a date in 1978 by waitress Alyn Chesselet, accountant Tom Horsley, from San Jose, California, decided to seek financial reimbursement for his wasted 100-mile journey. He filed a lawsuit against her on the grounds that she had "broken an oral contract to have dinner and see the musical *The Wiz*". He told the court that he intended to claim payment for the two-hour round trip at an accountant's minimum rate of $6 an hour plus mileage – a total of $27. When the court got in touch with Miss Chesselet, she said that Mr Horsley was "nuts".

BRIDE TAKES EXCEPTION TO HUSBAND'S HYGIENE

A Chinese bride burned her new husband to death in 2008 after he climbed into bed without first washing his feet. In the wake of a heavy drinking session, she set fire to the sheet in which he was sleeping.

100-YEAR-OLD ARRESTED FOR ATTACKING GIRLFRIEND

Police in Florida arrested a 100-year-old man in 2001 for allegedly attacking his girlfriend, whom he accused of paying too much attention to other men. Officers said Hermenergildo Rojas poured petrol on Janet Ali, 38, at a trailer park, but the case was dropped when Ali disappeared. Rojas had spent three days in jail when he was a comparatively youthful 98 following an incident in which he threatened a female bus driver with a fake sub-machine gun.

WIFE DIVORCES HUSBAND FOR DEFECATING IN POTS

A Nigerian woman demanded a divorce from her husband over his habit of defecating in the family cooking pots after he had been drinking. Oluwakele Ogundele said in 2009 that she no longer loved husband Oluwafemi, partly because he failed to provide for the family and also because she had to keep washing up after he relieved himself on her plates and pots.

LONELY ROMEO GETS MYSTERY DATE WITH MOTHER

When a 22-year-old Los Angeles man advertised in a magazine as a lonely Romeo looking for a girl to accompany him on vacation to South America, the first reply he received was from his widowed mother.

MAN FAKES HIS OWN KIDNAPPING TO TEST WIFE'S LOVE

A Colombian man faked his own kidnapping to see whether or not his wife still loved him. Jorge Giovanni Bravo Morales left his home in Medellin following a fight with his wife but a week later letters began arriving to say that he had been kidnapped. The letters demanded a $100,000 ransom but when police investigated they found that Mr Morales was the one sending the letters. He admitted: "I wanted to know if she still cared for me. I've always loved her but things were bad and I wanted her to notice me. I beg for her forgiveness."

DIVORCEE PESTERS EMERGENCY SERVICES FOR A DATE

Desperate divorcee Angela Stahl phoned the German emergency services more than 100 times in the hope of finding a new husband. She plagued the emergency line with endless calls claiming she couldn't afford dating agencies. Eventually two police officers visited her Berlin home and confiscated the battery from her cell phone. A police spokesman said: "Having no boyfriend is not an emergency."

LOVERS MISS EACH OTHER AFTER 11,000-MILE FLIGHT

Having taken a year off to travel round Australia, bricklayer Ian Johnstone realized he was missing girlfriend Amy Dolby so much that he flew all the way back to Britain to propose to her. The problem was, she did the same thing at the same time in the opposite direction. As a result they missed each other – even when they unwittingly shared a Singapore airport lounge while waiting for their respective connecting flights. So when Miss Dolby arrived at Johnstone's Sydney apartment, his stunned flatmate went white and asked what on earth she was doing there. Meanwhile 11,000 miles away in West Yorkshire, Johnstone, armed with engagement ring, champagne and flowers, thought Amy was winding him up when she phoned from Australia. Miss Dolby said: "The awful truth dawned when I found that Ian's rucksack and most of his clothes were missing. It was as though someone was playing a cruel joke. I sat on the end of his bed and cried my eyes out. I think our problem is that we are both quite impulsive people. We are always trying to surprise each other."

WOMAN BLAMES BREAK-UP ON VIAGRA

A woman sued her partner of ten years for $2.8 million in palimony in 1998 after claiming that Viagra wrecked their relationship. Roberta Burke, of Garden City, New York State, claimed that an hour after he took the impotence drug, 70-year-old retired construction executive Francis Bernardo had intercourse with her for the first time in years. However, two days later she said he walked out on her with the parting words: "It's time to be a stud again."

SPURNED LOVER RIPS OFF EX-BOYFRIEND'S TESTICLE

A Liverpool woman was jailed for two and a half years in 2005 for ripping off one of her former boyfriend's testicles with her bare hands after he had rejected her advances at a party. Amanda Monti pulled off Geoffrey Jones's left testicle and tried to swallow it, but she choked and spat it out into her hand. A friend then handed it back to Mr Jones, saying: "That's yours." Doctors were unable to reattach the organ. Mr Jones described how Monti had grabbed his genitals and "pulled hard. This caused my underpants to come off and I found I was completely naked and in excruciating pain." In a letter to the court, Monti apologized for her actions, adding: "I am in no way a violent person."

"MAN THREW CAT AT WIFE DURING ROW"

Police said a man from Palmyra, New York State, threw his pet cat at his wife during an argument in 2009. The cat, which wasn't declawed, struck his wife on the back, but neither she nor the animal was hurt in the incident. Officers said the husband also punched a hole in the wall of their trailer-park home.

DIVORCEE MAY LOSE HOUSE OVER UNPAID 50 CENTS

A Bulgarian divorcee faced the threat of having his house repossessed because he had forgotten to pay 50 cents to his ex-wife. Vasil Yordanov had been ordered to pay the sum as part of a divorce settlement 15 years earlier but it had slipped his mind. "I got a letter from the courts and at first thought someone was playing a joke on me," he said. "Then when I checked I found out they were being completely serious. It must have cost the courts and my ex-wife's legal team 20 times as much just to send me a letter to remind me. I am perfectly happy to pay up or if they would like I can offer them goods in exchange. I have had a look around for something in my house of similar value, and I thought maybe a toilet roll would be about right."

LUCKLESS LOVER SUES OVER LACK OF "LYNX EFFECT"

A luckless Indian lover sued Lynx after he failed to land a single girlfriend during seven years of using their products. Vaibhav Bedi, 26, sought $40,000 from parent company Unilever for the "depression and psychological damage" caused by the lack of any Lynx effect from its body washes, shampoos, anti-perspirants and hair gels. Marketed in India as Axe, Lynx is famous for its commercials showing scantily clad women throwing themselves at men, but Bedi protested: "The company cheated me because it says women will be attracted to you if you use Axe. I used it for seven years but no girl came to me."

BUSINESSMAN PAYS WIFE NOT TO NAG HIM

A Romanian businessman struck a deal to pay his wife $575 a month provided she didn't nag him when he came home from work. Nicolae Popa explained that running his food distribution company left him so exhausted at the end of the day that he just wanted to go to bed without being nagged. His wife Maria said she was happy with the arrangement but would ask for double money if they ever started a family.

WAITRESS TO MARRY BOY WHO TRIED TO THROW HER OFF BALCONY

In a touching display of forgiveness, a Hong Kong waitress announced her intention to marry the drug-addict boyfriend who tried to throw her off an 18th-floor balcony and then stamped on her hands as she clung to the railing. Eighteen-year-old Au Wing-sze was saved by a downstairs neighbour who grabbed her legs and pulled her to safety. Despite boyfriend Tang Kwok-wai subsequently being convicted for attempted murder, Au insisted they were still "very much in love" and would marry on his release from jail. His lawyer confirmed: "If anything, the incident has only strengthened their relationship."

WOMAN'S DATE LOOKED FAMILIAR

There was a simple reason why Barbara Lewis rejected the man offered to her by a dating agency in Slough, Berkshire, in 2002: he was the husband she had divorced in 1986.

WIFE SEEKS DIVORCE FROM SLIM HUSBAND

Maria Alexandru divorced her husband because he never got fat, no matter how much he ate. She complained to a divorce court in Focsani, Romania, that Toader Alexandru made her jealous because he said she only had to look at food to put on weight. "He's down at the refrigerator every night," she moaned, "and I'm sure he does it to provoke me."

DOCTOR DEMANDS CASH OR KIDNEY IN DIVORCE BATTLE

A New York doctor announced in 2009 that he was demanding from his estranged wife either the return of the kidney he had donated to her while they were still together or, failing that, $1.5 million as compensation. Dr Richard Batista had given his kidney to wife Dawnell in 2001 when she suffered renal failure. "My first priority was to save her life," he said. "The second bonus was to turn our marriage around." However, only the first part of the deal worked and she went on to file for divorce in 2005. He claimed he was suing for the kidney because she was now denying him access to their three children and had thrown him out of their luxury mansion.

1,480 ROSES FAIL TO WIN BACK SWEETHEART

An Italian Romeo named Roberto came up with the ultimate romantic gesture to persuade his fiancée Alessandra to reconsider her decision to break off their engagement: he sent her 1,480 roses – one for each day they were engaged. At a cost of $6,000, a florist delivered the roses to the restaurant near Verona where Alessandra was dining with her family. Then on cue Roberto arrived on horseback to deliver the last flower in person and make an impassioned plea to the woman he hoped to marry. Alessandra said, "Thanks but no thanks" and went back to her meal.

MAN SEPARATES FROM WIFE AND FINGER

Following an acrimonious divorce in 2006, a Viennese man cut off his ring finger and presented the severed digit, still holding his wedding band, to his ex-wife. Afterwards he claimed he had no regrets, insisting that "it was an act of breaking free". He added that he did not miss his finger, could work well without it and did not plan on getting married again anyway.

MARRIED COUPLE JAILED FOR GETTING BACK TOGETHER

A Spanish married couple who had separated in 2008 were jailed the following year for breaching a distancing order and reuniting. When their marriage went through a rocky phase, a court imposed an order forbidding the husband and wife to come within 500 metres of each other, but they were arrested more than 12 months later after Civil Guard officers discovered them together in their home town of Motril. Although they maintained they were with each other by mutual agreement having patched things up, the court found them guilty of breaking the order and sentenced the husband to six months in jail and the wife to four months.

MAN ACCUSED OF ASSAULTING EX-GIRLFRIEND WITH TURTLE

After the breakup of his relationship with Carol Cieslak in 1994, Dennis Amber, from Coraopolis, Pennsylvania, allegedly went over to her house with a snapper turtle and chased her with the reptile in an attempt to get it to bite her. He was charged with assault but she later dropped the charges because of the excessive media interest in the story.

JILTED WIFE SELLS LOVE RIVAL'S "HUGE" KNICKERS

A jilted Australian wife exacted revenge on her cheating husband in 2008 by selling on eBay his mistress's "huge" knickers and a "small-sized" condom wrapper that she said she had found in their bed. The wife – named only as Anna from Queensland – said of the black lace panties: "They are so huge I thought they may make someone a nice shawl or, even better, something for Halloween."

HUSBAND ENDS MARRIAGE ON FACEBOOK

A Lancashire wife only discovered that her six-year marriage was over after her husband posted a message on the social networking website Facebook. The message simply read: "Neil Brady has ended his marriage to Emma Brady." Mrs Brady said she first knew she was being divorced when she was telephoned by worried friends who had read the update.

MAN MISTAKES SEX LINE FOR MARRIAGE AGENCY

A man who mistook a sex line for a marriage bureau complained to his local phone company after running up a bill for $15,322. Kire Iliovski, from Prilep, Macedonia, spent over 135 hours on the phone to a woman he thought could be his future wife, and claimed he did not realize he was connected to a sex line until he saw the bill. "I couldn't believe my eyes when I saw the bill," he said. "I thought I was calling an agency for possible marriage connections. We were getting on so well, too."

ANGRY WIFE EATS EX-HUSBAND'S GOLDFISH

A row over jewellery between a Texas woman and her former common-law husband ended with her frying their pet goldfish and eating some of them. Acting on a complaint that the woman had stolen the fish, police officers visited her home to find four fried goldfish on a plate. She said she had already eaten the other three. The seven fish had been bought together by the couple during happier times.

POLICE CALLED OUT TO RESOLVE COLD FEET ROW

A woman telephoned the police in 2009 after her boyfriend refused to warm up her cold feet – and moments later the boyfriend phoned them to complain that she was too demanding. When the officer arrived at the apartment in Ningbo, China, the boyfriend told him: "Have you ever seen such a girlfriend? She put her cold legs on my belly, giving me stomach cramp. I asked her to take them away and she said she would only put them there for a short while. I agreed, but after ten minutes she still had them there, saying it was very comfortable." The officer eventually persuaded the boyfriend that it was a man's job to warm his girlfriend's feet but told the woman not to leave her feet there for too long. The young couple then thanked the officer for coming out to solve the dispute.

LOVING TATTOO PROVES PREMATURE

Alan Jenkins, from Port Talbot, South Wales, decided to express his love for his family by getting tattooed portraits of his wife and two daughters covering his entire back. He spent 20 hours under the needle at a cost of $1,600 but then Lisa, his wife of 15 years, ran off with a 25-year-old Latvian fitness instructor. Although her face follows him wherever he goes, Jenkins remained positive, saying: "I've still got plenty of room on my chest if I get hooked up again."

MAN STEALS WOMAN'S CAR ON FIRST DATE

In what was surely one of the worst-ever first dates, a Detroit man first slipped out of paying the restaurant bill and then stole his date's car. Terrance McCoy ate in a local diner with the woman, whom he had met a week earlier at a casino, but when it was time to pay, he said he had left his wallet in her car and asked for the keys. He then sped off in the car. In court his defence attorney described him as a "very nice man who made a bad decision".

HELP FOR MAN WHO HIT GIRLFRIEND WITH TUNA

In 1999, Nicholas Anthony Vitalich, of San Diego, California, hit his girlfriend several times with a ten-pound tuna. A judge ordered him to undergo counselling.

"WOMAN MADE 16,000 CALLS TO BLIND DATE"

Teruko Hamakawa, a 52-year-old Japanese woman, was arrested after allegedly calling a 54-year-old man at his Kawaguchi office more than 16,000 times over the course of a year. The pair had exchanged photographs as part of their romantic introduction but when he failed to follow up his interest with a phone call, police said she rang him over and over, hanging up each time. She told detectives that the man was "impolite as he turned down marriage with me without even seeing me".

HUSBAND WALKS OUT OVER CAKE NIGHTMARE

A husband left his wife after she forced him to eat cake for every meal. Cheng Yu, from Beijing, China, said he liked Tian Mae's sugary treats at first but eventually the merest mention of the word "cake" made him ill. "Egg cake, fruit cake, chocolate cake. I felt like a bakery dustbin," he wailed.

AFFAIR COUPLE FINED FOUR BUFFALOES AND A PIG

Two lovers found guilty of having an illicit affair were ordered by a Malaysian court in 2010 to pay a fine of four buffaloes and a pig. The court ruled that the cheating couple should compensate their communities with the animals, valued at around $1,500.

"LOVE WITCH" FAILS TO MEND BROKEN RELATIONSHIP

Desperate to be reunited with her boyfriend, a German woman paid a self-styled "love witch" $1,300 to cast a spell on him. The elderly witch promised that by conducting a series of rituals under the light of a full moon, she would be able to influence his mind and effect reconciliation, but when the plan failed the client demanded her money back. Ordering the witch to return the fee, a Munich court ruled in 2006 that the service she promised was "impossible to render".

WOMAN CHOOSES CROCODILE OVER HUSBAND

An Australian nurse revealed that she had divorced her husband in 2005 after he asked her to choose between him and her pet crocodile. Vicki Lowing's husband Greg said she spent too much time with the five-foot-long croc, Johnie, which was given the run of their Melbourne house and was even allowed to sleep with her son in bed. Mrs Lowing, who said the crocodile was like a second child to her, admitted: "As soon as I started looking after Johnie, Greg and I had problems. We did nothing but fight. There was a lot of tension in the house."

SULKING HUSBAND TURNED OUT TO BE DEAD

When 83-year-old Cayetano Sanchez didn't speak to his wife Margarita in their home in Huatusco, Mexico, for eight days in 1998, she thought he was simply angry with her. However it turned out that he was dead. According to reports, she told the police that she had tried talking to him but he hadn't responded. Later, when his body started to decompose, she sensed it was more than a prolonged sulk.

WOMAN JAILED FOR KILLING VIRTUAL HUSBAND

A Japanese woman was jailed in 2008 for killing her "husband" in a computer adventure game. She was so infuriated by her sudden virtual divorce from her online spouse in the popular game Maple Story that she logged on with his password and killed his digital persona. She was charged with illegally accessing a computer and manipulating electronic data.

WIFE CHANGES MIND OVER HUSBAND'S LIBERTY

A wife who spent 47 days and nearly $50,000 on a successful high-profile campaign to have her husband released from a Mexican jail called police three months later and had him arrested for assault. Merry Brunen, from Phoenix, Arizona, told police that husband James had head-butted her during an argument. Mrs Brunen, who had lobbied officials and driven to

Mexico almost every day during his incarceration to deliver bottled water, canned food and medical supplies, said the incident stemmed from his time in prison.

CHEATING HUSBAND REVEALS LOVER'S DETAILS IN SLEEP

A Chinese woman who suspected her husband of cheating on her had her fears confirmed when he revealed his secret lover's name and address in his sleep. Confronted with his slip of the tongue, he denied everything but when the wife later visited the address she found her husband there with his mistress.

RUSSIAN DIVORCES OVER PUMPKIN PIE

A **RUSSIAN MAN** divorced his wife of 18 years after discovering that she had been making him eat cheap pumpkins instead of courgettes. As soon as he found pumpkin rinds in the garbage bin, Ivan Dimitrov, from Voronezh, realized the truth about the pies his wife Irena had been feeding him for the last six months and instigated divorce proceedings. He said: "She knows I absolutely hate pumpkins and she lied to me for months about it just because the pumpkins were cheap. What else has she been lying about? What man could trust a woman who fed him pumpkins for half a year?" ●

DIVORCED COUPLE GO TO COURT TO DIVIDE UP BEANIE BABY COLLECTION

Following their 1999 divorce, Frances and Harold Mountain were unable to agree on how to divide up their large Beanie Baby collection, valued at around $5,000. To settle the petty feud, Las Vegas Family Court Judge Gerald Hardcastle ordered that all the stuffed toys be brought into the courtroom where first Frances and then Harold took turns, under the judge's supervision, in choosing Beanies. "It's ridiculous and embarrassing," snapped Frances, moments before squatting on the floor with her ex-husband to take first pick.

SPURNED WIFE BURNS 400 PHONES

A Chinese wife set fire to more than 400 new cell phones – worth a total of $42,000 – owned by her and her husband after he announced that he was leaving her. The couple had owned a retail phone business in Weifang until she burned the new stock and walked out of the house.

HUSBAND IS KEPT CHAINED UP IN KENNEL

A 75-year-old Polish man literally found himself in the doghouse in 2005 after his wife chained him up outside in a kennel as a punishment for repeatedly coming home drunk. According to reports, Zdzislawa Bukarowicza was tethered by his wife Helena and fed on dog food and water because she was sick of him spending all their money on vodka. He survived almost three weeks living on an old blanket and being fed from a dog bowl in temperatures of minus 20 degrees outside their home in Scinawa before friends, concerned that they hadn't seen him at his favourite bar, called the police.

MAN GETS DIVORCE FROM FURNITURE-SHIFTING WIFE

John Turner was granted a divorce in Middlesbrough in 2001 after complaining that he had finally had enough of his wife Pauline rearranging the furniture every single day of their 38-year marriage.

RADIO SHOW TRAPS CHEATING HUSBAND

A cheating husband was caught out in 2009 when, as a birthday surprise, his wife arranged a live phone call from his favourite radio show. Davor Ivanovic was supposed to be alone on a business trip to Zagreb, Croatia, but when DJ

Barbara Kolar called his room a woman answered and said he was taking a shower. When he came to the phone he claimed the woman was his wife – unaware that his real wife, Jasna, was listening in on another line. Ignoring pleas from radio station staff to keep quiet, Mrs Ivanovic screamed at him: "Who are you with? Who are you with?" Her husband hung up.

NAGGING MOTHER-IN-LAW SURVIVES ROCKET ATTACK

A vengeful Bosnian husband tried to kill his mother-in-law with an anti-tank missile launcher after claiming that she had turned his wife against him. Miroslav Milijici blamed his wife's mother for the break-up of his marriage, and when she survived the rocket attack on her home, he tried to finish her off with a machine gun. Yet incredibly she emerged from both attacks with barely a scratch. Jailed for six years for attempted murder, Milijici said in mitigation that he could no longer bear his mother-in-law's nagging.

"MAN ORDERED PET PYTHON TO ATTACK POLICE"

A man was arrested after allegedly ordering his pet python to attack two police officers. They were called to Victor Rodriguez's apartment in Bridgeport, Connecticut, after reports that he was threatening his girlfriend with the nine-foot-long snake. As they arrived he is said to have shouted at the snake: "Get them!" The snake took no notice of the command.

WEEPY GIRL WANTS TEAR DUCTS REMOVED TO SAVE RELATIONSHIP

A Chinese girl asked doctors to remove her tear glands because her continual crying was irritating her boyfriend. She said she wept while watching soap operas, listening to sentimental songs, and if she was wronged in any way, however minor. Her boyfriend had told her that if she didn't stop, he would leave her, which probably made her cry even more.

HUSBAND IS ORDERED TO DIVORCE 82 WIVES

An 84-year-old Nigerian man was given just two days in 2008 to divorce 82 of his 86 wives. Mohammadu Bello Abubakar had been sentenced to death by an Islamic court for having more than four spouses, so the only way he could save himself was to reduce the number to an acceptable amount. He said that his wives – most of whom were a quarter of his age – sought him out because of his reputation as a healer. "I don't go looking for them. They come to me," he added. One of the 86, who was still at school when Bello Abubakar proposed, recalled: "I said I couldn't marry an older man. But he said it was directly an order from God."

CUSTOMER BURNS DOWN SHOP OVER CALENDAR ROW

An irate customer burned down a barber's shop in Italy in 2008 after spotting a picture of his girlfriend in a pornographic calendar on the wall. Police said the customer torched the salon when the barber refused to take down the offending photograph.

EX-WIFE RECEIVES UNEXPECTED GIFT

Cory Quinn, from Sydney, Australia, committed suicide by locking himself in his estranged wife Mary's freezer when she went on holiday. He left a note for the 280-pound woman that said: "Gorge on this, you fat pig!"

JUDGES UPHOLD FERTILITY WAGER

Convinced that it was not his fault that wife Dorothy, 20 years his junior, was unable to conceive, 56-year-old Effas Ondya, of Lusaka, Zambia, bet her $200 that it was she who was infertile. Under the terms of the wager he said she could have sex with other men but if she was still not pregnant within three months, he would win the money. However when she willingly agreed to the conditions, he suddenly had second thoughts and sued her. The court found in her favour, ruling: "The bet remains a bet."

WOMAN SETTLES ROW BY HANDCUFFING HERSELF TO HUSBAND

In an attempt to resolve a marital dispute, Helen Sun took drastic action and handcuffed herself to husband Robert Drawbough as he slept in their Fairfield, Connecticut, home in 2009. But when Drawbough called police with his cell phone, Sun allegedly bit him on the arms and torso, prompting officers to break into the home and charge her with assault. One officer remarked: "Far from restoring matrimonial harmony, she only succeeded in making matters much worse."

CHEATING HUSBAND CAUGHT OUT BY BROCHURE PHOTO

After enjoying a secret tryst with his mistress in Normandy, a London businessman felt so guilty that he offered to take his wife on a foreign holiday the following year. His wife liked the idea of Normandy until, browsing through the brochures in the travel agents, she happened to turn to a photograph showing her husband leaning against a harbour wall and with his arm around a mystery woman. It was his clandestine mistress. Unbeknown to them, they had been photographed by the French Tourist Board 12 months earlier.

WOMAN ASSAULTS BOYFRIEND WITH STUFFED FISH

A woman in Detroit, Michigan, was arrested in 2004 for using a stuffed fish with a pointed nose to assault her boyfriend. The fish, which was described as resembling a swordfish, was used to stab the man who received a number of cuts to his arms and shoulders. She had apparently grabbed the decorative fish off the mantle of the fireplace during a violent argument and hit him repeatedly until he let her go.

FROG IN TEA IS GROUNDS FOR DIVORCE

A court in Zambia ruled in 2001 that a man was entitled to a divorce from his wife on the grounds that she had served him a cup of tea with a frog in it. The court heard that Andrew Nyoka had left his wife Catherine as a direct result of the frog-in-the-tea incident.

"WIFE STABBED HUSBAND FOR OPENING CHRISTMAS PRESENT EARLY"

Misty Johnson, from Rock Springs, Wyoming, was charged with aggravated assault and battery in December 2007 after police said she stabbed her husband of three months with a kitchen knife because he opened a Christmas present early.

MAN THROWS PENIS AT WIFE TO PROVE FIDELITY

A Filipino man cut off his penis in 2003 and hurled it through a window at his estranged wife in an attempt to prove his fidelity. The man wrapped the severed member in a newspaper and tossed it through the window of his wife's parents' house in the town of Malasiqui. He then shouted, "This is so you will not suspect I am courting another girl," before hobbling off into the night.

PARROT BLOWS WHISTLE ON CHEATING GIRLFRIEND

Parrot owner Chris Taylor realized that his girlfriend had been cheating on him when his talkative pet squawked in a perfect imitation of her voice: "I love you Gary." Suzy Collins had been secretly meeting ex-work colleague Gary in the Leeds apartment she shared with Taylor, but Ziggy the African Grey parrot with a talent for mimicry had overheard everything. Taylor first became suspicious after Ziggy croaked "Hiya Gary" when Collins answered her phone. The parrot also made smooching sounds whenever the name "Gary" was said on TV. Eventually in 2006, Taylor confronted the woman with whom he had lived for a year, and she confessed to the affair and moved out. He also said goodbye to his beloved Ziggy after the bird continued to call out Gary's name and refused to stop squawking the incriminating phrases in Collins's voice. "I wasn't sorry to see the back of Suzy after what she did," admitted Taylor, "but it really broke my heart to let Ziggy go. I love him to bits and I really miss having him around, but it was torture hearing him repeat that name over and over again." For her part, Collins was shocked but not disappointed to hear that Ziggy had gone. "I'm surprised to hear he's got rid of that bloody bird," she said. "He spent more time talking to it than he did to me. I couldn't stand Ziggy, and it looks now like the feeling was mutual."

WOMAN ACCUSES BOYFRIEND OF BEING PORN MOVIE ACTOR

A 20-year-old American woman was arrested after lashing out at her boyfriend with a knife because she thought he was an actor in a porn movie they were watching. Police said the woman was apparently happily watching the movie with her boyfriend at his home in Albuquerque, New Mexico, when she suddenly decided he was one of the actors in the film and went for him with a knife. After stabbing him in the face and biting him on the chest, she chased him down the street still angrily waving the knife. Wearing only a pair of shorts, he called the emergency services in desperation before managing to flag down a passing deputy.

NAKED MAN ARRESTED FOR SHOUTING AT TREES

A GERMAN MAN was arrested in 2005 for causing a public nuisance after visitors to a beauty spot saw him running around naked and shouting at trees. Dieter Braun revealed that he had been told to scream at trees by his marriage guidance counsellor as an alternative to venting his anger on his wife. He added that taking his clothes off at the same time helped him to relax further. ●

WOMAN CHARGED WITH BITING OFF EX-BOYFRIEND'S LIP

Police in Seattle charged a woman with assault in 2007 after she allegedly bit off her ex-boyfriend's lower lip while they kissed in bed. The pair had apparently kissed several times in the course of the evening, before, according to reports, she suddenly bit off his lip and spat it out. Other residents of the house were alerted by him yelling, "She's a devil woman", and police arrived to find him on the front porch, his face and neck covered in blood. They discovered his lip on the bedroom floor, covered in cat hair.

JILTED MAN SUES FOR COST OF EX-GIRLFRIEND'S BREAST IMPLANTS

In 1999, Neil Weekes, from Swindon, Wiltshire, unsuccessfully sued his former girlfriend for the $4,500 that he had paid for her breast enlargement operation before their relationship had soured. Weekes had paid for the chest of Joanna Kirby, nearly 20 years his junior, to be enhanced from a

34B to a generous DD-cup, but she later left him and moved back in with her parents. Finding himself no longer in a position to appreciate her implants, he wanted his money back.

WIFE SELLS DJ HUSBAND'S CAR AFTER ON-AIR FLIRTING

In 2005, the wife of Tim Shaw, a British radio DJ on Birmingham-based Kerrang! 105.2, sold his $50,000 Lotus Esprit sports car on eBay with a "Buy It Now" price of $1 after she heard him flirting on-air with model Jodie Marsh. Hayley Shaw took umbrage after her husband told listeners that he would leave her and their children for Marsh. The item description on eBay read: "I need to get rid of this car immediately – ideally in the next two to three hours before my husband gets home to find it gone and all his belongings in the street." The car was sold within five minutes.

NEW BOOTS SPARK TRIPLE SUICIDE BID

All three wives of a 67-year-old Iranian man took overdoses in an unsuccessful triple suicide bid in 2004 after the youngest wife sparked jealousy by buying an expensive pair of boots.

BOYFRIEND TORCHES CAR OVER DISAGREEMENT

A Raleigh, North Carolina, man was so incensed that his girlfriend didn't buy the car he wanted her to that he set fire to the vehicle she had just bought instead. The resultant explosion threw him over a fence and down a 35-foot drop, putting him in intensive care.

WOMAN KILLS HUSBAND WITH FOLDING COUCH

Annoyed with her couch potato husband for being drunk, a woman in St Petersburg, Russia, kicked the mechanism that automatically folds the couch up against a wall, an action that killed him by trapping him between the two halves. When she returned to check on him three hours later she thought he was unusually quiet.

WIFE PLASTERS HUSBAND'S INFIDELITIES ON CAR

A South African woman divorcing her husband of 36 years tried to shame him publicly into paying her maintenance money by plastering posters on her car giving details of his various infidelities. According to a poster on the rear of the car, these included "going out boozing each night" and "bedding cheap women".

GOING COMMANDO LEADS TO DIVORCE

Romanian Emese Nagy divorced her husband in 2001 because he refused to wear underpants. She said she didn't know about his little foible before they married.

MAN ACCUSED OF HITTING MOTHER WITH SAUSAGE

A man from Deland, Florida, was charged with battery in 2008 after police said he admitted hitting his mother on the head with a three-pound pack of Polish sausage. Gregory Allen Praeger, 46, had apparently been cooking in the kitchen when he argued with his mother and threw the sausage at her, grazing her head.

BANKING ERROR ENDS 35-YEAR MARRIAGE

A Brazilian couple were awarded over $16,000 compensation in 2003 after a banking error ended their 35-year marriage. Maria Rodrigues filed for divorce after her bank wrongly informed her that her husband, Luiz Gonzaga, had a joint account with another woman. Following a five-year struggle he finally managed to prove his innocence in a court of law but his ex-wife rather took the shine off his success by announcing that she was perfectly happy to stay divorced.

COUPLE ROW OVER CONDOM MIX-UP

A couple from Rotherham, Yorkshire, accused supermarket chain Tesco of nearly wrecking their four-year relationship after it mistakenly included condoms in their online shopping list. Lynn Newby was set to break up with boyfriend Andy Allott after discovering that one of his listed "Favourites" was a packet of 12 condoms. She knew she hadn't bought them, so she accused Mr Allott of having an affair behind her back. When he denied all knowledge of the condoms, the couple challenged Tesco whose internal investigation revealed that the error was the work of a new member of staff in the marketing department. Tesco sent them a letter of apology and a cheque for $200.

LOVESICK DANE RUNS UP $117,000 PHONE BILL ON CALLS TO INDIAN SWEETHEART

A 24-year-old man from Kolding, Denmark, loved the sound of his Indian sweetheart's voice so much that he ran up a phone bill of over $117,000. The long-distance lovebirds once spent 21 out of 24 hours on the phone to each other, and it was not unusual for him to spend more than $5,000 a week on calls to India. Yet bizarrely the two had never even met. They got in touch through a magazine that publishes the names and phone numbers of people all over the world who want to get to know foreigners.

HUSBAND SPENDS 50 YEARS IN TREE AFTER ROW

An Indian man has spent more than half a century living in a tree after a quarrel with his wife. Gayadhar Parida took to staying in a mango tree in Orissa state over a "tiny issue" with his wife in the 1950s and has since refused all pleas to come back to the house. He accepts food offered to him by family members but comes down from his tree house only to drink water from a pool.

RAMPANT SPANIARD SUES WIFE FOR NEGLECT

In 2004, a Spanish man tried to have his wife charged with domestic abuse because she refused to have sex with him on five consecutive nights.

MAN, 88, KILLS WIFE IN ROW OVER UROSTOMY BAG

An 88-year-old Canadian resident was convicted of the manslaughter of his wife of 56 years following an argument over who should change his urostomy bag. Joao Almeida strangled wife Evangelina in the kitchen of their Edmonton, Alberta, home in 2006 in a dispute over the surgical bag that diverts urine away from the bladder.

BOY TRIES TO WIN GIRL'S HEART WITH BLOOD INJECTION

A 22-year-old Cambodian man was arrested in 2007 after injecting a woman with his own blood in a desperate bid to win her affections. He had apparently fallen in love with her when they were classmates in 2004 but when she spurned his advances he took drastic action and injected a syringe of his blood into her rib cage and waist as she walked home from school. A police officer remarked: "He thought that if he could not marry her, at least his blood can stay inside her body."

WOMAN SETS FIRE TO EX-HUSBAND'S PENIS

A Russian woman set fire to her ex-husband's penis while he sat naked watching TV and drinking vodka. Although the couple had divorced three years previously they continued to share an apartment in Moscow. Describing his ordeal, the man said: "It was monstrously painful. I was burning like a torch. I don't know what I did to deserve it."

LOVE RIVAL "ASSAULTED WITH FROZEN FISH"

In 1991, a man was charged with assault in Cedar Rapids, Iowa, after hitting a love rival in the face with a frozen fish, thereby causing a broken nose.

PHONE COMPANY PROMOTION EXPOSES HUSBAND'S INFIDELITY

A cheating husband contemplated suing British Telecom in 1999 after a promotional campaign unwittingly alerted his wife to the fact that he was having an affair. Under pressure from competitors in the telephone sector, BT sent the couple a letter pointing out that a number which frequently appeared on their phone bills was not one of their cheap rate "friends and family" numbers. The puzzled wife soon dialled the number and discovered that her husband had been having an affair with one of their neighbours for several years. Thrown out of his house, the husband complained: "I wonder what my chances of suing BT would be. They have wrecked a 40-year marriage." A BT spokesman said only that the company was "always looking to encourage our customers to maximize any benefit of the discount scheme".

YOUNG RUNAWAYS SCRAP DEATH PACT

A real-life Romeo and Juliet ran away to the desert north of Phoenix, Arizona, vowing to kill themselves because their families disapproved of the relationship. Michael Tillery, 18, and Stefanie Townsend, 16, left a note saying that next time they were seen they would be dead in each other's arms. A frantic search was launched and finally the young lovers were spotted – making their way home again. After two days together they had realized they weren't compatible after all.

WIFE KILLED OVER LOUSY COFFEE

An Italian man admitted killing his 72-year-old wife in 2001 because she made him a bad cup of coffee.

HUSBAND BURNS DOWN HOUSE IN UNDERPANT TANTRUM

A husband who petulantly threw old clothes into the garden and set fire to them because he couldn't find any clean underpants ended up accidentally burning his house down. Ivo Jerbic was so angry about his wife's unwillingness to throw anything out of their house in Zagreb, Croatia, that he took matters into his own hands and started a fire of old clothes in the garden. But the blaze quickly spread to the house, burning it to the ground.

COUPLE DIVORCE OVER ONLINE AFFAIR

Trapped in an unhappy marriage, Sana and Adnan Klaric sought love in Internet chat rooms, only to end up romancing each other online under false names. The couple, from Zenica, Bosnia, met on an online forum while she was in an Internet café and he was at work, and began chatting under the names Sweetie and Prince of Joy. After pouring out their hearts to one other about their marriage problems, they arranged to meet outside a shop, each carrying a single rose for identification – but there was no happy ending when they realized what had happened. Instead both filed for divorce, with each accusing the other of being unfaithful. Adnan lamented: "I still find it hard to believe that the Sweetie who wrote such wonderful things to me on the Internet is actually the same woman I married and who has not said a nice word to me for years."

JUDGE ORDERS WALL TO SEPARATE WARRING SPOUSES

When Chana and Simon Taub both refused to move out of their Brooklyn home following the acrimonious break-up of their marriage, a judge came up with a novel solution to keep the bickering pair apart – he ordered a wall to be built straight down the middle of the ground floor accommodation. Erected at the end of 2006, the wall separated the living room from the staircase of the three-story house. Under the terms of the agreement Chana lived on the top floor and had access to the kitchen on the first floor while Simon got the ground floor living room and the dining room on the first floor. So that they didn't run into each other on the first floor, the door between the dining room and the kitchen was barricaded on both sides. The points of contention between the couple were numerous. She accused her husband of more than 20 years of bugging her phones, and she also said that she had to flush the toilet after him and put on his socks for him. He said she owned too many shoes.

WOMAN HITS BOYFRIEND WITH TOILET SEAT

Discovering her boyfriend smoking cocaine in the bathroom, an 18-year-old woman from Fort Pierce, Florida, turned on the shower with the intention of washing away the drugs. But when he refused to hand over his stash, a row broke out, which ended in her hitting him with the toilet seat. He was charged with possession of cocaine and she was charged with battery.

RUSSIAN JUMPS FIVE FLOORS – TWICE – TO ESCAPE NAGGING

A Russian man survived in 2009 after downing three bottles of vodka and leaping from the fifth-floor balcony of his Moscow apartment – twice. Alexei Roskov, 22, said he jumped the second time because he couldn't bear his wife's nagging about the first time. Wife Yekaterina had watched in horror as her drunken husband opened the kitchen window of their apartment and hurled himself out. Amazingly he managed to stagger back upstairs with barely a scratch after the 50-foot fall. But while his wife called an ambulance and berated him for his stupidity, he jumped again. He said afterwards: "I have no idea why I jumped the first time but when I came back up and heard my wife screaming angrily at me, I thought it was best if I left the room again – out of the window."

MAN BITES HEAD OFF GIRLFRIEND'S PYTHON

A man punished his girlfriend during a fight in 2007 by biting off the head of her pet snake. Shane Cooke, a 33-year-old bricklayer from Keady, Northern Ireland, picked up the cherished pet of Coleen McGleenon, put it in his mouth and threw its severed head at her, remarking: "Your snake tasted lovely." His lawyer said that Cooke had been consuming alcoholic drinks for several hours before the attack.

FORGETFUL HUSBAND LEAVES WIFE AT GAS STATION

A Macedonian man drove six hours across Italy and into Germany in 2005 before noticing that he had left his wife at a gas station. Ljubomir Ivanov, 35, only realized he had forgotten his wife Iskra when he received a call on his mobile phone from police to say that she was still waiting for him at the gas station near Pesaro in central Italy. He explained: "I filled up the tank with petrol, paid and then just drove off. I was very tired and not thinking straight. She usually sits in the back seat so I didn't really see she wasn't there."

EAT, DRINK AND BE WEIRD

DRUNK RIDES HORSE INTO BANK

Having had one too many drinks for the road at his local bar, a German equestrian decided to sleep it off for the night by riding his horse into a bank foyer. Wolfgang Heinrich, 40, had been out riding his horse Sammy in April 2007 when he stopped to have a drink with friends but on leaving the bar he realized he was too drunk to ride all the way back to his home in Wiesenburg. So, keen to get out of the cold, he decided to use his bank card to open up a nearby bank foyer and take himself and Sammy inside for the night. Heinrich was found fast asleep with his horse by customer Stephan Hanelt who went to the bank to withdraw money early the following morning. "It was a bit of a shock to find a man and horse asleep in the foyer of the bank," said Herr Hanelt. "I rang the police straight away." Heinrich was let off with a warning, but bank staff were less impressed when they had to clean up after the horse, who had left a deposit of his own on the floor of the foyer.

WOMAN MISTAKES HEARING AID FOR CANDY

An Idaho pensioner almost ate her own hearing aid in 2009 after mistaking it for a chocolate candy. Eighty-seven-year-old Violet Bishop, of Coeur d'Alene, was watching TV when she fancied a snack, so she decided to dip into a box of chocolate candies she had bought for Halloween trick or treaters. However one sweet was so chewy she had to remove it from her mouth – and that's when she realized it was her hearing aid that had fallen out of her ear and into the box. She said: "As I ate the Milk Duds, I was aware that one was not as fresh as the others. It was rather crunchy and I just could not get it to soften up, no matter how hard I tried."

HOSPITAL SERVES UP HUMAN TONGUE

Eating a chicken risotto at a hospital canteen in Izola, Slovenia, in 2008, a doctor was puzzled by a strange looking piece of meat. He insisted it was not chicken but was startled when tests showed that it was part of a human tongue. Hospital managers said the tongue portion may have been dropped accidentally into the food by a doctor who had gone to the canteen immediately after treating a patient. They added reassuringly that they have never used patients' parts in any of their dishes.

DRIVER BELTS IN BEER RATHER THAN YOUNG BOY

When police in Australia's Northern Territory pulled over a driver in 2008, they were amazed to see that he had secured a load of beer with a seat belt but not a five-year-old boy. The 30 cans of beer were safely buckled up on the rear seat but the child was left unrestrained. When officers pointed out the anomaly to the driver, they said he looked at them blankly.

MAN HIDES SEX TOYS IN SAUSAGE

Staff at a butcher's shop in Mannheim, Germany, were startled to find that a customer had hidden two sex toys in their sausages for transport to Dubai. After buying two large sausages earlier in the day, the man returned to the butcher's and asked a shop assistant to wrap and cool them until he left for Dubai the next day. But the assistant noticed the sausages were much heavier and when the police were called they found that the man had removed some of the meat and packed two dildos inside. A police spokesman revealed: "It was two latex dildos with a natural look."

STUDENTS MISTAKE GRANDAD'S ASHES FOR INSTANT COFFEE

Staying at a friend's country cottage in the Czech Republic in 2004, a group of students decided to relieve their hangovers with a cup of coffee. Spotting a tin full of grainy substance on the mantelpiece at Jakub Havlat's cottage, they thought it was instant coffee and made themselves a drink. It was only afterwards when Havlat returned that they discovered they had actually drunk his grandfather's ashes. One of the students said: "We grabbed the first tin we found, put what we thought was coffee in mugs and poured hot water over it. It was barely drinkable and we thought it was probably just a bit old but we needed a drink to sober up and so we just downed it. When our friend came home and realized what had happened, he said to us: 'You idiots, you've drunk my grandfather's remains.' We sobered up immediately."

POLICE CHIEF RESIGNS IN BURGER SCANDAL

Inverness, Florida, police chief Joseph Elizarde was forced to resign after arresting the proprietor of a Happy Days Diner in 2002 when the proprietor told him that the two hamburgers ordered 20 minutes earlier were still not ready.

QUEEN TAKES DELIVERY OF 2,000 PINTS OF BEER

A TRUCK CARRYING 2,000 pints of beer to a Berkshire pub called the Windsor Castle mistakenly took them to Queen Elizabeth II's nearby residence instead. The 12 barrels of lager had been ordered for England's 2008 World Cup soccer match against Croatia but when royal staff at Windsor Castle insisted they had no record of the order, the beer was finally taken to its correct destination – the pub of the same name at Maidenhead five miles away. The pub manager, Misko Coric, said: "We have received mail for the royal household before but I think this is the first time they have received anything meant for us." ●

DRUNK WAKES TO FIND PENIS TATTOO ON LEG

After a heavy vodka-drinking session, Joel Stefansson, 27, from Umea, Sweden, agreed to let a tattoo artist ink in any design he liked. However when he woke up, he found to his dismay that the artist had tattooed a six-inch penis on his right leg adjacent to his real one.

MAN EXISTS SOLELY ON MARS BARS

A Liverpool man claimed in 2008 that he had eaten nothing but Mars Bars for the previous 17 years. Keith Sorrell, 37, said he eats at least a dozen a day – for breakfast, lunch and dinner – and even orders Mars Bar drinks mixed with vodka or rum when he goes to the pub. Keith, who is single, said: "My love of Mars Bars started at school with one or two between meals. All my pocket money went on them and one day I realized I couldn't get by without them. Now I can easily polish off 12 a day, more at weekends. I'm totally addicted."

"YOU CAN'T BUY QUICHE BECAUSE YOU'RE NOT 21"

An over-zealous supermarket cashier refused to let an office worker buy a slice of cheese and onion quiche because she "looked under 21". Christine Cuddihy, who was in fact 24, wanted the quiche for supper but the checkout woman at the Tesco store near Coventry, West Midlands, had other ideas and demanded she produce her driving licence to prove that she was over 21. Miss Cuddihy said: "I told her I was certain the proof of age laws do not apply to quiche, but she was adamant. It was very embarrassing. What on earth is dangerous about a slice of quiche? It's not even like I was buying a whole quiche to binge on." Tesco apologized for the incident and confirmed that shoppers do not have to prove their age to buy quiche. "We're at a loss to say what happened here," added a spokesman.

DRUNK NEARLY CRUSHED BY GARBAGE TRUCK

William Bowen, from Muncie, Indiana, had a lucky escape in 2008 after waking up in a garbage truck just as the contents were on the point of being crushed. Bowen had fallen asleep in a garbage bin, which had then been emptied into the truck, but the driver heard screams as he was about to activate its compactor. "He looked up and this gentleman was standing out the top of our truck," said the waste disposal company supervisor. "This gentleman was extremely intoxicated." Bowen said he had no idea how he ended up in the bin. The last thing he remembered was drinking in a bar with some buddies around 3 a.m.

WIFE'S COOKING DRIVES MAN TO BLOW UP KITCHEN

A Romanian man tried to blow up his kitchen because his wife was such a lousy cook. Viorel Leahu, from Todiresti, said he decided to punish his wife for her terrible food. The explosion damaged the room and left him with an injured hand.

SUSPECT FORCED TO EAT 50 BANANAS

A man arrested in 2007 on suspicion of stealing and swallowing a $1,000 necklace was forced by Indian police to eat 50 bananas as a laxative so that the incriminating evidence could be retrieved. The man had initially denied any involvement in the theft until an X-ray of his stomach proved his guilt.

SWEDES MIX COCKTAIL FROM RED BULL AND SOAP

Teenagers at the 2004 Oestersjoe music festival in Karlshamn, Sweden, were so intent on getting drunk they downed containers of an alcohol-based liquid soap from the toilets. They mixed cocktails of energy drink Red Bull and soap containing 62 per cent alcohol from the portable toilets. The head of the firm that supplied the toilets said: "It only took one night for most of the soap to disappear. I thought either they were being fastidiously clean or something odd was going on, since the soap usually lasts for a month."

BEER-LOVER GETS STUCK IN OPEN DRAIN

A German man's love of beer proved his undoing in 2009 after he fell into an open drain – and couldn't get out because of his beer belly. Gerhard Wilder, 46, from Bochum, was wedged so tightly that he had to be freed by firefighters. After embarrassing pictures of his plight appeared in the German media, he vowed to stay off the beer and go on a diet.

STABBED MAN ORDERS COFFEE

A man walked into a restaurant in Warren, Michigan, in 2009 with a five-inch knife sticking in his chest and calmly ordered a cup of coffee. He told staff at the diner that he was waiting for an ambulance. It transpired that the 52-year-old man had been stabbed by a mugger and had then walked a mile to the restaurant after calling 911. One employee described the incident as "like something out of a movie", adding: "It kind of freaked us all out."

AMERICAN DINER LIBERATES LOBSTERS

An American tourist dining in a restaurant in Kinsale, County Cork, paid $900 for all of the 40 live lobsters sitting in a tank waiting to be cooked and released them unharmed into the sea. When the customer bought all 40, the restaurant manager said: "I thought he was throwing a party."

LIFEGUARD FINDS "LEMONADE" HAS EXTRA STING

Deciding that he needed a drink while working in the heat, a lifeguard in Queensland, Australia, went to the club house and drank what he thought was lemonade from a bottle. In fact, it was a sample bottle filled with the tentacles of the deadly Box jellyfish. The lifeguard survived – just.

ONLY CAKE IN CONTEST, BUT STILL CAME SECOND

When her Victoria sponge earned second place in a 2007 cake competition at her village fete, Jenny Brown was naturally delighted – that is, until she found out hers was the only entry. The 62-year-old grandmother from Wimblington, Cambridgeshire, said: "My friend came over to me at the fete and said I had come second. I asked her how many more entries there had been but she just started laughing and said I was the only one." Her effort was apparently marked down by the judges because of indentations on the top of her sponge from the oven rack.

MAN SETS CAB ON FIRE WHILE COOKING SAUSAGES

A drunken German accidentally set fire to the cab of his truck after deciding to cook himself some sausages while driving. Walter Reckling, who was three times over the legal alcohol limit, usually restricted the small gas cooker to roadside use but on this occasion he was running late with a delivery so he elected to cook while at the wheel. He was cooking two sausages while driving through Saxony when the cooker suddenly toppled over, setting fire to the truck cab and putting him in hospital, where he was treated for smoke inhalation.

SALAMI BATTLE PUTS GERMAN SHOPPERS IN HOSPITAL

TWO **GERMAN** shoppers needed hospital treatment after they fought a violent battle in a supermarket wielding salamis as clubs and brandishing a chunk of Parmesan cheese as a dagger. The fight took place in Aachen in December 2009 when a 74-year-old man and a 35-year-old woman laid claim to the same supermarket trolley. As the pensioner wrestled the cart from the hands of his rival, her 24-year-old brother stepped forward and floored him with a punch. Together with their 53-year-old mother, the brother and sister then took the trolley into the supermarket, but the OAP picked himself up off the floor and followed them to the cheese counter. There he clubbed the younger man with a salami while the mother tried to fend him off with a sharp four-pound piece of Parmesan. The pensioner responded by pushing the mother down on to a glass countertop, leaving her with a cut head. After police officers had arrived to break up the brawl and take the wounded to hospital, a spokesman said a sudden rush of shoppers on the penultimate Saturday before Christmas had depleted the supermarket's trolley reserves and "raised tensions" between customers. ●

CUSTOMER SUES OVER INADEQUATE SOUP CAN INSTRUCTIONS

David Sugar, from Petersburg, Ohio, sued Campbell's Soup Company in 2003 for facial burns he received when the contents of a soup can exploded – the result of him heating the can before opening it. He maintained that the accident was Campbell's fault because he simply followed the instructions on the can, which said "Heat, stirring occasionally" but did not stipulate that the can needed to be opened first in order to stir the soup.

GARLIC BREATH LANDS DRIVER IN TROUBLE

Stopped by a police patrol in Perth, Australia, in 1997, a motorist chewed on a clove of garlic before breathing in the face of an officer. He was charged with assault, which under Australian law includes "the direct or indirect application of force, including gas or odour, in such a manner as to cause personal discomfort".

CONFUSED DRUNK LOSES HIS BEARINGS

After a night's drinking in 2010, a teenager called the emergency services because he thought he was hanging perilously above the sea off the edge of a cliff – but his mind was so muddled, he was really a mile inland. Police officers, fire crews and the coastguard conducted a search of the seafront at Bournemouth, Dorset, only for the 19-year-old to be found clinging to a tree on a steep slope next to a car park over a mile away. Asked if the teenager was embarrassed, a coastguard official said: "We hope so."

DRUNKEN CROAT IN PENIS MISHAP

After swearing loudly at a woman in the street in 2003, a drunken Croat shoved his penis through her garden fence . . . unaware that her dog was on the other side. When the animal bit the intrusive member, the man reported the incident to the police.

FIFTY BRAWL IN ROW OVER LAST PACKET OF PEANUTS

An argument over who should have the last packet of peanuts in a club triggered a street fight involving 50 people. Dozens of police officers were called to the High Brooms Working Men's Club in Tunbridge Wells, Kent, in 2010 and used CS gas to quell the riot. One witness said: "Everything was fine until two guys started arguing at the bar over the last bag of dry roasted nuts. The next thing it was a mass brawl with half the club punching and kicking each other. To be perfectly honest, it spoiled the evening."

SNAKE DRINK PACKS A BITE

Preserving deadly snakes in alcohol makes for a popular drink in China, but a man named Li got more than he bargained for in 2003 when he uncorked a bottle of liquor in which a snake had been pickled for a year. As he lifted the bottle to his mouth, the snake, which had somehow survived its 12-month immersion, reared up and bit him on the neck.

MAN CALLS COPS OVER SANDWICH SAUCE

The ingredients for a spicy Italian sandwich were clearly so important to Reginald Peterson, from Jacksonville, Florida, that he twice called the police emergency number 911 after his local Subway shop left off the sauce. Locked out of the store after witnesses said he became belligerent, the burly construction worker initially rang 911 to ensure that the police could have his sandwiches made correctly. His second call was to complain that officers weren't arriving fast enough. When police officers did show up, they arrested Peterson on a charge of making false 911 calls. He told them to throw the sauceless sandwiches in the garbage.

TOURIST ACCIDENTALLY ORDERS $1,700 BOTTLE OF WINE

A British tourist in Prague misread the price on a restaurant wine list and ordered a $1,702 bottle of wine by mistake. Berkshire estate agent Andy Freegard was dining with girlfriend Helen Kelly in the Czech capital in 2003 when he picked a Chateau Margaux 1987 Premier Grand Cru Classe which he thought was $34. However he began to get worried when waiters started flocking to his table to sniff the cork, and when Miss Kelly asked the head waiter for the price in sterling, the reply came back "£1,000". Mr Freegard said: "We realized something was not right when the standard of service improved dramatically. And when they brought out the decanter I was very concerned. After we learned the truth we knew we couldn't send it back. Taking each sip was heartbreaking, knowing it was $85 worth a gulp."

DRUNK FALLS ASLEEP IN HIS OLD HOUSE

After an evening's drinking in 2003, a man staggered home and fell asleep – but in a house where he had last lived seven years earlier. Police were called when Giles Mottram found a complete stranger, Mark Norley, asleep in his bed at Axbridge, Somerset. Norley, a 34-year-old research scientist, was taken by police to his mother's home nearby "to sleep it off". Homeowner Harry Mottram said: "It was like a kind of latter-day Goldilocks and the Three Bears, except the sleeping drunk had dark hair and we are not a family of woodland bears."

GIRL SEES RELIGIOUS MESSAGE IN TOMATO

Shasta Aslam, a 14-year-old Muslim girl from Huddersfield, Yorkshire, cut a tomato in half in 1997 and found that the veins on the fruit spelled out in Arabic "There is only one God" on one side and "Mohammed is the messenger" on the other. Over 50 worshippers a day visited her home to see the fruit over the ensuing weeks. "God made me buy that tomato," said Shasta. The previous year, hundreds of people had flocked to the home of a man in Bolton who believed he had received a message from Allah in an aubergine.

THIEF INJURED BY FROZEN CHICKEN

Having stolen a frozen chicken in a raid on a butcher's shop at Macksville, near Sydney, an Australian thief then used the bird as a tool to break into a nearby café. But in doing so, he accidentally slashed his wrist open and was forced to phone an ambulance for help. He was arrested shortly after being treated by paramedics.

DRINKERS PAY TO CRY INTO THEIR BEER

A bar for depressed drinkers opened in Nanjing, China, in 2004 with customers paying $3 an hour, in addition to their drinks, to weep and wail to their heart's content. To help them burst into tears, tissues and menthol drops were provided at the bar, along with onions and red peppers. While melancholy music played in the background, dolls were made available for customers to throw around or beat to a pulp so that they could vent their anger and frustration over a broken relationship.

WOMAN FINDS CONDOM IN LOAF

A Slovakian woman cut into a loaf of freshly baked bread in 2006 – and found a condom inside. Petra Zeleznikova thought that the bread – purchased that morning from a local supermarket – had an unusually rubbery texture. The condom had not been used.

MAN DRINKS BOTTLE OF VODKA IN AIRPORT SECURITY LINE

A passenger nearly died at Germany's Nuremberg airport in 2007 after he drank a bottle of vodka at a security check instead of surrendering it to officials. The 64-year-old man, who was on his way home to Dresden from a holiday in Egypt, was told that under new regulations governing the carrying of liquids on board an airplane, he would either have to throw out the bottle or pay a fee to have his hand luggage checked as cargo. Instead he decided to down two pints of vodka on the spot – and was immediately rushed to a clinic with suspected alcohol poisoning, thereby delaying his journey home for at least a week.

ANGRY RESIDENTS URINATE ON RESTAURANT ROOF

Residents in a New York apartment block overlooking a newly opened delicatessen became so annoyed by what they considered to be excessive noise from patrons and garbage collections that they started urinating on the restaurant's glass roof. The owner put up a sign directing offenders to use a bathroom instead.

BUSINESSMAN BUYS $60,000 ROUND OF DRINKS

A German businessman walked into a London nightclub in 2001 and announced to everyone present: "The drinks are on me." His round came to a little under $60,000, including a ten per cent tip.

MAN CHANGES NAME TO "HAPPY ADJUSTABLE SPANNERS"

Daniel Westfallen, from Hornchurch, Essex, legally changed his name to Happy Adjustable Spanners for a bet on a drunken night out. All of his friends put names into a hat and Happy Spanners came out. His boss then picked Adjustable as a middle name.

FOOD HEALTH CHIEF STRUCK DOWN WITH SALMONELLA

Franz Fischler, the European food and farm commissioner, missed the launch of the new European Food Safety Authority in 2002 because he was struck down with salmonella poisoning.

WOMAN FINED FOR SMUGGLING SAUSAGE IN DIAPERS

A woman was fined $300 in 2008 for trying to smuggle spicy sausage across the US/Mexico border in babies diapers. Customs inspectors became suspicious when the 21-year-old from South Texas declared that the chunky diapers were "soiled". On examination, it was found that the diapers contained several links of pork sausage, or chorizo, and that they had been deliberately folded in such a way as to appear soiled.

PIONEERS LOSE FIRST CHEESE IN SPACE

An attempt by a group of English cheesemakers to celebrate the 40th anniversary of the first Moon landing by launching a lump of cheddar into space ended in ignominy in 2009 when organizers lost track of it minutes after lift-off. From a field in Wiltshire they had launched a weather balloon attached by a pole to a capsule containing a digital camera, a GPS tracking device and the 300-gram lump of cheddar glued to a plate. The idea was that the cheese would fly 19 miles into the upper atmosphere before the balloon burst and the capsule floated back to Earth on a parachute. However within ten minutes of taking off the tracking system failed. Dom Lane, one of the brains behind the mission, said: "We wanted to take a photograph of a piece of cheddar floating majestically in the firmament with the curve of the Earth below it, but we don't know where it's gone. We think it's somewhere in the East of England – possibly in Essex or Hertfordshire."

MAN STAPLES PENIS TO BURNING CRUCIFIX FOR $300

Thomas Hendry won a 1999 "How Far Will You Go?" contest at Trader McKendry's Tavern, Christchurch, New Zealand, by stapling his penis to a crucifix and setting it on fire. He said he coveted the $300 first prize because he had outstanding bills to pay and thought he could do better than an earlier contestant who had merely pierced his foreskin with a safety pin. Hendry's mother, who was watching, added: "I'm just very relieved that he won. I would have hated for someone to go through all that and lose."

MAN SAYS SUPERMARKET WINE RUINED HIS LOVE LIFE

A man demanded compensation from a supermarket in Aylesford, Kent, because he claimed that a bottle of wine he bought there had ruined his love life. He said his date didn't like the wine and consequently left early, and he never saw her again.

JAILBIRD SUES OVER POP TART

Christopher Lyons, a convicted drug dealer serving time in a US jail, filed a $310,000 lawsuit against Kellogg's in 1994 claiming that a "defective" Pop Tart had injured his mouth and caused him nightmares, resulting in 72 hours of sleep deprivation.

WOMAN SHOCKED BY EXPLODING ARTICHOKE

A 53-year-old woman from Trieste, Italy, was recovering from shock in 2003 after an artichoke she was peeling exploded. She said the vegetable emitted sparks, then a small flame before blowing up in her hands. At first police feared the exploding artichoke was the work of a terrorist who had been planting devices in food products in Italian supermarkets for the past ten years but forensic tests revealed no trace of explosives, leading experts to conclude that it was a bizarre natural phenomenon.

GRIM REAPER SEEN WALKING ALONG ENGLISH SEAFRONT

Having travelled all the way from Nelson, Lancashire, to the resort of Morecambe in 2007 to celebrate a friend's birthday, 31-year-old Christopher Kelly was determined to enjoy himself. So he downed several beers and vodkas, as a result of which he found himself wandering alone on the beach in the early hours of the morning. There, he contrived to become stuck in a pit of treacherous wet sand, from which he only escaped after losing his shoes, pants and jacket. Cold and wet, he staggered across to Morecambe Town Hall, spied an open window and climbed in. As he ambled through the building, he found a camera and a mobile phone, and tried without success to call his friends. He was now in such a state that he accidentally soiled himself and was forced to deposit his few remaining items of clothing in a bin bag. Inside one of the rooms he chanced upon a "Grim Reaper" fancy dress costume, with a mask attached to the hood. He put this on and, dressed as the harbinger of doom (minus scythe), left the building and wandered off along the seafront, where he was captured on CCTV cameras. He tried to turn himself in at a police station, but it was unmanned and he had to wait for three hours until officers arrived and arrested him for burglary. As the prosecutor at Lancaster Magistrates Court relayed details of Kelly's eventful night, one probation officer was forced to leave the courtroom in fits of laughter. Kelly was given a six-month conditional discharge and ordered to pay costs. His lawyer said: "He doesn't remember very much about all this."

SOZZLED SANTA FALLS THROUGH STORE WINDOW

A Santa Claus at a Southampton, England, department store thought it would be a good idea to drink red wine in his grotto so that his cheeks would acquire a nice rosy glow. But when Graham Webb stood up, he lost his balance and fell through a plate glass window.

RESTAURANT OWNER FORGETS TO EVACUATE GUESTS IN FIRE

When fire broke out at a restaurant in Vienna, Austria, in 2003, the owner fled the building together with his staff but in the commotion forgot to evacuate his guests. Around 20 diners were still sitting at their tables when firefighters arrived – even though the room was filled with smoke.

DRINKING CONTEST WINNER SUES ORGANIZERS FOR LETTING HIM GET DRUNK

The winner of a "drink-all-you-can" competition sued the organizers for $1 million after falling down drunk and knocking himself unconscious. John Remley, 67, claimed the owner of a café in Norwood, Ohio, should not have let him get drunk.

MAN FOUND NAKED AND COVERED IN NACHO CHEESE

Michael Monn was arrested in Maryville, Tennessee, in 2004 after officers spotted him running naked from the scene of a burglary, his body covered in nacho cheese. He had cheese in his hair, on his face and on his shoulders, and, according to the police, smelled strongly of alcohol. The court heard that Monn had marked his 23rd birthday by getting "highly intoxicated" and breaking into a pool bar where he stole a box of snacks and the cheese. He pleaded guilty to burglary, theft, vandalism, indecent exposure and public intoxication. It is thought his naked state and the cheesy dip may have been connected to the open bottle of vodka found in his Jeep.

CUSTOMERS CONFUSED BY RESTAURANT TOILETS

Customers at a pizza restaurant in Zhengzhou, China, were baffled when the diner began using banana and peach signs on the gents' and ladies' toilet doors. Research showed that every visitor to the toilets hesitated before going inside. One said: "We were not sure which one stands for men. Does the banana represent a slim woman or is it some sort of phallic symbol?"

COUPLE CELEBRATE WITH 50-YEAR-OLD TINNED CHICKEN

A Manchester, England, couple celebrated 50 years of marriage in 2006 by eating a tin of chicken they had been given on their wedding day. Les and Beryl Bailey had kept the can – part of a wedding gift hamper – as a memento of their big day in 1956 and vowed not to open it until their golden wedding anniversary. Les happily reported that the chicken was as good as new. He said: "I had it with some potatoes and vegetables and it went down a treat."

MAN DRESSED AS BREATHALYZER ARRESTED FOR DRINK-DRIVING

James Miller was stopped by Oxford, Ohio, police on suspicion of drink-driving in 2009 after he was spotted driving the wrong way down a one-way street while wearing a breathalyzer costume. After being pulled over by police, the 18-year-old, who was wearing the costume for a Halloween party, stuffed chewing gum into his mouth and insisted he hadn't been drinking. However officers said they found an open can of beer by the driver's seat, a partial case of beer on the front passenger seat and more alcohol in the trunk. Unfortunately for the fake breathalyzer, a real blood alcohol test showed him to be almost twice the legal limit.

TEETH IN CHOCOLATE BAR WERE HER OWN

Merryl Baker was appalled to find three teeth in a Galaxy Double Nut and Raisin chocolate bar in 1995. She complained to the manufacturer, Mars, and her story was widely reported in the UK press. Shortly afterwards she visited her dentist who, on examining her mouth, informed her that three of her back teeth were missing. "I feel such a fool," she said.

MAN CHOOSES BEER DESIGN FOR COFFIN

A Chicago man is planning to be buried in a coffin resembling a giant can of his favourite beer. Bill Bramanti paid $2,000 in 2008 to have a coffin painted in the design of Pabst Blue Ribbon beer and meanwhile the 67-year-old is using it as a cooler until his time is ready.

WOMAN SWALLOWS SPOON WHILE EATING PASTA

While eating a plate of pasta at a restaurant in Australia, a woman accidentally swallowed a six-inch-long spoon. The 26-year-old Sydney woman was devouring spaghetti when she suddenly had a laughing fit and gulped down the spoon as well.

DRUNKEN FARMER DRIVES TRACTOR DOWN STEPS

A Polish farmer tried to drive his two-ton tractor down steps in the centre of the city of Tczew in 2008 as part of a drunken bet. Tomasz Jankowski was arrested for damaging public property after the tractor became wedged against a wall of the steps as he attempted to negotiate a corner. He said later: "After a few vodkas the staircase seemed a lot wider than it really was and nowhere near as steep."

CARELESS WISPA FETCHES $400

A chocolate Wispa bar that had been stuffed down the back of a sofa for five years fetched $400 when it was sold on eBay in 2008. When student

Rebecca Wells from Stoke-on-Trent found the snack – which had a best before date of 28 April 2004 – her first instinct was to eat it but she then thought that because Cadbury's had stopped making Wispas in 2003, it might have some nostalgic value.

DRUNK DRIVER HANDS WHEEL TO ANOTHER DRUNK

Perhaps aware that he was being watched by a police patrol car, a drunk driver got out of his car and switched places with his passenger in Long Island in 2009. The problem was, the new driver was also drunk – and when they started moving again, their car began tailgating another vehicle, causing it to go onto the shoulder. Both men were charged with driving while intoxicated.

DEPUTY SHERIFF SUES OVER ANCHOVIES IN PIZZA

Wayne Andrews, a deputy sheriff from Boulder, Colorado, was a regular customer at a local restaurant, Pasta Jay's, where he particularly enjoyed the vegetarian pizza. However he could never figure out what the delicious secret ingredient in the sauce was – until he learned one day that it was anchovies, which were against his dietary restrictions. He promptly sued the restaurant for misrepresentation and in 1995 was awarded $463.24 – the cost of all the pizzas he had eaten there over the previous five years.

MAN LOSES 160 POUNDS ON GARLIC AND ONION DIET

Momir Zmiric, of Split, Croatia, saw his weight drop from 26 stone to 14½ stone in just six months – thanks to his new diet of garlic and onions. A friend said: "He looks great but his breath is really rancid."

PENSIONERS GO ON DRUNKEN RAMPAGE AT CARE HOME

Four elderly residents at a nursing home in Dumfries, Scotland, became so unruly during a vodka binge in 2008 that the police had to be called, after staff were unable to maintain control. One was so drunk that he apparently offered the other residents free sex.

OFFICERS UNEARTH VODKA PIPELINE

In 2006, Russian customs officers discovered a mile-long pipeline that was pumping vodka into Latvia. The tunnel had been laid six feet underground by crooks in order to pump homemade vodka across the border and into Latvia, where it was then sold. The discovery was made when council workmen dug holes to plant trees in the area.

FUGITIVE LEADS COPS ON 90 MILES PER HOUR CHASE FOR BURRITO

Wanted on multiple drugs charges, a man led police officers on a 90 miles per hour chase through two Indiana counties in 2009 – just so that he could taste a burrito. The high-speed pursuit lasted 16 minutes until the driver suddenly pulled into a Taco Bell outlet near Fort Wayne. He told officers he knew he was going to jail for a while and wanted to enjoy one last burrito.

WOMAN BUYS 10,000 CHOCOLATE BARS

A woman entered a branch of Woolworths in London in 2004 and bought 10,656 Mars Bars at a total cost of over $4,000. She asked for all the Mars Bars the store had – including ones in the stock room – and then watched her chauffeur load the 200 boxes into the back of a waiting car. A Woolworths spokesman said: "We have no idea what she wanted that many Mars Bars for but it raises all sorts of questions."

PRIEST FINDS FOETUS IN CHEESE SPREAD BOTTLE

Opening a food parcel from an unknown donor, a Filipino priest discovered a four-month-old human foetus inside a bottle of cheese spread. Monsignor Gerry Santos had just celebrated Mass at a church in Manila when he made the startling find. He said his family were unable to continue eating lunch.

PENSIONER CALLS 911 OVER PIZZA DELAY

Eighty-six-year-old Dorothy Densmore was arrested in 2005 for calling the emergency services because she couldn't get a single slice of pizza delivered to her apartment in Charlotte, North Carolina. She dialled 911 twenty times in less than half an hour and demanded that police arrest the pizza parlour employee who called her a "crazy old coot" over the phone. When the police arrived to calm the situation, she allegedly bit the hand of an officer.

UNFORGETTABLE JOURNEYS

MOTORCYCLIST FAILS TO NOTICE LEG MISSING

A 54-year-old Japanese motorcyclist rode his bike for over a mile in 2007 before realizing that he had lost a leg. It had become detached when he hit a central safety barrier while negotiating a bend. Despite being in great pain he didn't notice the limb was missing until he stopped at the next junction.

WOMAN CRASHES INTO STORE, THEN TRIES TO BUY BEER

A 74-year-old woman accidentally drove her car through the front window of a Los Angeles convenience store in 2008, causing $8,000 of damage, before stepping from the wreckage and trying to buy a six-pack of Budweiser. "I don't know how she managed to walk," said the cashier who declined to serve her and called the police instead.

SKYDIVER WATCHES AS BALLOON LEAVES WITHOUT HIM

A Frenchman's daring bid to skydive from the edge of space in 2008 ended in farce when the balloon that was to take him 25 miles up into the skies drifted off without him. After two decades of preparation and $20 million of investment, 64-year-old Michel Fournier was intending to ascend by balloon to an altitude four times higher than that of a cruising commercial jet and then freefall at speeds of more than 1,000 miles per hour, breaking the sound barrier in the process. Instead he could only look on helplessly as the helium balloon detached itself while being inflated at an airfield in Saskatchewan, Canada, and floated away into the heavens, leaving him stranded on the ground in his pressurized capsule. Mr Fournier is no stranger to failure: his 2003 attempt was aborted when strong winds shredded his balloon before it even became airborne.

FLIGHT DIVERTED DUE TO FART

A 2006 American Airlines flight from Washington to Dallas was forced to divert to Nashville, Tennessee, after passengers smelled smoke on the plane. It turned out to be the result of a woman passenger lighting matches in the bathroom to cover up the smell of her personal gas. American Airlines banned her from flying with them in future.

SAILOR WRECKS ROUND-THE-WORLD TRIP – TWICE

In 2002, British yachtsman Jim Hughes was preparing for an epic round-the-world voyage when his plans were scuppered by the intervention of Icelandic fisherman Eriker Olafsson. While Hughes's boat, *Dragon Song*, was moored in the Solent near Portsmouth, Olafsson's vessel managed to get tangled in its moorings and dragged it along, causing $40,000 of damage. By August 2003, Hughes was ready to try again, only for Olafsson to appear on the scene once more. A year and a day after the first collision, Olafsson, who had been drinking, spotted the *Dragon Song* moored in the Solent and sailed over to apologize. But he promptly smashed into it again, causing a further $30,000 worth of repairs. After Olafsson was fined for criminal damage, a distraught Hughes reflected: "Of all the yachts in all the harbours in all the world he has to crash into mine – twice. I can never rest sound or leave her alone again unless Olafsson has sailed off into the distance, never to return. I will never, ever sail anywhere near Iceland, just on the off chance that he will be there." Meanwhile Olafsson, who paid compensation for both accidents, was said to be planning his own round-the-world trip.

VANITY NUMBER PLATE LEADS TO $19,000 PARKING FINES

The owner of a car with the personalized number plate XXXXXXX received more than $19,000 worth of parking tickets intended for other vehicles. Traffic wardens in Birmingham, Alabama, automatically entered seven letter Xs onto their forms when issuing tickets to cars without plates. Unfortunately the default code for unidentified vehicles matched the vanity plate of Scottie Robinson from nearby Huntsville who at one stage was receiving up to ten fines a day – all for parking offences committed in different areas of a city that he had visited only once in five years.

ELDERLY WOMAN GOES DOWN AIRPORT BAGGAGE CHUTE

A 78-YEAR-OLD woman who misunderstood instructions while checking in at Sweden's Stockholm airport was whisked down a baggage chute after placing herself instead of her luggage on the belt. She was preparing to fly to Germany in 2008 when she lay down on an unmanned baggage belt in the belief that she was obeying check-in instructions. She was rapidly swept off to the baggage handling centre, where staff helped her get back on her feet. She suffered no serious injury and was able to catch her flight as planned. ●

NUNS FINED FOR SPEEDING ON WAY TO SEE POPE

Three nuns who hurried towards Pope Benedict XVI's holiday home after learning that he had suffered a minor accident in 2009 were fined nearly $500 after being stopped by police for speeding at 120 miles per hour. Asked why she was speeding, the driver of the Ford Fiesta, Sister Tavoletta, told police: "We had heard how the Pope had fallen over and we were on our way to make sure he was OK." A spokesman for Turin's police department said: "Hopefully Sister Tavoletta will mention her bad driving the next time she goes to confession."

WOMAN SELLS CAR AFTER DISCOVERING SPIDER

Shortly after buying a second-hand sports car, 27-year-old Michelle Holloway, from Yeovil, Somerset, felt compelled to sell it for a $250 loss because she had spotted a tiny spider on the driver's seat. Despite now having to rely on lifts to get to work at a local hospital, Miss Holloway insisted she had no regrets about selling her car. "I couldn't keep it after that," she said. "If the spider had come out while I was driving, I would have crashed."

MILLIPEDES BRING TRAIN TO A HALT

Rail passengers in Honshu, Japan, were delayed for two hours when their train was brought to a halt after running over an army of millipedes. As they were crushed, the insects' body fluids were squashed out, acting as a lubricant and causing the train's wheels to slip on the track.

PASSENGER LIES ABOUT BOMB TO SAVE MUM'S BLUSHES

A passenger told security staff at Chicago's O'Hare Airport that he had a bomb in his luggage – because he didn't want his mother to know it was really a penis pump. Twenty-nine-year-old Mardin Azad Amin was preparing to fly to Turkey in 2006 when security officers spotted the suspicious-looking black object in his bag but he decided to lie about it because his mother was standing nearby.

FLYING UNDERPANTS CAUSE HIGHWAY CRASH

A pair of flying underpants caused a crash on a German highway in 2003 when they landed on a driver's face and blocked his view. One of a group of naked men travelling in a van threw the underwear into a Volkswagen Passat as they overtook it on a busy stretch of autobahn near Gotha. Unable to see, the Volkswagen driver promptly rammed into the back of a truck. Nobody was hurt in the crash but police officers admitted they had no idea why the men in the van were driving along naked.

FLAMING NERVE! SEMI-NAKED MAN RIDES SPEEDING BARSTOOL WITH BACKSIDE ON FIRE

Police officers in Tauranga, New Zealand, dealt with one of their stranger cases in 2003 – that of a semi-naked man speeding down the street on a motorized barstool with his backside on fire. John Sullivan, who confessed to having "had a few" before his explicit ride and who claimed his barstool could reach 50 miles per hour, was sentenced to 200 hours' community service for driving his contraption in a public place with no warrant and no registration. The court heard that the flames came courtesy of one of his party tricks, which involved a piece of rolled-up newspaper and a cigarette lighter.

TOURIST GETS LOST IN AIRPORT FOR A WEEK

A confused Greek traveller managed to get lost in a tiny local airport in Germany for a whole week in 2008. Christianos Kaklamanis, 38, spent seven days wandering aimlessly around Hanover airport before travel agent Sabine Berger spotted him and alerted police. She said: "I saw him a few times and at first just thought he was flying in and out of the airport a lot."

PILOT ASKS PASSENGERS FOR LIFT HOME

A British Airways pilot about to land a plane in Manchester in 2006 asked passengers over the intercom whether any of them could give him a lift home. He then stood at the cabin door as everyone got off but there were no offers. A BA spokesman said of the unusual request: "Never let it be said our pilots lack ingenuity."

IMPATIENT DRIVER BITES DAWDLING PEDESTRIAN

In Iasi, Romania, in 2009, a road rage driver bit a pedestrian who was taking too long to cross the road. Mihai Nicoara told police that the furious motorist jumped from his car and sank his teeth into his stomach at a crossing.

WIFE BRINGS HOME WRONG CAR

Betty Vaughn was dreading telling her husband Edgar what had happened to their car while she had been on a shopping trip. The passenger-side mirror was missing and there was no sign of the garage door opener. When Edgar arrived home in Louisville, Kentucky, the retired schoolteacher nervously showed him the damage. Edgar walked round to the front of the car and noticed that the Transylvania University plate had also been removed. "I can't believe anybody would take that!" exclaimed Betty. "We've been vandalized!" Then Edgar noticed the tyres weren't the right brand – and, perhaps more significantly, the licence plate was different. He checked the glove compartment and confirmed that Betty had brought home the wrong car! It turned out that the Vaughns' blue 1992 Toyota Camry had been parked two cars away from Charles Lester's 1993 model. Both vehicles had been left unlocked. After the respective cars had been returned to their rightful owners, Betty said: "It could have happened to anyone."

MAN TRIES TO ENTER CANADA ON STREET SWEEPER

Damon J. Francis tried to cross the border from the US into Canada in 2001 . . . on a street sweeper. He had crashed a white Cadillac through a fence into the parking lot of the Michigan company where he had once worked and swapped it for a stolen street sweeper, which he then rode towards the Canadian border. He pleaded not guilty to theft by reason of insanity.

DRUNKEN GERMANS FLY 2,000 MILES DURING TOILET BREAK

Two drunken Germans, apparently looking for a toilet during a 2000 conference at Frankfurt airport, got on a plane by mistake and flew to Moscow, 1,000 miles away. The 20-year-old men were wandering round the airport when they found themselves on the tarmac and boarded a shuttle bus which drove to an aircraft bound for the Russian capital. "They got in and sat in the back of the airplane which then flew to Moscow," said the Frankfurt state prosecutor. "They weren't even at the airport to fly anywhere." On arrival in Moscow, they noticed it was cold and realized they had no passports, let alone entry visas. Russian police put them on a flight back to Frankfurt where they were met by Federal Border Police who charged them with joyriding.

ELDERLY WOMEN BRAWL OVER HANDICAPPED PARKING SPACE

A row in 1998 between two elderly ladies over a handicapped parking space left one in hospital with a broken hip and the other facing criminal charges. The trouble started when 88-year-old Edna Gilliam pulled into a handicapped parking space at the Kaiser Hospital, Santa Clara, California. Unfortunately 67-year-old Gloria Owens, who was bringing her 98-year-old mother for a hospital appointment, had been waiting patiently for the very same space. Owens immediately went over to Gilliam's car and knocked on the window, only to be totally ignored because Gilliam was hard of hearing. As Gilliam then left her car and began walking to the hospital, Owens approached her from behind, grabbed her sweater and spun her around. In the ensuing altercation, Gilliam was knocked to the pavement, fracturing her right hip. Owens was put on three years' probation and given 200 hours' community service. "It's somewhat bizarre for ladies of this age to be involved in physical confrontation," said a police officer. "Obviously there were some emotional hot buttons pushed."

TRUCK DRIVER TICKETED WHILE STUCK IN HOLE

Truck driver Michael Collins was on his way to collect a skip in London's Belsize Park when his 17-ton vehicle suddenly collapsed into a hole in the road created by a burst water main. With the front wheels stuck fast, Collins waited for assistance but instead saw a parking attendant appear and, standing on tiptoe, plaster a parking ticket on his windscreen. Helpfully she informed him: "You can appeal."

FIRST-TIME FLYER TRIES TO OPEN PLANE'S EMERGENCY DOOR

A Chinese man, flying for the first time, tried to open the airplane's emergency exit door in mid-air . . . because he wanted to spit. Luckily a fellow passenger managed to stop him just as he was about to push the door open. The man was arrested when the plane landed in Shanghai.

QUEEN IS STUCK BEHIND LEARNER DRIVER

The Queen missed a royal fly-past in 2002 – believed to be the first time in 50 years that she had been late for an official engagement – because her limo was stuck behind a learner driver on a rural road. The Queen was on her way from her residence at Sandringham in Norfolk to RAF Marham at Kings Lynn and was already running late after getting stuck behind a tractor for two miles when the royal entourage caught up with 19-year-old student Sarah Proctor who was taking her tenth driving lesson in a Vauxhall Corsa. After learning that the delay caused Her Majesty to be late for the fly-past, driving instructor Martin Underwood explained: "Both Sarah and I noticed the Queen was behind us. We were observing the correct speed and there was no place to pass." Sarah described the whole episode as "unreal", adding: "It was so weird having the Queen behind you on your driving lesson. I could see her hat but I could not see her."

JOY RIDER STEALS 30 FIAT UNOS IN THREE MONTHS

Police in Zagreb, Croatia, arrested a 20-year-old man on suspicion of stealing no fewer than 30 humble Fiat Uno cars for joy rides in a three-month crime spree in 2008. He abandoned the little cars in parking lots or alongside highways once they ran out of petrol.

LOST CYCLIST TAKES LONG DIVERSION

A Chinese cyclist's search for a Munich subway station ended with him pedalling for miles down the autobahn – completely oblivious to his mistake. When stopped by police, the 26-year-old student said he was at the end of a 50-mile ride from Augsburg and had wanted to finish his journey by subway. So he had followed blue "U" signs (which indicate subway stations in Germany), unaware that similar signs also mark diversions – "Umleitungen" – and they led him on to the A99 autobahn. The man was fined $10 for illegal highway use and sent on his way with a map.

MAN WAITS SIX YEARS FOR CAR TO BE REPAIRED

An Argentine pensioner revealed that he had been waiting for more than six years for a Buenos Aires garage to fix his car. Jose Orono said he took his Fiat 600 to the repair shop in 2000 but a week later the garage owner told him that he still needed another two weeks to fix the car. "It needed painting and some minor mechanical work," said Mr Orono, "but he kept making up excuses. One time, he said that his aunt had died and another that his shop had been broken into." Having finally run out of patience, Mr Orono announced in 2006 that he was going to sue the garage. It is not known whether he is still hoping that his car will be ready next week.

TRAIN STAFF BANG HEADS TO RELIEVE BOREDOM

A group of Russian train conductors needed hospital treatment in 2003 after smashing their heads repeatedly against a train window to find out who had the strongest forehead. The conductors thought the contest would help pass the time on the long 3,000-mile journey from Novosibirsk in Siberia to Vladivostok but barely halfway through they stopped the train and demanded medical help.

SAILOR ENDS VOYAGE TO SAVE WHALES AFTER HITTING ONE

A California sailor who set off on a solo voyage to Japan in 2000 to highlight the plight of whales had to abandon the attempt just one day into the adventure after his boat ran into one of the mammals. The collision damaged the rudder of Michael Reppy's 60-foot ocean racer *Thursday's Child*, making it almost impossible to steer. As the boat prepared to limp into Honolulu, Reppy acknowledged in his online log "the irony of sailing to save whales and running into them".

DRIVER IS DOWN IN THE DUMPS

A 65-year-old Swiss driver plunged 30 feet into a garbage bunker at a green recycling centre in Bazenheid in 2010 after accidentally hitting the accelerator instead of the brake as he was backing up. A shocked Heiner Mollard was winched to safety for treatment to cuts and bruises. To add insult to injury, he was fined $100 by dump bosses for leaving an "inappropriate item" – namely his car – in a recycling bin.

WOMAN CRASHES CAR AFTER BEING BITTEN BY TORTOISE

A driver crashed into an oncoming bus in Trimbach, Switzerland, after a tortoise bit her. The woman was travelling with two tortoises on the passenger seat of her car when one attacked her, causing her to swerve across the road and collide with the bus. Swiss police indicated that the tortoises were not wearing seat belts.

REFUGEE TRAVELS 30 HOURS STRAPPED BENEATH BUS – TO WRONG COUNTRY

A 19-year-old Afghan man survived a 30-hour journey strapped underneath a bus in 2009, only to discover that he had arrived in Poland instead of his chosen destination of Italy. The man used a belt to attach himself near the gearbox at the bus depot in Athens but unfortunately selected the wrong bus. So when he emerged from his hiding place at the end of the 1,700-mile journey and asked wearily, "Italia?" he was in for a nasty surprise. He was said to be exhausted, frozen and starving and had suffered a scratched face from the gear cable every time the bus changed gear.

DRIVER TAKES WRONG TURN ONTO AIRPORT RUNWAY

A Florida driver got lost and ended up on the runway of Tampa International Airport in 1998, causing a number of flights to be delayed. She had driven through a closed airport gate marked with "Do Not Enter" signs and, according to the airport's assistant director of operations, "was on a runway staring at a 737". She told police she had got lost while driving home from a party after fighting with her boyfriend.

JOURNALIST'S VOMIT GROUNDS MiG FIGHTER PLANE

A MiG fighter plane was put out of action for a week after a journalist vomited in the cockpit, damaging sensitive equipment. Kresimir Zabec from the Croatian daily *Jutarnji List* was researching a story with the Croatian Air Force but threw up as the MiG 21 sped through the air at 625 miles per hour during a flight that had been specially arranged for him. The plane was grounded for seven days while the hi-tech equipment was taken out and thoroughly cleaned.

HOTEL PARKING VALET WRITES OFF $175,000 FERRARI

Asked to park a $175,000 Ferrari 355 GTS for a guest, the 20-year-old parking valet at an upmarket hotel in Dana Point, California, merely succeeded in smashing the car into a palm tree just 30 feet from the hotel entrance. In a statement that was of little consolation to the Ferrari's owner, the hotel's executive assistant manager maintained: "We park hundreds of thousands of cars each year without a problem."

WOMAN HIT TWICE IN 24 HOURS BY SAME CAR

An Icelandic woman with an unblemished driving record of 20 years was hit twice in 24 hours by the same car in 1999. First, she was driving in Akureyri when a car suddenly came out of a parking lot and smashed into her vehicle, causing wholesale damage. After renting another car, the next day the woman was hit by the same vehicle as she drove through a green light at a junction.

BUS TOILET FAECES DUMPED THROUGH CAR SUNROOF

A family were driving through Ohio in 2006 when the Greyhound bus they were following allegedly dumped the contents of its toilet through their open car sunroof. Robert and Angela Stokes and their three children were returning from a Mother's Day meal in Toledo when they were suddenly covered with faeces, urine and toilet paper.

MAN FINED FOR SPEEDING IN WHEELCHAIR

A **GERMAN MAN** was stopped by police and fined $600 in 2007 for doing twice the speed limit in his electric wheelchair. After Guenther Eichmann, 54, was clocked at 40 miles per hour on a street in Geske, the former engineer revealed that he had modified the wheelchair's electric engine so that it could go faster. His souped-up wheelchair was confiscated. ●

LOST MAN DRIVES 370 MILES TO PICK UP MILK

Eighty-one-year-old Australian grandfather Eric Steward drove for nine hours and over 370 miles after setting off early one morning in 2009 to buy a newspaper. The former navy seaman had intended making a short trip to collect the newspaper from a store in Yass, New South Wales, where he and his wife Clare were staying with friends. However he took a wrong turn and just kept on driving – all the way into Victoria beyond Melbourne towards Geelong. There he finally stopped at a service station and asked a police officer to contact his wife. When she asked her husband if there were any signs around, he replied, "Uh, Westgate Bridge", in reference to the Melbourne landmark. That was when she knew he was hopelessly lost. Asked by the police why he had not stopped earlier, Mr Steward said brightly: "I just like to drive."

DRUNK DRIVER WAS ALSO BLIND

Estonian police who stopped a car in the centre of Tartu in 2008 found that the driver was not only drunk but also blind. Officers said 20-year-old Kristjan Gradolf was apparently being given directions by a friend in the passenger seat. Gradolf had also been stopped while driving erratically the previous year. On that occasion he only confessed to being blind after he could not find the tube to give a breath test.

ANGRY DAD HANGS SPEEDING SON'S CAR IN TREE

After his 16-year-old son Stephen picked up his third speeding ticket within just three months of getting his driving licence, Alan Cost decided to teach him a lesson. He used a chain to suspend the pick-up truck from a tree in front of the family home on a busy road in Birmingham, Alabama. He also put a sign in the vehicle's window, which read: "This is what happens when a teenager doesn't mind." Beneath was a smaller sign saying: "May be for sale."

FLATULENT PIGS FORCE JET TO MAKE U-TURN

Excessive flatulence from a consignment of 72 pigs in its cargo hold set off a fire alarm on a South African passenger jet in 1995 and forced it to turn back and make an emergency landing. The alarm automatically released fire-suppressing halon gas, which unfortunately suffocated 15 of the valuable stud pigs. The animals were travelling by passenger plane because, according to an airline spokesman, passenger flights are "less traumatic for them than going on a freighter flight".

COPS CHASE GARBAGE TRUCK FOR 57 MILES

A man in Minnesota led police on a 57-mile vehicle chase in 2009 – while driving a garbage truck. The chase began when police received a call about a drunken man trying to break into a house in Lastrup, but before they arrived he drove off in a garbage truck. In the course of the ensuing chase, he swerved the truck at police cars before accelerating away in reverse. After a deputy had unsuccessfully attempted to halt the truck's progress by firing a shotgun at its engine, the fugitive was apprehended by a police dog while trying to complete his getaway on foot.

SAFE DRIVER DID NOT HAVE LICENCE

A pensioner on his way to receive an award for 25 years of accident-free driving was stopped by police at a roadside check – and admitted he did not have a licence. Wilibald Schmidt had been forced to surrender his licence in 1978 but had continued driving illegally without it. The motoring club in Essen, Germany, where he was a member, had invited him to receive an award for his "careful driving and good example to other motorists".

PILOT JAILED FOR FLINTSTONES SINGALONG

Dutch airline pilot Wim de Nijs was sentenced to four months in jail after being convicted of jamming the air traffic control frequency and jeopardizing airport safety by singing the theme to *The Flintstones* over the radio for 20 minutes while landing his plane.

DRIVER WAKES UP IN COFFIN AFTER CRASH

A Croatian motorist who crashed through an undertakers' window in 2009 woke up to find himself in an open coffin. Radoslav Pokrajac was hurled from the car through an open window and landed in the funeral director's display of special offers. "He was very frightened," said one rescue worker. "When he woke up, he didn't know if he was alive or dead." Funeral director Miro Zirdum said it was not the first occasion a car had crashed into his shop in Sibinj. "This is the third or fourth time I've had a car in my shop," he said. "And none of them have brought me any business."

DISCARDED LEDERHOSEN CAUSE CITY GRIDLOCK

During an argument with his girlfriend, a 30-year-old German man angrily threw his lederhosen out of the window of his Augsburg apartment – and brought the entire city to a standstill. For the leather shorts landed on an overhead tram cable and short-circuited its power, forcing trams to a halt and blocking a busy arterial road for hours. Police had to retrieve the garment with a crane and made the lederhosen owner pay for the operation.

STOWAWAY DISAPPOINTED BY FIRST GLIMPSE OF NEW YORK

A Romanian who wanted to start a new life in the US set about realizing his ambition by stowing away in a cargo container on a ship bound for New York. When the ship eventually docked, he slipped ashore from his hiding place in eager anticipation of experiencing the Big Apple. But as he gazed out at his new homeland, he was puzzled that there wasn't a skyscraper in sight . . . or a yellow taxi . . . or the Statue of Liberty. It was only when he was arrested by docks police that he learned that the ship's first port of call was not New York but the English port of Felixstowe.

"BODY IN BOOT" IS FALSE ALARM

A woman in England phoned the police to report that she had seen a car being driven at Leigh-on-Sea with what appeared to be a body protruding from the open boot. Police quickly found the car – with two legs sticking out of the back. They belonged to a garage mechanic trying to trace a noise which was annoying the driver.

PILOTS OVERSHOOT DESTINATION BY 150 MILES

A Northwest Airlines flight carrying 144 passengers from San Diego, California, to Minneapolis, Minnesota, overshot its destination by 150 miles in 2009 because the pilots were busy on their personal laptop computers and lost track of time and place. The captain, Timothy Cheney, and first officer Richard Cole said they had been distracted looking at a new crew-scheduling system on their laptops. It was only when a flight attendant contacted them on the aircraft's intercom to ask what was going on that they realized they were flying over Wisconsin at 37,000 feet. Alerted to their lapse, Cheney told Cole to contact air traffic control because "we need to get this thing on the ground". They duly turned the Airbus A320 around and landed safely in Minneapolis. During the flight, the airplane was out of radio contact for 77 minutes, causing officials on the ground, fearful that the plane had been hijacked by terrorists, to prepare to scramble fighter jets to intercept it.

ITALIAN DRIVER IS LITERALLY STUCK IN TRAFFIC

A motorist and his car became stuck on an Italian road in 2001 after a truck shed its load of glue. The truck crashed into a tree on a bridge between Milan and Pavia, spilling gallons of extra strong construction glue all over the highway. When the driver of the car behind got out to investigate, his feet immediately stuck to the tarmac. For the next few hours he stood on the same spot calling for help on his cell phone until rescue workers arrived to dissolve the glue.

PASSENGER IS ORDERED TO DRINK HIS OWN URINE

Airport security staff in China ordered a retired policeman to drink his own urine sample before catching a flight in order to prove that it was safe to take on board. Yu Fahai was passing through security at Pudong International Airport, Shanghai, in 2009 when he was challenged about a bottle of liquid in his pocket. "The checker asked me what was inside," said Yu, who received a kidney transplant several years earlier and had to regularly test his urine for infection. "I told her it was my urine, and she told me to drink some to prove it." After Yu lodged a complaint, an airport spokesman said the security guard mistakenly heard the word "urine" as "beverage", and claimed Yu had his boarding card in his mouth, making his pronunciation unclear.

INTREPID FLIER TAKES TO SKIES IN LAWN CHAIR

California truck driver Larry Walters had always wanted to be an airplane pilot but poor eyesight prevented him from fulfilling his ambition.

Undeterred, he decided to build his own flying contraption, which resulted in a crazy adventure in the skies above Los Angeles in the summer of 1982. After buying 45 weather balloons and several tanks of helium from his local Army-Navy surplus store, Larry strapped the balloons to an aluminium lawn chair, which was in turn anchored to the bumper of his jeep. He then packed beer, sandwiches and a loaded pellet gun so that he could pop a few of the balloons when he was eventually ready to descend. His plan was to float gently up to a height of about 30 feet above his back yard and come back down a few hours later but when he severed the cord tying the lawn chair to his jeep, he instead streaked into the sky as if fired from a cannon. Rather than levelling out at 30 feet, he levelled out at 16,000 feet. There he stayed, drifting, cold and frightened, for more than 14 hours. To his horror, he found himself crossing the primary approach corridor of Los Angeles International Airport and a helicopter was sent to investigate after disbelieving airline pilots radioed in to report that they had passed a man in a lawn chair with a gun. Finally he summoned up the courage to shoot a few balloons and descend but as he came down the hanging tethers caught in a power line, blacking out a Long Beach neighbourhood. He eventually came to ground in a residential area of Long Beach and was immediately led away in handcuffs by waiting members of the Los Angeles Police Department. When a reporter asked him why he had done it, Larry replied nonchalantly: "A man can't just sit around." He was subsequently fined $1,500 for violating airspace and enjoyed fleeting fame as a talk show guest. Eleven years later, Larry Walters shot himself dead, aged 44.

TRAIN DELAYED BY GIANT PENGUIN

Passengers on a train in Germany were left stranded in 2005 after the driver pulled the emergency stop because he mistook a giant toy penguin lying on the tracks for a dead man in a tuxedo.

CABIN CREW "FREAK OUT" FRENCH WITH WRONG MESSAGE

A cabin crew caused chaos on a 2009 flight from Dublin to Paris by accidentally playing a message warning that the plane was about to ditch in the sea. An initial announcement in English had told passengers on the Aer Lingus flight to return to their seats and fasten their seat belts because of turbulence. But a second one in French said the plane, which at the time was heading south over the Irish Sea, was about to make an emergency landing. According to witnesses, French passengers, who made up most of the 70 people on board, immediately "freaked out" with many screaming and bursting into tears.

WOMAN CRASHES CAR AFTER DRIVING TEST

Moments after completing her driving test in Portage, Indiana, in 2006, Jessica Krasek crashed the car into the examiners' office. She was pulling into a parking space when she accidentally hit the accelerator instead of the brake. She failed the test.

FATHER LETS YOUNG SON DRIVE CAR AS A REWARD

As a reward for finishing his dinner, his homework and cleaning his room, a Florida man let his seven-year-old son drive the family car one evening in 2002. With his father sitting in the passenger seat, the boy, driving without lights, ran a stop sign and smashed into another car. Unrepentant, his father justified letting him take the wheel by saying: "Some kids play with dolls; my kid wants to drive."

TRACTOR FAN'S EPIC JOURNEY IS IN VAIN

For years, German farmer Wolfgang Mueller had dreamed of taking his 44-year-old red Massey Ferguson MF35 tractor back to Coventry, England, to visit the factory where it was built. So in 2007, two weeks after retiring, the 65-year-old left Stuttgart on the start of a 700-mile sentimental pilgrimage. Towing a caravan and chugging along sedately, he drove the tractor through Luxembourg and France before boarding a ferry at Calais. Once in England, he took minor roads and country lanes and eventually reached the site of the Massey Ferguson factory at Coventry – only to find that it had been knocked down years ago and was now a row of houses.

BOMB ALERT OVER WIND-BREAKING DOG

A novelty toy dog which breaks wind sparked a major security scare at an American airport in 2003. British passenger Dave Rogerson's life-size mechanical terrier set off a security detector at Norfolk airport, Virginia, prompting FBI agents to take a series of swabs from the toy's rear end. Rogerson said: "They told me it was the highest reading they had for explosives and they took it very seriously. They were convinced there was something explosive in the dog." Happily after a 20-minute examination they eventually decided the dog was not a security risk and handed it back to him.

FAKE PASSPORT BELONGED TO WANTED MURDERER

A 36-year-old man who bought a false passport to flee Russia in 2003 was unaware that the stolen paperwork belonged to a wanted murderer. Consequently as soon as he tried to cross the border into Latvia he was arrested on suspicion of murder. A police spokesman said: "He bought the passport on the black market in St Petersburg and inserted his own photo. Unfortunately for him, he did not know the passport's history."

TOURIST GETS LOST USING ANCIENT GUIDEBOOK

An elderly American tourist had to be rescued from the depths of a Bavarian forest in 2004 after losing his way while consulting a 90-year-old guidebook. Hank Edwards, 79, had longed to visit that part of Germany ever since reading "Beautiful Bayreuth", a guidebook bought by his father in 1914. Unfortunately following out-of-date directions from the book resulted in him getting stuck in the Bayreuth forest for two days. The local tourist board pointed out that two World Wars and a massive reforestation programme had considerably changed Bayreuth.

PENSIONER BANNED FROM DRIVING UNTIL YEAR 3000

An 84-year-old was banned from driving until the year 3000 after a magistrate in Sydney, Australia, ruled that her previous suspension – until 2999 – was inadequate. Luba Relic, who has appeared in court more than 70 times, had her disqualification increased after crashing her Honda Civic in a car park in 2008 while driving without a licence. She had previously had her licence revoked until 2999 for medical reasons but had defied the court by continuing to drive. Outside court she protested her innocence, claiming that she had been unfairly targeted by police. "I have been driving for so long and I am a good driver," she insisted.

NAKED CHESS FANATIC HITS THE ROAD

A bold nudist wrote to a newspaper in Des Moines, Iowa, claiming that he had driven 15,000 miles in the buff in the course of 2001. Dave Wolz, 47, said he mostly drove without clothes on trips to chess tournaments. He revealed that he had occasionally been spotted by passing motorists who had reported him to the police, but he had always managed to slip on a pair of shorts before being stopped.

PARAGLIDER STUCK IN TREE WITH CHIHUAHUA

An Australian man had to be rescued in 2008 after he became stuck 200 feet up a tree while paragliding with his pet Chihuahua. Paul Hansen was left dangling in a giant mountain ash tree near Melbourne for five hours with dog Emma strapped to his chest.

PASSENGERS SURVIVE BY SUCKING WOMAN'S BREAST MILK

Sixteen people who ran out of food and water when they become lost at sea for 12 days after fleeing the Dominican Republic in a homemade boat in 2001 survived by sucking a mother's breast milk. The eight men and seven women took turns suckling 31-year-old Faustina Mercedes for a few seconds a day. Mercedes managed to feed herself by getting her sister Elena to suck on her breast and then pass the milk on to her by mouth.

WOMAN EATS BOWL OF CEREAL WHILE DRIVING

Called to a single-vehicle crash near Woodstock, Ontario, in 2008, Canadian police found a 21-year-old woman covered in milk and cereal. She had apparently been trying to eat cereal with a bowl and spoon while driving in icy conditions when she lost control and crashed into guide posts on Highway 7.

DEAD PASSENGER GOES UNNOTICED ON BUS FOR SIX HOURS

A dead passenger remained on the top deck of a London bus for more than six hours in 2009 after staff failed to spot the corpse. Pawel Modzelewski died on the night bus but the driver thought he was asleep and then forgot to tell anyone at the depot about him before going home. Consequently, the dead man stayed in the bus garage overnight and was still slumped forward in his seat when the vehicle went out the following morning. Early morning commuters joined the bus, unaware that one of their fellow passengers was dead, until one finally raised the alarm.

OVULATING WIFE CAUSES DRIVER TO EXCEED LIMIT

A driver caught speeding in Philadelphia told police he had exceeded the limit because he and his wife were trying for a baby. He explained: "My wife is ovulating. I have to get home right now."

WOMEN TRY TO CHECK DEAD PASSENGER ONTO FLIGHT

Two German women were detained at Liverpool Airport in 2010 after staff discovered that the man with whom they were planning to board a flight to Berlin had been dead for at least 12 hours. Wearing sunglasses, 91-year-old Curt Willi Jarant arrived at the airport by taxi with his wife, Gitta Jarant, and stepdaughter Anke Anusic. Lifting him into a wheelchair, an airport worker immediately thought Mr Jarant was dead from the way his body slumped forward and felt ice cold, but the women claimed that he always slept like that. However when security officials tried to take a pulse, they confirmed that Mr Jarant had passed away. The women, who were suspected of attempting to avoid paying costly repatriation fees but were eventually released without charge, insisted they thought he was pale but alive – even though the post mortem indicated that he had been dead throughout the 45-minute taxi ride from their home in Manchester.

COUPLE FORGET TO TAKE MAP ON EUROPEAN JAUNT

Setting off in their motorhome from Dover in 1987, Mark and Laura Jones decided to cross the English Channel and spend a few days in Paris. They packed all the necessary provisions for their vacation – except a map. As soon as they arrived in France, they became hopelessly lost but simply continued driving without asking for directions. The result was that they finished up near the Swiss border. Realizing they had gone wrong, they decided to head back to Paris but thought that the route to the French capital took them through Luxembourg, Belgium and Holland. On reaching Rotterdam, they thought they had finally found the right road, only to end up in the German city of Bonn. By now they were short of money and had to beg for petrol cash. They eventually made it back to Dover a week later than expected and having driven over 1,000 miles without getting anywhere near Paris.

TOILET RIDE FOR CARAVANNER

German tourist Juergen Winkler had a surprise in 2008 when his caravan rolled 200 yards down a hill – while he was on the toilet. The caravan crashed into a lamppost and then into a ditch in Upper Austria, leaving Mr Winkler with cuts and bruises. He was still sitting on the toilet when fire crews arrived to pull the caravan from the ditch.

SPEEDY CYCLIST'S PANTS CATCH FIRE

A POLISH CYCLIST pedalled so hard that the friction from his pants caused them to catch fire. While enjoying a ride near Koroszyczyn in 2008, 55-year-old Mieczyslaw Jasinski started to smell burning and when he looked down he saw that his pants were on fire. He immediately jumped off his bike and rolled on the ground to extinguish the flames, but when passers-by arrived the tattered remains of his pants were still smoking. Witnesses described him as being like a flaming torch cycling along the road. ●

WOMAN PASSES DRIVER'S TEST AT 960TH ATTEMPT

A woman in South Korea passed her driving test in 2010 – at the 960th time of asking. Cha Sa-soon, 69, passed the driving part of the test at the tenth try, but only after making 949 unsuccessful attempts to achieve a pass mark of 60 per cent in the written exam, which she had taken almost daily between April 2005 and November 2009. She spent a total of $16,500, including application fees, to earn her licence.

WTF PLATE EMBARRASSES AMERICANS

North Carolina elementary school teacher Mary Ann Hardee couldn't understand why her teenage grandchildren kept giggling at the licence plate on her new car . . . until the connotations of the abbreviation WTF were explained to her. She became so self-conscious about it that she petitioned the Department of Motor Vehicles, which ordered that she and the other 9,999 drivers in the state who were issued with a WTF number plate in 2007 should receive new plates.

LINER PASSENGERS' HAIR TURNS GREEN

Nine passengers aboard the P&O liner *Oceana* were given free hairdos in 2003 after their hair turned bright green when they swam in the ship's swimming pool.

DRIVER FAILS TO SPOT SIX-FOOT-TALL ORANGE RABBIT

A driver told a court in Portland, Oregon, that he did not see a six-foot-tall woman wearing a bright orange rabbit costume and riding a pedicab before he ran into her. Edward Cespedes-Rodriguez was convicted of hit-and-run driving but was cleared of recklessly endangering another person after claiming he didn't spot the pedicab-riding orange rabbit because he was fumbling with his cell phone at the time. The rabbit in question, pedicab rider Kate Altermatt, told reporters that she was disappointed with the verdict, given that her vehicle was clearly visible, being equipped with reflectors and a blinking red light, plus the fact that she was dressed as an orange rabbit. She added that she initially struggled to persuade local police to take her complaint seriously – possibly because she was still wearing the rabbit suit.

PLANE CIRCLES WHILE AIR TRAFFIC CONTROLLER HAS LUNCH

A plane carrying 55 passengers circled an airport in western Scotland for half an hour because the air traffic controller was on her lunch break. The delayed flight from Glasgow to Benbecula in the Western Isles had to wait to land because national air traffic regulations prevented Benbecula's sole controller from working more than two hours without taking a break.

VILLAGER DRIVES WRONG WAY ON FREEWAY FOR 20 MILES

An 80-year-old man drove his vintage car against the flow of traffic on Malaysia's main freeway for 20 miles, blissfully unaware that he was on the wrong side of the road. After making a wrong turn on his way home in 2006, Ah Pee found himself on the busy six-lane North-South Expressway – the first time he had ever been on that road. Realizing he was heading in the wrong direction, he executed a U-turn in his Morris Minor but stayed on his side of the road divider, thereby putting him in the fast lane and heading straight into oncoming traffic. He drove like that for 20 miles – somehow avoiding a collision – until police officers finally intercepted him and steered him into the emergency lane. One officer who attended the incident said: "He was driving between 40 and 45 miles per hour, and I could see the befuddled look in his eyes as the oncoming vehicles flashed their headlights at him. We advised him to ask for a lift from his children the next time he went for a drive."

TRAIN COLLIDES WITH PASSING HOUSE

A house that was being moved from one location to another on the back of a truck was demolished in 2000 after being struck by an unscheduled train on a railroad crossing. Two men were keeping watch on the roof of the house, which was being escorted by a sheriff's car as it crossed the track at Sumner, Washington State, just before midnight. The house was barely halfway across when a special train carrying Seattle Seahawks fans home from a football game came roaring round a bend and smashed into it. Neither lookout was hurt although one ended up in a nearby field as a result of the impact.

DRUNK PILOT ASKS: "WHERE HAVE YOU HIDDEN THE RUNWAY?"

A 65-year-old amateur pilot who took a Cessna light aircraft to the skies over Germany in 2009 had so much to drink that he was unable to read the instruments telling him where the Schoengleida airfield was. After drinking copious amounts of beer and wine, he radioed the control tower saying: "Come on, I know you're down there. Where have you hidden the runway?" He then told staff to "pull your fingers out as I've got a party to go to". A rescue helicopter was sent out to escort the pilot down safely, but concerned airfield authorities notified the police who stopped and breathalyzed him as he drove home. As a result he lost his driving licence and pilot's licence on the same day.

THE IMPORTANCE OF BEING ERNEST

When Milwaukee police arrested a driver on a traffic violation, he kept insisting that they had the wrong man. Ernest Hickles repeatedly told police that it was his brother, Earnest Hickles, who was wanted on several warrants. After six days in jail, the police released Ernest, realizing that they already had his brother Earnest in another cell. Hickles' grandmother blamed their mother for the confusion. "She gave both kids the same name because she didn't want anyone to know she had another baby."

AIRPLANE GROUNDED BY SMELL OF CURRY

A British Airways flight to London was hastily returned to Belgrade's Nikola Tesla Airport in 2008 after passengers, fearing a terrorist attack, thought they could smell poison gas. The aircraft was contained on a special emergency procedure runway at the airport and workers wearing breathing apparatus helped screaming passengers from the plane until it emerged that the sinister fumes were from a giant container of curry spices in the cargo hold.

BAGGAGE HANDLER MAKES UNSCHEDULED FLIGHT

An airport baggage handler with contractor Servisair made an unplanned flight from Dallas to Mexico in 2001 after accidentally locking himself in the cargo hold of a jumbo jet. Crew members reported hearing a knocking sound at Dallas, but were unable to trace it.

COUPLE TAKE CAR FOR LONG TEST DRIVE

When a car dealer in Berlin allowed a couple to test drive a new BMW in 2004, they drove it 4,000 miles to Spain and back.

PASSENGER SUES AIRLINE OVER FLIGHT SPENT IN TOILET

A New York man, who said he was denied a seat on a five-hour flight and was instead told to "hang out" in the plane's bathroom, sued the airline for $2 million, claiming he had suffered "extreme humiliation". Gokhan Mutlu said that when he arrived to check in for a JetBlue flight from San Diego to New York in 2008, he was told the flight was full but was allowed to board after a flight attendant agreed to give up her seat and travel in a special "jump seat" reserved for airline employees only. But 90 minutes into the flight, Mutlu was informed by the pilot that the attendant was uncomfortable and needed her seat back. He said the pilot told him to stay in the bathroom for the rest of the flight. At one point, the airplane experienced turbulence and Mutlu sat on the toilet without a seat belt, causing him "tremendous fear", according to his lawsuit.

DRIVER MISTAKES CANAL FOR WET ROAD

Jozef Cene, a 38-year-old German police officer, left a pub in Wiltshire, England, in 2007 and drove straight into a canal after mistaking it for a wet road. He didn't even have the excuse of being drunk.

FLIGHT ATTENDANT STARTS FIRE TO AVOID GOING TO CANADA

A flight attendant on a 2008 Compass Airlines (Northwest) flight from Minneapolis to Regina, Saskatchewan, deliberately started a small fire in the plane's rear bathroom while the aircraft was in mid-air, because he was unhappy about having to work that route. The fire caused the plane to be diverted to Fargo, North Dakota.

MAN RELEASED WORMS ON TRAIN TO SCARE PASSENGERS

A Japanese man was arrested in 2008 on suspicion of releasing hundreds of beetle larvae inside a moving express train in an attempt to scare female passengers. Thirty-five-year-old Manabu Mizuta was said to have had ten containers in his backpack, estimated to house a total of 3,600 worms. "He would go close to women on the train, any woman, and pour out the worms from the containers," said the police who were investigating 19 similar incidents in the same region of Osaka. Mizuta was quoted by officers as saying: "I wanted to see women get scared and shake their legs."

NAKED MAN HIJACKS BUS

A naked man was arrested in 2008 after hijacking a Las Vegas bus. Police said he punched in a back window of the bus, climbed aboard, forced the driver off, and then drove the bus for about 200 yards before jumping off again while it was still moving. The arrested man was given a mental evaluation.

PASSENGER EATS WINNING SCRATCH CARD

An airline passenger ate his $18,000 winning scratch card in protest at not being able to claim the money immediately. The man was flying with Ryanair from Krakow in Poland to England's East Midlands Airport in 2010 when he won 10,000 euros with the scratch card. The flight crew confirmed that he had won the prize but told him that because it was such a large sum, he would have to collect the jackpot directly from the company that ran the competition. Ryanair said the man then became frustrated and started to eat his winning ticket, thus making it impossible for him to claim the prize money. A Ryanair spokesman said: "He clearly felt that we should have his 10,000 euro prize kicking around on the aircraft."

SHEIKH FLIES CAR TO LONDON FOR OIL CHANGE

A wealthy Arab sheikh spent $50,000 flying his luxury Lamborghini car from Qatar to London – for nothing more than an oil change.

DRIVER DOES 60 MILES PER HOUR ON HARD SHOULDER

Speeding along the breakdown lane on a highway in Ontario, a driver touched speeds of 62 miles per hour and passed more than 300 vehicles before he was eventually pulled over by police. By way of explanation, he told them that there was a chance his car was going to break down between Toronto and North Bay, and he wanted to be already on the shoulder when it did.

MOBILITY SCOOTER IN CASE OF MISTAKEN IDENTITY

Arnold Saunders was stunned to receive a parking fine for his mobility scooter in Birmingham – particularly as he had not left the Isle of Wight, 170 miles away, since moving there two years earlier. The 89-year-old said the journey to the Midlands would have taken nearly 30 hours if he had travelled at the scooter's top speed of 6 miles per hour. However he would have had to persuade eight people to let him recharge its battery en route, as it has a range of just 20 miles. A spokesman for Birmingham City Council speculated that a car was driving around the city with the same licence plate as Mr Saunders' electric buggy.

WOMAN FLASHES DRIVERS TO STAY OUT OF DEBT

A Pennsylvania woman was arrested in 2001 for standing by the side of the road and exposing her butt to drivers. She had apparently been told by her grandmother that doing so would keep her out of debt.

FLIGHT ATTENDANT RUNS SEMI-NAKED AROUND PLANE

After British Airways flight attendant Andrea O'Neill lost a bet with colleagues on whether her plane would land on time in Genoa, Italy, she fulfilled her side of the wager by stripping down to her panties, shoes, safety waistcoat and pilot's hat and ran a lap around the plane. There were no passengers in the vicinity at the time but fellow cabin crew, baggage handlers and cleaning staff all caught a glimpse of the semi-streak. British Airways said it was impressed by her dedication to punctuality. A spokesman said: "I guess we ought to take our hats off to her – but nothing else."

BANNED AFTER TAKING 11 YEARS TO PASS TEST

A 73-year-old man who took 11 years and eight attempts to pass his driving test was banned five weeks later for drink driving.

PEDESTRIAN HIT BY MICHAEL SCHUMACHER IN VAN

A pedestrian in Kent, England, who was hit by a van during an overtaking manoeuvre could hardly believe his ears when the police told him the van driver was none other than German Formula 1 ace Michael Schumacher. The seven-time world champion, who was on his way to a private airfield, dealt car salesman Martin Kingham only a glancing blow, but it was enough to throw him onto the hood of a parked vehicle. "I thought I recognized the driver," said Mr Kingham afterwards, "but my head was spinning. Then the penny suddenly dropped. When I phoned my business partner later and told him that 'you'll never guess who I've been run over by', he wouldn't believe me."

DRUNK DRIVES HOME IN GOLF CART

Stranded at a golf club in Richfield, Wisconsin, after drinking several beers, a 47-year-old man decided to "borrow" a golf cart and drive it home – for 40 miles. He was stopped by police driving the cart on Highway 175. Before hitting the road in the commandeered cart, he had not even taken the time to throw out the empty beer cans.

DRUNK DRIVER REPORTS HERSELF

A 17-year-old girl in Bismarck, North Dakota, called 911 on New Year's Eve 2008 to report that she was driving while drunk. She gave her location, and officers found her downtown in a parked car. Police Lt. Randy Ziegler said: "I've never heard of such a thing happening, and neither has anyone here."

FLIGHT IS GROUNDED BY MUSHROOM SOUP

A flight from Budapest to Dublin was forced to make an unscheduled landing in Germany in 2008 after a jar of mushroom soup in an overhead locker started leaking. With desperate misfortune, it dripped on to a passenger who happened to be severely allergic to mushroom soup. As the passenger's neck swelled up and he struggled for breath, the Ryanair flight was diverted to Frankfurt Hahn airport so that he could receive emergency medical aid.

MAN DRIVES TANK TO BUY ICE CREAM

A man drove a 12-ton tank through the centre of a historic Czech town in 2006 . . . just to buy his kids an ice cream. Miroslav Tucek told police he had to use the armoured personnel carrier through the narrow streets of Hradec Kralove because he had promised his children an ice cream and his car had broken down.

WOMAN WRECKS SIX CARS WHILE TRYING TO PARK

A 49-year-old woman driver on a 2001 shopping trip in Hamburg, Germany, wrecked six cars (plus her own) and caused an estimated $15,000 worth of damage – simply while trying to park. Her foot slipped as she tried to reverse into a parking space, and this sent her speeding back into two cars. The impact was so great that they in turn knocked into two others, one of which rolled into a main road where it collided with two cars heading down the street. To add to her woes, her insurance company refused her claim.

HIJACK ALERT TURNS OUT TO BE FRIENDLY GREETING

The FBI, a county SWAT team, and a squad of police officers were urgently summoned in 2000 after flight controllers at Oakland International Airport, Michigan, speaking with an incoming jet over the radio, heard the word "hijack". However when the plane landed, they realized there was no terrorist on board. Instead someone had simply stepped into the cockpit to say "hi" to the co-pilot, whose name was Jack.

AIRLINE LAUNCHES NAKED FLIGHTS

A German airline announced in 2008 that it was introducing special flights for naturists in a bid to recapture the spirit of old Communist East Germany. Enrico Hess, founder of the company OssiUrlaub.de, explained: "In the former East Germany, naturist holidays were a much-loved way of spending the best weeks of the year. All the passengers will fly naked, but they are only allowed to undress once they are in the plane. The pilots and cabin crew, however, will remain clothed."

"PEACE LOVING DRIVER LASHED OUT"

Frustrated that a truck ahead of her was moving too slowly along a two-lane road in Tustin, California, police said Lisa Lind pulled up alongside it in her car and aimed a series of blows at the vehicle with a baseball bat before throwing a can of air freshener at it. Her car had the personalized number plate PEACE 95. A Highway Patrol officer attending the incident said: "She told me she got it because there was so much violence going on in today's society."

PILOT LANDS AT WRONG AIRPORT

After completing a textbook landing, a Ryanair pilot announced to passengers: "This is your captain speaking. I may have landed at the wrong airport. Er, sorry." The 39 passengers on the March 2006 flight from Liverpool were supposed to be travelling to Ireland's City of Derry airport but the pilot mistakenly landed at Ballykelly military airbase five miles away. He said he only realized his error when dozens of surprised soldiers came running towards the plane.

STUTTER PREVENTS MAN BECOMING DRIVING EXAMINER

A man was barred from becoming a driving examiner in Southampton because his stutter meant that he could not say "Stop" in an emergency.

WOMAN KEEPS HAIR APPOINTMENT AFTER CRASH

Arriving for a 2007 hair appointment in Soldotna, Alaska, 73-year-old Della Miller saw her car skid on snow and crash through the front window of the salon, causing $15,000 damage and knocking a customer six feet across the room. Although shaken by the incident, Miller proceeded with her hair appointment.

AIRPLANE TAKES OFF WITHOUT PILOT

A pilot could only look on in horror as his plane took off without him. The 70-year-old pilot was taxiing the single-seater plane at Barton Aerodome, near Manchester, England, in 2006 when the engine cut out. He climbed from the cockpit to restart the motor manually but accidentally nudged the throttle lever open with the result that as soon as he spun the propeller, the plane surged down the runway. He desperately clung to the wing in the hope of preventing it taking off but he lost his grip and saw the plane soar into the sky where it performed an involuntary loop before crashing. The pilot said he hadn't realized he had knocked the throttle because he was wearing padded clothing.

BOY'S BICYCLE SOLD BY MISTAKE

Thirteen-year-old Cody Young made the mistake of parking his expensive BMX bicycle just inside the front door of a charity store in Salem, Oregon, in 2008. And while Cody was browsing around the store, an employee, thinking the bike was for sale, sold it to a customer for $6.99.

LOVELORN VIOLINIST CAUSES PLANE BOMB ALERT

At the end of a 1995 tour of the United States with a travelling theatre group, violinist Nuala Ni Chanainn was sitting on a plane at San Francisco Airport about to head home to Ireland. However just before the plane was due to take off, she suddenly jumped up, disembarked and ran to the terminal buildings. TWA officials thought she must have planted a bomb, and a sniffer dog was brought in to search the plane and her luggage, causing a delay of four hours. Finally she managed to convince them that there was no bomb – the reason she had left the plane in such a hurry was that she just couldn't bear to leave her new boyfriend.

MR BEAN GETS LOST

On his second day as a Glasgow bus driver, Barry Bean became hopelessly lost and ended up wedging his bus under a low bridge. Not content with one mishap, his attempts to release the vehicle saw him crash into a parked car, hit a lamppost, and demolish several garden fences. A passer-by commented: "It was chaos, but we couldn't keep a straight face when the driver said his name was Mr Bean."

FRIENDS SEND SLEEPING MAN ON RAIL JOURNEY

When Gerle Kittler nodded off on the couch during a party, his friends decided to play a joke on him. So they wheeled the still-sleeping Kittler more than a mile to the local railway station and put him on a train after buying a single ticket for him and a bike ticket for the couch. He woke up on a platform four miles down the line in Warngau, Germany, still stretched out on the sofa and being quizzed by police. He said afterwards: "I always sleep like a baby, so I didn't notice anything until the cops shook me awake and demanded my ID. I thought I was in the middle of a bad movie."

BOY TAKES AIRPLANE FOR JOY RIDE

A 14-year-old boy stole a Cessna light airplane in 2005 and went on a late-night joy ride. Finding the key in the unlocked plane at an airfield in Fort

Payne, Alabama, the teenager removed the tie-downs, started the engine, and began driving around. "The next thing he knew he was in the air," said the local police chief. Despite never having piloted a plane before, he stayed airborne for nearly 30 minutes, taking off and landing twice without suffering anything worse than minor cuts and bruises.

DRIVER HAS THREE CAR CRASHES IN AN HOUR

In the space of less than an hour in April 2009, a German woman was involved in three separate road accidents. The 69-year-old from Berlin began by crashing into three vehicles as she tried to leave a supermarket car park in Usedom. Next she accidentally stepped on the accelerator and sped across a lawn before crashing into a nearby house. As a result of her injuries, she was taken to hospital in an ambulance . . . only for the ambulance to be hit by a truck.

ANGRY PASSENGERS SET TRAIN ON FIRE

After spending hours stuck in a crowded commuter train that steadfastly remained stationary, frustrated passengers in Sao Paulo, Brazil, abandoned the train and set it on fire, completely destroying every carriage.

PLANE DROPS CEMENT ON HOUSE

Russian air force planes accidentally dropped a 25-kilogram sack of cement on a suburban Moscow home in June 2008, blasting a three-foot hole in the roof. The planes were seeding clouds above the city to empty the skies of moisture and prevent rain from spoiling a forthcoming national holiday but one of the packs of cement used in the process failed to pulverize completely at high altitude and fell onto the house.

ABSENT-MINDED DRIVER LOSES CAR FOR SEVEN MONTHS

On a sightseeing trip to Bury St Edmunds, Suffolk, in 2006, Eric King parked his black Ford Focus in a residential road and walked into the town centre. But when he went to return to the vehicle later that day, he realized that he had forgotten the name of the road and had no idea where it was. After four hours of fruitless searching, he had no option but to catch a coach back to his home in Milton Keynes, more than 60 miles away. Over the next seven months, he returned to Bury St Edmunds ten times to search for his lost motor, losing two stone pounding the streets in his quest. He finally got it back when two neighbours, who had both assumed that the car left outside their homes belonged to the other, finally realized that neither of them was the owner and contacted the local council.

FLAT CHAMPAGNE SPARKS TERRORIST ALERT

A Northwest Airlines flight attendant forced a 2003 flight from St Paul, Minneapolis, to make an emergency landing in Denver, Colorado, because she feared terrorist activity. Having opened a bottle of champagne and found it had gone flat, she apparently thought terrorists had sucked out all the bubbles.

PRONUNCIATION ERROR COSTS TOURIST COUPLE $5,000

A Spanish couple finished up with a taxi fare bill of over $5,000 because of their inability to pronounce the name of a Norwegian town. The elderly couple, who were touring Norway's fjords, wanted to travel from Stavanger to Olden on the country's west coast to rejoin their cruise ship but their poor command of Norwegian meant that the taxi driver took them instead to Halden, some 350 miles to the east, a trip that cost them $2,793. Oblivious to the mistake, the couple even gave the driver a $180 tip. It was only the next morning, after spending the night in a hotel, that they realized they were in the wrong destination and had to spend another $2,980 on a cab to take them to Olden.

PROFESSOR DRIVES WHEELCHAIR ON AUTOBAHN

Police in Germany stopped a retired astronomy professor as he tried to drive along a high-speed motorway in his electric wheelchair. While cars flashed past him at over 100 miles per hour, 67-year-old Wolfgang Hain plodded along the autobahn in North Rhine Westphalia at a steady 6 miles per hour. He told police that when he passed his driving test almost 50 years earlier any vehicle could travel on the motorway and he had not realized this had changed. He added that he was going home to Vechta, more than 110 miles way, after visiting family, and said he had already driven five miles. After Hain was escorted to the nearest B road, one of the officers attending the incident said: "He was fully aware of who he was and where he was going, but I'm not sure if he realized that it would take him 20 hours to get home."

CRASHED CAR GETS PARKING TICKET

A motorist in Oldham, Lancashire, was given a ticket for bad parking – even though her car had been shunted into a tree by another driver. Joanne Billington was fined by an overzealous traffic warden after her Ford Ka, which she had left parked, was hit from behind. Despite the fact that the front end of her car was in bushes, the traffic warden claimed he thought it had been parked that way.

DRUNK DRIVER RUNS HIMSELF OVER

A 21-year-old man was charged with driving while intoxicated in 2008 after leading police on a wild chase that ended with him contriving to run himself over. The man was spotted by police driving a pickup truck erratically on a highway near Sante Fe, New Mexico. As officers gave chase, the suspect narrowly missed other vehicles and drove through a ditch and a barbed-wire fence before finally stopping. He tried to park the truck but instead put the vehicle into reverse and as he fell from the open door on the driver's side, his legs were run over by the front wheel.

GOOD SAMARITAN LOSES ROOF OF CAR

A motorist who allowed a driver hurt in an accident to take refuge in his car after a crash could only watch in horror as firefighters cut off the roof of his vehicle to remove the injured man. Sean Carter was driving through Nottinghamshire in 2009 when he witnessed a crash in which a car overturned. He stopped, helped the driver out of the wreckage and then invited him to sit in his passenger seat to shelter from the cold. However, when paramedics arrived they said the injured man might have spinal injuries and that therefore they needed to take the roof off Mr Carter's Ford Focus in order to lift him into an ambulance. Mr Carter estimated that his Good Samaritan act left him £1,000 ($2,000) out of pocket. Meanwhile the other driver turned out to have no spinal injuries and was well enough to leave hospital the next day.

SAILOR RESCUED SEVEN TIMES ON CIRCUMNAVIGATION OF BRITAIN

Stuart Hill earned the nickname "Captain Calamity" in 2001 after his failed attempt to sail single-handed around the British coast resulted in five lifeboat launches and two rescue helicopter callouts. His problems began when the launch of his 15-foot-long converted dinghy, *Maximum Exposure*, was delayed for a month because he suffered an allergic reaction to resin he was using to treat the hull. Finally in May he set sail into the River Stour near his home in Manningtree, Essex, only for a friend to have to chase after him because he had forgotten an important item of equipment. Only minutes after leaving, he damaged his vessel by colliding with another boat. Six days and 100 miles later, he had to be towed ashore off Norfolk because his mast, which had been taken from a sailboard, had split. After a three-week delay he set off once more into high winds and what coastguards described as "the worst weather forecast possible". Consequently he managed just three miles in three days before a lifeboat and helicopter went to his aid. Numerous members of the public contacted coastguards over the ensuing days to report that he was in danger of sinking in a boat that was likened to "a glorified sailboard". A member of the Great Yarmouth coastguard said: "This type of craft is totally unsuitable for what he wanted to do. Even if you were Francis Drake, you would have trouble in a craft like that." But Hill pressed on regardless. At one point he was spotted drifting in circles 22 miles out to sea in busy shipping lanes and when he moved closer to shore, the Lowestoft lifeboat had to put to sea to warn him that he was in danger of running aground. He also blundered over to a target intended for a practice bombing run by RAF jet fighters. A member of the Cromer lifeboat crew said: "My coxswain described it as like putting someone blindfold in the middle of the M1 and telling everyone else to miss them." Against all the odds, Hill reached the Shetland Isles by August but there his luck ran out when the boat he had declared "unsinkable" turned over in a storm. He was rescued yet again but all he had left were the clothes he was wearing. Ironically his original plan had been to raise money for charity but his ill-fated voyage cost the rescue services an estimated $75,000. To complete his misery, his wife of 33 years telephoned him during his journey to say she was leaving him and selling their house. "She could have waited until I got back," he said, "but then again it was all taking much longer than planned."

BUS DRIVER GETS TICKET FOR PARKING AT STOP

A Manchester bus driver received a parking ticket in 2003 . . . while picking up passengers at a bus stop. Chris O'Mahoney pulled his No. 77 single-decker into a bay marked "Buses Only", next to a bus stop, but within seconds a zealous warden had swooped with a ticket, barking: "You can't stop here." After the city council agreed to scrap the fine and ordered the warden to be retrained, O'Mahoney said: "You have to park to let passengers on – you can't do it while the bus is moving. All my passengers queuing to get on were gobsmacked when the warden dashed over. He said the area was restricted. When I asked, restricted to whom, he replied: 'Buses.' I thought he must be blind."

HELPFUL HUSBAND SENDS CAR THROUGH SHOP WINDOW

In trying to remove the ignition key from the dashboard of his wife's car, a Polish pensioner accidentally started the vehicle up and sent it flying through the window of a Rybnik butcher's shop, causing $13,000 damage. Rudolf Wydra, 71, doesn't have a licence and can't drive. His wife Felicja moaned: "I've been driving for 30 years and I've never had an accident – until this disaster."

WOMAN IS STUCK TO TOILET DURING FLIGHT

An American woman travelling on a Scandinavian airline in 2002 made the mistake of flushing the toilet while she was still sitting on it. Clearing its contents by powerful suction, the toilet immediately formed a perfect air-tight seal with her butt, leaving her vacuum-stuck to it for the duration of the flight.

GIRL THROWN OFF BUS FOR BEING TOO SEXY

A 20-year-old girl was thrown off a bus in Germany in 2007 because the driver thought she was too sexy. The girl said: "He opened the door and shouted, 'Your cleavage is distracting me every time I look into my mirror and I can't concentrate on the traffic.'"

DRIVER LOSES BORROWED CAR IN FROZEN RIVER

A search for his lost dog ended in farce for Nathan Seely who, by virtue of a catalogue of errors, could only watch as the car he was driving disappeared beneath the surface of a frozen river. His first mistake was to drive the Buick onto the frozen surface of Black River, in Port Huron, Michigan. His second mistake was to lock his keys inside the car. His third was to leave the engine running, as a result of which he looked on in despair as the heat from the engine slowly melted the ice beneath the car, eventually sending it plunging into the water. To make matters worse, the car wasn't even his – it was on loan from a garage while his own vehicle was in for repairs. It is not known whether he ever found his dog.

POLAR TREKKERS FORGET FLAG

IN 2002, Eric Phillips and Jon Muir became the first Australians to walk unaided to the North Pole, trekking across barren wastes for 58 days, surviving frostbite, polar bears, and a near fatality after Muir fell through thin ice, only to realize when they finally reached their destination that they had nothing to mark their heroic deeds because they had forgotten to bring an Australian flag to plant at the Pole. They decided against going back to fetch one. ●

POLICE HELP MOTORIST OFF ROUNDABOUT

Police officers rescued a confused woman driver from a busy roundabout in Braunschweig, Germany, in 2009 after fellow motorists said she had completed at least 50 circuits in a bid to find an exit. Sixty-two-year-old Andrea Zimmer said: "I was breaking in a new car to see how it does in traffic and I couldn't seem to get to one of the exits. But I have to admit I got a very good feel for my new car and its handling. I think I can safely say it takes roundabouts pretty well."

WHEELCHAIR USER CHARGED WITH DRINK DRIVING

A man found asleep in a motorized wheelchair on a road in Queensland, Australia, in 2008 was charged with drink driving. The 64-year-old was spotted slumped in the stationary chair on an exit lane near Cairns, with cars swerving to avoid him. A breathalyzer test showed him to be more than six times the legal driving limit.

PILOT HITS COW AS HE MAKES EMERGENCY LANDING

The pilot of a vintage two-seater Tiger Moth plane hit a cow when he was forced to make an emergency landing in a Devon field in 2008. Rob Wotton had just taken off from Dunkeswell airfield, Honiton, when the 43-year-old airplane suffered engine trouble and he decided to land in a nearby field. There were a number of cows in the field but one animal was separate from the rest of the herd on the other side of the pasture. However, as Wotton touched down, the startled cow decided to run across to join the group and was clipped by the plane. "She went rolling away as I hit her, but she seemed unhurt and got up OK," said the relieved pilot.

DRIVERS USE BLOW-UP DOLLS TO OVERCOME LANE RULES

Motorists in Auckland, New Zealand, have turned to inflatable passengers to beat the city's transit lane rules, which stipulate that vehicles must have at least three occupants to drive in certain lanes. Auckland traffic safety managers say that some drivers have used blow-up dolls or shop mannequins as their third passenger while others have tried to meet the criteria by dressing dogs up as children.

MAN RUNS OVER WIFE . . . TWICE

An 84-year-old driver managed to run over his wife twice in a matter of seconds. Alex Ranson felt a bump as he reversed out of the garage in County Durham but thought it was a rock rather than his wife Olive. So he reversed again, accidentally hitting her a second time. The shock of seeing what he had done caused him to suffer a heart attack and end up in the same hospital where his wife was taken with a broken leg.

PASSENGER HAD SEVERED SEAL HEAD IN LUGGAGE

A man was arrested at Logan Airport, Boston, Massachusetts, in 2004 for trying to board a flight to Denver while carrying the severed head of a seal. When security officers made the gruesome find in a small canvas cooler, the man said that he was a biology professor who had found a dead seal on the beach and had cut off its head to take home for educational purposes. Airport authorities eventually allowed him to board the plane – but without the seal's head.

BRITISH AIRWAYS UPGRADES CORPSE TO FIRST CLASS

Passengers in the first-class section of a British Airways flight from Delhi to London Heathrow in 2007 were startled to see the crew placing the body of a dead woman in a seat and strapping her in. The Indian woman had died in economy class but had been moved to first class because there was more room.

DRIVER BLAMES CRASH ON PTERODACTYL

When police asked a 29-year-old man from Wenatchee, Washington State, what had caused him to drive his car into a street lamp in 2007, his one-word reply was "pterodactyl". A police spokesman said: "A breathalyzer test showed only a minimal amount of alcohol but the fact remains that there have been no sightings of the giant winged reptile for the past 65 million years."

POLISH BUILDERS BUNGLE TRAIN TUNNEL

Engineers in Poland were left embarrassed after building a railway tunnel that was too small for trains to pass through. The costly blunder was only discovered when inspectors measured the completed tunnel in Warsaw and realized the roof was so low that no trains would get under it. Rail bosses said the mix-up occurred because workers who were laying new tracks failed to liaise with the team that was building the tunnel. It was not the only misfortune to hit the Polish transport system in recent times. In 2007, the Polish road authority produced detailed plans for two sections of a major motorway that would have missed each other by five miles – each coming to a dead end in the middle of countryside.

PASSENGERS TOLD TO GET OUT OF PLANE AND PUSH

Passengers on a flight in China in 2008 were asked to get out and push when their plane broke down shortly after landing. The Shandong Airlines flight had arrived safely at Zhengzhou from Guilin but broke down before it could taxi to the passenger terminal. Airport staff were summoned to push the plane, but when it refused to budge, some of the 69 passengers on board were also asked to help. It took them nearly two hours to shove the 20-ton airplane half a mile to a side lane.

SKYDIVER LANDS ON ARMY BAND

Parachutist Scott Hallock, one of two skydivers taking part in a change of command ceremony at Fort Riley, Kansas, in 2008, missed his target and landed on the last two rows of the Army Band instead. Several musicians were injured in the collision and a number of their instruments destroyed. One of the musicians said: "You can't really hear anything when someone's overhead. Then at the last minute, you could hear some rustling. That's what I heard – 'Oh, shit,' and then crash!"

IRISH POLICE SOUGHT ELUSIVE MR LICENCE

In 2007, Irish police finally solved the case of the country's most reckless driver. According to their records he was a Pole named Prawo Jazdy who had clocked up 50 separate traffic offences but had always managed to escape with a ticket by giving a different home address each time. Their quest to bring the elusive Mr Jazdy to justice ended only when a bilingual officer pointed out that the name on the speeding fines and parking tickets, Prawo Jazdy, means "driving licence" in Polish.

ACCIDENTS WILL HAPPEN

WOMAN IS SHOT IN THE LEG BY HER OWN STOVE

A woman needed hospital treatment in 2008 after being shot in the leg by her own stove. Cory Davis, 56, of Sekiu, Washington State, had just stoked her cast-iron stove when something inside it exploded, hitting her on the inside of her left calf. At first she thought it was a piece of flying coal but then realized it was part of a .22-gauge shotgun shell that had been accidentally placed in the stove along with some newspaper. She said a case of ammunition had spilled out in her home the previous month and one shell must have landed inside the newspaper she used to light the stove. "It was just bad luck," she mused. "How many people get shot by your stove?"

VICAR HOSPITALIZED WITH POTATO UP HIS BUTT

A vicar had to undergo surgery in a Sheffield, England, hospital in 2008 to remove a potato that was wedged up his butt. Denying that the accident was the result of a sex game, the clergyman claimed the potato became stuck up his bottom after he fell backward onto the vegetable while hanging curtains naked in the kitchen. "It's not for me to question his story," remarked one of the nurses who treated him.

NAKED MAN RESCUED FROM PORTABLE POTTY

Rescue crews in Philadelphia had to cut apart a portable toilet to rescue a man who had become stuck naked inside the potty. Police had no idea why the 31-year-old had no clothes on or how he had come to immerse himself in the potty but they said he had been drinking.

DOG POUNCES AFTER MAN MISTAKES PENIS FOR CHICKEN'S NECK

Mistaking his penis for a chicken's neck, an elderly Romanian man hacked it off and could only watch in agony as his dog ate it. Sixty-seven-year-old Constantin Mocanu had rushed out into the yard in his underwear in 2004 to kill the noisy chicken that had been keeping him awake at night.

WOMAN STABS HERSELF IN FOOT DURING GOOD LUCK CEREMONY

A woman accidentally stabbed herself in the foot with a three-foot-long sword while performing a religious ritual at an Indiana cemetery. The Wiccan ceremony involves the driving of swords into the ground during a full moon but in 2008 Katherine Gunther inadvertently put the sword into her left foot instead. Asked why she was performing the ritual in the first place, she said it was to give thanks for a recent run of good luck.

PENSIONER TRAPPED UNDER SOFA SURVIVES ON WHISKY

A pensioner who became trapped under his own sofa for two and a half days survived the ordeal by drinking a conveniently placed bottle of whisky. Joe Galliott was ensnared by his sofa at his home in Yeovil, Somerset, when he tripped over a phone cord during a power cut. As he landed on the sofa, it flipped over, pinning him to the floor. Although unable to move, he was fortunate enough to have knocked a bottle of whisky within reach as he fell. The 65-year-old was finally rescued from his sofa hell when his grandson came to visit.

WOMAN CATCHES BELLY BUTTON RING IN NOSE

A 22-year-old woman from Sydney, Australia, called the emergency services in 2008 after getting her belly button ring caught in her nostril when she fell out of bed in the middle of the night.

COP MISTAKES REVOLVER FOR LIGHTER

An off-duty police officer in Newark, New Jersey, had a pistol-shaped cigarette lighter, which he had been using all night while drinking in a local bar. After many hours and drinks, he apparently mistook his revolver for the lighter and when he went to light his cigarette, he shot and killed John Fazzola, who was seated five stools away at the bar.

LIGHTNING EXITS FROM WOMAN'S BOTTOM

A Croatian woman suffered a severely burned anus in 2006 after a lightning strike that entered her body through her mouth departed through her bottom. The lightning struck Natasha Timarovic as she was cleaning her teeth with her mouth to the tap, sending the current surging through her body, but because she was wearing rubber-soled shoes, the lightning bolt was unable to earth through her feet and instead it shot out of her rectum. "It was incredibly painful," she said. "I felt it pass through my torso and then I don't remember much at all."

BEAUTY CONTESTANT'S FAKE BOOBS TRIP HER UP

THE FAVOURITE to win a 2009 Hungarian beauty contest only open to women who have had cosmetic surgery was forced to withdraw due to injury after her breast implants caused her to trip over her high heels. The silicone implants resulted in blonde Alexandra Horvath, 23, losing her balance as she tried to negotiate the catwalk. She tore a ligament in her foot and was taken to hospital. The untimely trip occurred moments after the Miss Plastic judges had admired the quality of her new breasts. A friend said tearfully: "She had not got used to the extra weight on top and her new hair extensions got in her eyes. It was just a tragic accident." ●

MAN LOSES BOTH LEGS IN SAME PLACE

Lying on railroad tracks in Littleville, Alabama in 1994, Terry Mills was hit by a train and lost his left leg. The incident occurred just a few feet from the spot where, in 1986, he had been hit by another train and had lost his right leg.

WORKMAN NAILS TESTICLE TO ROOF

An unfortunate slip at a crucial moment caused an Austrian workman to nail his own testicle to the roof of a house with a nail gun. After August Voegl from Jennersdorf shot the four-inch nail into his left testicle, it required the services of emergency medics to separate him from the roof.

TEENAGER IS IMPALED BY DEER ANTLERS

Having accidentally locked himself out of his grandmother's home in Carter Lake, Iowa, 16-year-old Todd Reynolds gained entry by climbing through a window, only to fall and impale himself on a set of deer antlers. The antlers stabbed him in the back, narrowly missing his spine. His grandmother said she had saved the antlers from a deer that her car had crashed into some years previously.

MAN SHOOTS TOILET WHILE HITCHING UP PANTS

While hitching up his pants after using the toilet at a Centreville, Utah, restaurant in 2009, a man managed to shoot the lavatory bowl, smashing it to pieces. The man's handgun fell out of a holster and hit the tile floor, going off as it did so.

CAFÉ USED BOMB AS TABLE LEG

Eight people were injured in 2002 when a Second World War bomb exploded in a Montenegro café where it had been used as a table leg.

HOLIDAY JINX ENDS IN THREE TRIPS TO HOSPITAL

A Hampshire man ended up in a New Zealand hospital three times in two days on what was supposed to be the holiday of a lifetime. Roy Dennis was visiting his son Edward in Auckland when his unlucky streak began. First he needed emergency surgery after breaking an ankle while skydiving and was released from hospital in a wheelchair. Undeterred, he continued with his holiday but the next day on a visit to an aquarium he was bitten by a poisonous puffer fish and needed a tetanus injection. Twenty-four hours later, Edward took his father to an adventure park where staff kindly put the wheelchair-bound 60-year-old in a special car to enjoy a tour of the facilities. However he and the chair somehow fell out and he careered into a window, breaking his nose. Back home in England, Roy sighed: "We wanted to make it a memorable trip and it was – for all the wrong reasons."

WAYWARD LETTERS MAILED IN DOG WASTE BIN

People mailing their letters in Easingwold, Yorkshire, in 2000 inadvertently put them in a red bin for dog waste, thinking it was a mailbox. The confusion arose because a local building firm supplied a red box instead of a green one. "When I found out what it was I was actually quite relieved," said one local woman. "I'd been posting my responses to lonely hearts adverts there and thought the reason I hadn't heard anything back was that no one fancied me."

SHORT-SIGHTED WOMAN PUTS RARE COIN IN PARKING METER

A South African woman who went shopping without her glasses mistakenly put a 100-year-old gold coin worth more than $1,000 into a parking meter near Cape Town. The woman said she also believed she had spent an 1890 sovereign, worth hundreds of dollars, as small change. She inherited the gold coins from her mother, but they became mixed up with loose coins she kept in a container and were accidentally transferred to her purse. Appealing to city authorities to keep a lookout for the valuable sovereigns, she said: "I didn't realize I had the coins with me when I went shopping, and I didn't have my glasses. I can't believe what I have done."

TRUCKER'S TOILET STOP LEAVES 49 TONS OF MESS

An American truck driver who was caught short while on the road made an unscheduled toilet break and left 49 tons of dirt spread across the highway. The driver tried to pull his vehicle over to the side of US Highway 2 in Washington State to answer the call of nature, little knowing that the side of the road was an embankment. The wheels of the truck promptly slipped down the gradient, spilling his load – tons of river sediment – all over the road.

HIT BY LIGHTNING AFTER SWEARING TO GOD

A Chinese man who swore to God that he didn't owe money to a neighbour was struck by lightning a minute later. The neighbour said the man, named Xu, owed him $80 but had always denied it. So Xu made an oath swearing his innocence before a crowd in Fuqing City in 2008, only to be hit seconds later by a bolt of lightning in what was seen as an act of judgement.

WOMAN GLUES EYE SHUT AFTER MISTAKING NAIL GLUE FOR EYE DROPS

Reaching into the bathroom cabinet early one morning, her vision blurred by sleep, Paula Griffin grabbed what she thought was a bottle of eye drops. But instead she picked up an almost identical bottle of powerful nail glue and squirted it in her eye. The mishap left her in agony and her eye glued shut for eight hours until doctors at Poole Hospital, Dorset, cut off her lashes and managed to prise the eye open. "As soon as I squeezed it, I knew something was wrong," she said. "It was really thick and gloopy – not like eye drops at all."

SMOKER LOSES SIX TEETH WHEN CIGARETTE EXPLODES

An Indonesian man lost six teeth in 2010 when the cigarette he was smoking suddenly exploded in his mouth. Security guard Andi Susanto said the Clas Mild cigarette inexplicably blew up while he was riding his motorcycle. Through bandaged lips, he told local media that he planned to quit smoking in future.

TEEN FLASHES MOTORISTS: HIT BY DISTRACTED DRIVER

A New Zealand teenager who flashed her breasts at passing cars ended up in hospital after a distracted motorist drove into her. Egged on by her friends and fuelled by alcohol, the 18-year-old girl flashed passing motorists from a traffic island in the middle of a four-lane highway in Invercargill. However the prank backfired when one vehicle crashed into her as she tried to run to the side of the road. Luckily the driver had slowed down to see what was going on.

WOMAN SUES AFTER GETTING STUCK IN TOILET BOWL

A woman sued a sports bar and restaurant in Allentown, Pennsylvania, saying she got stuck inside a toilet bowl for 20 minutes after the seat broke. Kathleen Hewko said she was in the bathroom when the handicapped toilet seat she was sitting on cracked and dumped her into the bowl, aggravating an existing hip injury.

RESCUER TRAPPED IN SHAFT AFTER COUPLE FORGET ABOUT HIM

When an elderly couple's dog fell into a 60-foot ventilation shaft in Budapest in 1998, a passer-by bravely lowered himself down the shaft on a rope. He then proceeded to tie the rope to the dog so that the animal could be pulled to safety. The dog's owners were so relieved to have their pet back safe and sound that they hurried off home, completely forgetting to throw the rope down to the rescuer. It was another four days before anyone heard his cries for help, and the poor hero ended up in a Hungarian hospital suffering from malnutrition and dehydration.

HUNTER KNOCKED OUT BY FALLING RACCOON

When Brad Davis, of Milledgeville, Georgia, went off on a hunting trip in 1998 with his friend Donnie Lamb, he took the opportunity to train his puppy to pick up the scent of a raccoon, which he had seen climb a nearby tree. Meanwhile Lamb decided to shoot the raccoon out of the tree. He hit it with his first shot but unfortunately Davis was still standing underneath the tree and the 15-pound animal crashed 60 feet onto his head, knocking him out and fracturing three vertebrae. Davis, who ended up wearing a neck brace for several weeks, said: "I heard him shoot, and the next thing I knew, I was seeing lights shining in my eyes."

MAN GETS PENIS STUCK TO BUS SHELTER

A man in Stravropol, Russia, got his penis frozen fast onto a metal bus shelter in 2003 after urinating in the street on a night when the temperature dropped to minus 30 degrees centigrade. He made the mistake of turning toward the shelter before zipping up his fly. A crowd gathered to watch the man's predicament but he remained firmly stuck to the shelter until rescue workers arrived with warm water.

WOMAN GETS HEAD STUCK UNDER CUBICLE DOOR AFTER FALLING OFF TOILET

A woman's 2000 Christmas celebrations lost their sparkle when she got drunk, fell off a seat in a public toilet and got her head stuck under the cubicle door. The woman was trapped in the public toilets in Huddersfield, West Yorkshire, for several hours until fire crews rescued her.

TRAINEE HYPNOTIST PUTS HIMSELF IN A TRANCE

A newly trained hypnotist accidentally put himself in a trance for five hours in 2010 while practising in front of a mirror. Helmut Kichmeier, whose stage name is Hannibal Helmurto, was found by his wife staring blankly ahead at their London home. It was only after she phoned his instructor, Dr Ray Roberts, and put the receiver to her husband's head that he was able to be talked out of the trance. She said her husband looked like a zombie when she first walked into the room. "I tried to ask him what was wrong but he didn't answer. Then I looked at the sofa behind him and saw a book titled *Hypnosis: Medicine of the Mind*. It was opened on page 45 and a chapter named hypnotic anaesthesia, and I realized there was something wrong."

WOMAN'S THREE-FOOT FINGERNAILS BROKEN IN CAR CRASH

A woman with record-breaking three-foot-long fingernails was devastated after all ten were broken off in a car smash in 2009. Grandmother Lee Redmond, who had not cut her nails for 30 years and who once turned down over $100,000 to have them clipped on live TV, lost her claim to fame when they were snapped off in a four-car smash near Salt Lake City, Utah.

GARDENER KNOCKED UNCONSCIOUS BY GIANT PUMPKIN

A keen Russian gardener announced his intention to sue a Moscow seed firm after he was knocked unconscious by a 40-pound pumpkin. Nikolay

Salakhov bought a small packet of pumpkin seeds in 2002 with the intention of growing them on the terrace of his country house in Pavlov-Posad. The description on the seed packet promised that the vegetables would be no bigger than the size of a pear but Mr Salakhov's reached epic proportions and when he slammed the door behind him, the vibration caused one of the pumpkins to fall and land on his head, leaving him with concussion.

BIRD-LOVER KNOCKED OUT BY DEAD GOOSE

Anne Osinger, chairperson of a bird protection society in Holland, was taken to hospital with concussion and a broken cheekbone after a dead goose plunged 75 feet from the sky and hit her on the head.

MAN TRAPPED IN OUTHOUSE FOR THREE DAYS

Coolidge Winesett, from Wytheville, Virginia, was trapped in his outhouse for three days in 2000 after it collapsed around him. The floor and part of a wall gave way leaving the 75-year-old sitting helplessly in a five-foot hole, trying to cope with the smell. After finally being rescued, he said: "I tell you what, it was hard to get one breath down there."

WOMAN HIT BY FALLING MOOSE HEAD IN BAR

A woman sued a New York City bar in 2009 after suffering concussion when she was hit by a stuffed moose head falling off a wall. Internet design consultant Raina Kumra said the blow from the 150-pound head, which had antlers spanning over three feet, caused her "chronic neck pain, anxiety, fatigue, dizziness and other serious and severe personal injuries," including "embarrassment".

MAN GETS LEG STUCK IN MELTING ROAD

A man had to be rescued by firefighters after his leg became stuck in a road that had melted in a heatwave. Keen amateur footballer Graham Merrington suffered torn ligaments and a damaged ankle after falling down the hole while crossing the road in Manchester, England, in 2009. He was stuck in the hole for 40 minutes while firefighters cut away the remaining road surface. "I was in a state of shock," he said afterwards. "You don't expect to be walking down a road and disappear down a hole."

TRESPASSER IS DETAINED BY VIRGIN MARY

A teenage boy trespassing at a school in Groton, Connecticut, suffered the ignominy of being detained by the Virgin Mary until police arrived. Stephen Miller, 16, was climbing the roof of the Sacred Heart School in 1995 when he lost his footing and fell, dislodging a 400-pound statue of Mary on the way down. He landed with a thud on the ground moments before the heavy statue came crashing down on his legs, pinning him to the spot for two hours before the authorities arrived.

STRAY THONG BLACKS OUT VILLAGE

The Lincolnshire village of Leadenham was blacked out in 2009 after a thong became entangled in overhead power lines. Heavy rain caused the thong to short circuit the cables, cutting power to homes and businesses in the village.

PELICAN BOMBS FLORIDA BATHER

A woman needed 20 stitches to her face after a pelican crashed into her in the sea off Florida while it was diving for fish. The bird, which died in the collision, ripped a gash in Debbie Shoemaker's face as she bathed near St Petersburg in 2008.

ELDERLY WOMAN POSTS FALSE TEETH BY MISTAKE

A harassed British grandmother was in such a hurry to post her Christmas cards in 1998 that she didn't notice that her new false teeth were wedged between them. The 74-year-old woman walked into the Post Office at Witham, Essex, and announced to stunned staff and customers that she had accidentally posted her teeth. "It's no joke," protested the unnamed granny. "I've had to put my old ones back in."

BURGLAR LEAVES FINGER BEHIND

A burglar in Hamburg, Germany, left behind a vital piece of evidence at the scene of the crime – his finger. As he fled after breaking into a leisure centre, a ring on his index finger caught on a metal fence and ripped his finger off. Police found the severed digit on the ground and used it to track him down, but it was too late for the finger to be re-attached.

COP COOKS GUN IN OVEN

Roasting a turkey at home in 1998, Wisconsin police chief Richard Williams forgot that he had left his gun in the oven. As the turkey cooked, the gun went off, sending a bullet through the gas stove and into a banister in the hall. Williams gave himself a one-day, unpaid suspension for violating his department's firearms policy. He added that the oven was one of his favourite hiding places for his gun.

BOY GETS HAND TRAPPED IN CONDOM MACHINE

To his acute embarrassment, 11-year-old Michael Steiner managed to get his fingers stuck in a condom machine in the toilet of a Braunau, Austria, cinema. After a female employee had tried to remove the hand, a doctor was called but he, too, failed. The boy's ordeal was eventually ended by the arrival of the local fire brigade who freed him by cutting the condom machine into pieces.

TODDLER RUNS UP $1,500 PHONE BILL

Playing with the family's phone, one-year-old Joe Williams, from Loddon, Norfolk, pushed the redial button and thereby connected to his great-grandparents on the Caribbean island of St Lucia. Unfortunately none of his family spotted that the phone was off the hook with the result that his 25-hour call ran up a bill of $1,575.

KNIFE TRICK HAS MAN IN STITCHES

A Chino Valley, Arizona, man was recovering in 2003 from having a 12-inch steak knife embedded in the back of his head. He had apparently been amusing himself by tossing the knife into the air.

JUMPER RESCUE LEAVES MAN STUCK IN GARBAGE CHUTE

A man who squeezed into a garbage chute in an apartment block in Stockholm, Sweden, to retrieve a favourite sweater that had been thrown out by his wife, had to be rescued by fire crews after getting stuck between floors. The 25-year-old Ecuadorian was so intent on recovering the old jumper – a present from his mother – that he managed to pull himself legs first through the chute's nine-inch-wide garbage hole on the third floor. But he became stuck after sliding down one floor and was unable to climb up a row of knotted bedsheets thoughtfully lowered into the chute by his guilt-ridden wife. After his rescue, the doors were unlocked to enable him to reclaim his now filthy sweater.

WORKER ACCIDENTALLY NAILS HEAD TO PLANK OF WOOD

A 44-year-old warehouse worker from Oldham, Lancashire, accidentally nailed his head to a 15-foot-long plank of wood. Jimmy McKenzie stood up suddenly without realizing there was a six-inch nail in a piece of wood above his head and was pinned in place for an hour until fire crews managed to separate the plank from his skull.

PRANKSTER GLUES MAN TO TOILET

In 2003, a customer was literally stuck on the toilet at a Home Depot store in Louisville, Kentucky, after a prankster had smeared glue on the seat. Bob Dougherty's repeated cries for help went unanswered because staff apparently thought it was a hoax. "They left me there, going through all that stress," he said. "They just let me rot." Paramedics eventually unbolted the entire commode and carried him out, still attached to the seat.

EASY-TO-OPEN DOOR TRAPS TEENS IN LOFT FOR 27 HOURS

It took 27 hours for four 17-year-olds to discover that they could open a door to the loft in which they were trapped by pulling rather than pushing it. Taking advantage of his mother's absence on holiday in 2002, Ali Wood invited three friends round to his house in Gillingham, Kent, to help organize a party. The quartet went up to the attic to fetch the food and alcohol they had secretly stashed there but got stuck when they were unable to open the trap door. Their frantic cries for help went unheard, and loft insulation ensured their cell phones could not get a signal. Meanwhile their guests, getting no answer at the front door, simply assumed the party had been cancelled and left. After the four boys finally realized that pulling the trap door was the answer, a red-faced Wood said: "We couldn't believe we had been stuck there so long when we could have been out in five minutes."

FOOD AID PARCEL CRASHES THROUGH ROOF

A FOOD PARCEL dropped by American airplanes crashed through the roof of a house in Herat. in Afghanistan, one night in 2001, narrowly missing the seven occupants and leaving a small boy covered in rubble. Surveying the gaping hole in his roof and the smashed windows, the homeowner, Golam Sediq, complained: "They should drop smaller packages or nothing at all. We'll have to pay at least 20 times more to repair the damage than we gain from the extra food." The package bore the label: "A gift from the people of the United States of America." ●

MAN SHOOTS HIMSELF ON FIRST DATE

On their first date, a former American Air Force fighter pilot decided to demonstrate to a woman how dangerous guns can be – and in doing so, accidentally shot himself in the leg. Kim Barnes and Susan MacDonald were enjoying a meal in Englewood, Colorado, in 2000 when the subject of accidental shootings cropped up in conversation. MacDonald, a hospital technician, was telling him about the gunshot victims she saw at work. Barnes, who had been handling guns since he was a boy, then produced his 9-millimetre pistol with the intention of showing his date how a bullet can be in the chamber even after a clip is detached. He then tried to expel the bullet from the gun, but the mechanism failed to work and the hammer went into the firing position. He attempted to engage a safety device, but the gun fired, hitting him in the left leg. "My finger was nowhere near the trigger," he protested from his hospital bed. "It was a misfire."

GIRL'S TATTOO HAS HIDDEN MEANING

In 2003, teenager Charlene Williams asked a tattooist in Poole, Dorset, to ink the word "mum" on her back in Chinese letters. But four years later, after a passing Chinese woman shouted, "Evil, evil, very bad" at her, Charlene discovered that the incompetent tattooist had really written "Friend from hell". Apparently the tattooist did not know that Chinese letters change their meaning when put together.

SKIER LEFT DANGLING FROM LIFT WITH PANTS DOWN

A hapless skier in the upmarket Colorado ski resort of Vail ended up unintentionally exposing himself to the world following a catalogue of calamities in 2009. The man and a child boarded a ski lift expecting a swift ride up the mountain but because the chairlift's seat was not in the correct position, as the man got on, he slipped through a gap between the chair and the seat back. His ski boot and ski then got lodged in the lift, preventing him from falling. But as he slid, his pants and underwear became caught and were pulled down, exposing him to tourists at the crowded resort. After he had been left red-cheeked, hanging helplessly upside down, 20 feet above the ground for some 15 minutes, resort staff were able to reverse the lift and free him – but not before a number of people had taken pictures of the dangling figure and posted them on the Internet.

MAN IMPALES BOTTOM ON PLUNGER

A man in Switzerland who used a sink plunger as a temporary bath plug impaled himself in the butt in 2007 after slipping on a bar of soap. Dieter Bayer, 79, used the plunger to keep the water in the bath because he couldn't find the plug, but as he stood up he slipped on the soap and fell heavily on the plunger, wedging its wooden handle deep inside his rectum. His wife Frieda rushed to the bathroom when she heard him screaming in pain but was unable to pull him free and had to call the emergency services.

After surgeons operated for eight hours to repair the damage, a hospital spokesman remarked: "There was a lot of blood, he could have died."

HOME BURNS TO GROUND IN IRONIC CIRCUMSTANCES

An abandoned cigarette burned a California mobile home to the ground in 2009, causing $200,000 worth of damage . . . while its occupants were attending a meeting to help them quit smoking.

ROGUE STAIRLIFT ACTS AS HUMAN CATAPULT

A disabled woman was awarded the equivalent of $15,000 after a faulty stairlift catapulted her down the stairs at her home in Pontypridd, Wales. The incident proved so traumatic that she decided to move to a bungalow.

WOMAN SWALLOWED BY FRIDGE

A woman in Roseville, California, spent four days trapped under her fridge in 2006 after the top-heavy appliance fell on her when she tried to open the door. Inga Walen finally managed to attract someone's attention by banging a wooden spoon on the lid of a pressure cooker and calling for help. The fridge ordeal left her with injured legs and a broken collarbone.

MAN HOPED BULLET WOULD FALL OUT OF HEAD

A man in Miskolc, Hungary, accidentally shot himself in the head while trying to fix a high-powered air gun in 2001, but didn't go to the doctor for two weeks because he was sure the bullet would fall out of its own accord.

TOPPLING CRANE CUTS HOUSE IN HALF

Kevin and Michelle McCarthy received a nasty shock in 2009 when they returned home to find that a 90-foot crane had sliced their house in two. The crane had been trying to move a 150-year-old oak tree from the property in Santa Rosa, California, but the tree was too heavy and the 100,000-pound crane toppled backwards, its boom crashing through the roof of the house. Earlier in the day Mrs McCarthy had been involved in a car accident and the couple were dealing with that incident when one of their neighbours called to tell them that their house had been destroyed. She said: "I kept saying to my husband, 'Tell me I'm having a really bad, vivid dream.'" The McCarthys had moved into the house three months previously and had been strongly advised by an arborist to have the ageing and sick tree removed for safety reasons. A neighbour said: "They were told that if they didn't have the tree taken down, it could fall onto their house."

CLIMBER SCALES MOUNTAIN BUT FALLS DOWN HOLE AT HOME

Shortly after making the first successful solo ascent of the treacherous south face of the world's seventh highest mountain – the 26,795-foot Himalayan peak Dhaulagiri – Slovenia's top climber, Tomaz Humar, broke both legs after falling into a hole at his home.

MOTHER'S EXTRA-LARGE UNDERWEAR DOUSES PAN FIRE

When a frying pan fire broke out in the kitchen of a house in Hartlepool, England, in 2008, Jenny Marsey's nephew extinguished it with a pair of her extra-large knickers. Darren Lines grabbed the blue underpants from a pile of washing, doused them in water and threw them over the pan. Mother-of-four Mrs Marsey said: "I'm just relieved that my parachute knickers have come in handy for something. I think if they had been my daughter's skimpy knickers they wouldn't have done any good."

MAN HIT BY TRAIN AND CAR ON SAME DAY

Just six hours after being knocked down by a car, unlucky cyclist Robert Evans ended up in the same Boulder, Colorado, hospital after being hit by a train. A doctor at the hospital said: "You know it's not your day when you manage to get run over by two different modes of transport."

RESIDENT BURNS DOWN CARE HOME DURING FIRE DRILL

A careless resident of a nursing home in Hamburg, Germany, panicked as she rushed out during a 1995 fire drill, dropped her cigarette and burned the home to the ground.

FLEEING ROBBER FALLS INTO CESSPIT

After robbing a teenage girl in 2007, a Romanian thief hid from police in an old lady's toilet. However his hopes of lying low for the night were dashed when the elderly householder needed to use the toilet in the small hours. Startled, he tried to run away, but the toilet floor collapsed and he fell through the hole into the cesspit below. A police spokesman said: "It was a really smelly business. We had to clean the robber and give him new clothes before even talking to him."

MAN SURVIVES LIFT PLUNGE BY LANDING ON WOMAN

A man survived a 25-foot plunge down an apartment block lift shaft in 2008 by landing on a woman who had fallen down it the previous day. Jens Wilhelms slipped while inspecting the open shaft in Frankfurt am Main, Germany, but his fall was broken by the woman who was already lying at the bottom. She was treated for injuries both from her original fall and from when Wilhelms landed on her.

SPIRITUAL HEALER SETS FIRE TO PATIENT

A self-styled spiritual healer in Puerto Rico accidentally knocked a candle into a bath where a client was bathing in alcohol, leaving her with burns over half of her body. The woman had sought the treatment as a result of marital and financial problems.

VICAR LEAVES MICROPHONE ON WHILE GOING TO TOILET

A Scottish minister who took a wee toilet break during his church service had his congregation squirming with embarrassment after he forgot to switch off his clip-on radio microphone. Stand-in vicar the Rev. John Hawdon went for a natural break during proceedings at Longforgan Parish Church, Perthshire, in 2006, unaware that he still had his microphone on. One parishioner said: "It was mortifying. Every sound boomed and echoed around the church. We all sat there looking at each other, totally embarrassed. Mr Hawdon is a very nice man and well-respected, and he certainly made a splash on this occasion."

GUNMAN SHOOTS OWN TESTICLE

After shooting at a teenager in a dispute over stereo speakers in Wichita, Kansas, in 2006, a 23-year-old gunman jammed the pistol back in the waistband of his pants – and it went off, hitting him in the left testicle. His reaction to the wound then caused the gun to fire again, this time hitting him in the left calf. He was arrested shortly afterwards when he limped into a medical centre seeking help.

TERMITES EAT TRADER'S MONEY

A trader in the Indian state of Bihar lost his life savings – around $20,000 – after termites infesting his bank's safe deposit boxes chewed the currency bills. Dwarika Prasad had started using the box in 2005 but when he opened it three years later, all he found was termite dust. The bank said it put up a notice warning customers about the termites but Mr Prasad did not see it in time.

MAN LOSES SAME LEG TWICE

A man from Poughkeepsie, New York, lost the same leg twice in the space of seven months. Scott Listemann lost his left leg below the knee in an accident with a dump truck in November 2007, and then in June 2008 his prosthetic leg, with a foot clad in a running shoe, flew off moments after he jumped out of an airplane while skydiving. The false leg literally vanished into thin air. "I looked down and it was gone," he said. "More than likely it's in the woods somewhere. When I told my instructor what had happened, he thought I was pulling his leg at first."

BIG CAT HUNTER TRAPS HIMSELF IN HIS OWN CAGE

For years the Beast of Exmoor – a mysterious big cat resembling a black panther – is said to have roamed the West of England, slaughtering farm animals. One man eager to put an end to the Beast's reign of terror was farmer Peter Bailey, of Tiverton, Devon, who had lost chickens, ducks and the family cat to an unknown predator. So in 1995 he set out to trap the Beast in a specially built wire cage on a remote stretch of moorland. Alas, while setting the bait, he accidentally triggered the cage door and spent the next three days trapped inside. He survived by eating the bait – which was pheasant – before eventually being freed by a passing shepherd.

BIKER'S PENIS HIT BY LIGHTNING

Motorcyclist Ante Djindjic from Zagreb, Croatia, was knocked unconscious in 2007 when lightning struck his penis while he was taking a roadside toilet break. His life was saved by the rubber boots he was wearing, which forced the lightning to seek an alternative exit from his body. Having been assured by doctors that his penis would eventually function normally, he said: "I just hope it is true that lightning doesn't strike twice."

GERMAN BLOWS UP APARTMENT WHILE FIXING AIRBED

A man from Dusseldorf, Germany, who tried to repair his leaking air mattress blew up his apartment instead. He had used tyre repair solvent to plug the hole but when he went to inflate it the next day, a spark from the electric air pump caused an explosion that wrecked his home and resulted in the entire apartment block being evacuated.

DOCTORS FIND DENTURES CLAMPED TO MAN'S BUTT

An elderly man from Nizhny Novgorod, Russia, turned up at a local hospital in 2002 to have his dentures removed from his butt. He had slipped in the bathroom and landed on his false teeth, causing them to clamp down tight on his left butt cheek.

PASSENGER GETS ARM STUCK IN TRAIN TOILET

A French train passenger had to be rescued in 2008 after having his arm sucked down the on-board toilet. The 26-year-old was travelling between La Rochelle and Paris when he accidentally dropped his mobile phone down the toilet. He tried to fish it out, but fell foul of the toilet's powerful suction system. The high-speed TGV train had to stop for two hours while fire crews cut through the train's pipework. One witness said: "He came out on a stretcher, with his hand still jammed in the toilet bowl."

ACCIDENT-PRONE SHEPHERD LEADS FLOCK INTO MINEFIELD

A shepherd who has become famous throughout Croatia for a history of mishaps made the headlines again in 2009 when he had to be rescued after following his flock into a live minefield. Mozambique-born Philimon Zandamela was led to safety by rescue workers in Sibenik after he had phoned for help from the middle of the field. He said: "I was walking along and I saw lots of strange bumps in the ground and suddenly realized where I was."

In the past Zandamela has survived shooting himself twice, accidentally drinking sulphuric acid and falling down a hole after crashing his moped.

LEG HAIR RECORD WRECKED BY FOOLHARDY TUG

A Taiwanese student's hopes of setting a record for having the world's longest leg hair were shattered in 2008 when he accidentally pulled it out. The tragedy occurred shortly after Lin Kuan-wei, from Pingting City, had displayed the impressive 13.4-centimetre-long hair to reporters. The hair, which he had been nurturing for a year, was one centimetre longer than the existing Guinness record holder.

WORKMAN FIRES NAILS IN HEAD TO EASE PAIN

After 25-year-old William A. Bartron accidentally cut off his left hand at the wrist while working on a house in Bethlehem, Pennsylvania, in 2001, he used a pneumatic nail gun to fire 15 one-inch nails into his skull. He explained that he shot the nails into his head to take his mind off the excruciating pain of the amputation.

STRIP CLUB CUSTOMER INJURED BY DANCER'S FLYING SHOE

A customer on his first visit to a strip club announced in 2009 that he was suing the management of the Akron, Ohio, venue after being struck in the face by an erotic dancer's flying shoe. Yusuf Evans needed surgery to his nose after being whacked by the 1970s-style platform heel as the result of a high kick by a dancer named Tiara. He said afterwards: "I probably have to live with this for the rest of my life."

MAN FALLS DOWN SAME CLIFF TWICE

While out for a country walk near Barnard Castle, County Durham, in 2009, 66-year-old George Stastny tripped on a narrow footpath and fell down a 20-foot cliff, breaking his nose and injuring his back. His wife Mary managed to drag him semi-conscious back to the top of the cliff before running to fetch help. No sooner had she turned to leave than her husband stood up, fainted, and fell back down the same cliff.

THAT'S LIFE

MIAMI ACCOUNTANT IS DESCENDED FROM GENGHIS KHAN

A mild-mannered Miami accountant was revealed in 2006 to be a descendant of the infamous thirteenth-century Mongolian warlord Genghis Khan. Genetic testing showed that 48-year-old Tom Robinson was related to the man who rampaged across Asia, killing thousands. Mr Robinson commented: "Obviously I've done nothing as big as Genghis Khan. I haven't conquered any countries, although I have headed up accounting groups."

SPEED-DATING EVENT ATTRACTS ONE PERSON

A village speed-dating event designed to appeal to young single men was cancelled in 2008 after attracting just one person – a 73-year-old. The event was organized following complaints about the lack of female company in Wolsingham, County Durham, but pensioner Jack Herdman was the only one prepared to say he was looking for love.

MEN ARGUE OVER CUSTODY OF SEVERED LEG

When Shannon Whisnant of Maiden, North Carolina, bought a barbecue smoker at auction in 2007, he got more than he bargained for – a severed leg. The leg had been kept there by the smoker's previous owner, John Wood from Greenville, South Carolina, who had lost the limb in a 2004 airplane crash and had then stored it with the intention of having it cremated with him when he died. "I want to be cremated whole," he stated. However Whisnant had other ideas and insisted that the leg was now his property. "It's a hell of a conversation piece," he argued. "I bought it. It's mine." As the feud over custody of the leg intensified, Whisnant saw the opportunity to make money out of it and reportedly planned to charge adults $3 and children $1 a time to view it. Eventually the police intervened and returned the limb to Wood, with Captain Tracy Ledford entering into the spirit by declaring: "The guy (Whisnant) don't have a leg to stand on." Wood later confirmed that he was now keeping the celebrated leg in his golf bag.

WOMAN BOASTS OF 100,000 COCKROACHES IN HER HOUSE

Rosemary Mitchell, from Tulsa, Oklahoma, won a 1994 contest run by an insecticide manufacturer to find the most cockroach-infested house in the US. She estimated that her small home harboured up to 100,000 roaches although she insisted: "I keep a pretty clean house." Her prize was a visit from entomologist Austin Frishman, also known as TV's Dr Cockroach.

MAN SELLS LIFE ON EBAY

A man from Perth, Australia, sold his life on the Internet auction site eBay for $380,000 in 2008. Forty-four-year-old Ian Usher was so distraught following the breakdown of his marriage that he put all the trappings of his life up for sale – his three-bedroom house, car, motorcycle, jet ski, a two-week trial in his job as sales assistant in a rug store, details of his favourite bars and restaurants, and even introductions to his friends. He had been hoping to raise at least $100,000 more but conceded sadly: "I have received what people think my life is worth and that's that."

GRANDFATHER COLLECTS WRONG CHILD

A 77-year-old man agreed to pick up his four-year-old grandson from school in Jacksonville, Florida, in 2007, only to arrive back home with the wrong child. The frantic mother of the collected child said the two boys "don't even look alike".

MAN FINDS SMALL SNAG WITH NEW HOME

When first-time buyer Ashley Parsons snapped up an old water tower for $60,000 with the intention of converting it into a house, he thought he had landed a bargain. It was only afterwards that he discovered that his new home at Weston-super-Mare, Somerset, could be reached only by air because the firm that owned the surrounding land refused to give him access rights. He moaned: "As things stand, the only way I can access my home legally would be by jumping from a helicopter onto the roof."

HOMELESS PEOPLE SLEPT ON A FORTUNE

A group of homeless drug addicts in New York slept on an abandoned sofa for a month without knowing that it was stuffed with over $10 million worth of cocaine. The discovery only came to light when garbage men disposed of the sofa.

FATHER POSES AS SON TO TAKE EXAM

A 54-year-old Japanese man was caught impersonating his 20-year-old son in an exam. The father, who ran a medical distribution company, sat a 2009 test for a licence to handle over-the-counter drugs so that his son could work with him. He even took off his glasses and had his hair permed to make himself look younger.

"DRIVER STAGED CRASHES TO FIND TRUE LOVE"

An unemployed Italian man from Turin was charged with fraud, harassment and damage to property after allegedly orchestrating at least 500 car crashes in a doomed effort to meet young women. Police said Andrea Cabiale had been seeking out vulnerable women drivers for at least a decade and when they searched his apartment they found 2,159 photographs of damaged vehicles and their female owners, all taken by Cabiale following his accidents. An address book was also found, containing hundreds of names and phone numbers, all belonging to women aged between 20 and 40. In one of Cabiale's cars, investigators found a mechanism that temporarily disabled the vehicle's brake lights. When the police contacted the women concerned, all told a similar story of running their car into the back of Cabiale's vehicle at traffic lights or a junction. He would then suggest an informal settlement. Happy not to lose their no-claims bonus, most women agreed and handed over contact details. But there then followed months of telephone calls and invitations to dinner as Cabiale was said to have turned the apparent accident into a dating game. Patrizia Calero, 28, who crashed into one of Cabiale's cars in 2001, said he "got out giving the impression that he was going to be really decent about it. He said he didn't want to make a formal claim . . . It became a nightmare. He was ringing me six or seven times a day". Although Cabiale, a shy-looking bearded man of 40, had amassed the largest number of accidents in Italian motoring history, he protested his innocence. The number of accidents, he insisted, was simply a result of bad Italian driving habits.

MAN PAID TEENS TO SPIT IN HIS FACE

A Southern California man was arrested in 2009 for allegedly paying a teenager $31 to spit in his face. According to a sheriff's statement the man also paid high school students to yell profanities and slap him in the face. His motive was unclear.

JAPANESE TOURISTS SUCCUMB TO PARIS SYNDROME

At least a dozen Japanese tourists a year have to undergo therapy after visiting Paris. The psychiatric problems are caused by a discrepancy between the tourists' expectations and their actual experiences while visiting the French capital. The condition, known as "Paris Syndrome", arises when their romantic vision of the city is shattered by a rude taxi driver or waiter. In 2006 alone, four traumatized Japanese visitors had to be sent home from France. Two women became convinced that their hotel was bugged and that there was a plot against them, another woman thought microwaves were attacking her, and a man believed he was the reincarnation of the French king Louis XVI.

WOMAN KEEPS POLICE TALKING FOR SEVEN HOURS

A woman who called the Roanoake, Virginia, Police Department set some kind of record by talking non-stop for seven hours and fifteen minutes. She called shortly before midnight to report a stolen watch but once that complaint had been dealt with she launched into a prolonged conversation which covered everything from politics to home furnishings. Busy officers answered other calls in the meantime but the woman just kept on talking. She finally ran out of steam around seven o'clock the following morning. She began to slur her words, then came what officers described as a soft bump followed by snoring.

COUPLE FIND FALSE LEGS HIDDEN UNDER FLOORBOARDS

MOVING INTO their new home in Bridport, Dorset, in 2007, Mike and Theresa Sutton discovered more than 100 artificial limbs, 100 crutches and numerous walking frames stashed under the floorboards. ●

NEIGHBOUR COMPLAINS ABOUT SNOWMAN'S BIG BREASTS

Police called on a woman in Kent, Ohio, in 2003 following complaints from a neighbour that a female snowman in her yard had disproportionately large breasts. Crystal Lynn's snowman had celery for the eyes, a carrot for the nose and two blobs of snow for the breasts. Lynn told reporters: "The officer said that I should cut off her breasts, but I said no woman wants that." In the end she agreed that the offending breasts be discreetly draped in a tablecloth.

FESTIVE BALLOONS LEAD TO FEARS OF ALIEN INVASION

Thousands of callers besieged a UFO hotline in Germany on New Year's Eve 2008 after mistaking mini hot-air balloons for a mass alien invasion. The red and gold lights that hung eerily in the night sky had UFO watchers across the country rushing for the phone but turned out to be nothing more sinister than new Chinese-style paper balloons which are lifted by a tiny burner and then hover in the sky until the paper burns up.

MAN IS STOPPED FROM CHANGING NAME TO SANTA CLAUS

Even though Robert Handley did holiday work dressed as Father Christmas and had a car licence plate 1MSANTA, Ohio magistrates turned down his application to change his name legally to Santa Claus. Their reason was that children would be upset when he died. Announcing his intention to appeal, Handley said: "Children who believe in Santa Claus generally don't read newspaper obituaries."

CHEF DISCOVERED LIVING IN FREEZER

Immigration officials who raided a Chinese restaurant in Llandudno, North Wales, found the chef living in its freezer. The man – a Chinese national who had overstayed his visa – had removed the freezer door and laid out a bed inside. He was arrested and deported within 72 hours.

PRANKSTERS TURN HISTORIC STATUE INTO HOMER SIMPSON

On New Year's Eve 2009, pranksters in Dunchurch, Warwickshire, turned the village statue of nineteenth-century benefactor and MP Lord John Scott into a replica of Homer Simpson, complete with yellow skin, bald head and pronounced overbite. The statue of Lord John, who died in 1860, was also dressed in Homer's standard attire of white short-sleeved shirt and blue pants. It was not the first time the statue had undergone an overnight transformation. In previous years Lord John had been decorated in the guise of such icons as Harry Potter, Spiderman and Shrek.

WOMAN INCLUDES HERSELF IN HOUSE PRICE

Deven Trabosh included an unusual optional extra in the sale price for her four-bedroom home in West Palm Beach, Florida – herself. The 42-year-old single mother listed the home for $340,000 on a sell-it-yourself Internet site, but increased the price to $840,000 if the buyer decided to take her as part of the package. "I figured, let's combine the ad because I'm looking for love and I'm looking to sell the house," said the tanned blonde. Her daughter reportedly described her as "embarrassing".

BOSNIAN SAYS ALIENS ARE TARGETING HIM

A Bosnian whose home was struck five times in the space of six months by meteorites told investigators in 2008 that he was convinced he was being targeted by aliens. Radivoje Lajic's house in the village of Gornja Lamovite was always hit during heavy rainfall and he became so disconcerted that he had his battered roof reinforced with a steel girder. "I am obviously being targeted by extraterrestrials," he said. "I don't know what I have done to annoy them but there is no other explanation that makes sense. They are playing games with me. When it rains I can't sleep for worrying about another strike."

ODD SHOES RIDDLE STUMPS POLICE

Mystified German police were trying to work out in 2002 how a hoard of 19 size eight shoes and 19 size nine and a half shoes came to be dumped. All of the shoes were new and the same brand, leading detectives to suspect they had been stolen from a shop display. However the truth was considerably more bizarre. It turned out that they had been thrown away by a man with odd-sized feet and who, because of his imbalance, always needed to buy two pairs of shoes at a time, one in each size, before discarding one from each pair.

HUSBAND GIVES BIRTHDAY GREETING IN MANURE

Stuck for a novel way of wishing his wife Carole a happy 67th birthday, farmer Dick Kleis used a manure spreader to spell out "HAP B DAY LUV U" in a field visible from the couple's home in Zwingle, Iowa. It took him three hours and four loads of liquid manure to create the message. "I was going to put a heart out there after the happy birthday," he said, "but I ran out of manure." His wife was surprisingly happy with the gift of more than 50 tons of dung. "He's done weird things before for birthdays," she told reporters, "but maybe not this weird."

MAN COMES BACK FROM THE DEAD TO WIN LOTTERY – TWICE

An Australian man who was pronounced clinically dead after a massive heart attack lived to win the lottery twice in the space of two weeks. Bill Morgan's heart stopped for 14 minutes and he spent 12 days in a coma in

1998 before defying the odds and pulling through. The following year a lottery win enabled him to buy a $17,000 car, and the story captured the imagination of a local TV station in Melbourne who filmed the 37-year-old truck driver returning to the store where he had bought the lucky ticket and re-creating the magic moment by scratching a duplicate card. As he did so, he held his face in disbelief at the realization that he had just scratched another winning ticket – this time for 250,000 Australian dollars ($170,000). "I've just won 250,000!" he exclaimed. "I am not joking! I don't believe this is happening. I think I will have another heart attack . . ."

WOMAN IS STRANGELY ATTRACTED TO GARBAGE BAGS

An elderly woman dumped 12 kilos of garbage in a man's garden in Owariasahi, Japan, in 2006 – just so that she could take home the bags. On 30 separate occasions, she picked up bags of household garbage from a collection spot, emptied the contents in a nearby garden and took the empty bags home. "I had an irresistible urge to collect rubbish bags," she told police. "I don't know why I wanted them."

WOMAN TAKES REVENGE ON JEHOVAH'S WITNESSES

A mother-of-three, who claimed she had been visited by Jehovah's Witnesses every month for 12 years, stormed into a hall in Peacehaven, East Sussex, during one of the religious group's services in 2002 and began handing out free magazines. "I just wanted to see if they would like any copies," she said, "as they have been doing to me month after month with *The Watchtower*. Nobody seemed to want them though".

"MAN IMPERSONATED DEAD MOTHER FOR SIX YEARS"

A New York man was charged with impersonating his dead mother for six years so that he could steal $117,000 in government benefits. Prosecutors said that following the death of his mother Irene in 2003, Thomas Prusik-Parkin wore a wig, thick make-up, nail polish, dark glasses, a long red dress and carried a cane and fake ID to collect benefit cheques, visit banks and even renew his dead mother's driving licence. On each occasion he was said to have been joined by an accomplice, Mhilton Rimolo, who, posing as her nephew, would help the supposedly frail old lady to walk and communicate with officials. When members of the district attorney's rackets squad arranged to interview Mrs Prusik in 2009, "she" turned up breathing through an oxygen tank. They claimed Prusik-Parkin wore a scarf around his neck to hide his Adam's apple but failed to conceal his "rather large hands". When arrested, he reportedly told authorities: "I held my mother when she was dying and breathed in her last breath, so I am my mother."

MAN WEARING SUPERMAN T-SHIRT SAVES FAMILY FROM FIRE

Wearing just the Superman T-shirt that he was sleeping in, father-of-two James Irvine single-handedly saved his wife, their children, their two dogs and seven puppies from a fire that swept through their home in Stowmarket, Suffolk, in 2009.

FRIEND ATTACKED WITH KNIFE IN ROW OVER HAIRY BUTTOCKS

An argument between two friends over which of them had the hairiest buttocks escalated into a brawl which ended with one allegedly slashing the other with a knife. Emmanuel Nieves, 23, and Erik Saporito, 21, were talking in the parking lot of an apartment complex in Mansfield Township, New Jersey, when the hairy butt debate got out of hand. Nieves boasted that he had the hairiest ass but Saporito begged to disagree. As tempers became frayed, police said Nieves then pulled out a knife and slashed Saporito's face and ear. A police spokesman remarked: "Some guys will fight over anything."

GIRL CHANGES NAME FROM CHICKEN DUNG

A Chinese girl who was named Chicken Dung by her father had it legally changed in 2009 when she reached the age of 18. The girl was named Ji Shi, which means Chicken Dung, on the advice of a doctor after chicken manure had been used to treat her as a baby. Her father Zhu Xiansheng said: "She had a serious illness when she was one and we didn't think she would survive, but a local medical practitioner advised us to paste her with chicken dung while taking medications he prescribed. She always hated the name but now at last she is no longer afraid to show anybody her ID card."

ROLLERCOASTER RELATIONSHIP: WOMAN IN LOVE WITH FAIRGROUND RIDE

Amy Wolfe's love life centres on objects rather than people. She has been in relationships with models of spaceships, the Twin Towers, a church organ, a banister, and the Empire State Building, but her main lover is an 80-foot-high fairground ride called 1001 Nacht, located at Knoebels, an amusement park in New York State, 80 miles from her Pennsylvania home. She joyously kisses, caresses and talks to the fairground ride and truly believes that it talks back to her. She has had a crush on 1001 for over 20 years, riding the machine 300 times a year and even gazing at a picture of it on her bedroom ceiling. "I was instantly attracted to him sexually and mentally," she told reporters. "I wasn't freaked out as it just felt so natural but I didn't tell anyone about it because I knew it wasn't 'normal' to have feelings for a fairground ride." Sympathetic staff allow Amy to go on 1001 after the theme park has closed. "I tell him how much I've missed him and what I've been up to since my last visit. And I kiss the bits I can reach. Obviously we could never have sex where he lives because it's public and it would be indecent, but I use photos of 1001 to help me in private. He makes me happier than any human ever could. I know we'll be together forever."

ANGRY AT BEING OFFLINE ON INTERNET STREET

After buying a house on Internet Street, Warsaw, Poland, Andrzej Gromek announced that he was selling it because he was unable to get a broadband connection.

GUN DUEL LEAVES BOTH PARTICIPANTS UNHARMED

Two old timers from Cleveland, Ohio, who decided to settle a long-standing feud with a gun duel in their apartment block, survived the experience without so much as a graze. Armed with antique pistols, the pair stood five feet apart in the hallway separating their apartments and each fired 12 bullets. Every shot hopelessly missed its target but left the walls peppered with bullet holes. Police officers speculated that the lack of accuracy may have been due to the fact that one antagonist needed a stick to prop himself up while firing and the other had difficulty seeing because of glaucoma.

WOMAN WINS COMPENSATION FOR SWEARING AT TOILET

A Scranton, Pennsylvania, woman who was arrested and prosecuted for swearing at her toilet was awarded $19,000 in compensation in 2008. Dawn Herb was arrested the previous year after a neighbour – an off-duty police officer – heard her swearing at her overflowing toilet through an open window. She was charged with disorderly conduct and faced the prospect of spending 90 days in jail, but the judge at her trial found her not guilty, ruling that swearing was not illegal and her language was constitutionally protected free speech.

GRANDMOTHER AUCTIONS SEAT IN FRONT OF TV

Fed up with petty arguments about who was going to sit in the favoured seat in front of the TV over Christmas, West Yorkshire grandmother Bev Stewart decided to auction the coveted spot on eBay. With 25 people descending on her Keighley home for Boxing Day, 2008, she advertised the seat as "a very comfy and popular item" and saw her daughter-in-law Alexis Stewart trump 17 other bids with a winning offer of $27. The enterprising grandma said: "There is always arguing over who gets it, it's the perfect seat. It is straight in front of the TV and has got the coffee table at the side for you to rest your drink on and the TV remote, so everybody wants to sit there."

HOMEOWNER DIGS 60-FOOT HOLE IN YARD IN SEARCH FOR GOLD

A homeowner digging for gold in his front yard said he got "carried away" and ended up with a hole that was 60 feet deep. Henry Mora, 63, began digging after his gold detector picked up a signal near the patio of his home in Montclair, California, in 2006. "I figured, well maybe there's something down there, so I started digging," he said. "I only intended to go down three or four feet but I started finding gold dust in the dirt and the detector was still beeping, so I kept digging." The excavation was eventually brought to a halt when fire officials, concerned for public safety, ordered Mora and his two helpers to stop digging. He was then informed that he would have to fill in the hole.

EX-CON SAYS GOD TOLD HIM TO DRESS AS A RED PEPPER

A former drug dealer and jailbird who travelled around stores dressed as a red pepper said God made him do it. Kenny Carter, of Rosedale, Maryland, started dressing as Peppy the Pepper in 1997 following a message from the Almighty. "It was a very powerful worship," he recalled. "I was crying out in the middle of church: 'Oh God! Oh God!' And suddenly I heard an audible male voice that said: 'You will be a vegetable.' I looked round, I thought I was going crazy. I began to worship again. I said: 'Lord, speak to me.' And I heard it again. 'You will be a vegetable.'" Following the Lord's guidance, Carter asked a friend to make him a costume, and his routine as a singing pepper proved so popular with shoppers that Super Fresh appointed him community relations manager and encouraged him to perform it at the company's different branches.

FISHERMAN HAS DAY THAT GOT AWAY

Staffordshire milkman Steve Carte enjoyed a remarkable day's fishing in 1995. He arrived at the River Teme only to find that all the best spots had gone, as indeed had his bait, which had fallen from his car roof somewhere between his home in Tamworth and the riverbank. So he hurried to Worcester to buy some more bait but in doing so collected a $25 fine for parking in a restricted zone. Back at the river, after nine hours' patient but unsuccessful fishing he finally got a bite but as he reeled in a large barbel, he stepped on his other rod – worth $150 – breaking it into three pieces. The shock caused him to lose the fish. Giving up, he decided to head home but as he was loading up the car he noticed that it had a puncture. He managed to repair it and called into a pub for a consolatory beer but there he succeeded in gashing his hand on a wall. When he finally arrived home, he accidentally locked all of his keys in his car and had to wait on the doorstep for several hours until his wife returned.

MAN CONFUSES VANDALISM AND SNOW

A Gambian man newly arrived in Germany called the police in December 2002 to report that vandals had painted his car white overnight. The "vandalism" turned out to be a snowfall, a form of weather with which the man was not familiar.

MAN FINDS CORPSE ON SOFA

A SWISS MAN returned home from vacation in 2006 to find a corpse lying on the sofa in his living room. Johann Rauber said: "Whenever you go away for a couple of weeks, you always return home expecting to find something that has gone off, but it's usually a lump of cheese or slice of bread, not a dead body." Berne police said the man had died a few days earlier but had no idea how or why he had entered Rauber's apartment. ●

TEENAGER PAINTS 60-FOOT PHALLUS ON ROOF OF FAMILY HOME

Inspired by a TV show about Google Earth, a teenager climbed on to the flat roof of his parents' house and daubed a 60-foot phallus in white paint. The parents of Rory McInnes did not discover their son's rude artwork for a year until a passing helicopter spotted it on top of their home near Hungerford, Berkshire.

FORGOTTEN BIFOCALS WIN $3 MILLION JACKPOT

A pair of forgotten bifocals helped a Roanoke, Indiana, man to a $3 million win in the Hoosier Lotto in 2008. Bobby Guffey usually plays the same combination of numbers representing the birthdays of his five children, but when he went to buy his ticket at a local service station, he realized he had left his glasses at home. Unable to see properly, he accidentally entered the last number as 48 instead of 46 – but it turned out to be the winning ticket. "My wife says it pays to be blind," smiled Guffey as he celebrated his win.

COCKNEY RHYMING SLANG CONFUSES OPERATOR

When a 19-year-old London girl phoned directory inquiries in 2008 asking for a taxi to take her to Bristol airport, she made the mistake of using the Cockney rhyming slang for "taxi", Joe Baksi. The operator said she couldn't find anyone by that name, whereupon the girl made her second mistake by replying: "It ain't a person, it's a cab, innit." At this, the operator found the nearest cabinet shop and put the girl through. The saleswoman at the shop sounded bemused until the girl demanded impatiently: "Look love, how hard is it? All I want is your cheapest cab, innit. I need it for 10 a.m. How much is it?" The girl duly paid $360 by credit card but was none too pleased when an office cabinet instead of a taxi arrived at her South London home the following morning. The cabinet firm's marketing manager said: "We thought it was a joke at first but the girl was absolutely livid. We have suggested that maybe she should speak a bit clearer on the phone."

FAMILY SUES MALEVOLENT GENIE

A family in Saudi Arabia took a genie to court in 2009 for throwing stones at them and stealing their cell phones. They said the genie's aggressive nature, which included strange sounds, verbal threats and stone throwing, forced them to move out of the Medina home where they had lived for 15 years. In Islamic theology, genies can harass or possess humans and are often said to be motivated by revenge or jealousy.

MAN WRITES 3,700 LETTERS IN SEARCH FOR LOVE

A Canadian man wrote to 3,700 Belgian women called Sabine following a romantic holiday encounter. Marc Lachance from Quebec fell for a Belgian Sabine while on vacation in Cuba but realized afterwards that he didn't get her full name and address. So he set about writing to every Belgian woman with that name and his quest paid dividends when the girl's brother heard about his mission on the radio and brought the two together.

WOMAN LIVES UNDETECTED IN MAN'S CLOSET FOR A YEAR

A homeless woman lived undetected in the closet of a Japanese man's house for a year before finally being discovered in 2008. Puzzled when food started disappearing from the kitchen of his home in Kasuya, the owner had installed security cameras that transmitted images to his mobile phone. When one of the cameras captured an image of a person moving, he notified the police who, after searching the house from top to bottom, eventually found a 58-year-old woman curled up in the top compartment of his closet. She had moved a mattress into the space and regularly took showers while the occupant was out, having first moved in 12 months earlier when he left the house unlocked.

MAN POSTS HIMSELF HOME

A homesick American shipping clerk packed himself in a crate and posted himself back home. Charles McKinley shipped himself from New York to Dallas by airplane in 2003 after a friend told him he could save money on the 15-hour flight by travelling in the cargo hold. He was even delivered to the door of his parents' house before emerging from the crate on their front lawn. His surprised father asked: "What are you doing in this crate?"

PAGAN COUPLE TAKE STONE CIRCLE TO SUBURBIA

A Dorset pagan couple who were downsizing from a Weymouth mansion to a suburban home in Dorchester alarmed their new neighbours by bringing an ancient stone circle with them. People watched in bewilderment as druid John Burton and his wife, hereditary witch Stuky, used a crane and a huge truck to deposit the six-foot-high stones in the garden of their new house. Mrs Burton then invited 20 witches from her coven to dedicate the stone circle during a night-time ritual. She said: "We had a blessing of the stones and we brought the energy back. You could feel it circling the stones. We feel they are a place between worlds. It's hard to describe the feeling you get when you are near these stones, but it is something extremely powerful. You can feel the energy pulsing around you, moving inside you – you feel at one with nature and get a real high." She added: "Although I think a few of the neighbours were a little surprised, on the whole I think it's been well received."

MAN LEAVES 3,000 WATERING CANS TO NIECE

When truck driver Ken Stickland died in 2010, he left his prized collection of 3,000 watering cans to his niece, Hilary Taylor. Mr Stickland – known unsurprisingly as "Watering Can Man" – had filled his shed, greenhouse, garden and even an entire floor of his house with his collection. Mrs Taylor, from Great Yarmouth, Norfolk, said: "He kept a meticulous record of every watering can he owned. He did not have a favourite, he just loved them all. He was such a fascinating person."

NEW ZEALANDER SELLS SOUL TO HELL

In 2008, a New Zealand man proudly sold his soul to hell – Hell Pizza, to be precise. Walter Scott, 24, had originally tried selling his soul on an online auction site, saying of the sale item: "I can't see it, touch it or feel it, but I can sell it, so I'm going to palm it off to the highest bidder." But the site withdrew it, considering the sale to be in bad taste, whereupon the New Zealand pizza chain snapped it up for $3,800. "The soul belongs to Hell, there is simply no better place for it," declared the firm's head of marketing.

MAN TRADES PAPERCLIP FOR HOUSE

In the space of a year, a Canadian man managed to turn a red paperclip into a house – just by trading on the Internet. In July 2005, 26-year-old Kyle MacDonald from Montreal posted the red paperclip on the barter section of an advertising website and was quickly offered a fish-shaped pen in exchange. He traded that for a ceramic doorknob, which he then swapped for a camping stove. Next came an electric generator, which he exchanged for a neon Budweiser beer sign. That was traded for a snowmobile, which in turn led to a ski vacation, a truck, and a recording contract. An aspiring singer snapped up the record deal, offering in exchange a year's rent in an apartment in Phoenix, Arizona, but the resourceful MacDonald managed to swap that for an afternoon with rock star Alice Cooper. Surprisingly he traded that for a Kiss snowglobe, but Kyle knew that Hollywood director Corbin Bernsen was an avid collector of snowglobes and sure enough he was able to trade the globe for a role in Bernsen's next movie. Finally in July 2006, the town of Kipling, Saskatchewan, offered to exchange a three-bedroom house in the town for the movie role. It had taken Kyle just 14 trades to move from a stationery item to a stationary home.

CAUTIOUS CASHPOINT USER IS ARRESTED

A wary German who had always avoided using cashpoint machines because of fears of identity fraud finally plucked up the courage to use one and was promptly arrested – on suspicion of identity fraud. Forty-year-old Hans Mauer spent so long checking the ATM at Muenster that other users became suspicious of his behaviour and called the police. He had begun by studiously inspecting the machine for hidden CCTV cameras, fingerprint powder on the keyboard, and any signs that the screen might have been tampered with. But the final straw was when he pulled on a pair of surgical gloves so that he wouldn't leave fingerprints as he entered his PIN number. On arrival, the police soon cleared the matter up after Mauer had explained his aversion to ATMs. "Unfortunately," said a police spokesman, "it is unlikely he will ever use a cash machine again."

COUPLE RAISE CABBAGE PATCH DOLL AS THEIR SON

Pat and Joe Posey raised a Cabbage Patch doll as their only son, for 20 years. The doll, christened Kevin, had his own playroom at the Poseys' Maryland home, a full wardrobe, and over $3,000 in savings. He even went off on regular fishing expeditions with "Dad" Joe. Admitting that some people found the relationship strange – especially in view of Joe's habit of conversing with Kevin in public – Pat Posey explained: "With every kid that you adopt, you promise to love them and be a good parent. And that's what we did with Kevin", whom she described as "easy-going, quiet and well-behaved".

MAN IDENTIFIES TOILET PAPER BRANDS – BY THEIR TASTE

Appearing on German television in 2001, Roger Weisskopf demonstrated his remarkable ability to distinguish between different brands of toilet paper by their taste. The blindfolded Swiss licked, sucked and chewed unused paper to identify the brand, name and country of origin. He had practised his art for a year, asking friends to bring back toilet paper rather than the usual souvenirs from their trips abroad. He said afterwards: "We Swiss have the best quality and best tasting toilet paper anywhere. We can be proud of it." However he was less complimentary about Japanese toilet paper which he described as tasting like moth balls. "It nearly turned my stomach when I was practising." Weisskopf's reward for his TV feat? A lifetime's supply of toilet paper.

WOMAN FINED FOR SNORING TOO LOUDLY

When a neighbour complained that her snoring was keeping him awake, Sari Zayed was roused in her Davis, California, home at 1.30 a.m. by a municipal noise-abatement officer who gave her a $50 citation for violating the city's anti-noise ordinance, which prohibits any wilful sound that disturbs the peace. Following the incident it was Mrs Zayed who could not get any sleep because she said she never knew when the police would knock on her door again to deliver another snoring summons. Eventually the city decided not to pursue the case because the snoring was not a "wilful act", whereupon Mrs Zayed sued them and was awarded $13,500 for lost wages, medical expenses and emotional distress.

GARDEN GNOME GOES ON WORLD TOUR

An ornamental garden gnome was returned to the house of a Gloucester, England, woman after seven months – together with a photo album showing all the places he had visited in the meantime. Eve Stuart-Kelso found the missing leprechaun, named Murphy, next to a carrier bag containing the album of 48 photos, which showed the gnome abseiling down a mountain, standing in a shark's mouth, swimming in the sea, and riding a motorbike. There were also stamped immigration permits to the countries he had visited on his world tour – South Africa, Swaziland, Mozambique, New Zealand, Australia, Singapore, Thailand, Cambodia, Vietnam, China, Hong Kong and Laos. An accompanying letter explained his absence. It read: "A gnome's life is full of time for reflection, and whilst surveying your garden one summer morning, I began to get itchy feet. I came to the conclusion that the world is a big place and there is more to life than watching the daily commuter traffic and allowing passing cats to urinate on you. So I decided to free myself from the doldrums of the Shire and seek adventure. My travels have taken me across three continents, 12 countries and more time zones than I can possibly remember. There have been high points, low points, and positively terrifying points. But I have survived – small thanks to the companion with whom I have shared all these moments." Mrs Stuart-Kelso had no idea of the gnomenabber's identity but was simply pleased to have Murphy back in just about one piece. "His feet were missing," she laughed, "but that's no real surprise given that he was sent abseiling down a mountain."

POLICE CALLED TO GET RID OF CHATTY FRIEND

When housewife Ingrid Schuettler invited her friend round to her home in Speyer, Germany, for a cup of tea and a chat in July 2008, she envisaged maybe an hour or two. But 30 hours later – all through the night and the next day – the friend was still babbling away and ignoring all of Ingrid's pleas to leave. Eventually the weary Ingrid became so desperate that she called the police who managed to persuade her friend to go.

COUPLE CLAIM THEIR SOFA IS HAUNTED

A family from Bristol claimed in 2009 that their sofa was haunted. Receptionist Christine Strange said her couch had started making weird squeaking noises which were getting so loud that her husband Nigel refused to sit on it and their Yorkshire terrier, Poppy, kept running away scared. "It could be an alien for all we know," said Mrs Strange. "I'm scared it's going to come bursting out one evening while we're watching TV."

WELSH POLICE SOLVE UFO MYSTERY

In 2008, a caller from South Wales rang the emergency services in a state of high anxiety. He said: "I need to inform you that across the mountain there's a bright stationary object in the air. It's been there at least half an hour and it's still there. If you've got a couple of minutes perhaps you could find out what it is?" The operator duly notified the local police who sent an officer to investigate. A few minutes later, the operator relayed the findings to the caller. "The bright object in the sky, we've ascertained what it is. It's the moon, sir."

TREE SWALLOWS BICYCLE

A bicycle has been eaten by a sycamore tree in Loch Lomond, Scotland. When a local boy, who had left his bicycle resting against the tree, failed to return from the First World War, the tree grew around it, devouring it so that only a few parts remain visible sticking out of the trunk. The iron-eating tree, which is located in an old blacksmith's yard, has swallowed hundreds of other metal items, including a ship's anchor and chain and a horse bridle bit.

WOMAN SAYS BEING DEAD HAS WRECKED HER LIFE

FOR EIGHT YEARS, Laura Todd, from Nashville, Tennessee, fought a battle to convince organizations including her bank, insurance companies and the IRS that she is not dead. Her problems started when a person in Florida died and Todd's Social Security number was typed in by mistake. She thought the matter had been resolved but when she went to refinance her house in 2002, she was told: "Your credit report says you're dead." She sorted that out but in 2006 the Internal Revenue Service refused to process her tax return on the grounds that she was dead. Her bank then closed her credit card account and attached a note of sympathy: "Please accept our condolences on the death of Laura Todd." During another of her dead periods, her health insurance was automatically cancelled. And in 2008, the IRS was still refusing to let her file her taxes electronically because it thought she had long since gone to meet her maker. Todd said: "At one point it was funny, but it has begun to get tiring. I don't think people realize how difficult it is to be alive when you're not." ●